# Operation
# Solomon

# Operation Solomon

## THE DARING RESCUE
## OF THE ETHIOPIAN JEWS

Stephen Spector

OXFORD
UNIVERSITY PRESS
2005

# OXFORD

UNIVERSITY PRESS

Oxford University Press, Inc., publishes works that further
Oxford University's objective of excellence
in research, scholarship, and education.

Oxford   New York
Auckland   Cape Town   Dar es Salaam   Hong Kong   Karachi
Kuala Lumpur   Madrid   Melbourne   Mexico City   Nairobi
New Delhi   Shanghai   Taipei   Toronto

With offices in
Argentina   Austria   Brazil   Chile   Czech Republic   France   Greece
Guatemala   Hungary   Italy   Japan   Poland   Portugal   Singapore
South Korea   Switzerland   Thailand   Turkey   Ukraine   Vietnam

Copyright © 2005 by Stephen Spector

Published by Oxford University Press, Inc.
198 Madison Avenue, New York, New York 10016
www.oup.com

Oxford is a registered trademark of Oxford University Press

Library of Congress Cataloging-in-Publication Data
Spector, Stephen, 1946–
Operation Solomon : the daring rescue of the Ethiopian Jews / Stephen Spector.
p.   cm.
Includes bibliographical references and index.
ISBN-10: 0–19–517782–7
ISBN-13: 978–0–19–517782–4
1. Jews—Ethiopia—History—20th century.
2. Operation Solomon, 1991.
3. Israel—Emigration and immigration—Government policy.
I. Title.
DS135.E75S64   2004
325'.263'09569409049—dc22   2004008347

1 3 5 7 9 8 6 4 2
Printed in the United States of America
on acid-free paper

For Mary, Dan, and Dave

# CONTENTS

# ACKNOWLEDGMENTS

I have been extraordinarily privileged to receive the quality of help and support that I got in writing this book. I am particularly grateful to Steven Kaplan, who read it in manuscript, correcting my errors and generously sharing his knowledge of Ethiopian history, religion, and culture. I am indebted to Shalva Weil for her many thoughtful observations about the text, her expert guidance, and her very kind encouragement. I especially want to thank Reuven Merhav, who read this book in successive drafts, supplied extensive factual information, and graciously shared his wisdom and unique historical perspective, all while respecting the integrity of my findings and conclusions. I am profoundly grateful to Bob Houdek, who carefully read the penultimate draft of the manuscript and offered extremely helpful observations, additions, and corrections, all imparted with his characteristic grace and good humor. I also owe a sincere debt of gratitude to Kay Kaufman Shelemay and Haggai Erlich for their excellent suggestions, to the late Harold Marcus for his welcome help and support, and to my son David, whose advice and encouragement I value greatly.

I thank the many people who gave their time to witness for this history. I also appreciate the advice, assistance, and encouragement that I received from Sandy Budick, Leona Toker, Robert Hoberman, Robert Goldenberg, Jonathan Levy, Robert Sokal, Bernie Dudock, Paul Dolan, Henry Abelove, and my other colleagues at Hebrew University, the State University of New York at Stony Brook, and Wesleyan University. All of my friends who gave their support have my heartfelt gratitude. My thanks go to Aida Miller, who brought me to visit Ethiopian families she assists in Netanya. I also warmly thank Rick Hodes for being a delightful host and guide during my visit to Ethiopia, and for allowing me to draw on his unpublished writing about Operation Solomon.

I am indebted to Michael Schneider, Gideon Taylor, Amir Shaviv, Will Recant, Arnon Mantber, Ami Bergman, and other members of the JDC for entrusting their confidential records to me for this project and for making themselves available to assist my research many times and in many ways. I am very grateful to the late Charles Hoffman, a fine journalist who gave me the notes of over sixty interviews that he conducted for an unpublished book shortly after Operation Solomon occurred. I have used them to enrich my own witnesses' accounts. I thank too Senator Rudy Boschwitz, who allowed me to quote extensively from his handwritten memoir of his mission as President Bush's envoy to Mengistu. He also carefully read the final draft of my manuscript, offering welcome corrections of detail and kind support.

I warmly thank Cynthia Read, my editor at Oxford University Press, for supporting this book so generously, and Theo Calderara, Sara Leopold, Catherine Humphries, and Woody Gilmartin for patiently shepherding it into the world. Thanks, too, to Susan Ann Protter, my agent, who believed in this book from the start.

This project was supported in 1996–97 by a sabbatical from the State University of New York at Stony Brook, which allowed me to spend that year in Israel.

# PREFACE

"I have chutzpah," Riki Mullah confided to me in a tone that sounded almost confessional. "Look at my toenails," she said, and raised her sandaled foot. "I painted them blue. If I had done that in Israel, everyone would be telling me I'm terrible. Here nobody cares. In Israel I feel safe. Here I feel free."

It was summer 1996, and Riki was the first Ethiopian Jew I had interviewed. She was also one of the most beautiful women I had ever seen, slender and strong, in her early thirties, with sharply defined facial features and a dark complexion. We were eating injera and vegetables in an Ethiopian restaurant on the Upper West Side of Manhattan. As Ethiopian music played in the background, Riki told me her story. She had been taken to Israel as a child in 1978, one of only a handful of Jews to get out of Ethiopia that year. An Israeli family adopted her, and for ten years she yearned for her parents and siblings, who were still in Ethiopia. Her brothers and sisters gradually reached Israel. Then in 1988, the Israeli government sent her back to Ethiopia, to bring out her parents. She spent eight months there, bribing officials, then finally succeeded: she brought her mother and father to Israel.

"It must have been very emotional for all of you," I intruded.

"Yes, it was," Riki said, so tersely and in a tone so reserved that it took me by surprise.

"Then what are you doing here in New York?" I asked.

"My mother criticized me all the time," she answered. "My mother said that I had become Israeli. I wasn't a nice Ethiopian girl. She kept telling me that I was too bold, I have too much chutzpah"—the Hebrew and Yiddish term for brazen self-confidence.

I didn't see a lot of chutzpah in her manner—not by the standards of the Upper West Side, anyway. But children were taught in Ethiopia to be deferential, to lower their eyes and speak softly in the presence of adults. Riki, like many other Ethiopian Jewish children who had been brought to Israel, had grown up without her parents and had acquired Israeli habits. Her mother didn't like the result. So, after her long struggle to bring her family to the Promised Land, Riki herself left it. Now she was living with a friend on Central Park West, which was about as far as she could get from the thatched-roof hut in which she had been born in the northern highlands of Ethiopia.[1]

The stereotype of Ethiopians is that they are patient, gentle, acquiescent, and polite—in short, the polar opposite of the popular image of Israelis. Riki exemplified the fact that the reality was far more complex than that.

Two weeks later I left for Israel, to spend my sabbatical year interviewing participants in Operation Solomon, the Israeli airlift of the Ethiopian Jews in 1991. I was showing some chutzpah of my own, having agreed to write a book on this subject. I was no expert on Ethiopian Jews at that point, but a friend, Liz Berney, had asked me if I would write on Operation Solomon. She pointed out that the American Jewish Joint Distribution Committee (JDC) in New York, which was crucially involved in the rescue, had hundreds of documents on the event, and nobody was using them. I was accustomed to working with historical documentary evidence, she argued, and I would finish in six months. The JDC offered me the unrestricted use of their archives and agreed that I was free to report what I discovered. Their only condition was that I should not write anything that endangered the lives of Israeli agents. And so I set off for Israel in August 1996 to begin my six-month project. Eight years later, with humility, I am completing this book. It tells the story of the rescuers, the rescued, and the others who played a part in Operation Solomon. Like Riki, it may not fit the stereotypes. But what ever does?

"Deception is the name of the game," Shalva Weil told me. Four months had passed since my conversation with Riki, and I was living in Jerusalem, teaching at Hebrew University and conducting interviews. Weil, a noted anthropologist at the university, was letting me know that I was in for trouble. "You're entering into a huge world that you're not going to get out of by the end of your sabbatical," she warned me over lunch one day in one of the university dining halls. "It's a rich world of trickery in storytelling. You're not going to get to what the truth is. Is there a truth?" she asked. "Obviously not, because you're not going to find it."[2]

Having done fifteen years of fieldwork with Ethiopian Jews, Weil alerted me that things were not going to be as they seemed. Ethiopians are suspicious and secretive by nature and would not talk freely to me, she said. Worse, manipulation is rampant in their culture. In fact, they come from a tradition of speaking, shall we say, creatively.[3]

In Western terms, one might call that deceitfulness. But indirection is an artistic quality in good Amharic, the native language of most of the Jews of Ethiopia (and of the Amhara, the Christian elite). Donald Levine's *Wax and Gold* argues that Ethiopians place a high value on invention in storytelling and on the art of using language ambiguously. The "wax" in the book's title is the obvious, outer meaning of language, which is lost when the "gold," or the hidden significance, is cast.[4] "If you're writing about Operation Solomon," Weil said, "I doubt that you're going to get a really true picture. But nevertheless, statements are worthy in themselves. They reflect a piece of reality."

Over the following year and beyond, as I conducted my interviews, I found that Weil was right. Several of the Ethiopian-Israeli activists I met had a clear agenda, especially regarding their countrymen who still were seeking to emigrate to Israel. And the Ethiopian immigrant families I visited often seemed to tell me either what they thought I wanted to hear or what would benefit them.

In other cases, the Ethiopians' accounts were so infused with spiritual mystery that I was confronted with another problem: how to integrate accounts of miracles into history. For example, an Ethiopian *qes* (Jewish priest) named Adane told me that his people had left for Israel for a simple and compelling reason: God had told them to. Hearing God's call, they quite suddenly had abandoned their villages and their homes, leaving their crops unharvested.

"Are you sure that they didn't leave because of some danger?" I asked him.

He replied, "There wasn't any problem in the area where we lived. We don't see by our eyes, we don't hear by our ear. But our *nefesh* [soul] hear the call of Zion, and it doesn't [allow] the people to rest. . . . Nobody was not stopping. It shows that this is the call of God."

Had God called only the priests? Had he spoken through the voice of the Americans, or perhaps the Israelis?

Adane answered: "There is no difference. Everybody hear it. Not a message by people, but from God. When I say this, also I can add that the same people who became awake by the call of God, when they got there, the Americans were there to help them."[5]

Though I suspect that Qes Adane understood Hebrew, he spoke in Amharic. The English quoted above was the translator's. And that adds an additional layer of uncertainty to the account, since several Israelis later warned me not to trust the translator, whose name is Yafet. "Yafet is a brilliant raconteur," one scholar told me, skilled in "the art of deception . . . the use of the imagination."

Adane took pleasure in illustrating this art for me. The *qes* told me that the governor of Gondar province in Ethiopia asked him in the mid-1980s why the Jews were leaving. Adane did not tell him the truth—that they were going to the refugee camps in Sudan, where they hoped the Israelis would find them and bring them to Israel. The *qes* was urging them to go, but he told local officials that he was telling them to stay. "In the daytime, I told people not to send their children to Sudan. At nighttime, I blessed them to do this," he told me. Then he misled the governor: "I said they were running to find jobs in Sudan. They will come back soon."

"You lied to the governor?" I asked.

"Yes, of course," Adane told me, beaming with quiet pride.

"And he believed you?"

"He's a *qes!*" Yafet observed enthusiastically.[6]

Were Yafet's translations reliable? I liked him and found his stories about his escape from Ethiopia charming, touched by miracle. But Israeli officials advised me that, in pursuing his political goals, Yafet was untrustworthy, even ruthless. He wanted Israel to gather in thousands of Ethiopians who were descended from converts to Christianity. This was and still is a controversial cause in Israel, as we shall see, and Yafet's conversation with me was no doubt informed by the fact that his wife's family included converts.

Clearly, political, religious, and personal investments heightened the question of trustworthiness in my witnesses' accounts. And disagreements among these narratives amounted to a contest to define history, often by impugning the motives and veracity of other individuals and groups. Against this contentious background, it was clear that no simple truth would issue from my interviews. Rather, many perspectives emerged and were challenged, sometimes heatedly. The Ethiopian Jews had suffered in the year prior to Operation Solomon, and many of them had relatives still living in Ethiopia, often in wretched conditions. As a result, my informants' accounts often were colored by anger and occasionally by guilt. At the same time, the Israelis and Americans had shown heroic dedication and patience in sustaining the community during its trials, and the airlift itself had been a triumph. Unsurprisingly, there often was competition for the credit, even for the same accomplishments.

All of these factors complicated the task of compiling oral evidence. The witnesses spoke about the Operation Solomon in their memories.[7] Many of them, I believe, tried to recover the reality of events fairly and honestly, sometimes even self-critically. But narratives based on memory and self-presentation are inescapably influenced by the need to reconstruct experience in ways that make sense, both personally and historically. As Hayden White says, "We give our lives meaning by retrospectively casting them in the form of stories," though we do not live them that way.[8]

The diverse smaller stories, those of individuals, gave form and substance to the larger ones, which we perceive as the patterns of history. And there were competing larger accounts. The Ethiopian Jews, for example, have transmitted a variety of foundational narratives, all of which establish their descent from ancient Israelites. For them, migration to Jerusalem would close a historical circle. The Ethiopian government leaders, by contrast, were living an entirely different story: the dream that their regime could survive if they could get sufficiently potent weapons from the almost mythically powerful Israelis. For the Israelis themselves, ingathering scattered Jewish communities was part of a grand enterprise following a long story of statelessness that had culminated in the Holocaust. Several Jews and non-Jews in America saw events in Ethiopia in the context of European anti-Semitism; some Israelis compared Ethiopian Jewish converts to the Marranos of Spain. These overarching patterns in turn shaped the private beliefs and decisions that determined the lives of individuals. The interplay between the two gave form to the motives that my informants felt, and those they spoke of. And, of course, under the public actions and postures lay unspoken issues: the desire to escape poverty and warfare, the search for personal meaning and usefulness, and other impulses to which people rarely testify.

The evidentiary base for the history that follows includes over two hundred original interviews with informants in Israel, Ethiopia, the United States, and England. Unless indicated otherwise, all oral evidence cited in this book is from that body of testimony. I employ as well a broad range of manuscript and printed materials, many of which were confidential during the period under study: memos, notes, reports, faxes, cables, correspondence, and memoirs by individuals and organizations involved in the rescue, intelligence briefings from Jerusalem and Washington, and State Department and National Security Council documents that were recently declassified under the Freedom of Information Act. The Joint Distribution Committee permitted me the use of their extensive handwritten records of the conversations of Americans and Israelis who planned and executed the rescue. These transcripts quote and paraphrase what many participants said day by day—and, toward the end, minute by minute—as events occurred. I also was given access to American Association for Ethiopian Jews internal and public reports and private correspondence, and to Senator Rudy Boschwitz's memoir of his mission as presidential envoy to Ethiopia. I have drawn in addition on hundreds of newspaper articles and on appropriate scholarly studies on the subject.

I include two chapters on the story of Chomanesh and her family, based on interviews with Ethiopians who participated in Operation Solomon. To protect the witnesses' identities and to offer a fuller sense of many Ethiopians' experience in these events, these characters are composites.

# Operation
# Solomon

## INTRODUCTION

# From King Solomon to Operation Solomon:
# History, Faith, and the Ethiopian Aliyah

In the late 1980s, as this history begins, the dark-skinned Jews of Ethiopia yearned to go home—to Jerusalem. They called themselves the Beta Israel, the "House of Israel," and they believed that the Holy Land was the birthplace of their ancestors. Their priests declared that God was calling them to Zion after a sojourn in Ethiopia that had spanned millennia: their "time of redemption" had arrived. But the Beta Israel's salvation would come at a cost that they could not have envisioned. This is the story of their exodus to Israel, and of the suffering and degradation that they endured along the way. It is an account of the international politics and secret dealings that led to their deliverance, and the obstacles and setbacks that nearly aborted it. And it is a report on the rescue mission itself: Operation Solomon, the majestic, massive, and astonishingly swift Israeli airlift of 14,310 Ethiopian Jews to Israel in less than a day and a half in May 1991.[1]

The Israelis plucked the Beta Israel from danger in that operation, flying them out of Addis Ababa at the climactic moment of a civil war, just as the city was about to fall to rebel forces. And yet this is not a simple chronicle of rescue. At the start of this story, in fact, the Ethiopian Jews were, by most accounts, at no imminent risk. To the contrary, they were relatively safe and secure in their villages, living much as they had for generations. They then placed themselves in jeopardy deliberately, even eagerly. There were claims that they did this to flee famine, but that was untrue. Conditions in the Jewish regions were hard, but there was no significant famine there at that point. Nor was there any other threat urgent enough to impel a community of tens of thousands of people to suddenly abandon their homes. Instead, the Jews left their villages because of a confluence of conviction, desire, and opportunity, as we shall see. Though it has been largely unreported till now, their wholesale migration was inspired and to a large extent enabled by an American advocacy group, and by one American woman in particular. Her name is Susan Pollack, and it was she, more than any other person, who created the crisis that necessitated Operation Solomon. She is the heroine of

1

the first part of this book, or the villain, depending on one's perspective. Her role and the extraordinary circumstances under which the Beta Israel moved to Addis have gone almost unnoted.[2]

## THE ANCESTRAL ORIGINS
## OF THE BETA ISRAEL

Until 1975, it was uncertain whether the Israelis would choose to gather in the Ethiopian Jews at all. Their decision depended on their judgment about whether these African villagers were authentically Jewish. The crucial questions were, who were the Beta Israel and what was the source of their Judaism? Were their ancestors ancient Israelites, Ethiopian converts to Judaism, or perhaps some mixture of both? In fact, the origins of the Beta Israel are obscure and contested, and attempts to reconstruct their history have been based principally on inference.

According to their own traditions, the Ethiopian Jews derive from ancient Hebrews. In the most famous and influential of these accounts, an elaboration on 1 Kings 10:1–13 and 2 Chronicles 9:1–12, the Beta Israel descend from no less a figure than King Solomon, through a union with the Queen of Sheba. Sheba in this narrative is the ruler of the Ethiopian kingdom of Aksum, the birthplace of Ethiopian civilization. Hearing of Solomon's wisdom, she visits him in Jerusalem, marvels at his sagacity and splendor, and accepts the God of Israel. Solomon then ingeniously tricks her into having sex with him. After her return to Aksum, she gives birth to a boy called Menelik, Solomon's first-born son. Later, Menelik visits his father. When the young man is ready to depart, the king commands the eldest sons of his counselors and officers to accompany Menelik back to Ethiopia, to establish a second Israelite kingdom there. Before leaving, however, these men steal the Ark of the Covenant from the Temple and bring it with them to Aksum (where many Ethiopians believe it remains today). With that, the Divine Presence moves from Jerusalem to Ethiopia, which becomes the new Israel.[3]

The Menelik story became the foundational account not only of the Beta Israel but of Ethiopian Christians as well, and was "woven into the very fabric of society and into the country's constitutional framework."[4] From the thirteenth century at least, it lent authority to a dynasty of Ethiopian kings who claimed descent from Solomon. Emperor Haile Selassie (r. 1930–74), the last of that line of rulers, also made this claim and took the title "Lion of Judah," as Ethiopian rulers had done since the nineteenth century.[5]

The Beta Israel have recounted other traditions about their genesis as well, and these too trace their ancestry to Israelites. In one account, they descend from Hebrews who left Egypt during the Exodus; in another, from refugees who accompanied the prophet Jeremiah to Egypt after the Babylonians destroyed the First Temple in 586 BCE. Still another story has the Beta Israel derive from Jews who came to Ethiopia after the destruction of the Second Temple in 70 CE.[6] In the last twenty years, according to Steven Kaplan, they have preferred the tradition that they are the tribe of Dan, one of the ten lost tribes of Israel.[7]

These various beliefs about an Israelite origin, as James Quirin points out, all assume that a substantial number of Jews migrated to Ethiopia. But there is no direct record that this ever happened. For that and other reasons, most academic scholars argue that the Beta Israel are not the descendants of Israelites, but are instead an indigenous Ethiopian people of Agaw stock who adopted Judaism.[8] Some scholars have contended that they converted under the influence of Jews from Egypt. The more widely accepted theory, though, is that Jews living in southern Arabia crossed the Red Sea at its narrowest point, then traveled to Aksum.[9] There are problems with this idea, however: although there is documentation that people migrated from southern Arabia to Ethiopia, there is no direct evidence that *Jews* did so before the twelfth or thirteenth century.[10] In addition, as Quirin notes, the Jews of southern Arabia knew Hebrew and rabbinic Judaism, including the Talmud, while the Beta Israel did not. Still, a number of prominent scholars conclude that the Arabian peninsula probably was the earliest and most important source of biblical Hebraic influence on Ethiopia.[11] But this does not necessarily mean the Ethiopian Jews are the biological descendants of Jews from southern Arabia.

## THE GENESIS OF THE BETA ISRAEL'S RITES AND CUSTOMS

Nor can one assume that the Beta Israel's Judaism derives directly from practices introduced by Jews in antiquity. There are clear implications of a Jewish impact at an early stage, in ancient Aksum (from the first to the fourth centuries CE), but then there are large gaps. And the evidence that does exist is almost entirely indirect. First, a number of Hebrew or Jewish Aramaic words appear in the Ge'ez language (classical Ethiopic). Some of these words, such as *meswat* (alms) and *ta'ot* (idol), have specifically Jewish connotations and "must have been introduced by Jewish merchants or migrants from Arabia . . . in pre-Christian times," says Edward Ullendorff.[12] In addition, striking Hebraic Old Testament elements survive in Ethiopian Christianity, testifying to a profound Jewish influence. Members of the Ethiopian Orthodox Church, for example, are perhaps the only Christians in the world who regularly circumcise boys on the eighth day after birth, as Jews do.[13] For a long time, Ethiopian Christians observed their Sabbath on Saturday, in the Jewish manner, and they still follow Old Testament dietary laws.[14] The Ark of the Covenant is central to their faith, and they proudly claim Israelite descent through Solomon and Menelik. Christians even refer to themselves as the "Children of Israel" (*Dakika Israel*). As Ullendorff says, it is unlikely that a people would have begun to boast of Jewish customs, institutions, and ancestry soon *after* being converted to Christianity.[15] Many scholars conclude, therefore, that these associations arose before Christianity was introduced into the country in the third and fourth centuries.[16] After that, there is a long blank in the historical record.

There are at least four allusions to Jews in Ethiopia between the ninth and thirteenth centuries, none of which academic experts generally accept as reliable. In the ninth century, Eldad Ha-Dani (the Danite) referred to the tribe of Dan and other lost tribes in Ethiopia. Scholars doubt his credibility as a witness, however. There are several attestations to a tenth-century queen who ruled for forty years; she is traditionally thought to have been Jewish, but probably was not, according to Quirin. The twelfth-century Benjamin of Tudela mentioned that Israelites lived in the mountains near Aden, or Eden, but Kaplan observes that Benjamin did not visit Ethiopia and that the mountain dwellers to whom he referred might be the Beja, not the Falasha. And Marco Polo wrote in the thirteenth century of Jews in Abyssinia with marks on their cheeks, but, as Quirin observes, it is uncertain what he meant by this.[17]

Between the seventh and the fourteenth centuries, in fact, there is no reliable evidence of the uninterrupted existence of a distinct Ethiopian Jewish community. Even the name *Falasha*, by which they were generally known, does not appear to apply specifically to Jewish groups until the sixteenth century. Kaplan suggests, therefore, that, rather than discuss the continuity of a Jewish community, we consider the survival of Jewish ideas and rituals.[18]

From that perspective, recent scholarship has offered a revolutionary understanding of the genesis of the Beta Israel's rites and customs. One such approach asserts that their religious practice does not derive directly from Hebrew tradition at all, but rather comes from Ethiopian Christianity.[19] The ethnomusicological research of Kay Kaufman Shelemay is a classic expression of this view. Shelemay argues that the Beta Israel liturgy does not appear to be distinctively Jewish. It does not survive from early Hebraic influence on Ethiopia, and it bears little resemblance to rituals known to be part of normative Jewish practice for nearly two thousand years.[20] Instead, it contains much of the liturgical text and music of the Ethiopian Orthodox Church and is conducted in the same language as the Christian liturgy, Ge'ez.[21] Shelemay concludes that the Beta Israel's Judaism emerged no earlier than the fourteenth or fifteenth century and that they received their prayers and their biblical and Jewish religious traditions from renegade Ethiopian Christian monks.[22]

Anyone interested in the religious and social history of the Beta Israel from early times should read Shelemay's groundbreaking *Music, Ritual, and Falasha History*, Kaplan's landmark *The Beta Israel (Falasha) in Ethiopia*, and Quirin's excellent *The Evolution of the Ethiopian Jews*. Our subject here is the Ethiopian Jews' tenacious struggle to reach the Promised Land.

## FALASHAS

For centuries the Beta Israel lived in their own villages, or in enclaves within larger ones, scattered across the northern highlands of Ethiopia. At one time there were more than five hundred such communities close to Lake Tana, the source of the Blue Nile, and north of it, in the Gondar, Tigre, and Wollo regions. By the late 1980s, most of the Jews in Ethiopia were concentrated in Gondar province. They dwelled there amid beautiful, arid terrain, principally as tenant farmers, working land that they leased from Christians. If a family owned a few animals, they considered themselves rich.

Often the Beta Israel supplemented their income through crafts, the men chiefly as smiths and weavers, the women most often as potters.[23] The men also worked as carpenters and masons and helped to build Ethiopia's new capital, Gondar town, in the seventeenth and eighteenth centuries. After that, construction decreased, and the Beta Israel became more dependent on crafts.[24] Their neighbors, mostly Christians, along with some Muslims, felt contempt for crafts, especially smithing, and despised the Beta Israel who practiced them. Jon Abbink argues that the dominant Christian Amhara forced the Falashas into the infamous smithing work in order to stigmatize them; the Amhara thereby degraded a group who laid claim to the same proud heritage of Israelite descent as they.[25] Hagar Salamon observes that some Christians even appended a religious association to this craft, charging that the smiths were the direct descendants of the Jews who forged the nails used to crucify Jesus. Yet at the same time, their neighbors needed the Beta Israel's handiwork and admired its quality, which many of them attributed to sorcery. They thought that people who work with fire, as the smiths and potters did, had magical powers. In fact, many of the people around them conceived of the Beta Israel as supernatural—as the dreaded *buda*, people who used the evil eye to cause sickness or death, and who took the form of hyenas at night to "eat" the blood from sick people or newly buried corpses.[26] The common factor in these charges was their neighbors' belief that the Beta Israel had the power to transform—metal, clay, and themselves.[27] This actually contained an ironic admiration for their spiritual power. Indeed, Christians would petition the Beta Israel priests to pray for them. During a drought, for example, the Christians reportedly would say, "Please, you pray, it only rains if the Jews pray." Christians also esteemed these priests as authorities on the Bible and sought them out for tolerant, even affable theological debates, a kind of "religious theater."[28]

The non-Jews called the Beta Israel "Falashas," and it was by that name that they generally became known to the rest of the world. *Falasha* means "landless one" and, by association, "stranger," "wanderer," or "exile."[29] The Beta Israel had been given this appellation because for hundreds of years they had been denied the right to inherit land unless they converted. This loss of land rights appears to date to the fifteenth century, during the reign of Emperor Yeshaq, who decreed, "He who is baptized in the Christian religion, may inherit the land of his father; otherwise let him be a *Falasi*."[30]

Although *Falasha* is a term of derision, the Beta Israel used it of themselves, and to a large extent the word encapsulated their way of confronting the world. Being landless and "strangers" in their own country engendered insecurity. Yet many Beta Israel felt that it also emboldened them. They had nothing to lose, which made them unafraid.[31] Since they were mobile, they were ready to take chances, an important factor in their willingness to risk everything to get to Israel.

Until fairly recently, the Beta Israel did not refer to themselves as Jews. American activists invented the term "Ethiopian Jews," and by the mid-1970s the Beta Israel had adopted it. In Israel, they now universally use this designation.[32] I employ it in discussing events in 1988 and later, when the parties involved in arranging Operation Solomon, the Western press, and, often, the Beta Israel themselves used it. Similarly, I refer to "Falashas" when presenting the views of people who used that term at the time under discussion.

Allusions to the Beta Israel as "black Jews," which have become current in Israel, also are problematic. The word *Ethiopian* means "burnt faces" in Greek, but many Ethiopians do not see themselves that way. An Ethiopian story tells that God created humans three different times: once the whites, once the blacks, and finally, when He got it right, the *queyy*, red or brown, Ethiopians. Despite the fact that their skin color can vary, the Ethiopian Jews did not consider themselves to be black while in Africa. Indeed, they specifically distinguished themselves from their African slaves, who, they said, had black skin, frizzy hair, and dazzling white teeth.[33]

## THEIR JUDAISM

Despite prejudice and discrimination, the Beta Israel persisted in their faith, a form of Judaism that until relatively recently was quite different from mainstream, postbiblical Jewish practice. Their religion was based on the Bible and other sacred writings translated into Ge'ez. Their canon included the entire Old Testament, as well as apocrypha and pseudepigrapha, including the books of Enoch and Jubilees. They were unaware of the Talmud, or rabbinic tradition, or even Hebrew. They did not know Hanukkah or the joyous celebration of Purim. They had no bar mitzvahs, *kipot* (skullcaps), or prayer shawls, and they did not light Sabbath candles.

They had unique rites and customs of their own. They placed a special emphasis on purity, and practiced ritual immersion to the extent that their neighbors said that they smelled of water. Following biblical injunctions, they believed that females were impure during menstrual periods and after childbirth. The Beta Israel interpreted this so stringently, however, that the women stayed at those times in a separate "blood hut" (*yedem gojo*) behind a stone fence on the periphery of the village. Touching outsiders was considered contaminating, in large part because they did not observe the scriptural menstrual laws (though this was less strictly observed in recent times). So some Ethiopians called the Falashas "Attenkun," meaning "don't touch me." The Beta Israel held midwives and people who performed circumcisions or clitoridectomies to be unclean. They believed that touching a corpse was spiritually polluting, and anyone coming into contact with one spent a week in solitary confinement. To avoid losing Falasha workers during this period, Christians offered to help carry the deceased.[34]

The Beta Israel kept an annual pilgrimage and feast holiday called the Sigd, which included climbing a mountain and reciting the Ten Commandments, recalling Moses' ascent of Mount Sinai. Their priests danced with the books of the law carried before them, as David did as he followed the Ark of the Covenant. They also recited passages from the prophets Nehemiah and Jeremiah, and bowed their foreheads to the ground repeatedly.[35]

The Beta Israel venerated the Sabbath and observed it strictly. They ritually cleansed themselves and extinguished all fires on Friday afternoons. They avoided sex on Sabbath evening—unlike normative Orthodox Jews, for whom marital sex on Friday nights is highly appropriate (and a particular obligation for scholars, according to the Talmud).[36] In addition, the Beta Israel personified the Sabbath as a woman who intercedes with God in behalf of mankind.[37] Their practice of animal sacrifice also set them apart from mainstream Jews. In fact, Protestant missionaries used this to discredit their faith, since it contradicted Old Testament precepts.[38] Their customs differed from those of normative Jews too during their equivalent of Yom Kippur, the Day of Atonement. On that day they jumped up and down, ululating and hissing, and broke into dance, a ritual that they considered purgative of sins.[39] And, though they had no rabbis, they venerated white-turbaned priests called *qessotch* (*qessim* in Hebrew). Remarkably, the Beta Israel had monks, who for centuries were the proprietors of the Falasha liturgical tradition, and who trained the *qessotch*. They also had nuns as well as educated but unordained clergy called *dabtaras*. Shelemay observes that by the early 1970s there were few or no monks and no nuns in the Falasha villages she visited. One Ethiopian Jewish monk, however, evidently the last of his kind, did reach Israel in 1990.[40]

## THE INDIFFERENCE OF WESTERN JEWS

In view of these religious distinctions, compounded by the racial difference between them, many Western Jews did not accept the Falashas as authentically Jewish. Still less did they consider them descendants of the ancient Israelites who, according to the Bible, lived in the land of Cush. (Though often translated as "Ethiopia," the term *Cush* typically designated the southern portion of Nubia and is not necessarily associated with the country now known as Ethiopia.) Until the nineteenth century, in fact, most Western Jews were indifferent to the Falashas' existence. Then in 1867, alarmed by Protestant missionizing among the Beta Israel, the Alliance Israélite Universelle sent a Jewish Semiticist named Joseph Halévy to Ethiopia. Halévy affirmed that the Beta Israel were Jews and tried to "purify" their religious ideas. He also called for efforts to fortify them against Christian missionizing. Still, Western Jews showed little further interest in the Falashas until 1904, when Halévy's pupil Jacques Faitlovitch traveled to Ethiopia. Faitlovitch introduced mainstream Jewish practices and brought their community to the attention of world Jewry. He also started a school for their children in Addis Ababa in 1924. And he arranged trips abroad for young Beta Israel, who then returned to take leadership roles in their villages and in the Ethiopian government. In keeping with this westernizing orientation, by the late 1950s Western schools established in the Gondar region taught the Hebrew language as well as Jewish liturgy and mainstream Jewish practices. Around 1950 the Falasha liturgical calendar began to incorporate postbiblical holidays.[41]

Once the Beta Israel had been rulers and warriors known for their bravery. Less than two centuries ago, by some estimates, there had been hundreds of thousands of them, though this may well be exaggerated. Extrapolating from the Scottish traveler James Bruce's assertion that the Falashas included 100,000 "effective men" in the seventeenth century, David Kessler supposes that the entire community may have numbered up to 500,000 at that time. Halévy put their population at 150,000 to 200,000 in the midnineteenth century. Kaplan argues, though, that the Beta Israel probably never exceeded 100,000.[42] By the twentieth century, they were much reduced by famine (especially the great famine of 1888–92, in which half to two-thirds of all Beta Israel probably died),[43] as well as by war, disease, enslavement, and conversion, both forced and voluntary. At the start of the present history, in 1988, no one could calculate their exact numbers, and estimates ran as high as 18,000 or more.[44] The Israeli Foreign Ministry, however, initially supposed that there were as few as 7,000 to 9,000 Falashas in Ethiopia. By 1990, that number was revised to over 20,000. In the years following Operation Solomon, events would cause Israeli authorities to more than double that figure as they reconsidered the question of who is an Ethiopian Jew.

## ISRAEL, ETHIOPIA, AND THE ETHIOPIAN ALIYAH

The ingathering of dispersed Jewish communities is a principal mission of Israel and a main reason for its existence. As Israel's Law of Return, passed in 1950, stated, "Every Jew has the right to come to this country." Despite this, the Jewish state for many years did not welcome the Beta Israel. Having opened a consulate in Addis Ababa in 1956, Israel chose to safeguard its relationship with Emperor Haile Selassie, who did not want the Falashas to leave. Isolated by their Arab neighbors, Israeli officials considered Africa to be crucial to their diplomatic efforts at the time.[45] In fact, many Israelis felt that Ethiopia, with its strategic location in the Horn of Africa, was their most important ally in Africa, a vital link precluding total Arab dominance of the Red Sea. The long Red Sea coastline of the Ethiopian province of Eritrea provided Israeli ships with their first friendly port of entry to Africa. Eritrea also offered a site for Israeli intelligence to monitor activities in Sudan, as well as Saudi Arabia and other Arab states. As most African countries gained independence, Addis Ababa became the seat of the Organization of African Unity and the UN Economic Commission for Africa. It was a hub of African politics and a very important listening post for Israel.

Haile Selassie's posture toward Israel was shaped by long-standing traditions of both trust and fear. As Haggai Erlich observes, the trust issued from the Ethiopian Christians' belief in their biblical connection with Israel, which engendered a sense of a shared destiny. The emperor feared provoking the Arab states, however. This anxiety was heightened, Erlich argues, by the traumatic historical memory of the Islamic conquest of Ethiopia in the sixteenth century. Since that time, he observes, it has been part of the Ethiopian consciousness to fear the emergence of a politically revitalized Islam. By 1958, Haile Selassie was wary of the rising pan-Arab and antimonarchic sentiment in the Arab Middle East. The emperor worried that these forces could harness the power of Islam in neighboring Somalia, in Eritrea, and within Ethiopia to threaten his regime. He therefore adopted a policy of placating the Arabs, and consequently kept relations with Israel low-key. Faced with a common threat from Egypt's Gamal Abd al-Nasser, however, Israel and Ethiopia gradually grew closer. The emperor was receptive to David Ben-Gurion's Periphery Policy, in which Israel would join with Ethiopia,

Turkey, and Iran under the shah to create a coalition of non-Arab nations in the Near East.[46] In 1960, the Israelis helped Haile Selassie crush an attempted coup. Israel also reportedly trained an elite counterinsurgency group, the Emergency Police, who attempted to put down a revolt in Eritrea.[47] Jerusalem and Addis established full diplomatic relations in 1962. There was never any doubt about popular Ethiopian enthusiasm for Israel, which became effusive after the Israeli victory in the Six-Day War in 1967. Israel's ambassador to Addis at the time wrote that the Ethiopian Christians displayed an astonishingly deep and broad identification with Israel; many Orthodox churches stayed open for twenty-four hours as people prayed for an Israeli victory. Even some Muslims expressed sympathy. After the 1967 war, the influence of pan-Arabism declined and official Ethiopian trust in Israel increased.[48]

To nurture their connection with Ethiopia, the Israelis helped build some of its major institutions. They served as faculty and deans at Haile Selassie I University, organized the country's postal and telegraph services, helped develop its banks, transportation, agriculture, and industry, and played a role in establishing its medical sector. They also supplied the emperor's armed forces with weapons and training. By the late 1960s and early 1970s, Israel's diplomatic community in Addis Ababa was its second largest in the world, second only to the one in New York. Israel became so involved in Ethiopian affairs that its ambassador, Uri Lubrani, joked in 1970 that he briefed the emperor at least once a week about what was going on in Ethiopia.[49] (Some twenty years later, as we shall see, Lubrani returned to Addis and became a central figure in Operation Solomon.)

In view of its connection with Haile Selassie and the doubts about the Falashas' ancestry, Israel showed little enthusiasm for them into the mid-1970s. Golda Meir, who was prime minister from 1969 to 1974, reportedly said of them, "Don't we have enough problems?"[50] In early 1973, the Israeli Ministry of Immigrant Absorption, noting the skepticism about the Beta Israel's Judaism, concluded that Israel should cease all association with them. Before this report was released, however, the Sephardi chief rabbi in Israel, Ovadiah Yosef, recognized the Falashas' legitimacy as Jews. Citing two sixteenth-century responsa by the Egyptian halakhic (religious legal) authority David Ben Abi Zimra (the Radbaz), Yosef determined that the Falashas were indeed descendants of the lost tribe of Dan. In 1975, the Ashkenazi chief rabbi somewhat reluctantly concurred. In April of that year, the state of Israel translated that into civil law, acknowledging the Ethiopian Jews' right to immigrate under the Law of Return.[51] And so their aliyah, or emigration (literally, "ascension") to Israel, gradually began.

The timing was unlucky. Only months after Rabbi Yosef's ruling, the October 1973 Yom Kippur War broke out and Haile Selassie ended diplomatic relations with Israel. Soon after that, he expelled the Israelis from

Ethiopia. Then in 1974 a military junta deposed the aged and ineffectual emperor. The Derg, the Marxist regime that replaced him, had no diplomatic ties with Jerusalem and would not allow the Ethiopian Jews to leave, at least not officially.

## MOSHE DAYAN'S "BLUNDER"

Covert security cooperation and information gathering persisted, though, largely through the Mossad, the Israeli secret intelligence service that deals with operations outside of Israel. In 1975, the Ethiopian head of state, Mengistu Haile Mariam, invited Israel to rebuild part of the Ethiopian army, which had become politicized and had been disbanded.[52] Jerusalem sent arms to the new government and was allowed to take a limited number of Falashas to Israel, on condition of complete secrecy.[53] This arrangement was unexpectedly sabotaged, however, by Moshe Dayan. In 1977, Dayan was foreign minister under Menachem Begin, the recently elected Israeli prime minister. Animated by an attachment to Oriental Jews, who made up much of his constituency, and seeking to controvert the 1975 United Nations resolution that equated Zionism with racism, Begin made the Ethiopian aliyah a high Zionist priority.[54] He therefore worked out a secret deal with Mengistu to send Israeli weapons in exchange for the emigration of the Falashas. He then ordered the Mossad to do whatever it took to bring them to Israel. Dayan, for his part, personally supported the aliyah. But in February 1978, during an interview in Zurich, he undermined it by explicitly confirming published reports that Israel secretly was supplying arms to Ethiopia. Arab nations responded to this public revelation with stinging criticism, and Ethiopia halted the exchange of Falashas for Israeli weapons. The official tally shows that only three Beta Israel were permitted to leave Ethiopia in 1978. Mengistu by then was certain that he could receive arms from other sources, and for the second time in less than five years, Ethiopia expelled the Israelis.

Why did Dayan do it? "Because he was Moshe Dayan. He opened his big mouth," one high official in the Foreign Ministry told me later. "It was stupidity, or a slip of the tongue," said another. Some Americans who doubted the sincerity of Israel's commitment to the aliyah were not so sure about that. Nor was Mengistu, who took this as proof that the Israelis could not be trusted.[55] An Israeli diplomat said in an interview with *Ha'aretz* that Dayan had spoken with forethought, anticipating that his revelation would force the Ethiopians to cancel the aliyah.[56] Dayan himself said that he was just setting the record straight, pointing out that Israel was not providing men or warplanes.[57] Former prime minister Yitzhak Shamir insisted, though, that Dayan simply had misspoken: "It was a blunder," he told me in an interview. "Nobody could explain it. Nothing could justify it."[58]

But Haim Halachmi did offer an explanation for Dayan's "blunder." Halachmi was the grandfather of the Ethiopian aliyah. In 1976, the Jewish Agency recruited him to initiate the Falasha immigration, and the following year, Prime Minister Yitzhak Rabin asked him to continue the job. Coincidentally, just at that time, Ethiopia began to change its international allegiances. Until 1977, it had received Western support in its war against its neighbor Somalia, which in turn got assistance from the USSR. These alliances then reversed. In April and May 1977, by agreement with the Soviets, Ethiopia ordered the United States to close its military facilities there, and a massive airlift of Cuban troops and Russian supplies then began to arrive. By February 1978, when Dayan made his disclosure, over ten thousand Cubans had reached Ethiopia, as well as four hundred Soviet tanks and fifty MiG jet fighters.[59] This, Halachmi told me in an interview, was why Dayan spoke out: to embarrass Ethiopia because it had become a Soviet client state.[60] Israel may well have been uncomfortable being in what looked like military collaboration with the USSR and Cuba. By that time, in any case, Jerusalem had come to place far less value on its connection with Addis Ababa than it had previously. Egypt's Anwar el-Sadat had embarked in 1977 on a course of reconciliation with the Jewish state that culminated in the Camp David accords in 1978 and a peace treaty in 1979, greatly diminishing Ethiopia's strategic importance to Israel.[61]

## THE TREK TO SUDAN

After the Dayan incident, the thousands of Beta Israel who tried to get to Israel had to do so covertly, by making a long, dangerous trek to Sudan, to the west. They traveled for weeks or even months across the desert, usually at night. A tragically high number of them died dreadful deaths on the way, including many children and elderly people. Some sources, including Ethiopian Jews, estimate that four thousand died en route, though Israeli authorities cannot confirm this figure, and some consider it an exaggeration.[62]

The Beta Israel's suffering did not end with the walk to Sudan. Once they got there, very many more died in pestilential refugee compounds. "Sudan is a kingdom of death and sorrow," one young Ethiopian Jewish woman later recalled.[63] The Mossad performed heroically, finding thousands of survivors in Sudan and bringing them to Israel. Every service of the Israeli Defense Forces ultimately became involved, including elite commando units, air force pilots and crew, and navy seamen and even frogmen. Then, in Operation Moses, the airlift of November 1984 to January 1985, the Israelis brought approximately sixty-five hundred Falashas to Israel.[64] "For the first time in history," William Safire wrote in the *New York Times*, "thousands of black people are being brought into a country not in chains but in dignity, not as slaves but as citizens."[65]

The Sudanese suspended the operation when it was revealed in the press. At the end of March 1985, the American government, which had supported Operation Moses financially, carried out a follow-up airlift called Operation Sheba (also known as Operation Joshua) that brought to Israel perhaps six hundred Beta Israel who had been left behind in Sudan. In the four years that followed, the Mossad secretly took out nearly two thousand more.[66]

By the late 1980s, the Ethiopian Jewish community was split in two. Between 1977 and 1988, 15,826 of them had reached Israel.[67] Almost every Beta Israel family in the Gondar region had photos and letters from relatives they had not seen in years. The separation of parents from children was especially hard for them to bear. Many of those who had reached Israel endured the guilt of having been unable to bury their loved ones, or having survived at all. They mourned parents whom they feared they had left behind forever. Often, young Ethiopian-Israelis pleaded with officials to send them back to Ethiopia to bring out their families.

## A SECRET GAME OF POLITICAL POKER

By the start of 1990, perhaps two thousand more of the Beta Israel in Ethiopia had put themselves at risk. They had sold their possessions, left their villages, and made their way south to Addis Ababa, the sprawling, impoverished shantytown that is the capital city. There they waited for the Israelis to rescue them. Ultimately, most of the remaining Jews of Ethiopia also traveled to Addis, which already was swollen with the refugees of a long civil war. The Jews expected the Israelis to reunite them quickly with their children, their families, and their friends in Israel. They could not know how much suffering awaited them before they would be allowed to leave Ethiopia.

The Beta Israel were not entirely naive. When they left their homes, they knew that they were risking everything. Most of them never had even seen a town before. They perceived themselves as self-reliant, however, and they valued bold and clever action. They knew that Ethiopia's Marxist government did not permit them to emigrate, but they depended on the Israelis, the Americans, and God to help them.

What they could not foresee was that they would become living chips in a secret game of political poker in which the stakes were the Ethiopian government's survival, and their own. The hands of this game were played in Addis. But the cards often were dealt in Jerusalem and Tel Aviv, in Washington, New York, and Illinois, as well as in Moscow, London, and Khartoum. By the time it was over, many Jewish children had died. Thousands of the Beta Israel had endured up to a year or longer in degrading slum conditions.

Fathers had lost their traditional means of livelihood, and with it, often, their authority and self-esteem. Virtually the entire people had become dependent on Israeli and American relief workers, and for many this bred a habitual dependency. Values corroded; families fell apart. And a significant number of the Jews contracted HIV, which had been unknown in their villages. Especially among the Falash Mura, Christian Ethiopians of Jewish descent, the virus reached disturbing proportions. Most of them were left behind after Operation Solomon, and the longer they remained in Addis, the higher their rate of infection became.

Through it all, Israelis and American Jewish rescue organizations worked to sustain the Ethiopian Jews. These groups acted with amazing dedication, though not always with mutual trust or respect. At the time, the disharmony among them seemed chaotic. Actually, it was, on a strategic level, deliberate and necessary. The American Association for Ethiopian Jews (AAEJ), a maverick advocacy group that often aggressively challenged Israeli policy, played a major part in creating the early scenes of this drama. They were soon joined by the North American Conference on Ethiopian Jewry (NACOEJ), an organization that came to develop a particular interest in the Falash Mura. The American Jewish Joint Distribution Committee (JDC or "Joint"), which had been supporting Ethiopian Jews in their villages for several years, ultimately played a crucial role in maintaining them in Addis. This group provided for their daily expenses, ran a day school for over four thousand of their children, created jobs for the adults, and operated a spectacularly successful medical clinic. Though officially nonpolitical, the Joint also was involved in potentiating and facilitating the rescue in ways that have not been revealed previously.

Against this background, the Israelis negotiated for the release of the Ethiopian Jews. In these talks, they had to deal with a despotic government that desperately wanted the one thing that the Americans insisted that Israel should not give them: lethal weapons. Logically, the Israelis could not succeed. And yet they did, at the last moment, as the government collapsed and the rebels stood outside Addis Ababa, ready to capture the city.

## A MODEST INGATHERING

This aliyah initially promised to be a comparatively minor event carried out at a time when the governments of Israel, the United States, and Ethiopia were each focused on much larger concerns.

From Israel's perspective, the original estimate that no more than 9,000 Falashas remained in Ethiopia made this appear to be a modest ingathering relative to earlier aliyot (immigrations). Operation Magic Carpet, for example, had airlifted nearly the entire Jewish population of Yemen, some 50,000 people, to Israel between December 1949 and January 1951. In Operation Ezra and Nehemiah in 1950, Israel had brought in 121,512 Jews from Iraq and Kurdistan. More than 200,000 Soviet and Eastern European Jews had come to Israel in the 1970s, and in 1989 the largest aliyah of all began, from the Soviet Union. Over 185,000 people from the Soviet republics emigrated to Israel in 1990 alone (and more than 1,116,000 in all by the start of 2004).[68] The comparatively diminutive Ethiopian immigration was carried out while Israel's absorptive capacities were straining under the burden of this huge Soviet influx. Much of Israel's attention at the time was concentrated on the challenges of the first intifada, the civil resistance and violent protests in the West Bank and Gaza Strip, which Israel had seized from Jordan in the 1967 Six-Day War. Prime Minister Shamir also was dealing with Palestinian Liberation Organization demands for a Palestinian state, and with American pressure on Israel to stop settlement activity in the occupied territories. Then, early in 1991, the Gulf War began, and Iraq launched thirty-nine Scud missiles at Israel. In the context of these challenges, the Beta Israel aliyah was a secondary concern.

In the end, however, both the drama of Operation Solomon and the dimensions of the Ethiopian aliyah far exceeded what Israeli officials originally had anticipated. Some 22,000 Ethiopians arrived from November 1989 through May 1991. Approximately 4,000 came in the next year, in follow-up flights that brought Beta Israel who had been left behind in Addis and the remote region of Quara. Another 2,500 Quaran Jews were brought over seven years later. The decision to admit the Falash Mura brought thousands more to the Jewish state in a controversial process that is not completed as of this writing. The Ethiopian community in Israel now numbers more than 94,000, constituting nearly 2 percent of the country's Jewish population.[69]

From Washington's vantage point, the Falasha emigration was a relatively insignificant issue that became embedded in larger strategic decisions and, ultimately, in the deposition of Mengistu. The aliyah in itself advanced no strategic American goals and in fact complicated key objectives in the Horn of Africa. U.S. foreign policy in 1990 and 1991 was concentrated principally on the collapse of the Soviet Union, the political liberalization in Eastern European states, the Iraqi invasion of Kuwait, and the Gulf War. The United States had little strategic interest in Ethiopia at that point. American Jewish leaders did a great deal, however, to direct official American attention to the Ethiopian Jews on a humanitarian basis. Washington's relationship with the Shamir government was increasingly strained in those years, owing in large part to Israel's policy of expanding settlements in the West Bank and Gaza Strip. This did not diminish official American sympathy for Israel's ingathering of scattered Jewish communities. Dedicated and effective officials at the U.S. embassy in Addis, the State Department, and the National Security

Council (NSC) worked in virtual collegial harmony with the Israelis to advance the Falasha emigration. In addition, as it happened, President George H. W. Bush had had personal experience with the Ethiopian Jews during the earlier rescues from Sudan. That predisposed him to take an interest in them in this instance, and his interventions were critical in launching Operation Solomon.

America's inclination to take an active role in the Middle East and Africa was amplified by its victory in the Gulf War, as was its influence in the region.[70] Washington's concern for Ethiopia's future and the Jews' safe departure from Addis was further heightened by two events in 1990 and 1991 in which the United States did not intervene: the bloody episodes in Somalia and Iraq. The civil war in Somalia degenerated into murderous violence in the capital city, Mogadishu, in 1990 and 1991. Washington did not want a similar conclusion to the Ethiopian hostilities. In addition, the Bush administration, after calling on the Kurds and Shiites of Iraq to rise up against Saddam Hussein at the close of the Gulf War, stood by as Iraqi troops crushed them brutally. Officials at the NSC felt that the United States could not allow the possibility of another slaughter, this time in Addis, especially if Jews might be among the principal victims. The State Department, by contrast, was not persuaded that the Falashas were in serious jeopardy. Some American Jewish leaders, however, saw the danger in Addis through the prism of European anti-Semitism and pogroms, or even of the Holocaust. Ethiopian Jews themselves played an important part in inspiring the foreboding of a massacre, ultimately through a nightmare vision that became known as the Doomsday Scenario. As much as any other single factor, fear of this possible doomsday outcome in Addis Ababa triggered American intervention at critical moments in this story.

Still, the United States had broader geopolitical considerations in the region to which it was willing to subordinate the Falasha emigration, if necessary. In 1989, Bush reached a secret understanding with Soviet leader Mikhail Gorbachev to help Moscow withdraw from its commitments in Ethiopia with dignity. To accomplish that, State Department officials favored negotiations to bring the Ethiopian civil war to a peaceful end. If not for this policy, the United States would have had little political contact with Addis Ababa, and Operation Solomon might never have happened. The United States supported the aliyah only to the extent that it was consonant with this larger objective, however. In early April 1991, for example, in order to spur Mengistu to accelerate the emigration, the NSC declared that the proposed peace talks would be contingent on the prompt release of the Ethiopian Jews from Addis. The policy ultimately was a bluff, though: within a month the NSC abandoned it so that the peace talks could go ahead even if the Jews were still in the Ethiopian capital. This decision was intended to prevent further bloodshed on the battlefield, but it carried the price of putting the Falashas at potential risk. In taking this position, the NSC rejected the wishes of the Israelis and American Jewish groups, and placed itself at odds with the State Department. The NSC then covertly arranged Mengistu's departure from office, clearing the way for a transitional government and a rebel victory. This had the incidental effect of threatening to actualize the Doomsday Scenario: the Beta Israel might be slaughtered in a fight for the capital or in the chaos that might occur before the new rebel regime was firmly in place. At the same time, though, with Mengistu out of the picture, it was more likely that, when the Jews did leave Addis, the entire community would be permitted to go. At this moment of danger and opportunity, Israel put the rescue in motion. The United States provided crucial assistance, asserting its influence with both the Ethiopian government and the rebels. Bush sent a letter to the acting president in Addis urging the Ethiopians to permit the airlift. This allowed the Ethiopian regime, in its final hours, to portray the release of the Jews as a humanitarian act, rather than in the light in which it might otherwise have been seen: as the last-minute sale of over fourteen thousand human beings in desperate circumstances. Then, three days after Mengistu's flight from Ethiopia, Operation Solomon began and Washington intervened with the insurgents, having them stand down until the Israelis completed the rescue.

Certain officials in the United States and elsewhere suspected that, in conducting this aliyah, Israel was pursuing unspoken policy concerns. The leaders of the AAEJ felt that the Jewish state was showing too little zeal. Influential figures in Washington, by contrast, suspected that Israel was showing too much, using the immigration as a cover for its true goal: to back Mengistu and regain Ethiopia as an ally.[71] The Mengistu government, for its part, impeached Israel's motives from still another perspective, accusing the Jewish state of allying with Ethiopia solely in order to gather in the Falashas.[72] Jerusalem did in fact seek to reestablish its strategic alliance with Addis Ababa, but the aliyah was neither a pretext nor a political side effect. Israel's dedication of people and material resources to the Ethiopian Jews at a time of economic distress evinced its ongoing concern for them. And the extraordinary devotion and effort with which the Israelis planned and executed Operation Solomon demonstrated beyond question their genuine commitment to the Beta Israel. The airlift itself set off a spontaneous expression of popular joy and pride among Israelis. Many of them took the ingathering of the Ethiopian community as a sign that their nation had been faithful to its original Zionist principles. Some declared that it was a step in ushering in the Messiah.

Almost immediately, the charge came from Arab quarters that Israel had brought in the Falashas for the purpose of settling them in the West Bank and Gaza Strip.[73] Palestinians wanted these occupied territories for their own independent state and fervently objected to the expansion of Jewish settlements there. Among the most ardent Israeli supporters of the Ethiopian aliyah were, in fact, religious nationalist groups who sought to deploy new immigrants to the settlements. These groups did not bring pressure to bear, however, until late in this story, specifically with reference to the Falash Mura. And it was chiefly the convert families who, years later and in comparatively small numbers, were settled in the territories.[74]

For the Ethiopians especially, the Falasha emigration turned out to be far more consequential than it originally had seemed. The Falashas were a marginalized, minor religious group, and as this history opens, in 1988, Mengistu was focused not on their strivings, but on the threat posed by rebel forces that were deployed against him. Though vastly outnumbered, the insurgents were scoring battlefield victories, and the Ethiopian leader indulged in the vain hope that by acquiring more weapons he could reverse his fortunes. His attention, as a result, was directed toward getting those arms from friendly nations: North Korea, East Germany, and in particular Russia. It is therefore in the Kremlin that this history begins in Chapter 1. With Moscow's declining role in the world, however, and its sharply diminished support for Ethiopia, Mengistu came to see Israel as his best prospect for military sponsorship. He realized that the Falashas were his most effective leverage in securing Jerusalem's aid, and he used them to try to coerce the Israelis to supply the weapons, despite their declared policy to the contrary. The Ethiopian aliyah thus became entangled in the politics of the region and inextricably linked to Mengistu's struggle to survive.

The history that follows chronicles these events, beginning in the summer of 1988.

# ONE

# Restoring Diplomatic Relations— Conceiving the Aliyah

## JULY 1988–JANUARY 1990

> On that day the Lord will exert his power a second time to recover the remnant
> of his people from Assyria and Egypt, from Pathros and Ethiopia. . . . He will
> assemble Judah's scattered people from the four corners of the earth.
> —Isaiah 11:11–12

The airlift of the Ethiopian Jews in May 1991 was the unlikely consequence of international politics that initially had nothing whatsoever to do with them. Indeed, the chain of events that culminated in Operation Solomon could be said to have begun neither in the Jewish villages of Ethiopia nor in Jerusalem, but in Moscow. In July 1988, the Ethiopian dictator, Mengistu Haile Mariam, traveled to the Kremlin to ask Mikhail Gorbachev to increase Soviet military aid to his regime. Rebel forces in the northern provinces of Eritrea and Tigre had inflicted serious defeats on the Ethiopian army, and Mengistu imagined that an influx of Russian weaponry would allow his troops to stem the insurgent advances. The Soviet military commitment to Ethiopia went back to the time of Leonid Brezhnev, who, Mengistu recalled later, had aided him generously after the Americans and the Chinese had turned him down.[1] But on this trip, the Ethiopian leader was told that he was losing his most important patron.[2]

The Russians had come to regard Mengistu as a bad investment. The wars against his regime had cost the lives of between half a million and a million Ethiopian combatants and civilians. The fighting and the disruption it caused, in concert with periodic famine and Mengistu's misguided domestic policies, also were destroying the country economically, despite massive infusions from the Soviet bloc: Russia, East Germany, Czechoslovakia, and Poland had given Ethiopia at least $12 billion in grants and loans since 1977. The Soviets, facing their own financial crisis, had tired of carrying Ethiopia as a client state. In addition to arms, they were sending 250,000 tons of grain to Ethiopia annually at a time when they themselves were net importers of cereals. Moreover, the Ethiopian army had become ineffectual, and it often abandoned its Russian-made weapons and equipment to the rebels. So Gorbachev put Mengistu on notice that the USSR would curtail its military aid drastically in 1990.[3] If the Ethiopians wanted additional weapons, they would have to pay for them, and they did not have the foreign currency to do that. Gorbachev advised Mengistu to reconcile with the West, and to reach a negotiated settlement with the rebels.[4]

Mengistu also traveled to China and North Korea in search of arms that summer, with little success. At the same time, he made initial gestures toward courting American goodwill. In August 1988, he met with former president Jimmy Carter in Addis Ababa. Both men expressed regret over the rift between their nations, which had occurred in 1977, early in Carter's term. In November, giving his first interview to a Western news organization in several years, Mengistu called the recent election of President George H. W. Bush "a new opportunity" to improve relations.[5] This initiative bore no immediate fruit.

Mengistu's fortunes declined rapidly from there. During the following winter and spring, insurgent forces in the north of Ethiopia made major advances. In particular, rebels in Tigre inflicted a stunning defeat on the army at the town of Enda Selassie in February and March 1989. Government forces withdrew, leaving Tigre province in the hands of the insurgents. In May, mindful of this devastating setback, one-third of the army's general command attempted a coup. Mengistu, who was in East Germany at the time seeking weapons, flew home and had his security chief arrest 176 high-ranking military officers. Mengistu executed eighteen senior officers and placed twelve generals under arrest. In October, the East German leader, Erich Honecker, fell from power and East Germany soon halted the arms shipments that he had promised Ethiopia.[6] East German advisers, who had trained the ruthless Ethiopian security services and had been crucial in putting down the coup, were called home. At the same time, the Ethiopian rebels were scoring one victory after another. Mengistu's army was demoralized, his cadre of competent senior officers was severely depleted, and his sources of armaments were contracting. His best remaining option was to resume his courtship of the United States.

The Bush administration, however, considered Ethiopia under Mengistu to be a pariah state, in a category with Cuba and North Korea. People in the State Department privately referred to Mengistu as the "Butcher of Addis"; Bush himself found the dictator particularly distasteful. As Ronald Reagan's vice president, Bush had been personally involved in Operations Moses and Sheba, the airlifts of Falashas from Sudan in 1984–85. In his dealings with the Ethiopian regime, he had come to dislike Mengistu.[7] He had no intention of sending weapons to prop up the repressive Ethiopian leader.

American relations with Addis had been strained for fifteen years. This stood in marked contrast with the friendship that Washington had enjoyed with Emperor Haile Selassie for more than three decades prior to his overthrow in 1974. U.S. officials had appreciated the emperor's strong support in the Cold War and his dispatching a brigade to fight in the Korean conflict from 1950 to 1953.[8] Overlooking the corruption and venality of Haile Selassie's feudal regime, Washington had seen in Ethiopia a rare case: an African state that was historically independent, strategically located, predominantly Christian, and well disposed toward the West. As part of a global transition of power from Britain to America after the Second World War, Washington had become Ethiopia's principal military sponsor, and half of all American military aid to Africa from 1950 until 1974 had gone to Ethiopia. The United States also had initiated limited agricultural and educational initiatives, as well as commodities development and export projects. Haile Selassie, in turn, had given the United States access to the supply and oil depot at Ethiopia's port of Massawa, and the use of an important signals facility at Kagnew Station in Eritrea. The Pentagon had had misgivings about Ethiopia's strategic military value. Diplomats in the State Department, however, had considered the country a stable and trustworthy ally in a volatile region, and a potential base for any future projection of U.S. power in the Red Sea area. This latter view had taken on greater importance after Nasser alienated the United States by reaching an arms deal with the Soviet Union and recognizing the People's Republic of China.[9] Just as Ben-Gurion's Periphery Policy made Ethiopia a cornerstone in a non-Arab alliance with Israel, by 1957 the Eisenhower Doctrine envisioned Addis as a stronghold containing Soviet expansionism in the region.

Ethiopia's significance for the United States waned in the late 1960s as American space satellite technology lessened the usefulness of the listening post at Kagnew Station. Then, after Nasser's death in 1970, Sadat formed an alliance with the United States, and Egypt's crucial location on the western shore of the Red Sea further diminished Ethiopia's centrality for Washington.[10] Relations between the United States and Ethiopia cooled when a military junta called the Derg deposed Haile Selassie in the Revolution of 1974. The emperor had become incompetent to cope with the internal and external threats that Ethiopia faced. Washington came to disdain the new regime, however, and specifically Mengistu, who ultimately emerged as its leader, as unreconstructed Stalinists. Still, the Ford administration continued diplomatic ties with Addis, participated actively in famine relief, and enhanced its military assistance program.[11]

President Carter took a properly harsh view of the Derg's appalling human rights record and halted military aid to Ethiopia in 1977, when the Soviets switched sides in the Horn of Africa and armed the Ethiopians against the Somalis. The area became a flash point between Washington and Moscow. Zbigniew Brzezinski, Carter's national security adviser, said that the second strategic arms treaty all but perished as a result of these events.[12] When the American ambassador left Addis Ababa in 1980, he was not replaced. The U.S. embassy remained open, however, with a chargé d'affaires representing American interests.

Washington cautiously renewed its interest in Ethiopia in 1989, when the Russians withdrew from contests with the West, seeking instead cooperation in resolving regional problems. Bush agreed to collaborate closely with Gorbachev, and Moscow made a special request for assistance in withdrawing from its commitments to Ethiopia and Angola. Wanting to help the reformist Gorbachev regime look good, the Bush administration sought to create the conditions that would let it exit Ethiopia gracefully. U.S. policy therefore was to bring about a negotiated peace in the Ethiopian civil war as the Soviets faded away. Despite the administration's contempt for Mengistu, this necessitated a diplomatic initiative toward his government.[13] That, in turn, provided the occasion for intervention in behalf of the Falashas. American Jewish leaders, particularly the American Association for Ethiopian Jews, had alerted key figures in Congress and the State Department to the plight of the Ethiopian Jews. Bush was sympathetic, owing to his earlier experience with Operations Moses and Sheba. Now, as president, he was sensitive to the Falashas' longing to be reunited with their relatives who had already reached Israel.

In August 1989, Herman Cohen, assistant secretary of state for African affairs, traveled to Addis to explore brokering peace in the Ethiopian conflict. Cohen told Mengistu that improved relations with the United States would be conditioned on several principal points: the Ethiopians would have to move toward an accord with the rebels, moderate their policies on human rights and emigration, and liberalize their Marxist economic system. Declaring that he was the last holdout against the Arabization of the Horn of Africa, Mengistu indicated that he was receptive to the American terms and agreed to ask Carter to mediate at peace discussions. Although Cohen had not specifically mentioned the Falasha aliyah, Mengistu said that he knew what Cohen was referring to. He did not understand America's interest in the Falashas, Mengistu told his guest, but he promised to respond to it.[14] An Ethiopian official informed Cohen that the government already was in secret negotiations with Israel, was discussing the reunification of Falasha families, and was issuing passports to about two hundred Falashas each month.[15] The Ethiopians were, in fact, allowing Jews to leave, but this number was exaggerated. In all of 1988, only 220 immigrants reached Israel directly from Ethiopia. The rate remained more or less the same in the first six months of 1989, then increased in the latter half of the year.[16]

On September 9, 1989, in Atlanta, Carter presided over the first round of talks between the Ethiopian government and the Eritrean rebels. At the same time, however, in an act of duplicity typical of Mengistu, the Ethiopians still sought the weapons that they hoped would give them victory on the battlefield. For the Bush administration, arming Ethiopia was out of the question. But in Addis a plan emerged. One of Mengistu's key advisers calculated that they might be able to get the arms they sought from Israel. To accomplish that, it would be necessary to reestablish diplomatic relations with Jerusalem. Perhaps Israel, with its special connection with the United States, could then help ameliorate the American attitude toward Mengistu. The Israelis, for their part, had been encouraging the Ethiopians for two years to reopen diplomatic ties. From their perspective, that not only would restore an important, traditional strategic alliance but also would reenergize the Falasha aliyah.

## REUVEN MERHAV: A TURNING POINT

In the autumn of 1989, Prime Minister Yitzhak Shamir had authorized the ingathering of the Falashas, and Reuven Merhav was assigned the responsibility for overseeing Israel's policy toward Ethiopia. Merhav had been a high official in the "Office of the Prime Minister," the discreet Israeli term for the Mossad, and had served in Ethiopia as well as Kenya and Iran. Then, in a very unusual career path, he had moved to the Israeli Foreign Ministry. In late 1989, at the age of fifty-two, Merhav was in his first year as director-general of that ministry, a position immediately beneath Foreign Minister Moshe Arens. At that moment, Merhav recalled later, the circumstances seemed especially propitious for a change in Ethiopia's relations with Israel. The Russians had lost the ability or the desire to invest in proxy wars and could not maintain their role in Ethiopia or the rest of the world. At the same time, Ethiopia's economy was close to catastrophe. In addition to incurring enormous costs in the war, Mengistu had forcibly imposed socialist policies of resettlement and villagization on his people, with disastrous results.[17] The resettlement plan, initiated during the drought and famine of 1984–85, had uprooted over eight hundred thousand farmers who were sympathetic to the northern insurgents and moved them to remote areas to the south and west. Villagization, which was intended to create a collective farm system quickly, had failed utterly, affecting twelve million to fifteen million people. Mengistu asserted later that he had moved rural populations to prevent future famines. In fact. these policies had exacerbated the famine conditions, resulting in many deaths.[18]

The Israelis had known for over a year that the Ethiopians were desperately seeking an ally to compensate for the reduced Soviet presence. So when

Mengistu decided to restore diplomatic relations with Israel in November 1989, Merhav was certain that they wanted Israel to give them the weapons that the Russians would not.[19]

On November 3, 1989, the Ethiopians announced the renewal of diplomatic ties, after a break of sixteen years. Two days later, Mengistu dispatched one of his closest advisers, Kassa Kebede, to Jerusalem. Kassa met with Benjamin Netanyahu, who was then deputy foreign minister, and with high officials of the Mossad. He also had an audience with Prime Minister Shamir, presenting him with a letter from Mengistu. The Ethiopians offered the renewal of "old strategic bonds" as well as the use of part of the Dahlak Islands in the Red Sea for Israel's defense purposes. Mengistu also promised that Ethiopia would permit five hundred to a thousand Beta Israel to leave for Israel each month.[20]

What did the Ethiopians ask in return? Kassa always insisted that the restored ties and the Jewish emigration were not linked to a request for military aid. Reports circulated immediately, however, that Ethiopia was seeking weapons, and that the Israelis had acquiesced. American officials correctly maintained that, even before renewing diplomatic relations, Israel had resumed providing Addis with military hardware, including communications equipment.[21] Shortly thereafter, former president Jimmy Carter charged that Israel had sent Mengistu a particularly devastating weapon: cluster bombs.[22]

Merhav confirmed later that Kassa brought with him "a voluminous shopping list for matériel, including lethal weapons," on his trip to Jerusalem that November.[23] The question of precisely what commitments Shamir actually made at that time remains a matter of dispute. But the Ethiopians were convinced that Israel had undertaken to send them the arms, covertly formalizing earlier arrangements with the Mossad.

Merhav said, however, that at his initiative, and with the support of colleagues at the Foreign Ministry, Israel had decided that it would no longer arm Mengistu under any circumstances.[24] Kassa's shopping list for lethal weapons had triggered a hot debate in Israeli foreign affairs, intelligence, and defense quarters. The arms industry was then the biggest sector in Israel's economy, and the Israeli defense establishment was eager to provide the Ethiopians with war matériel. To send Mengistu weapons would be the key to reestablishing a presence in Ethiopia. Even Ethiopian-Israeli activists tried to pressure Israel to do it, and whatever else was necessary to get the Jews out.[25] Providing the weapons would create a political symmetry, since Israeli intelligence reported that radical Arab nations were arming the rebels. And it would assuage Ethiopian fears that allying with Israel would provoke Arab states to increase military aid to the rebels. But, Merhav recalled, during a trip to Addis Ababa in January 1990 he became firmly convinced that Israel must not become involved in an arms deal with Ethiopia. After discussions with Mengistu and some senior officials there, as well as candid conversations with old friends, Merhav concluded that the weapons would be used against civilians, perhaps including Jews. Mengistu was doomed anyway. Why support him at the end of his rule?[26]

By far the most compelling consideration, though, was that the United States strongly opposed Israel's sending arms to Mengistu, in particular any weapons containing American-made components. American intelligence assets were watching closely, and Israeli defiance in this matter would place a strain on their relations.[27]

Instead of supplying weapons, Merhav recalled, he proposed that the Israelis offer economic and agricultural aid, as well as medical assistance. And most importantly, they would mobilize American goodwill toward Ethiopia. After consulting with the veteran Israeli diplomat Uri Lubrani, Arens agreed to this strategy, and got Shamir's approval as well, Merhav told me. That marked a turning point. From that moment on, the Foreign Ministry, rather than the Mossad or the defense establishment, would make policy toward Ethiopia.[28]

In the early months of 1990, however, there were persistent reports that Israel was in fact sending weapons to Ethiopia. Diplomatic sources in Addis said that two ships carried Israeli arms into the Ethiopian port of Assab early in January 1990. A senior Israeli Foreign Ministry official conceded that the United States and Israel were at odds because of Israel's policy of arming Mengistu. The *New York Times* noted on February 7 that an Israeli official had acknowledged that Israel had given Ethiopia 150,000 bolt-action rifles.[29] Also in February, the Morrison Report, a secret assessment prepared for the House Subcommittee on Africa, reiterated Carter's charge that Israel had given Mengistu cluster bombs in 1989. Based on information from the State and Defense Departments, a classified briefing at the American embassy in Addis, and conversations with the Eritrean rebels, the report added that Israel had shown the Ethiopians how to adopt a mobile, small-unit, helicopter-borne approach to troop movement.[30] Helping the Ethiopian commanders rethink strategy and tactics was, in fact, the main Israeli contribution, noted Steve Morrison, the author of the report.[31] It was the cluster bombs that most urgently concerned American officials, though, as we shall see.

In March, *Ha'aretz* broke the story that the Bush administration had incontrovertible evidence of extensive Israeli military involvement in Ethiopia. American officials reportedly were furious with Israel for sending weapons and several hundred military advisers to support Mengistu's "brutal Stalinist dictatorship." Pro-Israeli senators and congressmen had summoned Moshe Arad, the Israeli ambassador to Washington, to hear strong protests about this policy. Merhav insisted at the time that there were no Israeli advisers in Ethiopia, but he refused to confirm or deny that Israel was arming Mengistu.[32]

Merhav conceded later that some minor arms shipments may have gone through initially. But the new policy then went right into effect, and Israel sought to reach its goals without compromising it, he said.[33] Every Israeli official I spoke with confirmed that Israel refused to supply the weapons that the Ethiopians wanted. Asher Naim, who became Israeli ambassador to Addis in November 1990, remarked that, in their eagerness to renew ties with Ethiopia in 1988–89, the Israelis had "overpromised. We gave them hope, expectation actually. We said, 'Come, see these weapons and plants.'" But Naim said emphatically that Israel had not delivered the weapons during his term in Addis. In the end, "the military equipment we promised never operated," Naim recalled, "and several dozen men sent [to Israel] for training never went back."[34]

Mengistu and his advisers viewed Israel's position as a betrayal and complained about it bitterly. Feeling abandoned by the Russians and despised by the Americans, they now felt deceived by the Israelis. Former CIA official Paul Henze observed in a Rand Foundation report, "How much weaponry and advice Israel originally promised him is still unknown, but Mengistu was clearly disappointed at the scale and tempo of arms deliveries, for his needs were insatiable."[35] Ultimately, the Ethiopians would try to coerce Israel into giving them the weapons that they demanded, using the Falashas as hostages. By any logic, the Israelis faced an insoluble problem. They wanted the Jews but had determined not to give weaponry for them. The Ethiopians, for their part, wanted the arms but did not want to give up the Falashas, certainly not all of them. If they did, they feared that Israel and the Americans would lose interest in Ethiopia. The Ethiopians also calculated that a gradual Falasha exit would guarantee them an ongoing source of cash from Israel. And, ultimately, Mengistu felt that he needed to keep at least some of the Jews as a shield against a final rebel attack on Addis. Bob Frasure, the American assistant chargé d'affaires in Addis, who went on to serve on the National Security Council, warned Merhav about trying to outmaneuver Mengistu's advisers under these circumstances. "These guys are not a banana republic," Frasure told him. "They're smart, dangerous people. You can't run a shell game with no beans: you can't trade Jews for guns with no guns." Merhav could only respond that Shamir had asked him to sort this problem out.[36]

Merhav prevailed on a senior diplomat, Meir Yoffe, to serve as Israel's ambassador to Addis Ababa. Yoffe had folded the Israeli flag when the embassy closed in the Ethiopian capital in 1973; now it would be he who raised it again.[37] Then Merhav continued to put the pieces in place in Jerusalem, creating and chairing a steering committee to monitor events in Ethiopia and to oversee the aliyah. It included members of the Foreign Ministry, the Mossad, the Israeli Defense Forces, the Jewish Agency, and the Joint Distribution Committee, as well as ad hoc invitees. He gave instructions to prepare the old Israeli embassy compound in Addis for the thousands of Jews who, he felt sure, would make their way there once the news reached them that the embassy had been reopened. There would have to be a school, a medical clinic, soup kitchens, and a processing center for aliyah applications. And it all would have to be set up quickly, before the rainy season began in mid-June.[38]

In an unusual move for the Foreign Ministry, Merhav selected a Jewish Agency employee, Micha Feldman, and gave him the title of "special consul on family reunification." Feldman, then forty-six years old, had worked with the Ethiopian aliyah for years and spoke fluent Amharic.[39] He would have the critical responsibility of checking the identity of every Ethiopian Jew against the official Israeli list of approved names, which the Israelis called the "Book of Jewishness" or simply the "bible."[40] When the Israeli embassy compound reopened on January 22, 1990, he was there.

The Israelis wanted the Ethiopian aliyah to be orderly and safe. They intended to develop a pilot transport program that would bus a modest number of Jews, perhaps five hundred a month, from Gondar province down to Addis Ababa. They expected to fly a similar number to Israel in monthly installments, as Mengistu had promised Shamir. They planned to keep a critical mass of Jews in Addis, up to two thousand at any given time, to apply constant pressure on the Ethiopians for further exit permits. By moving only small numbers of the Beta Israel to the capital on each bus, they hoped to minimize the risk that the buses would become targets for the rebels.[41] But the Israeli officials soon would have to adjust to totally different circumstances beyond their control.

## SUSAN POLLACK: "WE ARE LOSING PEOPLE, AND BEFORE WE LOSE THEM, THEY SUFFER"

Neither the Israelis nor the Ethiopians reckoned on the intervention of an obscure young American woman named Susan Pollack. In December 1989, she was starting her second year as the resident director for the American Association for Ethiopian Jews (AAEJ) in Addis Ababa.

Pollack, who was then in her mid-thirties, had been working on behalf of the Ethiopian Jews since the early 1980s. She had grown up in the only Jewish family in a small town in Maine. She learned about the Ethiopian Jews in 1981, in Jerusalem, from an inspiring lecture and slide show by AAEJ president Howard Lenhoff and an Ethiopian-Israeli. Pollack volunteered to work for the Canadian Association for Ethiopian Jews for a time, then associated with the AAEJ, doing public speaking, raising money, and even smuggling medicine to the Jewish villages in the Gondar region.[42] The fact that she represented the AAEJ seemed improbable. The AAEJ was a dedicated advocacy group that had successfully aroused public awareness of the plight of the Ethiopian Jews. It had been particularly effective in cultivating the support of U.S. government officials. But it sometimes went too far, to the point of recklessness.

Graenum Berger, the first president of the AAEJ, was a social worker with the Federation of Jewish Philanthropies in New York. He had visited Gondar in 1965 and had been both shocked by the Jews' living conditions and moved by their commitment to their faith. He raised money for the Falashas privately at first; then in 1974 he and a few other pro-Falasha activists established the AAEJ. For the first several years the group was small enough to meet in Berger's home. Then it grew into a national organization. They raised money through speaking engagements, mostly in synagogues, and direct mailing campaigns. Their annual budget eventually reached $1.5 million, and at different points they were partially reimbursed by the JDC and the Jewish Agency.[43]

Berger and his colleagues, including Lenhoff and Nate Shapiro, had been frustrated by some Israeli leaders' overt indifference to the Ethiopian Jews in the mid-1970s. They were further disturbed by what they saw as Israel's subsequent reluctance or even hostility regarding the aliyah. In response, the AAEJ activists became confrontational and provocative, willing to take controversial steps to push the emigration along. Among other things, AAEJ officers accused Israel of prejudice against the black Jews. Israeli officials insisted that the AAEJ was unaware of their secret efforts and of the difficulty of reaching agreements with the Ethiopian government. The Israelis were offended by what seemed to them to be the arrogance of these American amateurs. They also feared that the charge of bias would play into the hands of their enemies, who in 1975 had devised UN Resolution 3379, which held that Zionism is a form of racism. Then, in 1981, an AAEJ publicity campaign endangered covert Mossad rescue activities in Sudan, Israeli sources said. Two years later, the AAEJ's public references to Sudan, and their own failed rescue attempts there, almost ended the entire operation. The AAEJ ultimately reached an agreement that it would not go into Sudan again, and the Mossad would clean out the camps. Still, the American group claimed credit for having been the first to locate the Ethiopian Jews in Sudan, and for having inspired Operation Moses by showing that rescue from Sudan was possible.[44]

The AAEJ, one of the organization's officers told me later, was willing to play the role of the crazies of the Jewish advocacy groups if that was what it took to get the Ethiopian Jews to Israel. Soft-spoken and exceptionally pretty, Pollack did not fit this image. She seemed too gentle and well-mannered, too circumspect.

In late 1989, the AAEJ officers felt that the Israelis were moving too slowly, not even greasing the right wheels financially. Someone on the scene had to accelerate the aliyah, especially now, with the reopening of relations with Israel, since the Jews finally could emigrate legally. That job fell to Pollack, though by any objective standard her prospects looked bleak. She was in Addis on a tourist visa that had to be renewed each month, leaving her vulnerable if the Ethiopian government did not like what she was doing. She represented an organization with no legal standing in the country. She did not even have an office.[45] Within a matter of months, however, Pollack and the AAEJ would alter events in Ethiopia dramatically, utterly disrupting the Israelis' plans for a gradual and orderly aliyah.

Pollack believed the Jews' situation in Ethiopia was desperate. In February 1989, she had gone from village to village in the Gondar region and had seen their pain and suffering. Traveling with a Muslim interpreter, Pollack saw "teenagers with rotting hands or feet, pretty young women with goiters, old men and women (dozens of them per village) gone blind with milky white eyes."[46] She was not expert in Ethiopian culture; she was not fluent in Amharic. But her intuition told her that the Jews were desperate, and she could see that they were sick. She reported to the AAEJ that they suffered from polio, tuberculosis, malaria, skin fungi, goiters, skin ulcers, and infected wounds. She spoke of babies with their eyes swollen or crusted shut and covered with flies. Every other person in the villages needed medical attention, she said. "We are losing people," she told the AAEJ, "and before we lose them, they suffer."[47]

In her formal report, Pollack recommended only that the organization intensify its advocacy programs, pressuring Washington, Israel, and Western Europe to insist on human rights in Ethiopia, as well as free emigration and family unification. But what she really wanted was to get the Jews out of Gondar province. However implausible it seemed at that moment, that was exactly what she was going to do, profoundly changing the lives of tens of thousands of people.

By December 1989, perhaps two thousand Jews had made their way to Addis from the Gondar highlands.[48] Ethiopia is like Switzerland without roads, said one relief worker. To walk over four hundred miles from the Jews' villages in the north down through the mountains and on to the capital was extremely difficult, even for the healthiest people. Yet many of the Beta Israel had done it, often arriving sick and malnourished. Others had sold their homes and cattle and had walked to Gondar town, north of Lake Tana, or to the town of Bahr-Dar on the southern tip of the lake. There they had used their money to pay bribes and to buy tickets to come the rest of the way down to Addis Ababa by bus.

When they reached the city, many of them came to Pollack for help. She shepherded them through the complex emigration process and gave them funds to keep them going for the month. She also gave some of them money to go back to the Gondar region and bring their families to the capital.

Pollack knew that conditions in the north were getting worse. The Jewish community had been weakened by the loss of the thousands of people who already had gone to Israel. The rebels had moved into Gondar province, and she had heard reports of close fighting there, and of forced conscription of Jews into the army. There were stories of vandalism, of Jews abandoning whole villages, and of Christian neighbors burning Jewish homes.[49] She believed that the Jews would be safer in Addis Ababa, and she wanted to get them there. But the incipient AAEJ transport program, which united family members with relatives who were already in the capital, brought down only fifty people in December. Then Susan reported a consequential turn of events: five Beta Israel elders came down from their villages in the north and told her that the Gondar area was in chaos. They were in a war zone, they said, and pleaded, "Get us out!" God had told them to forget about escaping through Sudan, they told her; the Sudanese were expelling refugees. The elders knew that the Israelis were reopening their embassy in Addis. "We have to go there," they declared. "They will take us to Israel. Will you help us go to Addis Ababa?" "There was no holding them back," Pollack said later.[50]

The AAEJ already had considered various proposals to transport the Beta Israel out of Ethiopia. In the early 1980s, Jonathan Pollard, an American who later was imprisoned as a spy for Israel, had suggested a naval route for bringing them out. The organization had rejected that as too far out. They also had considered a plan to move the Jews to Addis. Nate Shapiro, the president of the AAEJ at that time, had decided, however, that to bring large numbers of Jews to the capital would create chaos, in addition to costing a lot of money. And to bring more people down than could be moved to Israel each month would, he thought, have been wrong and bad for credibility. But when Pollack told him about the Jewish elders' request and described the deteriorating situation of the American Jews' "brothers and sisters" in the Gondar region, Shapiro and the AAEJ board of directors decided to act despite the consequences. "Do what you have to do," he told Pollack. "Spend whatever you have to, $1 million or $100 million."

Shapiro did not discuss this decision with the Jewish Agency, which was responsible for immigration to Israel, or with the JDC. "There was no time," he recalled. "I was one hundred percent confident that it was right. And very seldom am I one hundred percent certain." He also was certain that money would not be an obstacle. As long as it meant saving a life, he was sure that the American Jewish community would give whatever was necessary.[51]

# TWO

# The AAEJ Accelerates the Process

## FEBRUARY–APRIL 1990

In the early months of 1990, rebel victories in Ethiopia helped set the future course for both Mengistu and the Beta Israel. Advances by the Eritrean insurgents brought their home province to the verge of independence, and Tigrean forces pushed southward, into the region in which most of the Jews lived. According to most sources, this did not profoundly impact the daily life of the Beta Israel. The AAEJ, however, considered that the Jews were in immediate danger and accelerated its transport program. The peril in which Mengistu now found himself would soon become entangled with the fate of the Jews, who would become political capital in his dealings with Israel.

### KASSA KEBEDE

While Reuven Merhav and the Israelis constructed the mechanisms for an orderly aliyah, and as Susan Pollack and the AAEJ determined to speed things up, Kassa Kebede watched. Kassa was the Ethiopian who had realized that Israel was the country that could open doors to the Americans. The Falashas were crucial to that strategy, and Kassa was empowered to deal with them.

Kassa was widely regarded as one of the most adept of all Mengistu's advisers, far more intelligent than the dictator himself. His information network was awesomely efficient, at home and abroad, and it drove the Israelis crazy when he complained about events and media reports from Israel even before they had heard about them. Before long, he would learn about the AAEJ transport program and turn it to his advantage.

Kassa, who was in his mid-forties at the time, came from an aristocratic family. His father, Kebede Tessema, had been Haile Selassie's minister of the Imperial Court and had held the title *dejazmach*, which was given to senior dignitaries and district chiefs and was roughly equivalent to *count*.[1] Kassa's manner was patrician, charming when appropriate. Mengistu had made a superb choice in selecting him to deal with the Israelis. Kassa spoke perfect Hebrew (though he switched to English when he wanted to show the Israelis that he was displeased with them). He had been educated in Jerusalem, where he had studied social work at Hebrew University from 1960 to 1965. During that time, he had had a very active social life in Jerusalem, and stories survive of his remarkable success with Israeli girls.[2]

Kassa enjoyed Mengistu's trust, though how close their relationship was remains a matter of speculation. It was said that they were half-brothers, and the American and Israeli press often accepted this uncritically. Mengistu's parents are thought to have been servants in the household of Kassa's father, though popular stories lent noble lineage to this humble descent. One variant proposed that the *dejazmach* himself was Mengistu's actual father. By this account, Kassa's father had sired Mengistu by a servant girl, then married her off to his night watchman. In another version, Kebede Tessema actually was Mengistu's grandfather, which makes Kassa his uncle.[3] Rumors of a blood relationship between Kassa and Mengistu could only have been strengthened in 1985 when Mengistu attended the *dejazmach*'s funeral, which resembled a state occasion.[4]

The putative family tie between Mengistu and Kassa served them both: Kassa because it connected him to the president of the state, and Mengistu because it tied him to Kassa's aristocratic family. Kassa did little to discourage this until after Mengistu fell from power. In an interview in 1992, he cited proof that he and Mengistu were not related: Kassa's father had been a refugee in Jerusalem nine months before Mengistu was born, and so could not have been his father.[5] Haile Selassie and a small group of his closest associates went into exile in Jerusalem and elsewhere during Mussolini's occupation of Ethiopia, from May 1936 until May 1941, and Kebede Tessema is said to have been among them. Mengistu's birth is variously dated at between 1937 and 1941, a period when Kebede was living abroad.[6] Whatever the true nature of Kebede Tessema's relationship with Mengistu, it may well have accounted for the fact that he survived the 1974 revolution unscathed. The same may apply to Kassa, the son of a minor noble who improbably rose to a position of influence in a Marxist regime.

By 1990, Kassa was an experienced diplomat. The former Ethiopian ambassador to the European headquarters of the UN in Geneva, he now he held the powerful post of secretary for foreign relations for the Central Committee of the Communist Party. In addition, he headed the organization known as the Cadre, which dealt with political indoctrination.[7] Kassa also was Mengistu's principal adviser about the Falashas and Israel, and it was he whom Mengistu had dispatched to Jerusalem to reopen diplomatic relations.

Kassa knew both the American organizations and the Israelis very well. And, more than anyone else, he understood that the Falashas could be the key to the survival of the Mengistu regime. Israeli, American, and Ethiopian sources agree that Kassa quickly came to understand that by controlling the Falasha emigration, he could give Mengistu leverage in his demands for Israeli arms. To pressure Jerusalem, the Ethiopians could simply reduce the flow of exits to Israel or turn off the tap altogether. In that way, they could transform a marginalized religious minority, the Falashas, into a critical fac-

tor in Mengistu's struggle to stay in power. This elegantly simple and devi-
ous approach was by no means self-evident. In 1990, the Jews comprised a
mere one-twentieth of 1 percent of the population of Ethiopia, a country of
over fifty million people. Linking Mengistu's future to them was the approximate equivalent, proportionally, of tying the fate of the United States
to a group the size of the Old Order Amish.[8] But, despite the Falashas' small
numbers, Kassa appreciated their political value.

Ironically, he had been instructed in this by two American Jews, members
of the AAEJ, during a visit to the United States two years earlier. One of
them, Gil Kulick, a former officer at the American embassy in Addis and a
board member of the AAEJ from the time of its inception, later recalled that
he had laid out the whole Falasha issue for Kassa. "I said, 'This is your key.
American Jews are very interested in the Falashas.' (I lied.)" Kulick assured
him that American Jews had a great deal of political influence and would use
it to improve Ethiopia's relations with the United States if Kassa's government let the Falashas go. Then Nate Shapiro, the president of the AAEJ,
flew to Atlanta and told Kassa the same. "Nate felt that it was possible to do
business with him," Kulick recalled. "From then on, [Kassa] was the big person on the Falasha issue."[9] Kulick and Shapiro had intended to show the
Ethiopian that it was in his nation's interest to permit the aliyah, and to win
his cooperation. They succeeded in both. Their conversations revealed to
him, however, how keenly the American Jewish organizations and the Israelis wanted the Falashas' release.

This put Kassa in an influential but conflicted position. He could ma-
nipulate the Falasha emigration in order to press Mengistu's increasingly
desperate demands for weapons. Yet he ardently did not want to be accused
of doing that. He was acutely sensitive to world opinion and the way that
history would depict him, and he did not want the Americans or the Arab
states to charge that Ethiopia was selling Jews for arms. In time, Kassa's
situation would become further complicated by his need to safeguard his
own future. He was loyal to Mengistu and was trying to save his regime. But
as the rebels advanced, Kassa would become dependent on the Israelis for his
security, even while he was their adversary in negotiating the release of the
Falashas. According to American and Israeli sources, he also would reach a
private financial arrangement with the AAEJ, contingent on his cooperation.[10] The strategy that he adopted to deal with these contrary demands
shapes much of the rest of this history.

Kassa's tactics vexed and occasionally enraged the Israelis, some of whom
later called him a liar. "Kassa never tells the whole truth," said one. "He can
lie to your face."[11] Another, more diplomatically, said that he had never known
anyone who related to the truth in quite the way that Kassa did. Bob Houdek,
who was the U.S. chargé d'affaires in Addis during the time of this story,

observed that indirection is a value in Ethiopian culture. "This was very, very frustrating," Houdek recalled in an interview. "As applied to political discourse, it meant that it was harder than hell to get a straight answer on an issue. . . . Rather, there were all kinds of smoke."[12]

From the Ethiopian perspective, by contrast, it was the Israelis who were untrustworthy. Mengistu had distrusted them since the Moshe Dayan incident in 1978.[13] Given that fact, Kassa had taken a chance by championing renewed relations with Jerusalem. And now, as Mengistu saw it, Israel had broken its promises, cutting off the supply of arms that his regime needed to survive. And the cultural differences that disturbed the Western diplomats worked both ways: the Israelis and Americans at times unknowingly offended Ethiopian sensibilities, as we shall see. Kassa, with his deep understanding of Israel, was positioned to bridge that cultural divide—and to use his formidable skill and influence to gain the best advantage for his country in a perilous time.

Several of the Israelis and Americans became fond of Kassa and respected his intelligence and subtlety. Asher Naim, who later would serve as Israel's ambassador to Addis, considered Kassa to be a believing Christian who on some level had a genuine feeling for the Jews in his charge. "Mengistu didn't care if he put them in the fire tomorrow," Naim told me in an interview, but Kassa "cared more about Israel and the Falashas than any other Ethiopian."[14] Uri Lubrani, who later locked horns with Kassa as the chief Israeli negotiator for the release of the Jews, told me that he needed an interlocutor who could deliver. "I knew that this was my man," he said of Kassa. "I had rapport with him. He was erudite, a man of the world. But I also always knew that he was a wily fox, and greedy." Kassa was a good emissary of a rogue regime, Lubrani said.[15] His value to Mengistu increased as the rebels advanced and Ethiopia's demands for Israeli arms became more urgent.

## "THE MACBETH OF AFRICA"

In early 1990, Mengistu's circumstances became more precarious, and his response was characteristically brutal. In mid-February, the Eritrean rebels in the north scored a major victory: the Eritrean People's Liberation Front (EPLF) captured the crucial port city of Massawa. Ethiopia proper is landlocked and depends on Eritrea, with its sprawling six-hundred-mile-long Red Sea coastline, for access to international waters. The loss of Massawa, one of only two seaports in Eritrea, was a disastrous setback for Mengistu. It severely curtailed Ethiopia's ability to import arms and other goods, and it isolated Asmara, the provincial capital, which now in effect was under siege by the EPLF.[16] The fall of the port also severed the sea link to the one hundred thousand men of the Ethiopian Second Army, the best element of

Mengistu's forces. Rebels had driven government forces from the province of Tigre the year before, denying Mengistu a land route by which to supply his army in Eritrea. Now, with the loss of Massawa, Mengistu was unable to reach his troops by sea. This obliged him to provision them through the only remaining means, an airlift—a very expensive recourse that sapped the country's economy and its meager fuel reserves.

Mengistu launched indiscriminate retaliatory bombing raids on Massawa, during which, EPLF spokesmen claimed, government MiGs dropped cluster bombs, causing great damage. The fighting and the subsequent bombardment destroyed most of the fifty thousand tons of imported grain that had been stored there for relief purposes. The air strikes also damaged the port and forced its closure, halting a United Nations effort to deliver food shipments. This seriously exacerbated the famine conditions in the region, leaving one million people in the area at risk. The *Times* of London now called Mengistu "the Macbeth of Africa."[17]

In carrying on this fight, the EPLF sought independence for their province, which had endured a long history of colonization and exploitation. As Haggai Erlich notes, Eritrea was a creation of European imperialism. The Italians seized the region in 1885–89, gave it its name (from "Red Sea" in Greek), and established Asmara as its capital.[18] They used Eritrea as a launching site for an 1896 attack on Ethiopia that was crushed at the battle of Adwa, and for a successful invasion in 1935, under Mussolini. In 1941, British-led forces defeated the Italians, ending their occupation. London subsequently adopted a rapacious policy toward Eritrea's assets, removing the modern sector that the Italians had built.[19] The United Nations confederated Eritrea and Ethiopia in 1952.

The emperor degraded Eritrea's autonomy and freedoms for ten years, then dissolved the federation in 1962, reducing Eritrea to an Ethiopian province. Eritrean rebels began a struggle for independence, led by the predominantly Muslim Eritrean Liberation Front (ELF). After the Derg came to power, Mengistu inflamed this insurgency by taking a leading role in the regime's decision to subdue Eritrea by force. By 1977, the rebels held 95 percent of the region.[20] Mengistu shifted his troops northward to deal with the rebellion, leaving southeastern Ethiopia vulnerable. The irredentist Somali leader Mohammed Siad Barre then sent regular army forces into the Ogaden in southeast Ethiopia, where they supported a secessionist insurgency by ethnic Somalis. By September 1977, these forces controlled 90 percent of that region.

Under assault in both the north and the southeast, Mengistu faced the possibility of defeat and the breakup of Ethiopia. The Soviet Union, Cuba, and South Yemen forestalled that, however. Replacing the United States as Ethiopia's principal ally, the Soviets sent Ethiopia advisers and arms, while

Cuba dispatched over ten thousand troops and the South Yemenis provided training in the use of Soviet tanks.[21] By March 1978, the Somali forces had been decisively beaten back and Mengistu was free to focus on Eritrea. His army, supported by the Soviet bombers and warships, rolled back the insurgents, who were able to hold on to only a corner of the province.

Still, the Eritrean struggle continued. The EPLF, founded in 1972, had eclipsed the ELF as the dominant rebel force in the region by the 1980s. Comprising mostly Christians, the EPLF espoused a strict Marxist platform. In 1987, however, its party congress called for a mixed economy and a multiparty system. Known for its egalitarianism, the EPLF included women in combat roles and called for a referendum in which Eritreans could decide if they wanted independence. In 1988 and 1989, the EPLF achieved significant battlefield successes in what was by then the longest ongoing war in Africa. Mengistu could not afford to lose: retaining control of Eritrea was the one point on which he had the support of his people, his only political asset.[22] But after the generals' failed coup in May 1989, the Ethiopian army was disheartened and the Eritreans were emboldened. With the capture of Massawa in February 1990, the EPLF leaders were becoming confident that Mengistu could not last much longer.

At the same time, another rebel group, the Tigre People's Liberation Front (TPLF), also was anticipating victory over Mengistu. The TPLF had been founded in 1975 by eight Addis Ababa University students opposed to the Derg who fled to Eritrea for training by an EPLF commander, then went home to the mountains of Tigre province. As this group grew, it drew support from Tigrean peasants who were angered by the regime's harsh policy outlawing seasonal labor migration and by its hostility to religion. The TPLF, many of whose members were devoutly Christian, initially professed an orthodox Albanian Marxism. Isolationist and taking no military aid from abroad, they armed themselves with tanks, heavy artillery, and other weapons that they captured from fleeing government troops. By the late 1980s, the Tigreans began to cooperate with the EPLF militarily and politically, resulting in victories for both, including the TPLF successes that liberated Tigre in 1989.[23]

The Tigrean rebels were fighting not for the right to independence, as the Eritreans were, but for the removal of Mengistu and for democracy. To create a national anti-Mengistu movement, the TPLF merged in 1989 with a predominantly Amharic rebel force, the Ethiopian People's Democratic Movement. Together, they formed the Ethiopian People's Revolutionary Democratic Front (EPRDF). Their principles included basic democratic freedoms, the release of political prisoners, the dismantling of the repressive state security apparatus, and Eritrean self-determination.[24] The closer the Tigrean rebels came to victory, the more moderate their charismatic young leader, Meles Zenawe, became. He took his lesson from the liberalization of socialist states in Eastern Europe and realized that if the EPRDF came to power, it would need American support.

Though vastly outnumbered, the sixty-five thousand EPRDF fighters continued to beat the army back in early 1990. With the cream of Mengistu's forces pinned down in Eritrea in the north, the EPRDF was able to push south and west into ethnic Amharic regions, including Gondar and even Shoa, the province in which Addis Ababa sits. By early March, in a battle in which they claimed to have killed or wounded sixteen thousand government soldiers, the EPRDF closed in on the strategically important airbase at Bahr-Dar, south of Lake Tana. "We are in a position to launch the final offensive," Meles declared boldly, though prematurely.[25]

Against these rebel groups Mengistu fielded the largest army in sub-Saharan Africa, up to four hundred thousand men or more—reportedly including conscripts as young as fourteen—assisted by Soviet and North Korean advisers.[26] As the insurgents advanced, however, his prospects became increasingly dire.

## ERITREA ON THE VERGE OF INDEPENDENCE

The rebel successes early in 1990 complicated matters politically. With the victory at Massawa, the Eritreans were on the verge of independence, which would mean the dismemberment of Ethiopia. Neither Washington, Moscow, nor Beijing supported that outcome. Even Meles, the EPRDF leader, reportedly preferred that the region remain part of Ethiopia. Meles sought to forge a coalition with the Eritreans while not outraging those who insisted that Ethiopia remain unified. So he agreed with the EPLF to form a transitional government first, then to have Eritrea hold a referendum on independence at some later date.[27]

For the Israelis, an independent Eritrea could be problematic. Approximately half of the population of the region is Sunni Muslim, and Israeli intelligence reported that radical Arab nations were arming the Eritrean rebels. If the province achieved independence, it might join the Arab camp.[28] Meir Yoffe, the new Israeli ambassador to Addis, said as much at the time, warning that an independent Eritrea would make the Red Sea an Arab sea.[29] Saudi Arabia and North and South Yemen controlled the eastern banks of the Red Sea. If Massawa on the western shore came into the hands of a hostile regime, Israeli shipping could be imperiled. The situation seemed all the more ominous because in June 1989 an Islamist regime had come to power in Sudan, Eritrea's neighbor to the north and west, which also stands along the Red Sea. Another significant consideration for Jerusalem was that an unfriendly government in

Eritrea might end the existing Ethiopian policy of allowing Israeli planes to overfly the province en route to Kenya and South Africa.

Haggai Erlich noted at the time, however, that the EPLF was not particularly threatening: in addition to being predominantly Christian, it had no close ties with Syria or Libya, and it had been wooing the West.[30] Indeed, its young Christian members reportedly resented the ELF's earlier Arabization of the independence movement.[31] Still, from Jerusalem's perspective, a rebel victory and the breakup of Ethiopia would represent a destabilizing change in the equation of power. This put the Israelis in a delicate position. Mengistu kept Ethiopia unified, he had restored it as an ally, and he was letting Falashas go. The Israelis needed his goodwill. Under American constraint, though, their declared policy was not to arm him. Now they had another compelling reason: they did not want to alienate the insurgents, for whom victory seemed probable. Rebel leaders already resented what they charged was Israel's military support for Mengistu. If the Eritreans won independence, Israel would need the new government to safeguard its air and sea routes. And if the EPRDF came to power in Addis, Israel would have to turn to Meles to maintain Ethiopia's friendship and complete the aliyah.

In the meantime, the rebel advance might affect the emigration of the Jews in ways that were impossible to calculate. The Israelis and most American observers did not think this danger was at all imminent. But Susan Pollack did, and she and the AAEJ decided to act on it before this historic moment passed.

## BOB FRASURE:
## "THEY WERE PLAYING A RISKY GAME"

In April 1990 Pollack and the AAEJ became convinced that conditions in Gondar required an aggressive remedy. Bob Frasure, the deputy chief of mission at the U.S. embassy in Addis, had urged her to get all of the remaining Jews out of the province, she told AAEJ officers in the United States that month. Frasure had advised her that the rebels had closed the road from Gondar to Addis, she said, and that advance rebel forces were within hours of the capital. She added that he had warned her to transport the Jews quickly, before the rainy season started. He even had directed her to Ethiopian Airlines officials who might help with airlifts out of the Gondar area.[32] According to Pollack, Frasure had told her that the situation was critical. It was time to act.[33]

Frasure would not confirm this in an interview. Self-confident, colorfully outspoken, and exceptionally capable, Frasure, who was forty-eight years old in 1990, was a career foreign service officer. He had served in Addis Ababa since 1988 and would be leaving soon for Washington, to serve as the National Security Council's director of African affairs. He knew that the Ethiopians were holding the Jews hostage for guns and he wanted the emigration to proceed, but he was uncertain about moving them to Addis at all, he said in an interview. He worried about a reiteration of the chaos, rape, and murder that had occurred there when Haile Selassie fled Mussolini's troops in 1936. After the emperor's flight, patriots had begun to destroy the capital in order to deny it to the Italians, and this had given way to mob violence. "This was part of the collective memory," Frasure noted. "Everyone who lived in Addis Ababa knew about it." He warned at the time that if the Falashas were in Addis when Mengistu fell, they would be singled out, "not as Jews, but as strangers, country people with food and money, a target." In transporting the Jews to the capital, "Susan wanted to raise the stakes," Frasure recalled. "I told them they were playing a risky game," he said of the AAEJ. He didn't urge Pollack to bring the Falashas down, he said, but he didn't advise her not to, either. He did warn her about the danger of having thousands of people sitting in the mud in Addis Ababa, though.[34]

Frasure also helped smooth over the fact that the Beta Israel were coming to Addis Ababa illegally, Pollack recalled in an interview. In the complex Ethiopian bureaucracy, people needed a *meshenya,* a document from the local peasant farmers' association permitting them to leave their area. (Later Pollack would buy a stamp and produce her own.)[35] They then needed a *kebele* stamp in Addis to permit them to buy food, use the bank, or pay rent (a *kebele* was a local Communist Party organization). The Jews would come from Gondar without any permission, but Frasure told the authorities not to harass them about this, Pollack recalled. "An organization will take care of them," he told the authorities in Addis. "You will look good, and make money."[36]

The urgency of this moment was heightened by the fact that the other main escape route to Israel, through Sudan, now officially was closed.[37] Even after Operation Moses was terminated abruptly in 1985, smaller-scale rescues had continued secretly from Sudan. But the Islamist government that had seized power in Khartoum, Sudan's capital, in June 1989 had halted these missions. Then in January 1990, Sudan expelled the nearly one thousand remaining Jews from the refugee camps, depositing them at the Ethiopian border.[38] (At the same time, the Sudanese welcomed anyone from an Arab country without requiring a visa. Among those who found refuge there two years later was Osama bin Laden, who was fleeing from Saudi Arabia.)[39] Of these one thousand Jews, fewer than seven hundred survived. Meir Yoffe, the Israeli ambassador, recalled in an interview that he fought successfully to keep them from coming to Addis. "We didn't want the situation to deteriorate to refugees in tents," he said.[40] Susan Pollack responded very differently. These people had walked from Gondar to Sudan, where they had suffered in refugee camps, hoping to be taken to Israel, she said later. Many of them were sick, often with yellow fever or malaria. Then they had walked all the way to Addis, only to be trucked back to Gondar. It was the only time that she allowed herself to cry during the years that she worked in Ethiopia.[41]

## "MAY GOD HELP YOU"

Against this background, in April 1990, on Passover, the AAEJ's Will Recant arrived in Addis Ababa. During this brief trip, Recant's only visit to Ethiopia, he and Pollack took a decision that altered the course of the aliyah. They reviewed the progress of the emigration and determined that the conditions were right to expedite the AAEJ transport program. This decision would have far more immediate consequences than they imagined: it would trigger the mass migration of almost the entire Jewish community from Gondar to Addis within a matter of months.

Exit applications were being processed quickly at that point, with some 250 Jews leaving for Israel in the first week of April, and the fighting had stopped temporarily in the Gondar region.[42] Those two factors created a window of opportunity for the transport program. A committee of twenty-two locals who worked for the AAEJ, led by an Ethiopian Christian named Berhanu Yiradu, asked to bring the Falashas down more quickly.

At just that time, Kassa Kebede was about to leave on an extended trip to the United States and elsewhere. With him out of the country, this was the ideal moment for the AAEJ to act, and Pollack and Recant determined to exploit it. Up until then, the organization had been bringing down only the relatives of their cases in Addis Ababa. Now they would speed up the transport program and move *all* of the Jews.[43] Nate Shapiro, the head of the AAEJ, said later that he had agreed with this decision. "We knew what Susan was doing," he stated. "We said, 'Accelerate it.' I can't even recall if she asked our approval."[44]

Pollack and Recant secured the private consent of the JDC's Michael Schneider, too, though not his public support or the cooperation of his organization.[45] Indeed, Pollack and the AAEJ did not coordinate their plan with anyone. They made no preparations sufficient to deal with the massive movement of people that was about to occur, and with the sickness and social disruption that would follow.

The trickle of Jews reaching Addis soon would become a stream, then a deluge. From January through April, the transport program moved a modest number of Beta Israel to the capital city, fewer than a hundred a week, according to AAEJ records. In May, by the organization's own count, it would triple that amount. Then it would move an astounding ten thousand people in June and July.[46] Thousands more would arrive on their own, often after having been inspired to leave by AAEJ agents.[47] To spur the emigration further, the AAEJ secretly would fund Ethiopian demonstrations in Israel demanding faster immigration from Addis. Some Israeli officials believed that the activists coordinated this with Kassa, who wanted to turn up the pressure on Israel for his own purposes.[48]

Once the migration started, no one wanted to be left behind. In all, over twenty thousand people, including many families of Jewish converts to Christianity, would leave their homes in the north illegally and come to Addis (see Appendix 1). This mass migration would far outstrip the rate of Beta Israel exits to Israel, creating a glut in a city already swollen with refugees.

The Jews expected the Americans and Israelis to take care of them. And they expected to be taken to Jerusalem "immediately, tomorrow," as one AAEJ agent told me later.[49] Instead, they were trapped in squalid conditions in Addis Ababa, in some cases for a year or more. When the migration began, there was no infrastructure to accommodate them in Addis: no adequate housing, medical staff, or supplies of food and clothing. Many Jews died there, especially children. The Ethiopian Jews came believing that they were reliving the Exodus. But for many families, it was their own firstborn who would die in the wretched slums of Addis Ababa. And very many of the adults would prove to be the "generation of the wilderness" (in Hebrew, *dor ha-midbar*), the generation that would be sacrificed on their way to the Promised Land. "Whether AAEJ made the right decision or not, history will judge," a JDC report observed in December 1990.[50]

"May God help you. I hope you know what you are doing," Henry Gold told Pollack when he learned about the transport program. As executive director of Canadian Physicians for Aid and Relief, Gold had worked with the Ethiopian Jews in the refugee camps of Sudan. The son of an Auschwitz survivor, he had seen great suffering in Sudan in the eighties. Now, in mid-1990, as the Jews began to descend on Addis in great numbers, he had a sense of impending tragedy.

"That sounds like Henry: dour and melancholy," Pollack told me years later, with a smile.[51]

## WHY?

Was the danger in the Beta Israel villages so compelling that it justified moving an entire population? Virtually none of the people who worked for the Jewish Agency, the Israeli government, or the Joint thought so. U.S. State Department officials perceived no urgency in the Falashas' circumstances in their villages. Nor did most of the Ethiopian Jews who were interviewed for this book, including some who worked for the AAEJ and the other rescue organizations.

Contrary to claims being made in the West, for example, the people on the scene knew that there was no significant famine in the Jewish areas in Gondar at that time.[52] Very many of the Jews were poor, and most of the children were mildly or severely malnourished. But, the Beta Israel said later, famine was not the reason that they left their villages.

Nor did they leave because they were in a war zone. At almost precisely the time that Pollack and Will Recant were deciding to transport them more quickly, the Jewish Agency's Micha Feldman determined that the Jews were not in significant danger. He told John Hall, a visiting U.S. State Department official, that he had checked out reports of violence against the Jews in the north but could not verify any of them. No Jewish villagers had been caught in military crossfire, he added. Hundreds of Jews had been conscripted into the army, Feldman noted, but this had happened to everyone else as well. Ethiopian Jews confirmed later that in general they had not been in peril. In my interviews with them, none spoke of cluster bomb attacks in their region. They may have feared being caught in a battle, they said, but they were not afraid of the rebels, and they passed freely through rebel-held areas on their way to Addis.[53]

Their Christian neighbors did not drive them out. Several Ethiopian-Israelis told me about prejudice and isolated attacks against them in the villages. One, a graduate student at Hebrew University, said somewhat dramatically that if not for Susan Pollack, the Beta Israel now "would be extinct in Gondar. The [Christian] Amharas would have killed them."[54] But none of the Ethiopian Jews I interviewed, including him, said that they had left because of tensions with non-Jews. Their Christian neighbors did not steal from them until after they had left, Feldman told Hall, adding that, far from pressing Jews to leave, Christians tried to persuade them to stay.[55] The Jews were the blacksmiths, and, though the non-Jews despised smiths, they needed them.

The Beta Israel did not leave because of illness, either. There was disease in the villages, but Dr. Rick Hodes, who later ran the JDC clinic in Addis, told me that Pollack's estimate that half of the Jews needed medical attention seems extremely high. There was no medical emergency at the time, he said. "Susan Pollack is not a doctor," Hodes commented. There was no urgency of *any* kind, he added.[56]

That is not what the elders had told Pollack. They had said that the Jews' lives were in danger, and perhaps that was how they perceived their circumstances at that moment. Or they may have exaggerated in order to get their people to Zion.

But why did they want to? Their lives were relatively stable in Gondar. If the Beta Israel were not at risk, why did they abandon their villages and their way of life? Ethiopia had a brutal government that was losing a civil war, and one Ethiopian Jew who had lived in Addis admitted to me that he left only because of the instability in the country. Another consideration was that they certainly anticipated having more prosperous lives in Israel. Ethiopia was the poorest nation in the world, according to the World Bank, and a confidential JDC memo of two years earlier conjectured that the Jews were coming to Addis because of the level of support they expected to get there.[57] But none of the Beta Israel I spoke with cited financial comfort as his incentive. Motives can be unrecognized, misrepresented, and complex, but the answer every Ethiopian Jew gave me was unambiguous: they wanted to go to Zion. The flag of Israel was flying in Addis Ababa. If they could get there, they believed that the Israelis would take them to Jerusalem. The migration had already been partially completed: thousands of their people were already in Israel. The Jews of Gondar saw this as their chance to be reunited with their children, their parents, and other dear ones in Zion. Their relatives in Israel were sending letters, urging the remaining Beta Israel to make their way to Addis. The AAEJ gave many of them the means, and the rest came on their own.

They were seriously mistaken in thinking that they would be taken to Jerusalem quickly, but Ethiopians place a special value on acting shrewdly and boldly. The Amharic word *gobez* captures this central concept. As the Israeli scholar Haim Rosen notes, every Ethiopian wants to be considered *gobez:* "smart, brilliant, clever, strong, brave, and, finally, quite a fellow." The Jews believed that people had been *gobez* to make the long trek to Sudan. And they were *gobez* now to abandon their villages and risk everything in the hope of going to the Promised Land.[58]

Shamay Balay, like most of the other Ethiopian Jews I spoke to in Israel, told me that people did not leave their villages because of bad conditions, but rather because they "dreamed of life." They were going to Jerusalem at last.[59]

"I heard about Jerusalem every day, as if my parents had just left a year ago," Babu Yacov, an Ethiopian-Israeli, told me. "Jerusalem, Jerusalem. I heard it in the prayers," said another, Tevege Tegenye.[60] "Our ancestors all hoped and prayed that they themselves would make it to Jerusalem," said an elderly *qes* (Jewish priest). "They did not make it. We are on the brink of reaching Zion. Our children are there. I don't want to die without seeing my son, and without seeing Jerusalem."[61]

Another *qes*, Menashe Zimru, was the oldest of the Ethiopian religious leaders, in his eighties. Most of the other *qessotch* had been his students, and his words spoke for all of them: "The thirsty go to water, the hungry go to food, and I go to Jerusalem," he said.[62]

Why did the AAEJ believe that the Jews were in peril in Gondar? The Joint accused AAEJ officials of resorting to "emotional and sometimes irresponsible exaggeration of the condition of Ethiopian Jewry" in order to promote their fund-raising.[63] But the fact that the AAEJ leadership undertook to uproot a community, putting thousands of people in jeopardy and incurring huge expense, demonstrates that their concern for the immediate safety of the Jews was no mere posture. Frasure's concerns had had a profound impact on them, and the Beta Israel elders' pleas that Pollack reported also had had an effect.

Pollack and the other AAEJ officials believed that the Jews faced imminent threat: the war had created an emergency, with security and civil administration in Gondar progressively degenerating in the face of the rebel advance. The AAEJ knew that the Jews wanted urgently to go to Jerusalem and would take the necessary risks to get there. Pollack and her colleagues saw their role as actualizing that wish.[64]

Another factor that impelled the AAEJ leaders to approve the transport program was their drive for action in the aliyah, informed by their historical impatience with what they saw as Israel's lack of a sense of urgency. I asked Will Recant directly why there was such a disparity between the AAEJ's perception of the situation in Gondar and that of other observers. There was a basic philosophical difference, he responded. Micha Feldman and the Jewish Agency felt that the Jews were not starving, so they were willing to take them out slowly, slowly. They considered that since the Jewish community had sustained itself for generations, it could continue to do so indefinitely. The AAEJ, by contrast, felt that the Jews were in present danger from civil war and conditions in the area. Even if there was no famine, there were certainly crop failures and food shortages; even if the Jews were not caught in battlefield crossfire, they were subject to forced conscription. The community had waited long enough.[65]

# THREE

# A Potential Catastrophe

## MAY–JUNE 1990

In May 1990, the movement of people down from Gondar turned into a flood. Hundreds of Jews each week, often hundreds a day, arrived in Addis, where the AAEJ had made no plans adequate to their needs. The resulting disorder angered both Ethiopian and Israeli officials, and the death rate among the Beta Israel, especially the children, alarmed everyone who worked with the community.

## A QUIET, DISCREET MIGRATION

In early May, AAEJ agents were in the north arranging transport and Susan Pollack was preparing for more arrivals. She rented a large compound from a sympathetic Ethiopian Christian priest to serve as a reception center. The priest believed that the Messiah would not return until all Jews had returned to Israel, and that by helping the AAEJ he was speeding the process.

Nobody was prepared for what happened next, however. On May 12, the first AAEJ truck carrying Jews from Gondar reached the city. By the fifteenth, two hundred or more people were arriving every day, often malnourished and ill with fever. Then on a single day, May 23, AAEJ agents delivered five hundred Beta Israel to what became known as the "Susan Compound" in Addis.[1] Pollock was taken by surprise: there was no place to put the new arrivals. She called Bob Frasure, who showed up at the compound two hours later, in jeans, with a U.S. Army truck and helped offload three tents and a supply of high-energy protein biscuits. Later he brought firewood, which was hard to come by in Addis Ababa, to use for cooking.[2]

In the month of May, Pollack reported, the AAEJ agents transported 1,366 Jews from Gondar province to Addis Ababa. They brought them by chartered plane, then, when the road reopened at the end of the month, by truck, bus, and minivan.[3] In addition, many people sold their possessions and made their way to Addis on their own. Observers in the capital at the time confirmed the dimensions of the migration. A JDC memo of May 21 noted the influx, saying that there were 6,000 Jews in the city at that point. By the beginning of June, 400 to 700 Jews were reaching Addis every day, according to another JDC memo.[4] Micha Feldman notes that most of them were brought on buses hired by the AAEJ and taken directly to the Susan Compound. By June 7, there were 8,500 Jews in Addis, and the rate of their arrival was accelerating.[5] On June 9, two physicians in Addis corroborated the increase, observing that 1,026 Jews had reached the city in a period of just four days.[6] Pollack reported bringing down a total of 6,023 people in June, which seems feasible in view of an estimate by the JDC's Kobi Friedman that 6,000 arrived in that month.[7]

The AAEJ gave one of the three tents to the Israeli embassy so that Beta Israel registering to emigrate could stay out of sight of the main road. The Ethiopian officials wanted the process to be low-profile, hoping that the Arab states, the rebels, and Ethiopian Muslims would not notice. Buses and trucks would deposit their passengers in Addis as quickly and quietly as possible. Nobody would show money or documents in public, and children were forbidden to run around.[8] It was supposed to be a quiet, discreet migration of a community of over 20,000 people.

Finding housing for the newcomers became an urgent need. AAEJ workers began to reserve ten to fifteen houses a day, five days a week. In all, the AAEJ staff managed to rent 490 buildings in an overcrowded city whose population had doubled to perhaps two million in recent years.[9] Of necessity, much of the housing they found was in appalling condition. In late May, Micha Feldman moved fourteen families out of a building that formerly was a cowshed into more suitable lodgings.[10] The Joint helped too, renting accommodations for five hundred people that month.[11] It was a good effort, but that many people could arrive in a single day.

Berhanu, the Ethiopian Christian who worked for the AAEJ, organized the entire transport program. With the other AAEJ workers, he set up committees that rented twenty-six trucks and forty-three buses, paying the astonishing price, by Ethiopian standards, of up to 8,000 birr ($1,600) to bring a hundred people to the city. It cost even more when the main road was closed and the trucks had to take the bad route around Lake Tana. The work was dangerous for the AAEJ agents. They carried what for them were enormous sums—$5,000 to $10,000 in birr each—and brought guns for self-protection.[12] (Berhanu also carried his gun in Addis to protect Pollack.) It was all supposed to be secret, but the government knew, said Berhanu. Micha Feldman also knew, and participated, Berhanu added: "He sent a guide to Gondar to bring people. He gave me lists. . . . He sent messages to Gondar for people to come."[13]

The fact that government officials were aware of the transport program from the beginning was confirmed by Dr. Girma Tolossa, an Ethiopian Christian who represented the JDC in Addis. "Everyone in government must have known that the Jews were coming," he said. "Security must know. . . . We used to go frequently to Gondar because we had projects. I saw pamphlets: 'It is time to go to Israel now.' This was at the end of 1989, eight to ten months before the flood [of Jews to Addis]. This is foolish. There were always government people in the villages. They knew it. This used to be like a police state."[14]

## "WHAT HAVE WE DONE?"

The sheer number of people who made their way south was overwhelming. "We didn't know that thousands and thousands would come," Recant recalled. "We thought it would be a long process. . . . But it snowballed. . . . If we had known, we would have planned for it."[15] Pollack remembered it differently, however: "I *did* expect twenty thousand to come," she said later. "I figured the agencies would take care of them. Nate [Shapiro] said, 'Spend whatever you have to.'"[16]

Pollack reported a very orderly registration process: the Jews would arrive at dusk, when they would attract the least attention. They would register at the AAEJ compound, be given a meal, and spend the night. By arrangement with Micha Feldman, the AAEJ gave the Jews cash for their first month's rent and an orientation to the emigration process. Then they sent them to register at the Israeli embassy. That would give Feldman and the Jewish Agency workers one month in which to confirm that they were really Jewish and to register them.[17]

The reality for the Jews was extremely harsh, however. The number reaching Addis Ababa grew out of all proportion to the city's capacity to absorb them. In June, when the AAEJ reported bringing down well over six thousand Beta Israel, only eighty or ninety were allowed to leave for Israel each week. "We saw a refugee camp at our feet, with great needs," Recant recalled later.[18] In the middle of the month, the rains began.

Crowding and lack of sanitation contributed to a serious level of illness, especially among children. The Beta Israel had always been an outdoor people, but in Addis they lived indoors, in overcrowded rooms. This facilitated the spread of tuberculosis and other contagious diseases. In the absence of a functional drainage system, wastewater flooded the rooms where many of the Jews were staying, further heightening the risk of illness.[19] During the move to the city, many already malnourished people had gone hungry for days or weeks, and this too degraded their health. Dr. Rick Hodes, who later became the medical director of the JDC clinic in Addis, noted in an interview that the new arrivals' main problems were intestinal parasites, pneumonia, malnutrition, and tuberculosis. Measles was a major danger, especially for children, most of whom had arrived malnourished. And there was another threat in Addis that had been unknown in the Jewish villages: HIV. Up to 60 percent of the prostitutes in the city were later found to carry it.[20]

Many of the Beta Israel men would become infected with the deadly virus during their stay there.

Zimna Berhane, a veteran Ethiopian-Israeli who had taken part in secret rescues from Sudan, was dismayed by the conditions in Addis that June. He had just arrived to work with the Jewish Agency, he recalled in an interview, and he was appalled by what he found at the Israeli embassy: "I saw a sea of people. It is hard to describe their condition. . . . I was in a camp in Sudan, but these people were in worse shape. There was pouring rain, mud. They were practically naked and malnourished. It was hard to accept this. People had lost human decency. They were pushing and trampling old people and kids. . . . They fell in the mud. They were filthy. It was hard to see."[21]

"I had a feeling of 'What have we done?'" Recant recalled. "No, not exactly. We had to deal with their needs. There was no panic."[22]

Pollack rose to the challenge, despite the fact that she had only recently recovered from a case of typhoid. Micha Odenheimer, an Israeli-American rabbi who came to Addis to cover the Beta Israel story as a journalist, recalled later that Pollack was like a field general in the middle of a battle. "It was impressive but scary," he told me. She fought to obtain and distribute high-protein biscuits and blankets, hired a medical staff, helped start a school.[23] The need to hire doctors and nurses was particularly urgent, and Pollack, with her limited Amharic, gave the job to Berhanu. Under the pressure of the moment, he found someone within a day. But Rick Hodes said later, "The doctor they hired wasn't a medical doctor. He was a businessman. [He] set up an injection factory."[24]

Pollack tried to be accessible to all of the new arrivals and was baffled when, despite her invitations, none of them came to ask her for help. Then she realized that they had never encountered a doorknob before and did not know how to enter her office. "I'm learning every day," she told Bob Houdek, and, after fixing that problem, made herself available to each of the Ethiopians who sought her out.[25]

The usual tensions among the Jewish relief organizations exploded into conflict that spring and summer. Pollack had never been timid about berating the JDC and the Israelis, and she blasted them now for not doing more. She was especially frustrated that her staff carried the burden of medical care when the crisis began. The Joint had clinics in the north but did not start one in the capital until July, and then it was only for referrals to other medical services in the city. The JDC simply was not prepared for the huge Jewish migration from Gondar, so the job of saving lives fell to Pollack.

Inevitably, the Jews suffered. It was an especially cold rainy season, and when the bad weather came, they started dying at an alarming rate. "Every day we would bury kids," a JDC official who worked in Addis recalled later. "I was afraid to come to the embassy. Each day people would come for a burial grant."[26] Whenever a child died, Micha Feldman would fast for the rest of the day, honoring the Ethiopian Jewish tradition of fasting from the time of a death until after the funeral.[27] Odenheimer wrote on August 20 that there was reason to believe that far more Ethiopian Jews died in June, July, and August than the one hundred that Israeli officials reported. In the preceding month alone, over seventy Jews were known to have died in Addis Ababa, he reported, as against the published figure of thirty-three.[28] A visiting Ethiopian-Israeli social worker reached a similar conclusion, saying that three to nine Jews died in Addis every day that July.[29] The Israelis consulted the *qessotch*, however, who confirmed that the official mortality figures were accurate.[30]

To put these tragic deaths in perspective, it must be said that statistics about the Ethiopian aliyah are often estimates, and virtually all of those vary with the source. One also must bear in mind that Ethiopia has one of the worst infant malnutrition rates in the world, and the overall mortality rate in the country was very high: on average, in a population the size of the Jewish community in Addis, forty-four people could be expected to die each month.[31] In the worst month, July 1990, the JDC reported thirty-nine deaths. Every month after that, the mortality rate declined, sometimes precipitously.

Whatever the true numbers, Jews were dying, especially children. Pollack reported that the twelve-by-sixteen-inch boxes that had contained biscuits now were used for baby coffins. "One day, an old man came with a box tied up," said Pollack. "I opened it. There was a dead baby inside. That was the worst." Later, in the months after she left Ethiopia, Pollack recalled, she cried whenever she talked about this.[32]

On June 4, 1990, the JDC-Israel's Eli Eliezri and Ami Bergman sent an urgent fax from Addis Ababa to Michael Schneider in New York reporting that the Ethiopian Jews were arriving in Addis by the thousands "with no means to handle them." They warned, "In case a delay in departures occurs, due either to slow processing or problems on the part of the Government, we will face a very difficult situation." It would be no exaggeration if they called it a catastrophe, they said.[33]

That delay happened almost immediately. At the end of June the Ethiopians tightened the requirements to apply for a passport. In July they stopped issuing exit permits at all, and migration to Israel virtually halted. The Falashas were trapped in the cold and mud of a strange and hostile city.

## "WE NEEDED A JEWISH SHERIFF"

While the migration to Addis was quickening that spring, Kassa spent five weeks in America. His mission was to secure loans and to restore ambassadorial-level relations with the United States, which had been suspended since 1980. Kassa proposed a package of concessions designed to satisfy American demands: he offered to halt the bombing of Massawa, open the port for emergency humanitarian food shipments, and allow the immediate departure of three thousand Falashas from Addis. In exchange, Ethiopia would be permitted to send an ambassador to the United States. Kassa argued that Ethiopia was liberalizing and cited as proof Mengistu's pledge to give clemency to the twelve generals who had been imprisoned after the coup attempt in May 1989. Mengistu, however, then abruptly had the generals executed, reportedly after torturing them.[34] Kassa left Washington on May 18, the day that he was supposed to meet with Deputy Secretary of State Lawrence Eagleburger to formalize the agreement. Kassa said later that Mengistu's rash act had given him no choice but to abort his trip. But American officials drew a different conclusion: that Kassa left because he could not deliver the bargain he had proposed.[35]

When he got home, Kassa saw firsthand what had happened in Addis Ababa during his absence, and he was appalled. The Israeli embassy was beginning to look like a refugee camp.[36] The Ethiopians had wanted to keep a low profile on the Falashas so their Arab neighbors would not accuse them of selling Jews for arms. They certainly did not want a reenactment of what had happened in Sudan five years earlier. In that country, the Gaffar el-Nimeiri regime had taken American aid in return for letting the Israelis and Americans fly Ethiopian Jews out of the refugee camps in the 1980s, especially during Operations Moses and Sheba in 1984–85. In April 1985, only a few days after Operation Sheba, Nimeiri was overthrown. The new government then imprisoned or executed those Sudanese who were thought to have cooperated with these rescues.[37] With these dangers in mind, Kassa had warned Pollack to keep things quiet and out of sight in Addis. Now, as thousands of Jews reached Addis Ababa, that had become impossible.

As the transport program created an increasing sense of urgency in the capital, and as new arrivals had to find housing in degrading slums, Kassa confronted Pollack: "I know what you are doing," he recalled telling her. "Please do it intelligently." In June, Pollack petitioned for the release of an AAEJ worker who had been imprisoned while bringing Jews down from the mountains. Kassa arranged to let him go, but warned Pollack, "This happened because of your excess. Be careful."[38] Tesfaye Wolde Selassie, who headed the Stasi-style Internal Affairs Ministry, called her into his office to intimidate her.[39] The transport program was declared illegal, and Pollack promised to stop it. But she did not. "We could not stop the mechanism we had created, nor did we want to," she commented later.[40]

Kassa allowed the AAEJ to continue to work in Addis, despite the fact that the organization had no legal standing in Ethiopia. He noted later that the AAEJ had been the only ones who helped him in Washington in May, and he was grateful to them. In addition, he recalled, he liked Susan. She was always quiet and polite with him and would do whatever he told her, he said. To her face, he told Pollack that she should have been the head of organization for the Communist Party.[41] (She had been that effective—at making a mess.)

That is not what he said about her to the Israelis, however. "I would shoot her," a furious Kassa told Arnon Mantber, the director-general of the Jewish Agency's Absorption Department at the time. (It was only a figure of speech, Mantber hastened to add.)[42] The massive AAEJ transport program had corrupted the government, Kassa said. There were bribes to the government bus company and bribes to protect the program from the Internal Affairs Ministry. "This is jeopardizing my position," Kassa told the Israeli ambassador, Meir Yoffe. "This has got to stop." The Israelis and the American Jewish rescue organizations were now at odds, he said: "The Israeli embassy complained about Pollack, the JDC complained about the AAEJ, Mossad complained. . . . I had Israelis come to me saying, 'Something crazy is taking place. Why don't you stop it?' . . . We needed a Jewish sheriff!"[43]

"Will you please do something about Susan Pollack?" Ambassador Yoffe implored Bob Houdek. Pollack was American; maybe Houdek, as chargé d'affaires at the American embassy, could rein her in. Pollack's transport program was ruining Yoffe's relationship with the Ethiopian government, he complained. Yoffe yelled at Pollack, but the Jews kept coming. "I tried to stop Susan," he said in an interview. "I couldn't."

Yoffe understood that the Ethiopians were afraid to let too many Jews go to Israel at once, he recalled. If they did, Iraq, Libya, Sudan, and Yemen, which, according to intelligence reports, were arming the rebels, might increase their shipments of weapons. Now, thanks to the AAEJ, there were thousands of Falashas waiting outside of his embassy, Yoffe said. "We weren't able to handle it," he added. "The Ethiopians complained horribly. They said that Israel had organized this. They were especially angry about having more refugees in Addis Ababa, added to thousands of others!"[44]

Yoffe was only one of many Israelis who were angry with the AAEJ. The Jewish Agency's Mantber complained later that the transport program was "a very brutal intervention in internal affairs. . . . You played with the destiny of people!"[45] Micha Feldman's relationship with Pollack also became very tense. He had wanted to bring the Jews from Gondar earlier in the year, at a rate that would have allowed them to complete the aliyah within two and a half years.[46] The Jewish Agency had vetoed such a program when Addis became too congested to accommodate more arrivals. The AAEJ refused to accept this decision, however. Conditions in the north were horrible, they said, so they considered it their duty to bring the Jews down, regardless of the Israeli position.[47] Susan's decision was a dangerous one, Feldman told me.[48]

Other Israelis who worked with the Ethiopian Jews also were upset. One Foreign Ministry official told me, "We thought it was irresponsible. It was a cynical play with lives. . . . We would have achieved the same results without her. They came all of the time without her. . . . If she's such a great humanitarian, why didn't she take them to the U.S.? Why embarrass Israel?"[49]

Kassa and the Israelis discussed whether Pollack should be expelled from Ethiopia. One official of the Israeli Foreign Ministry said that the Israelis decided that "kicking her out would have created bad publicity. It would have made her a great martyr. So we stopped taking interest in her."[50] On the Ethiopian side, Kassa prevented her from being expelled, but, he recalled, "I cursed her at night."[51]

The Israelis worried that the mass migration not only had put the Beta Israel at risk, but had jeopardized the entire mission. Foreign Ministry officials feared a repeat of Operation Moses, which Israel had been forced to abort when it was made public in 1985. Now the Israelis were apprehensive that the Ethiopians would halt this rescue because of the chaos in Addis Ababa.[52]

Mengistu and the internal affairs minister had decided to send the Falashas back to Gondar. "We said, 'You can't do this,'" Yoffe recalled. They had nowhere to go back to, he argued at the time, and it would cause a crisis in relations with Washington.[53]

According to one veteran Ethiopian-Israeli, Prime Minister Shamir also wanted the Beta Israel to return to Gondar.[54] Yoffe was right, though. The Jews could not return to their villages. "Honor is the highest value in Ethiopian culture, not life," Micha Feldman observed later. "So the Ethiopians couldn't go back [to their villages] and say, 'I was defeated.'"[55] The Beta Israel would remain in Addis. The Israelis decided to stop the AAEJ, however, and to restore order.

No one disputed the AAEJ's dedication, but now the JDC and the Jewish Agency were determined to take over.[56] On June 25, 1990, the Israelis and representatives of American Jewish groups met in Jerusalem to put an end to AAEJ activities in Ethiopia. At the meeting, Feldman expressed concern that the AAEJ was still active. Embassy and Jewish Agency workers received their instructions from Israel, he said, but the AAEJ did whatever it chose. Pollack responded that Micha knew about all of her activities. She added that the Jewish Agency could take over. "You do it and we'll leave, but not before," she said. Everyone present agreed that the AAEJ would turn over full responsibility to Feldman by August 1 and would remain in Addis as observers.[57]

"Running a relief camp is overwhelming, an exhausting job," Pollack said later. "I was glad to hand it over."[58] She would leave by the end of August. The Ethiopians had said that they would not expel her from the country, but "Kassa was unhappy with her after his trip to the U.S.," Recant recalled.

"Susan was on a tourist visa. She had to come out every month to renew it. She heard from Kassa that her visa would not be renewed." The AAEJ had planned for Pollack to leave in September anyway. "She was sick, and she had been there for a long time," Recant observed.[59]

By the time Pollack left Ethiopia, most of the Jewish community had come to Addis.[60] She had been seriously ill for weeks. Back in America, she would be hospitalized and would spend four months in bed recuperating from typhoid and a bronchial infection.[61]

## "I GAVE THEM THE NOD.
## THEY WERE RIGHT"

Years later, key American and Israeli figures who had condemned the AAEJ transport program officially at the time acknowledged that they nevertheless had given it their blessing privately. They approved it not because they thought that the Jews were in danger in Gondar, but because the aliyah would be much more efficient if it was conducted out of Addis. These officials knew that somebody would have to induce the Jews to leave their villages and to bring them down to the capital. In the spring of 1990, they had agreed that the AAEJ would do that, in the process taking on the role of irresponsible extremists. The AAEJ was used to it, and only they could take the criticism that came with it.

That spring in Jerusalem, Michael Schneider gave Susan Pollack and Will Recant his approval to bring the Jews down from Gondar, as noted above. "When Will and Susan said they wanted to bring people from Gondar," Schneider told me in 1997, "I knew Israel and my colleagues would be against me. But frankly, I gave them the nod. They were right. They forced the issue. The rescue could never have been done from the villages in the north." Schneider knew that his own organization, as a government-approved NGO in Ethiopia, was restricted from doing what the AAEJ planned to do. A group such as the AAEJ, by contrast, had greater latitude. Schneider let them use it, allowing them to move the process along.

In consequence, the tensions that emerged and eventually exploded in Addis Ababa were inevitable. "It was necessary to have our staff criticized by the AAEJ," Schneider said. "I allowed this dynamic to play. . . . Susan was a bruiser, a fighter." She "created merry hell" attacking the JDC and the Jewish Agency for not doing more in Addis. But Schneider sympathized with the AAEJ's strategic goals. And once the Jewish community was in the city, the Joint and the Jewish Agency would take over.

At the same time, the JDC soon would play a crucial role in the negotiations that led to Operation Solomon. To help accomplish that, Schneider would bring the AAEJ leadership into the fold, even though the mainstream organizations had shut down the AAEJ's role in Addis. In the spring of 1991, he would invite Nate Shapiro and Will Recant into the "kitchen cabinet," the small working group that would be critically involved in the negotiations to complete the exodus. "I was probably closer to the AAEJ than any of my staff were," Schneider said later.[62] This act of allying with a sometimes troublesome adversary was a brilliant decision. It harnessed the advocacy group's energy and political connections. The Israelis, for their part, were gratified that the American Jewish mavericks had become part of a unified effort, rather than critical outsiders.

Like Schneider, Micha Feldman was constrained, though by different forces. Officially, he opposed the AAEJ's program. Back in February 1990, however, he reminded Pollack that she was not bound to follow Jewish Agency policy, she reported. "His meaning to me is clear," she wrote at the time: Feldman, like Schneider, privately approved of her carrying out a program that his organization could not.[63]

"We saw it as Exodus," Feldman told me. "I was very excited, and my people were. . . . The Jewish Agency spoke with her and got an agreement that she won't do anything on her own."[64] But, of course, Pollack did. Feldman became angry, not that the migration was happening, but that it was so hurried and unplanned. Feldman's displeasure with the AAEJ led to competition and tension. "He was a real pain in the ass," said Pollack. "You can quote me."[65]

Some Israeli officials still become livid when they speak of the chaos that the AAEJ caused that spring and summer in Addis Ababa. But virtually every Ethiopian Jew with whom I spoke expressed warm enthusiasm for Susan Pollack and the AAEJ. Several were quick to point out that Susan and her colleagues had truly helped and cared about them. And Uri Lubrani, Reuven Merhav, and others who were crucial to the mission now say that Operation Solomon could not have happened without the contribution that Pollack made. "She created a fact on the ground," said Merhav. "This white woman with an American accent did what no state could do. She did a great thing. I honestly think so. Israel couldn't do it."[66]

Henry Gold, the head of a Canadian physicians' rescue group, saw a deeper significance behind Pollack's actions. He told me that when he worked in the refugee camps of Sudan in the 1980s, he had been called a hero. "I did it only to save me," Gold confided, "for my own sense of well-being." Then what did he think had motivated Pollack? In mid-1990, when Susan was planning to transport the entire Ethiopian Jewish population to Addis, Henry recalled, he had doubted her. "Susan said, 'We've got to get planes, helicopters!' I wondered, 'Is this woman nuts?'" But, he said, sometimes you can see that a person's entire life was organized around a single point in time. "I think Susan's destiny was for that particular moment."

"You can say that because the whole thing worked," I countered.

"It worked because it was her instinct," he replied. "I don't have a rosy picture of the world. I am not a believer. But there are moments in life when even a nonbeliever has to accept that things happen for a reason."[67]

## THE NORTH AMERICAN CONFERENCE ON ETHIOPIAN JEWRY

In mid-1990, as the AAEJ was dealing with the transport program and its consequences, another support organization established a presence in Addis: the North American Conference on Ethiopian Jewry (NACOEJ). Founded in early 1982, the members of NACOEJ took pride in being quieter and more cooperative than the AAEJ, yet they were dedicated and had a track record. Unlike the AAEJ, NACOEJ had faith in Israel's commitment to the Ethiopian Jews and felt that attacking Israel as racist was wrong, Barbara Ribakove Gordon, the executive director of the organization, noted in an interview. NACOEJ sought to address the human needs that might otherwise have been overlooked in Addis. The organization's founding principles were to inform American Jews about Ethiopian Jewry, assist the Falashas in Ethiopia and in transit to Israel, ease the absorption process when they got there, and work to preserve their culture.[68]

NACOEJ attracted a base of over forty-five thousand supporters through direct-mail campaigns, raising several hundred thousand dollars a year. With the encouragement of the Israeli Foreign Ministry and the Jewish Agency, the organization sent eighteen missions to Gondar between 1983 and 1989, bringing duffel bags with $10,000 worth of sweatshirts for children and $50,000 worth of medicine. They also brought doctors and nurses, school supplies, and religious articles, along with "goodwill gifts" for non-Jews. The NACOEJ agents pretended that they were tourists, and customs officials played along, encouraged by a lot of bribes.

NACOEJ secretly sent money to the Jews in their villages in Gondar. The organization did not participate in the AAEJ's attempts at rescue in the 1980s, Gordon recalled, but instead developed the so-called legal method of facilitating emigration. That involved providing phony college scholarship and job offers and other bogus documents to Jews in order to satisfy the Ethiopian bureaucracy's requirement that people have formal invitations in order to leave. An Ethiopian-Israeli NACOEJ agent named Solomon Ezra was the architect of this method, which was adopted by the other support groups as well as the Israelis, Gordon recalled. In Addis, NACOEJ helped fund the AAEJ transport program.[69]

In spring 1990, as the Jews began to stream into the city, Joe Feit, a tax attorney from New York who was then NACOEJ's head of relief and rescue, spent a month working alongside Susan Pollack in her compound. Feit recalled that he registered at least fifty families a day, giving each their first month's stipend and arranging for their housing. Solomon Ezra found hundreds of rooms for the NACOEJ clients to live in, and the organization filled out exit applications for the families on its list. Its representatives also dealt with emergencies. One night in April, for example, Feit, Susan Pollack, and Micha Feldman learned that people who had just arrived from Gondar, knowing no place else to go, were sleeping in a road. The area was dark and unsafe, so the two Americans and the Israeli loaded the families on a truck and brought them to the Susan Compound. Then Feit and Pollack stayed with them the rest of the night as animals howled in the distance.[70]

NACOEJ also provided children's clothing to the Jewish community. Andy Goldman, who later represented the organization in the city, bought twelve thousand outfits, a few at a time, then distributed them, Gordon said later. In addition, NACOEJ taught the adults to embroider aprons, which were sold in the United States, and set up after-school recreation programs, with board games, volleyball, and video games in Hebrew. They arranged for two *qessotch* to give religious instruction in Amharic and Ge'ez, in order to foster the preservation of Ethiopian Jewish culture. And Goldman planned to put on a circus, the "Humblest Show on Earth," with children juggling and walking tightropes. Those children who participated had more self-confidence and poise when they got to Israel, Goldman said later.[71]

Michael Strum, who worked for NACOEJ in Addis for several months, said that he was especially concerned that hundreds of Ethiopian Jews were being missed in the registration process. They did not feel that the Jewish Agency had enough staff on site, he recalled. Feldman protested that all genuine Jews were in fact being accepted. But the next day, Strum asserted, he brought sixty-five people to the embassy, virtually all of whom had been denied entry, and every one of them eventually was confirmed as being Jewish.[72]

Israeli officials regarded NACOEJ as interfering amateurs, though perhaps less noxious ones than the AAEJ. "Israel always said, 'We don't want or need you,'" Strum recalled. But as far as he could see, the Israelis never had enough staff to handle the Jews' registration or visa applications. Strum was especially concerned about the people whom the Jewish Agency had turned away as non-Jews, dreading the possibility that people starving in the street later might be identified as Jewish.[73] In early 1991, NACOEJ would extend its role, supporting Jewish families that had converted to Christianity. That was a controversial decision, as we shall see.

# Chomanesh and Dan'el

One of the Beta Israel who made their way to Addis Ababa in June 1990 was a young woman named Chomanesh. Her name means "full of fat," a very optimistic name to give a child in Ethiopia, where fat is considered a sign of good health. Chomanesh, like almost all Ethiopians, was not the least bit fat. She was slow, however, and she walked deliberately, delicately, as she left her village for the last time.

This trip evoked awful memories for her of her first attempt to go to Jerusalem. Nine years earlier, Chomanesh had left her home and set off for Sudan. She wanted to be free to be a Jew, and there was nothing to keep her in her village anyway. She had been betrothed, but the boy had gone to Zion, leaving her an "old virgin" by local standards.[1] She was around sixteen years old at the time. She and other young people in her village knew that the government did not allow its citizens to leave, and threatened to torture their families if they did, but they determined to go to Jerusalem anyway. They decided not to tell their parents, so there would be no arguments. One night they slipped into the moonlight. The next morning, they took a bus part of the way, then they walked, and at each town an army guard checked their papers. "You are so young," one soldier said to them. "We go to find work," Chomanesh answered.

There wasn't enough money, and the children got hungry and tired. In one town, people gave them food and housing, but the older boys got suspicious and began to sneak away. Guards had put empty soda cans around the house, though, to make noise if anybody tried to escape. When Chomanesh woke that morning, she saw the older boys digging their own graves. "We will kill you!" yelled the local guards who had caught them. "You are leaving your country. You are going to be slaves of the *farenj* [whites]." Rather than kill them, though, the soldiers handed the group over to the police, who took them by helicopter to the provincial capital, Gondar town. There were eighty-eight of them, including twenty-two girls.

They brought the children first to the police station, where the military governor shouted at them, "We saved you! If you go to Sudan, bandits along the way will rob you. They will rape and murder you. If you get there alive, they try to kidnap you to the other place"—by which he meant Israel. Then the police took Chomanesh and the other children to the main jail, where they kept murderers. Every morning they tied her to a wooden rod and hung her upside down from the roof. "Who told you to leave your home?" the police demanded, and they beat her feet with a wooden cudgel called a bastinado.

In Israel, a group of Ethiopian-Israelis heard that the eighty-eight young people had been imprisoned. This group had become activists, working to help new Ethiopian immigrants and urging the government to speed up the emigration. They had held demonstrations, surprising Israelis who supposed that Ethiopians were always quiet and acquiescent. Now the Ethiopian-Israelis protested the jailing of the young Beta Israel, and the Israeli newspapers carried the story. In response, the police in Gondar town released the Jews with the warning that if they caught them again, they would kill them without a trial. They had beaten Chomanesh's feet for six months, and she would never walk without pain again.

Now, shortly before the rainy season in June 1990, Chomanesh left her home again. An AAEJ agent had told the people in her village that this was the time to leave for Addis Ababa, and Chomanesh's father told her and her sisters to go. He would stay behind with her mother and her four young brothers, and would sell their animals and other possessions.

Despite the constant ache in her feet, Chomanesh walked. With her were her sisters, Yewot and Tagenich, and Tagenich's son, who was named Or, along with many of the other people of their village—about forty in all. They brought with them only small parcels of possessions, a few birr (the Ethiopian currency), and as much food as they could carry. As they approached the town at dusk, a horror ran through Chomanesh as she remembered what she had endured there years before. Still, she walked, slowly and in pain. She and her group reached the city as darkness fell, and the AAEJ agent met them. He took them to a house, and they waited there while others from the villages joined them. On the morning of the second day, the agent returned and hurried them into an old truck as a driver jumped behind the wheel.

Two days later, almost at dusk, they reached Addis. They were hungry and exhausted, and Or was coughing more than usual. A bus took them into the city and stopped near a large tent outside of a big building where a very long line of other Jews stood. They were waiting quietly for the *farenj* woman inside to speak to them and to give them money. As Chomanesh and her family joined the line, an old man who had been with them on the truck advised Tagenich to claim that she had two sons, not one. They would give her more money if she said that. "The *farenj*, like children, believe everything they are told," he said, citing an Ethiopian proverb. When they got closer, they heard the *farenj* woman tell one man in limping but forceful Amharic, "Israel will allow you to bring only *one* wife!" He had brought two, presenting one as his former spouse, the other as his current one. It had not worked. One of the wives would have to go back to Gondar. Finally, Chomanesh and her family's turn came to meet the woman, who told them that her name was Susan.

A nurse gave them a checkup. Then Chomanesh and the others ate a hot meal that the AAEJ workers provided. Some of the older Jews asked repeatedly if the *farenj* woman was Jewish and if the food really was kosher. They had not eaten in days but would not take food until they were reassured. Later, Chomanesh and the others washed themselves while many of the young people washed the elders' feet. That night they slept on hides in a tent in the Susan Compound. The next morning, Chomanesh, Yewot, Tagenich, and Or were sent to the Israeli embassy, where an Ethiopian-Israeli named Zimna registered them. Then one of the AAEJ committee members took them to find a place to stay.

Chomanesh was shaken by what she saw. In dirty, mud-walled houses with tin roofs, large families of Jews were crowded into tiny single rooms with no running water, or into latrines. Chomanesh agreed that they would share a six-by-ten-foot room with another family in a dingy, windowless shack. Taking the money that Susan had given her, she counted out the birr that the landlord demanded as rent. She had no idea if the price was fair.

Yewot missed her parents and their *tukul*, the family's circular hut with walls of tree trunks and branches covered by mud, clay, and straw, with a conical thatched roof. She cried for days. Everything that they had known had changed. There would be no running stream here, but instead a leaky communal faucet. They all would have to sleep on a single hay-filled mattress. Most of all Yewot longed for the family's cows. Tagenich worried that there was no open place with trees, to meet the needs of the body. She accepted these indignities, though, since she was certain that they would be leaving for Israel soon. It might not be in a couple of days, as she had hoped, but the AAEJ committee member had told her that many Falashas were leaving for Israel every week. She certainly would be there by July, she thought.

One of the veteran Ethiopian-Israelis who had protested the jailing of Chomanesh and the eighty-seven other young Jews in Gondar town in 1981 was a young man named Dan'el.

He had heard about Jerusalem every day during his childhood, as if his parents had just left there. One day in 1967, when he was perhaps ten, he saw his father kneel and pray. His father did this every day for six days, and refused to sleep on a hide that week. "Israel is at war," he recalled his father saying, "I wish I was there." His father was regarded as a *tanqway* (a wizard and healer), famous for his wisdom and rarely taken by surprise. But he was stunned one day two years later when Dan'el asked for permission to go to Israel. "The Messiah will come and we'll all go together," his father responded.

"I am not waiting for the Messiah," Dan'el replied.

"You are young," said his father, "you cannot go yourself."

"I gave him to choose," Dan'el told me. "One is, I will go to Israel. The other is, I will go to the Ethiopian army."

His father said, "You don't know. All you hear is on the radio. How can you go?"

Dan'el left the village where he had been born, his parents, and his twelve brothers and sisters, and walked to Gondar town. From there he took a bus to Addis. For six months he asked for permission to leave, but there was no legal emigration; Israel did not even recognize the Beta Israel as Jews then. Dan'el persisted. He traveled north to Asmara in Eritrea, two more days on a bus. He had heard that fishing boats were taking Falashas from the port of Massawa to Eilat in southern Israel, and he tried for four more months to get permission to go, but failed again and went home.

"You see," said his father, "we are waiting for five thousand years. You want to go in one year."

Dan'el returned to Addis again six years later, when he was about eighteen years old. A wealthy Italian named Mario who knew Dan'el's father offered to help. He took Dan'el to the Israeli ambassador, who told Dan'el that if he could show him a round-trip ticket and $500, he would get Dan'el a tourist visa. Mario got him the ticket and withdrew the cash from the bank. Dan'el brought them to the embassy, got the visa, then gave the ticket and the money back to Mario. Dan'el's father ultimately paid for his airfare, and Dan'el flew to Israel. It was 1975.

"Were you frightened?" I asked him.

"I don't remember," Dan'el replied, then quoted an Ethiopian proverb: "When a monkey falls from a tree onto a bush, he must first find someone to remove . . ." Unable to recall the English word that he wanted, Dan'el got out an electronic translator. "Thorns!" he cried out, finding the word. Then he recited the complete saying: "When a monkey falls from a tree onto a bush, he must first find someone to remove the thorns from his backside," the thing he cannot do for himself. But when Dan'el reached the Promised Land, there was no one there to help remove the thorns from a poor African boy. So Dan'el made his way to Eilat and stayed with an Ethiopian. He had $40 in his pocket. He worked during the day, cleaning in a hotel in return for a room and food. After half a year, he attended an *ulpan* (where people learn Hebrew through total immersion) on a kibbutz, then joined the army for four years.

By 1989, he had not seen his parents for fourteen years. "I saw myself alone," he told me. The Mossad provided airplane tickets, and he returned to Ethiopia, then brought his parents and three of his brothers down from Gondar by boat, across Lake Tana, and down to Addis Ababa.

Now his father worried about a conversation that he had had with God. Many Ethiopian Jews talk to God often, and Dan'el's father had made a deal with Him. "In Ethiopia," said Dan'el, "a man will pray, 'Please God, let my bad neighbor die, and I will die the next day.' Then the next day, the neighbor dies and the man says, 'Please, God, forget what I said.'" His father had prayed, "Please, God, let me go to see Jerusalem, then let me die the next day." Now he actually might get to Jerusalem, and Dan'el's father would have to pray his way out of the bargain. As it turned out, the contract with God did not take effect quite yet. The brothers were able to leave, but the government would not let Dan'el's nephews out. He paid bribes, but that did not help. So his parents stayed in Addis Ababa to take care of the children while Dan'el and his brothers went to Israel.

He went back to Addis to get his parents and his nephews in June 1990. When he brought them to the Israeli embassy, they happened to meet Chomanesh, and Dan'el's father, the man who was not easily surprised, was astonished. He and his wife quickly realized that they had a very close connection to her: her parents and they had arranged many years before, when Dan'el and Chomanesh were still children in different villages, for them to be married. In Ethiopia, betrothal of children as young as ten is not uncommon, and, as in Talmudic Judaism, is almost as binding as marriage. But Dan'el had left for Israel before they could meet. Now they had found each other in the most improbable circumstances. Dan'el returned to Israel, but Chomanesh had to wait until the Ethiopian government allowed her to leave. They would not see each other again until Operation Solomon.

# FOUR

# Eggs—Uri Lubrani—Cluster Bombs

**JULY–OCTOBER 1990**

Beginning in July 1990, with the AAEJ officially sidelined and with Susan Pollack out of the country, the JDC and the Jewish Agency took on the full responsibility for the Jews in Addis Ababa. The Jewish Agency determined who qualified to go to Israel, and the Joint and its offshoot Almaya saw to the community's daily care and maintenance. Equally important, these organizations tried to prepare the Jews for the culture shock of life in Israel. At the same time, the Ethiopians curtailed Jewish emigration, trapping the Beta Israel in the slums of Addis.

## AN EGG, A POTATO, AN ORANGE, AND A ROLL

By the time the JDC took over the care of the Jewish community in Addis, the organization had had years of experience offering nonsectarian relief services in Ethiopia. After establishing a presence there in 1982, the Joint had set up a health center and a dozen satellite clinics in the Gondar region, built wells, reforested, provided electricity, and supplied agricultural assistance. It also secretly had sent money to thousands of Ethiopian Jews. To identify them, the JDC's Ami Bergman had computerized and updated a handwritten list of Beta Israel originally compiled in 1976 by the Organization for Rehabilitation through Training (ORT). Since there were no official birth records or ID cards in Ethiopia, this list now became a crucial reference, the Israelis' "bible." It was their only written source for determining who really was a Falasha.[1]

With the arrival of the Beta Israel in the capital in mid-1990, the Joint set up a quasi-official organization called Almaya to continue to work with them in case the Ethiopians expelled the JDC itself or closed the Israeli embassy. JDC/Almaya supplied the Jews' monthly maintenance stipends, but they were concerned about fostering a culture of dependency. They therefore created jobs, ultimately employing some two thousand of the Beta Israel as security guards, social workers, health workers, and mattress and brick makers. Others built housing for new arrivals, and a synagogue on the embassy grounds.[2]

Almaya also ran a day school with an enrollment variously estimated at between 3,400 and 5,000 children ages six to eighteen, meeting in shifts. Israelis taught seventy Ethiopian teachers some Hebrew each morning, then

63

the teachers passed it on to the students during the day. The vast majority of the children were illiterate, and all learning initially was by rote. As the pedagogical approach shifted toward active participation, the children began to play, laugh, and become creative.[3] Orna Mizrachi, the director of the school, noted in an interview that the children wanted to learn as much Hebrew as possible. "They wanted to become Israelis fast. We saw it didn't always work," she recalled.[4]

The school's primary aim was the children's survival.[5] In Ethiopia, Mizrachi observed, adults eat first, which meant that food might not always reach the children. A confidential JDC memo of February 1991 raised the question of whether family heads were selling their food rather than feeding their children.[6] So in the school, every student got an egg, a potato, an orange, and a roll. The Israelis also taught the children to speak up when they were ill, since parents typically sent sick kids to school rather than to a doctor. In addition, the school changed the Ethiopian tradition of teachers beating pupils who misbehaved.[7]

The Israelis motivated the Ethiopian parents to put their children in the school by making their monthly stipends conditional on their enrolling their children.[8] School officials then used this leverage to intervene, especially in behalf of the children and the women. "In the Ethiopian family, the child has the lowest priority," Mizrachi said. "The father would come in a suit and tie—the kids without shoes and clothes, even in the winter. . . . We made sure that the parents bought them clothes." The school officials also urged families not to marry off their daughters before the girls could make their own choices in Israel. And they intervened if girls showed an inclination to prostitute themselves, sending them to Youth Aliyah in Israel immediately.[9] Wife beating appears to have been common in Ethiopia, where men hit their wives anytime they failed significantly to fulfill their duties. (An Ethiopian proverb asserts that women and donkeys can be beaten.)[10] With the collapse of normal social patterns in Addis Ababa, domestic violence was occurring more often, and the school officials encouraged women to complain. "This led to arguments and fights," Mizrachi recalled. "There were already bad family problems when we arrived. They got worse."[11]

The school provided the occasion for a number of other interventions by the Israelis. They taught hygiene, including how to take a shower. And they encouraged a Western sense of time. "In Ethiopia, time is not money," one Israeli official told me, laughing. "Time does not control people in that culture, people control time," said another. Bringing their kids to the school sessions fostered in the mothers a habit of keeping appointments. The school also gave two hundred men work constructing more than forty school buildings in the style of traditional straw-thatched homes, or *tukuls,* to provide some sense of continuity with village life. The Israeli embassy soon began to look like an Ethiopian village.[12]

The JDC responded to the health crisis in Addis belatedly but, in the end, with brilliant results. The organization was spurred to act when veteran Ethiopian-Israeli activists demonstrated in front of the Knesset, protesting the death rate among their relatives in Addis. Having previously run only a referral clinic, the Joint quickly developed a comprehensive medical program.[13]

To bring down the death rate, Dr. Ted Myers, the JDC's director of East African medical programs, started an outreach program in which a hundred Ethiopians were trained to be "health facilitators." Each visited fifty Jewish families in the city twice a week.[14] "Just finding the families was a problem," Dr. Rick Hodes said later. "Getting them to have faith in Western medical care was also an issue."[15] For example, Myers noted in an interview, Ethiopians traditionally did not seek treatment for elderly people when they became ill: "If an old person gets sick, put him in a corner of the *tukul* and he dies." Myers had them bring the elders in for examinations. "We had no more deaths from 'old age,'" he said. It also was customary among Ethiopians not to seek medical care until the late stages of an illness, said Myers. That too had to change.

"The situation was catastrophic," Myers recalled. "I had to be tough to get the job done." If the Jews wanted their monthly stipends, they would have to follow the medical procedures that Myers set in place. The health facilitators gave the families stars, which they needed to get their stipends at the embassy. If someone was sick, his family had to bring him to the JDC clinic in order to get their star.[16]

Myers also started a nutritional rehabilitation program to address the fact that 80 percent of the children were below 80 percent of their proper body weight. Malnourished people were given *fafa*, a mixture of wheat, soy, and powdered milk, which a specialist in pediatric nursing taught the mothers how to make.[17] In addition, the Israelis coordinated a mass inoculation program against measles and meningitis. By the end of November 1990, the entire community was vaccinated.[18]

Hodes came to work for the Joint in Addis that November. When he got there, he had five Ethiopian doctors and one Israeli to help him serve over twenty thousand people. "In the U.S., there is one doctor for every eight hundred people," he said. "In Ethiopia, we had one for every three thousand."[19] Yet by the time he arrived, the clinic had already cut the death rate among the Ethiopian Jews in half. And by March 1991 they had reduced it to less than one-third that of the general population of the United States. Hodes's major success was the tuberculosis program he created. Most Ethiopians tested positive, but for 90 percent of them the disease was dormant and it was not clear who was suffering actively from it. So Hodes aggressively treated anyone who showed symptoms, using the most potent drugs in existence.[20]

Hodes and the Israelis tried to alter some cultural views and practices through health education, but certain habits would change only when the Falashas arrived in Israel. Like other Ethiopians, for example, the Jews performed female circumcision, which they justified as preventing women from being hyperactive and hypersexual. Hodes estimated that clitoridectomies of this kind were performed on 90 percent of the Jewish girls in Ethiopia, though examinations in Israel indicated that only a third of the Ethiopian immigrant women showed signs of some form of ritual genital surgery. Once in Israel, Ethiopians reportedly abandoned this ritual practice entirely.[21] Other Ethiopian folk beliefs included the idea that venereal disease is caused by urinating under a full moon, and that traditional healers could cure HIV with an onion and herbs.[22] The longer the Beta Israel remained in Addis, the graver the problem of HIV would become among them.

### "WE WERE IN THEIR HANDS"

During the rainy season of 1990, with the Jews mired in the mud of Addis Ababa, the Ethiopian authorities intensified their pressure on Israel to provide lethal weapons. Soviet support for Ethiopia was falling off precipitously, with arms deliveries declining from almost $1 billion in 1989 to $300 million in 1990. The 1,500 Soviet advisers in Ethiopia were reduced to about 350 over the same period.[23] The Mengistu government, seeking to compensate for these losses, realized that its power in negotiations with the Israelis grew with each truckload of new arrivals from Gondar.

In bringing the Jews from their villages, the AAEJ had wanted not only to rescue them from the dangers in the north but also to put pressure on Israel. Their plan succeeded in ways they had not intended. As the rebels advanced toward Addis, the government stepped up their demands for arms, using the Falashas as bait. Kassa had assured American officials that he was not selling Jews for arms, that there was no linkage between the Israelis' providing weapons and the emigration of the Falashas. The delays in their departure resulted, he insisted, simply from problems in getting the paperwork right. But a bottleneck in emigration would give Mengistu a tremendous advantage in negotiations, and, with Jews pouring into Addis, the Ethiopians made no attempt to stop the illegal migration. Then, in July, they virtually cut off the aliyah. "We were in their hands," said one Foreign Ministry official.[24] "Mengistu knew that he could squeeze us," Asher Naim, who would replace Yoffe as ambassador in November, told me in an interview.[25]

The Ethiopians blamed the Israelis for the slowdown, saying that Israel needed time to sort out the Jews from the non-Jews who had descended on the capital in the hope of getting to Israel. Another explanation offered at the time was that Mengistu had temporarily halted the emigration during the meeting of the Organization of African Unity (OAU) in Addis Ababa that month. The Ethiopians, according to this account, did not want to provoke Arab and Muslim OAU member states. Informed Israeli and American officials say, however, that the Ethiopians in fact were punishing the Israelis for not giving them weapons. Early in July, Mengistu had made a widely reported "secret" trip to Israel for which Kassa Kebede had laid the groundwork on his way back from Washington that spring. Mengistu had brought along another long shopping list of lethal weapons, according to reliable Israeli sources, but had left disappointed. The Ethiopians then cut off the aliyah.

In August 1990, Mengistu sent Kassa and the Ethiopian army chief of staff to Israel, also with a shopping list for arms, and their trip took a surprising turn. The Ethiopians were frustrated until they met with Benjamin "Bibi" Netanyahu. Netanyahu was then deputy to David Levy, who had become foreign minister in June. Netanyahu had met with Kassa ten months earlier at the renewal of diplomatic ties, and now quite abruptly he took an active role, offering Kassa a dramatic deal. Despite the American opposition to Israel's selling arms to Mengistu, Netanyahu agreed to supply lethal weapons that were on Mengistu's list. In return, Netanyahu required a commitment that all of the Ethiopian Jews would be allowed to leave within two months. This was called the "Bibi formula." The United States would have to approve it, Netanyahu said at the time.[26]

Netanyahu did not respond to an invitation to comment on this.[27] Former prime minister Shamir told me that he did not remember Netanyahu's offer, which he called irresponsible.[28] In any event, Mengistu would not accept such explicit linkage of arms for Jews, and the deal did not go through. As a result, the Ethiopians seriously slowed the emigration. Only 82 Ethiopian Jews reached Israel in July, and only slightly more than that in each of the next two months: 128 in August and 177 in September.[29]

## URI LUBRANI

By October 1990, Reuven Merhav's careful plans of the year before seemed to be in jeopardy. Over two thousand Jews had left Ethiopia for Israel since January, but at that rate it would take eight to ten years to complete the aliyah. The proposed orderly movement of Jews from their villages to Addis had been turned on its head by the AAEJ transport program and the deluge of people from the Gondar region. And Israel no longer had an ambassador in Addis Ababa. Meir Yoffe had barely escaped assassination by a Libyan terrorist and had left Ethiopia in July, concerned about his health.[30]

Israeli diplomats once had regarded a posting to Addis Ababa as a prize, but no longer, and Merhav had been unable to find a replacement for Yoffe. Worst of all, the Ethiopians had refused to accept applications for exit visas during the summer, and by now had almost halted the emigration. A mere fifty-eight Jews were allowed to leave Ethiopia in October.[31] Meanwhile, Ethiopian-Israelis, organized under an umbrella organization, held a violent demonstration to press for results in the aliyah.[32]

Merhav now was distracted by other matters, most importantly Iraq's invasion of Kuwait in early August and the impending Gulf War. Even more than he needed an ambassador, Merhav needed a top-level commander to take over the entire Ethiopian project, and he made an inspired choice: Uri Lubrani. Then sixty-three years old, Lubrani was one of Israel's most accomplished diplomats. He had been Israel's ambassador to Ethiopia from 1967 to 1971, in the time of Haile Selassie, and before that, ambassador to Uganda. (Later Lubrani survived a plane crash with Ugandan dictator Idi Amin; he and Amin became blood brothers after the crash, Lubrani said.)[33] He also had been Israel's representative to Iran, where he and Merhav had predicted the shah's fall six months before it happened. Since 1983, Lubrani had been the coordinator for Lebanese affairs, a sensitive position in view of the ongoing battles in southern Lebanon at the time. Ten years older than Merhav, Lubrani had been his boss in Lebanon, his mentor and friend. "We both had served the state in unconventional ways," Merhav observed later, "not in the usual diplomatic green pastures, frequently under harsh conditions."[34]

Now Merhav needed Lubrani to get the emigration going again and to coordinate the organizations that would take part: not only the Jewish Agency, the JDC, and the Foreign Ministry, but also the Ministry of Defense. Up to this point, the Jews were being flown out of Addis Ababa on Ethiopian Airlines planes. But Merhav foresaw that the Israel Defense Forces (IDF) might play a role, and he knew that Lubrani had access to the highest-ranking officers of the IDF. Merhav arranged for Lubrani to report directly to Shamir as the prime minister's special representative to Ethiopia, intentionally bypassing David Levy. Shamir had problems with the new foreign minister and wanted him kept out of the loop on Ethiopia, Lubrani recalled. Levy was not particularly interested in the rescue at the time anyway, though he would be later, when he realized that it would be a major PR coup, Lubrani told me in an interview.[35] The prime minister agreed to make Lubrani his personal envoy. "I appointed him, more or less," Shamir told me.[36] Shamir's choice of words reflected the fact that he was under pressure at the time from Ethiopian-Israeli activists to appoint a high-level official to expedite the aliyah. Once Merhav had chosen Lubrani, the deal essentially was done.

Lubrani was the perfect choice. He knew Ethiopia and still had friends there from his days as ambassador twenty years earlier. Interestingly, one of them was Kassa Kebede. As ambassador, Lubrani had visited Kassa's father, and he remembered seeing the young Kassa around the house, closing doors. Now Lubrani was going back, and he needed a negotiating partner with clout. Kassa, with his close connections to Mengistu, was his man. And Lubrani was ideally suited to deal with the challenges that Kassa would pose. "He has lots of patience, is very good at preparation, gives a very sincere impression, has a lot of charm, but can also be a bit of a *mamzer* ['bastard' or 'shrewd dealer']," said Merhav.[37] "Sometimes," said Lubrani, "when you deal with mafiosi, you have to be a bit of a *mamzer*. Otherwise, they'll eat you alive."[38]

When I interviewed Lubrani in February 1997, first in Jerusalem, then at his office in the Defense Ministry in Tel Aviv, he seemed pleasantly irritated to be asked to discuss a topic about which he had spoken many times over the years. He obliged me by describing his personal impressions of the players, the details, and the flavor of the negotiations. Lubrani often speaks of his "gut feeling" about people and situations. That was what I wanted to hear from him, starting with Mengistu.

Before taking up the assignment in Addis in 1990, he had never met Mengistu, Lubrani told me. "They told me that he's a ruthless son of a bitch, that he'll try to, how shall I say, bamboozle me, to demonstrate his knowledge of Ethiopian history, his patriotism, the justice of his case, the perniciousness of . . . his enemies." That, Lubrani recalled, is exactly what Mengistu did. In two very long meetings with the Israeli in mid-October, Mengistu reviewed Ethiopian history, explained his government's policies, and detailed Israel's broken promises to help him. "You come after we have had all these disappointments," Mengistu told him. The Israelis had failed to send him the arms they had promised. Israel had undermined its traditional relationship with the Ethiopian people, said Mengistu.

Lubrani believed that there are two ways to make tyrants give you what you want: to browbeat them or to express extreme interest in anything that they tell you. Knowing Ethiopians, he recalled, he decided that browbeating would not be the right choice, so he chose the second strategy. In their initial meetings, as Mengistu spoke for a total of nine hours, Lubrani politely asked for further details as he downed one cup of coffee after another. "These were very tiring hours," Lubrani told me.

Lubrani did not even raise the issue of the Ethiopian Jews in their first meeting.[39] He was more interested in establishing rapport with the Ethiopian ruler, and he evidently succeeded. "Mengistu was unbalanced, suspicious, tense, but Lubrani felt at home with him," recalled an Israeli Foreign Ministry official.[40] Lubrani may have given that impression, but later, when the rescue was over, he would describe the Ethiopian dictator as a moron with a warped mind, "a narrow-minded and perverted tyrant."[41]

In their second meeting, Mengistu told Lubrani that most Ethiopian Christians were descended from Jews who had converted. By that reasoning, Mengistu told him, he himself was a Falasha. Did the Israelis want to take all of them? Still, the Ethiopians were cooperating in the Jewish emigration, he said.

In addition to promising to intervene with the Americans, Lubrani offered health and agricultural assistance and two water purification plants, as well as help with Jewish investment from abroad. In return, he asked Mengistu to allow a thousand Jews to leave each month. "It was like extracting teeth to get a thousand," Lubrani recalled. "Mengistu said he cannot afford it, he had difficulties . . . the Arab League was at his throat, Egypt, and so forth. He had to do it in slow portions."

Lubrani observed in our conversations that he knew from his own time as ambassador how sensitive the Ethiopians were about letting the Falashas go. Some Ethiopian-Israeli activists believe that the true obstacle to the aliyah in the 1960s and 1970s was Israel's lack of interest in the Falashas, owing to doubts about their Jewishness, and perhaps to racism.[42] But Lubrani disagreed. He had asked an official in Haile Selassie's court twenty years earlier, he recalled, why the emperor opposed the emigration of the Falashas. "If the Jews leave," the official had told him, "Ethiopia will lose a particle of genius in our society."[43] The emperor himself had said that the Falashas' departure would be a national disaster for Ethiopia.[44] Now, as Mengistu fought for his life, the Beta Israel's value to Ethiopia was becoming even more compelling. Lubrani needed to exploit all of the factors that he was finding in order to get the Ethiopians to let the Jews go. He would have to restore order to the emigration process. And he would need a lot of money.

The first step was to have an ambassador assigned to Ethiopia. Mengistu considered it a blatant insult that Israel had not yet replaced Yoffe. Ultimately Merhav chose Asher Naim, who had just returned from an ambassadorial assignment in Finland. Naim had been born in Libya and had feelings about saving African Jews, but he was not interested in Ethiopia. "For three days, Reuven Merhav worked on me," Naim recalled in an interview. Merhav phoned him repeatedly, then held him "hostage" in his office until Naim accepted the offer. This was a once-in-a-lifetime chance for a retiring diplomat to take part in a historical event, Merhav argued. Naim saw no choice but to pack and go.[45]

## CLUSTER BOMBS

In late October 1990, as Lubrani and Naim prepared to go to Addis, Merhav flew to Washington to persuade the Americans to hold their first official meeting with Mengistu. Merhav knew that American intervention to end the civil war would be the carrot he needed to persuade Mengistu to let the Jews leave. The key to that cooperation was the Israelis' agreement not to arm the Ethiopians. But Merhav had to deal with American officials' suspicions that, prior to or during the renewal of relations with Ethiopia in November 1989, Israel in fact had met Mengistu's requests.

Paul Henze, for example, in reports for the Rand Corporation, deplored Israel's sending arms to Mengistu. By the end of 1989, he wrote, "weapons deliveries, including arms covertly supplied from Chile and Argentina, had begun."[46] Henze considered that Israel's policy was driven chiefly by the desire to regain Ethiopia as an ally against the Arabs, a view shared by some officials in the State Department.[47] "This appealed to certain Israeli hawks," Henze told me later. "What advantage there would have been in embracing a character as odious as Mengistu is really hard to see."[48]

What worried the Americans was the possible delivery of extremely destructive devices, such as cluster bombs (CBUs).[49] One kind of cluster bomb, the CBU-87/B, contains over two hundred small bomblets that disperse in midair, then explode, shooting out shrapnel, an antitank warhead, and incendiary zirconium. U.S. Air Force officials described this bomb as the "weapon of choice in the Middle East."[50]

Mengistu reportedly had used cluster bombs on civilians.[51] As early as December 1989, former president Jimmy Carter had said that he had been told that the Ethiopians had obtained such bombs "from one of our Middle East allies," i.e., Israel. The Ethiopian government was quite happy to get them because they thought that this weapon would be destructive enough to end the war, Carter noted. One of Carter's former aides said that the ex-president was especially sensitive about this issue because it was he who originally had approved the sale of cluster bombs to Israel.[52] American officials added that Israel had sent CBUs to Ethiopia during the Carter administration and that Mengistu had employed them to great effect against the Somalis in the Ogaden.[53]

On January 18, 1990, Secretary of State James Baker III had met with Israeli defense minister Yitzhak Rabin and impressed on him the intensity of the Bush administration's opposition to Israel's sending cluster bombs to Ethiopia. Rabin had assured him that Israel was not providing such weapons and would not do so in the future. Two days later, officials from the State and Defense Departments said that they strongly suspected that Israel had sent CBUs to Mengistu, though they did not say when.[54]

On February 13, the Morrison Report, prepared for the House Subcommittee on Africa, had concluded that Israel had indeed provided Ethiopia with cluster bombs. The report stated that Israel had sent Mengistu approximately a hundred CBUs in 1989, perhaps forty of which were deployed either in practice exercises or on the battlefield. The report speculated that, rather than supplying these bombs directly, Israel may have sent them through a "cutout," a third nation, such as Chile. (There were suspicions that Israel had financed the Chilean firm Industrias Cardoen's deal to sell such bombs to Ethiopia in September 1989.) Morrison noted that Ethiopia had pressed Jerusalem to send another thousand CBUs in late 1989, but in the face of strong American opposition, Israel probably had halted any further deliveries. The *Wall Street Journal* later cited "overwhelming evidence" from classified intelligence reports that Israel had sent cluster bombs to Ethiopia at some point.[55]

Bob Frasure, who by late 1990 was serving on the National Security Council, was one of those who suspected that Israel had sent Mengistu more than they admitted. "It was all smoke and haze," Frasure said later. "I got tired of hearing Israel say they'd sent 'only fifteen thousand rusty rifles.' I don't know the truth," he said. But he thought that the Israelis had to do something after the renewal of relations with Ethiopia.[56]

The *New York Times* had reported in January 1990 that the United States had asked the Israelis repeatedly about selling cluster bombs, and that each time the Israelis had denied it. But their denial was less definite when they were asked if they had done so in the recent past.[57] That was consistent with Merhav's account that Israel had changed policy and refused Mengistu's arms requests sometime after January 1990. It also was consonant with Morrison's conclusion that Israel probably had backed off from arming Ethiopia by that time. Merhav later conceded, "It is possible that when the explicit policy of 'only non-lethal equipment for Ethiopia' was adopted, a shipment, either direct or indirect, had been on the way." On the other hand, he said, "it would not be beyond the Ethiopians to have floated an old bomb story in order to embarrass us with the Americans and uplift their own spirit."[58] Frasure said the same: "The Ethiopians had an interest in spreading stories about Israeli aid, to bolster morale."[59] In any case, the Americans' suspicions were based on descriptions of attacks, not on actual physical evidence of cluster bombs. "Since we found none, we had no reason to protest," concluded Herman Cohen, who was assistant secretary of state for African affairs at the time.[60]

# FIVE

# Carrots, Not Carats—The Kitchen Cabinet

## NOVEMBER–DECEMBER 1990

In November 1990, as Reuven Merhav secured American cooperation in dealing with Mengistu, the living conditions and social mores of the Jewish community in Addis continued to degrade. In December, Uri Lubrani made a crucial connection with the JDC in New York that allowed him to bypass the Jewish Agency, in the process creating tensions between those organizations that would threaten the rescue later.

### IMPROVED AMERICAN RELATIONS WITH MENGISTU

To enlist American support, Merhav met in Washington with the State Department's Herman Cohen on November 1, 1990, almost one year to the day after the renewal of diplomatic ties with Ethiopia. Merhav assured Cohen that Israel would stand by its policy of not supplying arms to Ethiopia. The Israelis would offer instead medical and agricultural aid, economic training, and trade opportunities, and would try to help Ethiopia get credit with the International Monetary Fund. But they needed Cohen to provide political leverage, to substantiate the Israeli claim to Mengistu that they had clout with the United States.[1]

Cohen agreed. American relations with the Mengistu regime had improved in recent months, owing in part to a series of conciliatory gestures by the Ethiopians. They had been cooperative about the Falasha emigration, albeit inconsistently. They also had agreed to halt the bombing of Massawa in June, allowing emergency food shipments to enter through the port.[2] Then, with the Iraqi invasion of Kuwait on August 2, Mengistu's goodwill suddenly had become important to Washington. Ethiopia was serving a term on the UN Security Council at that time and was one of three African states whose votes would become crucial when President Bush sought a resolution authorizing the use of force if Iraq failed to withdraw. The Ethiopians had worked closely with the United States on this matter. Secretary of State James Baker had rewarded Mengistu by meeting with his foreign minister, Tesfaye Dinka, at the UN in September.[3]

In recognition of these friendly Ethiopian gestures, Washington had agreed to Tesfaye's request for help in restoring the peace process. Jimmy Carter's mediation efforts had foundered because of what State Department officials saw as bad faith on Mengistu's part. Battlefield setbacks had awakened the Ethiopians' interest in talks, however. As a result, Cohen had presided over a trilateral meeting in Washington with the Ethiopian government and the EPLF in October.[4] When Merhav approached him now, in early November, and proposed a three-way meeting with the Israelis and Ethiopians, Cohen saw no problem. The Americans believed that Mengistu was doomed, but while he was still in place, they had to deal with him. Moreover, the meeting held the prospect of improving the exit process for the Jews. Cohen considered this a human rights issue. U.S. policy encouraged unrestricted emigration, especially of Jews, from Communist countries, and Cohen, who was Jewish, shared this view. In addition, he was aware of the pressure applied by the AAEJ and the Canadian Association for Ethiopian Jews, and of congressional support for the Falashas.[5]

Cohen was guided, however, by a U.S. policy that he did not disclose to Merhav: President Bush's decision to help Mikhail Gorbachev's regime withdraw from Soviet involvement in Ethiopia. The administration intended to facilitate a negotiated peace that would permit the Russians to make a dignified exit. That priority had prompted Cohen's visit to Mengistu in August 1989, and, he said later, it continued to help shape the United States' posture toward Ethiopia. The three-way meeting presented no obstacle to this plan, and so it was set for mid-November. As soon as the American embassy in Addis confirmed Cohen's agreement, Mengistu ordered the Jewish emigration to be resumed.[6]

### "THIS WAS THE WORST OF TIMES"

As Merhav made progress in Washington, Lubrani and Naim prepared to set off for Addis. They arrived there on November 8, 1990, and took rooms at the Addis Ababa Hilton, a beautifully landscaped luxury hotel. But the Jews they had come to rescue were enduring very different circumstances.

Lubrani already had seen and been shaken by the shocking conditions in which the Beta Israel lived.[7] The Falashas had been stuck there for months, and they were suffering. Fathers who always had supported their families were reduced to dependency on monthly stipends. Most had never managed cash before, and many spent the money on liquor and prostitutes. The whores of Addis, one American relief worker commented later, were beautiful, and were available for a dollar. The HIV that many of them carried now began to infect the Jewish community.

One Israeli diplomat posted in the Ethiopian capital told me that big-city life came as a complete shock to the Jews. The dangers and temptations were unlike anything most of them had known before, and their communal social restraints all but vanished. In the villages, there was very little alcohol; in

Addis it was everywhere. In the villages, sexual availability followed known rules; in the social disorder of Addis, said the diplomat, the rules began to corrode in the face of the need to survive. His views inevitably reflected Israeli values. The anthropologist Shalva Weil points out, for example, that social workers in Israel considered Ethiopian Jews to have loose morals, since the women easily accepted men into their homes and the men aligned themselves with different women. Ironically, the Ethiopians drew a similar conclusion about Israelis.[8] In any event, there were among the Jews in Addis many single-parent families, most often headed by a woman. Many of these and other single women married for protection after they left their homes. As Weil notes, women in Ethiopia who are not attached to a man are perceived as defenseless targets of sexual predation.[9]

The "body trade" also degraded traditional Beta Israel family patterns. Christian men would marry Jewish women, and pay them, in order to become eligible to get to Israel. Or Christian families would pay Jews to claim that the Christians' children were their own and to take the children to Israel.[10] Often, non-Jews would exchange living space in their apartments for this favor. One reliable source estimated that this illegal barter accounted for 10 percent of all of the Ethiopian youngsters who reached Israel.

In addition, the schedule for determining stipends caused families to break up. A couple would get only 150 birr a month, but as individuals they were given 100 birr each. So married couples would split up in order to get more money. Or girls as young as twelve would marry, since the child bride would get a larger stipend in a separate family unit than she did in her parents' family.[11] The Jewish Agency responded by refusing to recognize divorces, a decision that some observers called outrageous. The Israelis also put a freeze on marriages between Jews and Christians in an effort to prevent "hitchhiker weddings." And they gave family stipends to newly married couples only if the girl was over sixteen, though that could be hard to tell.[12]

"There was great damage," Zimna Berhane, an Ethiopian-Israeli who was working for the Jewish Agency in Addis, recalled in an interview. He saw immediately the degradation of values and family life among the Beta Israel in the shacks, former animal sheds, and latrines in which they were living. Husbands left their wives; young people, who were traditionally brought up to respect parents and elders and to speak very softly in their presence, were now rebelling against them. "We couldn't stop the disintegration of families," Zimna recalled with agitation. "We couldn't stop desertions, or young girls from being spoiled. The young criminals of Addis Ababa got our girls. They said they are their husbands." He did not add any of these men to the list of people eligible for reunification with families in Israel. "We had to use force to get these girls back," he added.[13]

The JDC and the Jewish Agency had taken the deliberate decision to give the Jews only a minimal monthly allowance to pay for their housing. The non-Jews already called the Beta Israel the "people who get money from the sky" because American Jewish groups had sent them support for years.[14] Now, in Addis, they were getting cash at the embassy, and sometimes were robbed. The Beta Israel were proud and would not part with their money easily, and to give them too much would only make them more conspicuous targets. In addition, the more money they had, the higher rents would go. So the stipends were minimal.[15] But for a man from a village, said Zimna, it seemed like a lot of money, and he might squander it. "As soon as a man got money," he noted, "the wife would come in a week later and complain that she had no money. I saw this in literally a few weeks."[16]

The Israelis and Americans were working with enormous dedication to help the Ethiopian Jews, but it would be up to Lubrani and Naim to save them. And to do that, they would have to deal with Mengistu.

## THE TRIPARTITE MEETING

### November 12–13, 1990

To encourage their renewed friendship with the Ethiopian president, the Israelis sent a "dowry" with Naim. In political romance, gifts often are measured in carrots, not carats, and the Israeli dowry was meant to induce the Ethiopians to release the Jews more quickly. The most important carrot was the tripartite meeting with the Americans to which Herman Cohen had agreed a few weeks earlier. Cohen kept his promise and came himself to represent the United States at the meeting. He was joined by Bob Houdek, an experienced Africanist who had been the chargé d'affaires at the United States embassy in Addis since 1988. Naim, Lubrani, and Haim Divon, the Ethiopia desk officer at the Foreign Ministry, represented the Israelis. Kassa and Colonel Mersha Ketsela, the deputy internal affairs minister, were there for Ethiopia, as was Mengistu's chief of protocol.[17]

At the meeting, on November 12–13, 1990, the Americans called for human rights and the hastened emigration of the Jews. They declared that only negotiations could resolve the civil war, and they endorsed a unified Ethiopia. The Ethiopians promised to comply with the American demands. Kassa then made what Naim later called an unexpected appeal for the United States to supply Ethiopia with arms, or to permit others (i.e., Israel) to do so. Cohen deflected the request, reiterating American support for a negotiated peace.[18]

In all, little new was said, but it was important that the meeting took place, Lubrani recalled later. "The Ethiopians saw that the Americans acted as we said they would, that America was officially committed to the integrity and unity of Ethiopia. This created new ties for Ethiopia with the U.S."[19] Cohen agreed that the most important value of the trilateral meeting was that it took place at all. He did anticipate one practical benefit, though: since Washington had become the de facto mediator between Addis and the EPLF, he expected the Ethiopians to comply with the American demand for improvement in the Falasha emigration rate.[20]

For Mengistu, the meeting was both a symbol of the dramatic turn that he had taken in foreign policy and also a measure of his desperation. His career previously had been marked by revolutionary fervor, admiration for the Soviet Union, affinity for socialist economic and political models, and hostility to the United States. He also had harbored a deep distrust of Israel since Moshe Dayan's revelation of the secret arms deal between their countries twelve years earlier.[21] Of necessity, Mengistu now had reversed course.[22] Although Cohen had not put new commitments on the table, for Mengistu the meeting in itself implied a level of recognition that would diminish the uncomfortable sense that his was a pariah regime. Perhaps that would restore morale to the army and open the door to further American acceptance. Mengistu at this moment had reached the apex of his influence with the United States. Washington appreciated Ethiopia's recent collaboration against Iraq on the UN Security Council, and the Ethiopians knew that their vote would be crucial to the upcoming resolution to authorize the use of force in Kuwait.[23] That may have emboldened them to take their futile stab at asking the United States to look away as Israel sold them arms. In any case, if Mengistu had gained little of substance at this meeting, he had given little. Even if he permitted an enhanced rate of Falasha departures, he could contrive to keep hundreds or even thousands of them in Addis for years to come. It is doubtful that Mengistu ever had any intention of letting the entire community go. As long as he had them, he could count on the continued political interest of Israel and the United States, and on a constant infusion of cash paying for the departures that his government did allow.

Mengistu was elated with the tripartite meeting and told the Israelis that he personally had given orders to smooth the way for the Falasha emigration.[24] The aliyah rose accordingly, from 58 departures in October to 428 in November and 532 in December.[25] A few days after the meeting, however, a visiting delegation of Knesset members put this new spirit of cooperation in jeopardy. After meeting with Ethiopian foreign minister Tesfaye Dinka, one of the Israelis was quoted as saying that Ethiopia would permit one thousand Jews to emigrate in December.[26] Kassa was appalled by this announcement. "It was totally unfounded, a sheer lie!" he said later in an interview. The Knesset member had in effect made a public declaration that Ethiopia was bargaining for the release of Jews. Imagine what Mengistu thought when he read it, Kassa told me. "Many radical Communists in our camp felt that collaborating with the Zionist entity was the worst thing to do," he said. "They feared that the Arabs would strengthen the rebels. And the Arabs *were* arming the rebels. The Israelis had lots of intelligence on that. They had found notes in the PLO headquarters in Beirut."[27] The Palestinians were in fact alarmed by the aliyah from Addis. The PLO charged that the Ethiopian Jews would become Israeli soldiers and would "kill the children of the Intifada." In fact, PLO chairman Yasser Arafat called on Palestinians to "open fire on the new Jewish immigrants, be they Soviet, Falasha, or anything else."[28] Public statements like the one that upset Kassa could only exacerbate this situation.

Naim learned from these early encounters how closely Kassa's network in Israel followed the Israeli press. Indeed, after this first week of meetings, he concluded that Kassa was the only strategist among the Ethiopians. The others were assistants, he said later. The Ethiopian foreign minister, Tesfaye Dinka, was not even in the loop. In Naim's judgment, Kassa was the only Westerner there. He was the architect of the change in orientation from the Soviets to the Americans, and of the revived Israeli-Ethiopian relations.[29] Tesfaye himself confirmed Kassa's role later: "Everybody left it to Kassa to handle everything" regarding Israel, he told me.[30]

## HE *WAS* THE COMMITTEE

Even though the rate of Beta Israel departures had returned to the levels of the previous spring, the actual process of preparing exit applications was dauntingly complex. Ethiopia was one of the most bureaucratic countries in the world, and the Israelis had been forced to fill out a painful assortment of forms for each visa application. One showed that the applicant had no debts to the bank; another confirmed that he owed no taxes; a third was a *meshenya* indicating that he had permission to migrate from Gondar province. Each applicant had to have a notarized invitation to come to Israel for the purpose of family unification, as well as authorization establishing that he was Jewish. At the end of October, Kassa had offered to streamline this paperwork. He proposed that a single form would suffice for each applicant, along with three photographs of each family member over the age of four. To simplify the process, Micha Feldman, as the Israeli consul, agreed to take responsibility for any claim against the emigrant by a government ministry, organization, bank, or individual.[31] A social worker himself, Kassa said that the forms would be checked by the Ethiopian Committee of Social Workers, headed by Colonel Mersha. There would be no quotas, Kassa assured them. Whoever filled out the forms would be permitted to leave.[32]

Initially, Feldman was enthusiastic about the offer. It would allow the Israelis to set priorities for who would get out first, which in turn would reduce the private bribery to Ethiopian officials. In consultation with the *qessotch*, the Israelis settled on a general guideline for who would leave each month: 50 percent would be people who had been in Addis Ababa for a long time, 30 percent would be veterans of camps in Sudan, 10 percent would be the old and sick, and 10 percent would be families who had lost children. Two *qessotch* also were selected to go every month.[33] The Israelis would tweak these numbers if they needed to fly people out for urgent political or other reasons.

In December, when Mersha said that his committee had found errors in the first batch of forms, Feldman accepted it. "I was pretty naive then. We believed them," he recalled.[34] But Feldman and Lubrani soon concluded that the true function of Kassa's forms was to control the Jewish emigration in any given month. The Ethiopians would approve only the number of applications that they had determined in advance, turning all others back because the committee had discovered "errors." Only later did the Israelis learn that this "committee" never existed. Rather, it consisted of Mersha alone, acting on the monthly allocations of exit permits that Kassa gave him. He *was* the committee, Mersha confessed when Operation Solomon was all over, exploding with laughter.[35] Such subterfuge was only fitting for a man who, in addition to checking emigration applications, was the deputy head of the Stasi-style state security apparatus.

## "DON'T COME TO ME FOR MONEY"

In the late autumn of 1990 in Jerusalem, Lubrani sought to trump these bureaucratic obstacles and get the Jews out of Addis Ababa quickly. Prime Minister Shamir gave his approval for Israel to take dramatic steps, but insisted that the funding would have to come from Diaspora Jews. "Don't come to me for money," Shamir warned Lubrani.[36]

So Lubrani turned to America. He was not particularly familiar with the American Jewish philanthropic community and he did not have a nuanced grasp of U.S. politics. Lubrani did know, though, that Jewish-black relations were a sensitive subject for American Jews. Jews in the United States historically had supported African-American civil rights, an alliance perhaps most memorably imaged when Rabbi Abraham Joshua Heschel marched side by side with Dr. Martin Luther King Jr. in Selma, Alabama, in 1965. But in recent years, tensions had arisen between the two groups. In addition, American Jews, like other Jews around the world, bitterly resented the United Nations resolution that equated Zionism and racism. (Ironically, the General Assembly passed that resolution in November 1975, seven months after the Israeli government had extended the right of Israeli citizenship to Ethiopian Jews under the Law of Return.) Lubrani was aware that the Ethiopian rescue could be a powerful statement about both of those issues.[37] His job now was to find a practical way to enlist American support for it, politically and financially.

In December, the Joint brought Lubrani to New York, to a JDC board meeting, where he impressed the Americans with his candor and his ability to inspire confidence. He in turn was impressed by the fact that Michael Schneider was accepted by all of the American organizations. Lubrani made the JDC his base, and the Joint gave him full office facilities, hotel rooms, and plane tickets. It was at this point that he first told Schneider that it might be necessary to get the Jews out of Addis through a massive one-shot rescue mission.[38]

Schneider appointed Gideon Taylor, a young Jewish attorney from Dublin, as the Joint's desk person in New York covering Lubrani's negotiations with the Ethiopians. He also assigned JDC-Israel's Eli Eliezri as liaison between Lubrani and the Joint. From that point on, Eliezri became Lubrani's almost constant companion and associate on business related to Ethiopia. An intense, energetic man, then around fifty, Eliezri was a veteran of Israeli intelligence services. Though he stayed in the background, he was connected to virtually every aspect of the operation—more so than some of the key participants knew. In addition to his role with Lubrani, he was the chairman of Almaya. A friend of Merhav's from their days in the same paratroop regiment, and then in the Mossad, he also sat on Merhav's steering committee in Jerusalem. He was a conduit to the JDC for confidential political and military information. And when things got tough in Addis, he was an effective field operative.

Schneider, Lubrani, Eliezri, and Taylor, along with Nate Shapiro and Will Recant of the AAEJ, formed a "kitchen cabinet," the inner working group that spearheaded the American Jewish community's part in the Ethiopian aliyah. Shapiro and Lubrani were wonderfully odd bedfellows. Shapiro had distrusted and bedeviled the Israeli government for years, and Lubrani was the quintessential Israeli insider, yet the chemistry between them was good. Later, former U.S. senator Rudy Boschwitz would become the seventh member of their team.

Much of this might not have happened if not for the fact that Lubrani was making an end run around the Jewish Agency and its chairman, Simcha Dinitz. Lubrani wanted latitude in bargaining with the Ethiopians about money. A few months earlier, he had had a run-in with Zvi Barak, the Jewish Agency's director-general of finance, over the $10 million aid package that Lubrani initially had offered Mengistu.[39] The Ethiopians had taken the aid but had not delivered a significant increase in exits, and the leaders of the Jewish Agency were not pleased. They were all the more disturbed because this was the second time that this had happened. The Jewish Agency had made a large payment to the Ethiopians before Lubrani was appointed, and that too had resulted in no major increase in the aliyah. "We paid and no fruit," Barak told me. The Israelis treated this first payment as a state secret, he noted.[40] So, at a stormy meeting in Dinitz's office, Barak had insisted on seeing results before he authorized yet another payment, and he and Lubrani had quarreled, nearly becoming violent.[41]

Now Lubrani was after a much larger sum, and he did not want to have to go to Dinitz and Barak for it. He knew that if the American organizations were guaranteeing the payment, he could have the freedom he wanted in negotiating a figure with Kassa when the time came. In addition, Lubrani may have had another motive: he might have been afraid that Dinitz would leak news about interim stages. Lubrani came from a security background and liked to work in secrecy. Dinitz, by contrast, was a politician, and for him publicity was valuable currency.[42]

Dinitz resented the Joint's involvement. It was the responsibility of the Jewish Agency to bring Jews to Israel, while the JDC's role was to provide assistance and support services to endangered Jewish communities. As the JDC blurred this line, the relationship between the two organizations deteriorated to a degree that eventually endangered the operation.

## SEEKING AN AMBASSADOR AND WEAPONS

Kassa chose this moment in December 1990 to return to the States on a "confidence-building mission." In reality, he intended to join Lubrani in pursuit of two goals: an exchange of ambassadors between Washington and Addis, and American military and economic aid for Ethiopia. If they failed to achieve the latter, they intended to seek an end to U.S. restrictions on Israel's supplying the arms.[43]

Kassa certainly came in search of weapons, according to Congressman Gary Ackerman. During this trip, Kassa was frustrated, though—not least in Queens, New York, which, he found, had some neighborhoods as tough as Mengistu's palace. Lubrani and Kassa had an appointment to visit the congressman at his home in Queens late one night. Their driver called to say that they were lost, Ackerman recalled later. "Then he phoned again from a neighborhood where you don't want to be in the middle of the night. My administrative assistant goes to get them, and finds Uri Lubrani and Kassa Kebede watching people strip a car on a corner." When they finally got to the congressman's house at midnight, Kassa was alarmed to find security officers everywhere. Ackerman assured Kassa that the security had nothing to do with him. The week before, Meir Kahane of the militant Jewish Defense League had been murdered, and Ackerman's name was found on the top of the killer's hit list. So there was a policeman outside of his house, as well as two federal officers inside.

After this strange start, Kassa finally made his case. "He knew that the United States wouldn't directly give arms," Ackerman recalled, "but he wanted us to look the other way if Israel provides them." Ackerman knew that Israel could not give them what they wanted: "It couldn't give them victory in a war that they couldn't win," he said. "The Ethiopians were being shot with their own arms by the Tigreans." If the Israelis gave them weapons, sooner or later the army would abandon them to the rebels. In fact, Kassa said later, he already knew at that point that the military situation was hopeless, and had for months. But the Ethiopians evidently hoped that getting the arms would in itself raise the army's morale enough for them to start to fight. Kassa also hoped to secure a loan, but left the United States unsatisfied.[44]

Lubrani had promised Mengistu that he would try to soften the American opposition to arming Ethiopia, and that was his declared purpose on this trip. In fact, however, when he traveled to Washington, Lubrani sabotaged that mission. During testimony before the House subcommittee on African affairs, he frankly admitted that Israel had supplied weapons to the Ethiopians in the past. "He said, 'Yes, we did this, under certain pressures,'" congressional aide Steve Morrison said in an interview. Lubrani then asked Howard Wolpe and the others on the subcommittee to keep telling the Ethiopians that Israel must not send them arms. "This helps us," he told the legislators. Morrison, who had authored a report that accused Israel of having surreptitiously armed Mengistu in 1989, remarked that Lubrani impressed people on Capital Hill with his openness. The Israeli was persuasive and really boosted his own credibility, Morrison observed.[45]

# SIX

# The Doomsday Scenario—
# The Falash Mura

**JANUARY–FEBRUARY 1991**

By the close of 1990, the Israelis, with American help, had put the Ethiopian aliyah back on course. From its low point of only fifty-eight exits in October, the emigration had returned to an average of about a hundred departures a week in November and December. In the early months of 1991, however, a series of events posed actual and potential obstacles to the emigration. In addition, the Ethiopians insisted that Israel deal with the vexed question of the Falash Mura, whose complexly ambiguous status presented the Israelis with a divisive and enduring problem.

## "IT WAS A GAME"

For the Israelis, one of the most frustrating impediments to the aliyah was the Ethiopians' rejection of exit applications because of minor errors in the way that they were filled out. At the end of 1990 and at the start of 1991, Colonel Mersha Ketsela turned back many of these forms, saying that they listed false or incomplete information. Naim yelled at the Israeli social workers, demanding that the Jewish Agency do better. He still believed that the success of the aliyah depended on filling in the forms properly, but, like Feldman, Lubrani, and other principal figures in the aliyah, he concluded that Kassa actually was using the paperwork as a ploy to control the number of exits.[1]

Mersha's Social Affairs Committee, for example, would return an application because it said a woman had four children by three husbands. That, however, was not an uncommon family structure in Ethiopia. Mersha rejected another form because, he said, a woman seemed too old to have a child. In the elastic Ethiopian *zemed* (extended family, traced back seven generations), a grandmother might be given a grandson to raise, and she would call him her son, so the Israelis would list him that way.[2] That was reason enough for Mersha's committee to turn the application back. "Case 159: The woman is 60 years old. It is difficult to believe that she would have a 3 years [*sic*] old baby," the report on this case commented.[3] Mersha was hardly naive in this respect; indeed, it was he who explained the complexity of Ethiopian family structures to the Israelis.[4] As deputy head of the Ethiopian state security, he was doing his job: creating difficulties to slow the aliyah.

The forms certainly did contain mistakes. The Israelis' record keeping was complicated by the fact that there are no family names in Ethiopia. Among Amharic-speakers, a man typically is known by his first name, followed by his father's first name. So Kassa (whose name means "compensation") was addressed as "Mr. Kassa," followed by his father's first name, Kebede. Children born to a woman by different fathers, therefore, usually have different surnames. In addition, different family members used differing names for each other in addition to the official ones that they were given at birth. And since some Ethiopian names have two components, naming patterns alone could confuse the Israelis. Another complicating factor was that there were no official birth records, and Ethiopians generally had no reason to keep track of their age. So, in almost all cases, ages were guesses, arrived at with reference to historical events, such as the end of the Italian occupation in 1941.[5]

A lot of the errors were simply careless. In addition, the Israeli social workers invented or concealed details quite often. A number of them spoke openly of filling in false information in order to deceive the Ethiopians.[6] And the Beta Israel could be very inventive themselves. It was not uncommon for a family head to exaggerate the number of children or other relatives in his or her family in order to get a larger living allowance.[7] The result, in one instance, was that the Israelis submitted a form for a father listing three children, then sent in a second form for the same man—only this time he had five offspring. Naim later described a typical experience: Mersha would ask the details about an invitation from relatives in Israel, and the Israelis would supply them. Mersha then would return the form, wanting it to state how much the relatives earned. The Israelis would resubmit it, hiding the fact that the relatives were unemployed. "It was a game," Naim said later.[8] But the game had serious consequences for people divided from their families, living in squalor, and unable to leave Ethiopia.

## THE GULF WAR

A potentially far more dangerous threat to the aliyah arose in January 1991 with the outbreak of the Gulf War. In that month, President Bush made good on his promise to retaliate against Iraq for Saddam Hussein's invasion of Kuwait. As an American-led coalition of Western and Arab forces struck at the Iraqis, the Israelis, uncharacteristically, were obliged to restrain themselves. Scud missiles fell on Tel Aviv, and Israelis sat in sealed rooms with gas masks. But Israel, at American insistence, did not strike back. If it had, the Arabs might have withdrawn from the coalition.

In Addis Ababa, the Ethiopian Jews surprised the Israelis and the Americans by the quiet intensity of their identification with Israel and their determination to continue the aliyah despite the war. Jewish Agency workers showed them gas masks so the Jews would know what to expect in Israel. They were undaunted. "We are going to Israel. We are going to die if Israel is going to die. We are going to fight if Israel is going to fight," one of the Jews said.[9] They made symbolic gestures of support, such as not listening to music again until Israel was safe.[10] And they prayed. In the JDC clinic, Rick Hodes listened to BBC radio while his patients, who liked to participate in their own medical care, shook their medicine, a mixture of water and streptomycin. As Hodes heard the news of the war, he passed it on in Amharic to his patients. While they were shaking the medicine on one particular day, Hodes asked them to pray. "All Ethiopians have great faith and communicate very well with God," he told me later. "The women prayed, and shook their fingers. One woman quoted Psalm 121: 'The God of Israel never sleeps.' Everybody had relatives in Israel," Hodes recalled. "Everyone wanted to go to Israel during the Gulf War."[11]

At the start of February, the senior *qes*, Menashe Zimru, eighty-six years old, would make aliyah. Israel was still under attack, and he and the other Ethiopian *olim* who landed with him were greeted with gas masks, along with a song, flowers, and sandwiches. Wearing a white cloak and turban, and carrying a cane and a fly whisk made of monkey hair, the *qes* asked, "Are we really in Israel?" and jumped for joy. "I feel happy like a lamb," he explained, "because now all of my wishes have been fulfilled. It is better to die as a free Jew than to continue living in exile in Ethiopia," he said. "If I was young, I would fight with a rifle alongside the soldiers to defend Israel. But I have another rifle—my prayer. I will pray."[12]

The Israelis continued to dedicate resources to the aliyah, despite their preoccupation with defense at home. One thousand and thirty-eight Ethiopian Jews reached Israel in January, the best month of the aliyah since Operation Moses six years earlier.[13] By contrast, with Israel under attack, the immigration from the former Soviet Union declined drastically that month. The massive Soviet influx dwarfed the Ethiopian arrivals, and placed a tremendous strain on the Israeli economy. In 1989, 12,721 people had arrived from the USSR; this number had exploded to 185,232 in 1990. More than a thousand a day had come in December 1990 alone. But in January 1991, that rate dropped by 60 percent, with 13,360 Soviet Jews immigrating to Israel.[14]

## KASSA OPENED HIS HEART

In January 1991, while the Gulf War was under way, Kassa spent three weeks in Israel trying to get the arms or money that he had failed to secure in the States. During this visit, Kassa opened his heart to the Israelis and confessed the troubles that awaited him back home. He was under pressure from hardliners in Mengistu's government who opposed the aliyah, Kassa confided to them. If Israel refused his requests, it would weaken his personal position, and with it, the Ethiopian Jews' chances of leaving. The argument did not work; the Israelis offered economic aid instead. Kassa returned home empty-handed and, according to a reliable Israeli official, in effect sabotaged a planned visit by Simcha Dinitz.[15]

The Americans helped keep the pressure on Kassa, though. Bob Houdek showed constant interest in the numbers, and Herman Cohen had scheduled the next trilateral meeting for February 12. Although Cohen ultimately canceled the meeting, these factors together resulted in much better results. With a record number of Jews allowed out in January, Lubrani supposed that he had succeeded. "I thought my mission was over," he said in an interview.[16] He urged American Jewish leaders not to release the immigration figures, thinking that Kassa might not realize how high they were.[17] The press reported them, though, and added that Jewish Agency officials were hopeful that the aliyah would soon reach fifteen hundred to two thousand a month. At that rate, the Jews would be out by January 1992.[18]

## THE DOOMSDAY SCENARIO

There was reason to fear that the Jewish community would not survive in Addis until 1992, however. Susan Pollack and the AAEJ had brought the Jews down from the Gondar region because of a premonition of a disaster that might have descended on them in their villages. Now their exodus was hastened by another harrowing vision—of what could happen to them if they remained in the slums of Addis Ababa. This took shape during the third of Lubrani's recent visits to Ethiopia, in a disquieting conversation with his old friend Zimna Berhane. Zimna, an Ethiopian-Israeli, was working with the Jewish Agency in Addis. One day in mid-February 1991, he described what Lubrani and the American Jewish leaders later would refer to as the "Doomsday Scenario."

A catastrophe was coming, Zimna told Lubrani. The Jewish community was under great threat. Families were falling apart, and their values were corroding under the influence of prostitution and alcohol. If the government fell, anarchy could break out, and that could lead to a bloodbath. It would be no problem, Zimna said, for the people of Addis to slaughter all of the heads of Jewish households in the city. "We are Falasha [i.e., strangers]," he told the Israeli. "We left our villages. We can't protect ourselves. Do everything to get us out of here!"

Zimna made it personal. "If this community would be the victim of a pogrom, they will throw all the mud on you," he told Lubrani. "If you succeed, you get all of the credit—from me too. . . . See all these children?

Remember Germany! If all these children are slaughtered, it will be on your conscience." Lubrani became emotional. "Don't talk like that," he replied.[19]

Zimna's account expressed the worst possible case, reaching beyond his own cultural context to evoke pogroms and the Holocaust. Lubrani would assert this Doomsday account at critical moments in the negotiations, and others then would restate it until it reached the highest levels in Washington. Ultimately, the Doomsday Scenario would become a principal factor in persuading American officials to intervene in the crisis.

"When I was in Uganda I saw several revolutions," Lubrani recalled in an interview. The conflict was tribal. In one night, sixty thousand people were murdered, he said. "This was always at the back of my mind" as the rebels approached Addis Ababa, he noted. "This could happen all at once. All the time I felt this in my gut." Lubrani feared that if the Israelis waited until the new regime established itself, the rescue could take a year or more to complete. It would be impossible to predict what the rebels, and the citizens of Addis, might do to the Jews in the meantime. "Our conception changed," Lubrani recalled. Now it was necessary to think in terms of a dramatic rescue.[20]

In fact, more than a year earlier Jewish Agency officials had proposed a quick, large-scale evacuation. Micha Feldman had filed a report in January 1990 calling for such an operation. The Jewish Agency passed the idea on to the Israeli embassy in Addis, which forwarded it to the Foreign Ministry in Jerusalem.[21] However the proposal reached Lubrani, he already was thinking in these terms by the time of the conversation with Zimna. Indeed, he had told Michael Schneider during his visit to New York in December 1990 about the need to think of a mass exodus, as noted above. By February 1991, when Lubrani's conversation with Zimna took place, plans for the operation already were being developed in Israel.[22] Now Lubrani would have to get the American government to support it.

## "A HEN THAT LAYS GOLDEN EGGS"

Despite fears of what might happen in the future, in the early months of 1991 the aliyah was proceeding well, and the JDC and the Israelis were infusing vast amounts of money into Ethiopia to keep things moving smoothly. The monthly cash and maintenance stipends that the Joint provided to the Jewish families in Addis made their way into the Ethiopian economy in the form of exorbitant rents and other living expenses. The Americans and Israelis also provided various "incentives," including Jewish Agency payments to the Ethiopian Internal Affairs Ministry to issue immigration licenses. "The Jewish Agency . . . had to pay them off," one highly placed Israeli source told me later. The Israelis also paid inflated rates for seats on Ethiopian Airlines planes for the Jews who were allowed to leave. In addition,

Mashav, the Israeli Foreign Ministry's economic assistance agency, made Ethiopia an offer of $2.5 million in nonsectarian aid for the coming year. The JDC, which secretly assisted Mashav financially, calculated that by January 1991 it already had transferred $300,000 into the country.[23] In the twelve months prior to Operation Solomon, the Joint expended $9 million on Ethiopia, out of a total annual budget of $60 million.[24]

The Ethiopians thought "that they have a hen that lays golden eggs," Eliezri now reported to the JDC. "This hen lays every day golden eggs of tens of thousands of dollars."[25] Michael Schneider calculated at the time that the Joint was providing the sixth or seventh largest stream of cash into Ethiopia, following such sources as coffee exports and the Addis Ababa Hilton.[26]

On his trip to Addis in February, Lubrani brought with him two wealthy British Jewish businessmen, David Alliance and Sammi Shamoon. Alliance, a textile manufacturer, was "a billion-dollar man," Lubrani enthusiastically told the Ethiopians. Alliance offered to give the Ethiopians a textile mill and promised to buy anything that they produced in it for the next three years. Shamoun, a financier who worked with agricultural marketing, proposed that the Ethiopians grow fruit and vegetables for export to Saudi Arabia. "The Ethiopians realized that this was *tachlis*," Lubrani recalled in an interview, meaning that they thought of these offers of assistance as concrete and real. But, Lubrani added, with the rebels advancing, the Ethiopians were deceiving themselves.[27]

## THE ETHIOPIAN GOVERNMENT TURNS OFF THE TAP

February opens the prime season for military attack in Ethiopia, and the rebel offensive in 1991 was more effective that month than in earlier years. For the first time, government forces fell apart on all fronts and made no effort to counterattack.[28] The insurgents had surrounded Gondar town, north of Lake Tana. They had taken the important military base of Bahr-Dar, on the southern shore of the lake, with no real opposition, and were deep within the ethnic Amhara regions. Stories were spreading about officers deserting or going over to the other side, and of thousands of new recruits being coerced to go to the front. Oil reserves were running out, and the Saudis reportedly had refused to sell any more oil to Ethiopia. Despite the failure of the generals' coup attempt in May 1989, Ethiopian army officers now reportedly plotted again to overthrow Mengistu. According to this report, they abandoned the plan when Bahr-Dar came under attack, however.[29]

The Ethiopians now desperately pushed the Israelis for arms and again took steps to close down the aliyah. In February, nearly a thousand Jews were allowed to leave, many of them early in the month.[30] Menashe Zimru, for example, the aged *qes* who jumped for joy on landing in Israel, arrived on February 5 along with 223 other *olim*. But at the end of February, the Ethiopian government turned off the tap, just as it had the previous summer and fall. Mersha turned back nearly all exit applications that month, then announced that he would accept no new applications. He had a thousand pending, and that was enough, he said. Two weeks later, he still was not accepting forms.

## THE FALASH MURA

In the early months of 1991, with the aliyah about to slow down, the Ethiopian government pressured the Israelis and Americans to address another problem that had arisen, one that would have increasingly urgent implications. Since May 1990, many of the people who had made their way to Addis, or whom the AAEJ had transported, were the descendants of Jewish converts to Christianity. By January 1991, there were two thousand of them in Addis.[31] These people hoped to be taken to Israel, but they were not Jewish under Israeli law. They were known by the name Falash Mura, Feres Moura, or some similar variant—recently invented terms of uncertain meaning. Others called the converts the *Mariam wodid*, "lovers of Mary."[32]

The Beta Israel did not consider the convert families to be an entirely distinct group, but the Israelis, working under the guidelines of Israel's Law of Return, did. According to rabbinic law, a Jew who converts to another religion normally remains Jewish. Israeli civil law does not necessarily agree, though. The Law of Return guarantees that any Jew, as well as the child or grandchild of a Jew, has the right to live in Israel, as do their spouses. The law specifically excludes, however, Jews who have converted to another religion voluntarily. The Falash Mura said that they wanted to return to the Judaism of their ancestors, which would entitle them to live in Israel. Micha Feldman talked with many of them, however, and concluded that they definitely were not Jews. They knew nothing about Judaism, they baptized their children, and they buried their dead in Christian cemeteries, he recalled later. Obliged to make a decision at the time, Feldman declared the Falash Mura ineligible for aliyah and told them to return to their villages.[33] He knew, though, that many of them would not leave, that their codes of honor did not allow them to go home in defeat.[34] Many of the converts did anything that they could to be accepted. A JDC official recalled that when he told one to get out of the Israeli embassy, the man responded, "I swear by Jesus Christ that I am a Jew!" Rick Hodes recalled that one of the Falash Mura leaders "claims that he's not a missionary. But I've seen him sign, 'Yours in Christ.'"[35]

The AAEJ was willing to round the convert families up and bring them back to Gondar.[36] There were claims in some quarters in Israel, however, that these people had been the victims of forced conversion. Some of their advocates compared them to the Marranos, the Jews of Spain who converted under pressure prior to the expulsion in 1492 but then in many cases practiced Judaism secretly. As Steven Kaplan noted in "Falasha Christians: A Brief History," however, the reality of Ethiopian history was more complex than that. Contrary to what often was claimed, the Christian Falashas typically had not been coerced into conversion. It was only in the modern period that missionizing, by the London Society for Promoting Christianity Amongst the Jews, had led to a distinct community of Falasha Christians. Still, in 1885 there were only eight hundred or nine hundred converts. During the great famine of 1888–92, in which half to two-thirds of the Beta Israel died, many Jews left their villages in search of food. They assimilated among Christians and, to a lesser extent, Muslims. Under these conditions, they converted, not through coercion, but for the chance to own land, to get a good education in a missionary school, or to advance in official positions. Converts may have resembled Marranos because they continued to practice circumcision and follow biblical dietary laws. In Ethiopia, though, Christians do this as well. A convert to Christianity might therefore appear to an outside observer to be clinging to his Jewish traditions and convictions.

At all times, the converts continued to be identified as Falasha, and to enjoy contacts with their Jewish families and friends. They attended Jewish religious celebrations, and converted men sometimes married Beta Israel women. Kaplan cited one researcher's estimate that there might be as many as fifty thousand of these "nonpracticing Falashas" in Ethiopia. The decision on whether to accept the few thousand of them who were in Addis would apply to everyone in this group.[37]

Hagar Salamon adds that, according to Ethiopian-Israelis, Jews often converted on the promise of marriage to Christian girls, but in the end had no choice except to marry other converts. Or they converted to get money or land but ultimately were not accepted into the Christian community. In consequence, the Falash Mura were stuck in a state of permanent liminality, between Judaism and Christianity. In the eyes of many Ethiopian Jews, the Falash Mura conversions were never completed: they had become Christian on the outside, but their hearts were still Jewish.[38] Thus the Jews saw the converts' status as ambiguous. The Israelis, however, needed to make a simple yes-or-no decision about whether to let them immigrate.

There was a further complication: some Ethiopians from convert families had reached Israel in the 1980s. So had some Christians who made no claim to recent Jewish ancestry, usually former neighbors of Jews, who sponsored them under false pretenses after arriving in Israel.[39] Their Christian first-degree relatives in Ethiopia could claim the right to emigrate under Israel's Law of Entry, which provides for family reunification. This law guarantees that anyone with a parent, child, or spouse already settled in Israel is entitled to live there too. The liberal Israeli Law of Entry and the complexly elaborate and inclusive Ethiopian family structure were a volatile combination. A single Ethiopian child in Israel could bring in eighty relatives, one Israeli official observed.[40]

The most assertive advocates of the converts were veteran Ethiopian-Israelis, in many cases their relatives. Leaders of the religious nationalist group Gush Emunim (Bloc of the Faithful) also favored the convert families' immigration, but with a specific agenda in mind: they believed that Jewish settlement of the West Bank and Gaza Strip was integral to the process of messianic redemption, and they wanted the Ethiopians to be deployed as settlers.[41] What to do with the Falash Mura was already a vexed question. The prospect of settling them in the territories outside the Green Line (the Israeli borders prior to the 1967 war) embedded the whole issue in a political hornets' nest. The Shamir government's policy of expanding settlements in the territories occupied in 1967 was a principal factor in Israel's increasingly strained relations with the Bush administration at the time. Secretary of State James Baker repeatedly identified the settlements as obstacles to peace. This took on particular significance for new immigrants early in 1990 when Shamir, in an act of defiance toward the United States, declared that the huge Soviet aliyah required a "big Israel." Shamir's formulation triggered American and Arab fears that he intended to settle many of the new *olim* in the occupied territories of a Greater Israel. To forestall that, Baker linked $400 million in U.S. loan guarantees for new housing for Soviet immigrants to a freeze on settlement expansion. Ariel Sharon, who was minister of housing and head of a cabinet committee overseeing immigration, announced in June 1990 that no Soviet immigrants would be sent to the territories. But a U.S. Department of State report found that by the spring of 1991 some three thousand of them had been settled on the West Bank and the Golan Heights.[42] At that point, the debate turned on the aliyah from the former Soviet Union, not the Beta Israel, but Ethiopian officials were concerned and sought Israel's assurance that the Falashas would not be settled on the West Bank.[43] The Falash Mura were a very minor factor, if they figured at all. The decision whether to bring them over had not even been made yet. Still, the possibility of settling them outside the Green Line would drive a last-minute push to bring them along during Operation Solomon, as we shall see.

There were forceful opponents to the converts' emigration as well. Among the most outspoken were the Ethiopian Church and the government in Addis, which strongly resisted anything that smacked of converting Christians to Judaism. And some Israelis feared that the Falash Mura would missionize for Christianity if they reached to Israel.

The Israelis felt that their mission was to rescue Jews, and any decision on the converts would have to wait. The AAEJ refused to support the converts, and in February 1991 the JDC declared that it would accept no new Falash Mura cases.[44] NACOEJ, however, decided to take the convert families in Addis into its care. That, said Michael Strum, a NACOEJ official, was why his organization had opened its own compound in Addis in the summer of 1990.[45] Barbara Ribakove Gordon, the executive director of NACOEJ, expressed her perspective starkly in an interview: "We do not attempt to say who is a Jew. We leave that up to the rabbis." But there were reports that the Falash Mura were destitute. "We did not want them to starve to death while Israel was deciding whether they were Jews or not," she said.[46] Asher Naim suggests that NACOEJ was influenced by political support it received from right-wing Israeli religious groups who wanted to bring in Jews of any origin in order to people the territories.[47] That devalues the dedication that NACOEJ has shown over many years, however.

Whether to accept or disown the Falash Mura would become one of the most heartrending problems that the Israelis would face in this aliyah. "We're tough during the day, but cry at night," Almaya's Kobi Friedman said at the time.[48] The problem would persist into the next century, and would divide the Ethiopian Jewish community in Israel.

# SEVEN

# Mengistu's Chestnuts—The Ante

## MARCH 1991

In March 1991 the Ethiopians shut down the aliyah completely. The result-ing delay in departures extended the Jews' exposure to the many dangers of Addis, including HIV, which had reached alarming levels in the Ethiopian capital. American Jewish leaders succeeded in rallying official American pres-sure to force Ethiopia to restart the emigration. More ambitious diplomatic steps, however, proved elusive.

### "THE DOOR FELL OVER"

By early March, it seemed certain that the Mengistu regime would collapse; the only question was when. Though battlefield reports by the rebels and the government disagreed wildly, the regime's military situation was very grave, as Bob Frasure informed American Jewish leaders. The EPRDF had ad-vanced as far as the Gojjam region, south of Gondar, and had taken the important airbase at Bahr-Dar. Farther north, the Eritrean fighters were only slightly more than thirty miles from Assab in Eritrea, the last port un-der government control. If Assab were cut off, the government might be unable to import vital supplies, especially fuel, and that in itself would mean the end of the war. This was Mengistu's last gasp, Frasure concluded. Some officials expected the dictator to fall within two to three weeks, but other informed parties cautioned that Mengistu was a notorious survivor.[1] And Eliezri, in one of his intelligence reports to the Joint, said that, although the fuel shortage could lead to rioting in Addis, the Ethiopian army thought that it could hold out for months.[2] Still, large-scale desertions from the army persuaded Bob Houdek that a trip wire had been crossed: the government would fall soon, perhaps within a matter of weeks. On March 8 he ordered the evacuation of dependents and nonessential personnel from the Ameri-can embassy.[3]

By mid-March, Tigrean forces were reported to have advanced to within seventy to a hundred miles of Addis Ababa. "They knocked on the door and the door fell over," said one Western diplomat.[4] The Ethiopian army was disintegrating, with increasing numbers of officers and soldiers surrendering without a fight or defecting to the rebel side.

Life in Addis Ababa had become precarious. With the EPRDF in control of the farmlands north of the capital, the price of grain had doubled in the city and people could not afford basic foodstuffs.[5] Many Ethiopians believed that if the situation got any worse, there might be a popular uprising in Addis. Western embassies in the capital advised nonessential personnel to leave Ethiopia. The Russian embassy denied having issued a similar directive, but one Russian official conceded that several embassy staff had taken their vacations early.[6] As for the Israelis, Passover was coming, and that would provide a good cover for nonessential staff and families to leave the country. All flights out of Addis were full.

## THE AMERICAN STICK

Facing dire circumstances, the Ethiopians stopped the aliyah cold in order to pressure Israel to send them weapons and fuel. During the first week of March, for the first time since early November, not one Ethiopian Jew arrived in Israel.[7] On Friday, March 8, in a conference call from New York, Michael Schneider told American Jewish leaders and Israeli officials that the Ethiopians were holding the emigration hostage to extortionate demands on Israel. The American Jews, in concert with Israelis, now showed rare unanimity. The carrots were not working. The time had come to summon the American stick.

Some participants in the call suggested bringing the matter to the national security adviser, Brent Scowcroft, or directly to Bush. But Malcolm Hoenlein, the executive vice chairman of the Conference of Presidents of Major American Jewish Organizations, was not sure that a meeting with the president was necessary now. Lubrani concurred. Going to Scowcroft might do the job, he said. "Let's save some ammunition till later." So the group agreed to press the issue on three fronts. First they would approach Herman Cohen at the State Department. Then they would ask Shamir to raise the matter on Tuesday with Secretary of State Baker, who was in Israel to promote peace talks with the Arabs. And Hoenlein, who had access to high American government officials, would meet with Scowcroft.[8]

That Friday, the day of the conference call, Gondar town fell to the rebels. Most of the Ethiopian army's 603rd Corps reportedly surrendered without a fight.[9]

## HIV IN A "REFUGEE CAMP"

One of the most troubling consequences of the suspension of the aliyah was the danger that it posed to the health of the Jewish community in Addis. The longer the Beta Israel remained in the capital, the greater their exposure would be to HIV. On March 11, in a phone call to Jerusalem, Schneider told the Jewish Agency's Arnon Mantber that the emigration could be blocked for two to three months. Such a delay could lead to a significant spread of

HIV among the Jews, particularly the men. Mantber noted that one estimate showed that 2 percent of the Ethiopian Jews who had reached Israel
were HIV-positive. Israelis in Addis were providing intensive education on
HIV, Mantber said, but it was not having much effect.[10]

Israel could have kept the infected Falashas out, yet chose not to. The
Law of Return has a provision that prevents people from entering the country if they endanger public health, but the Israelis decided not to apply it for
moral and political reasons. An Israeli doctor told Moshe Yegar, a Foreign
Ministry official, that every month they were sending people with AIDS to
Israel. "This is a tragic thing you are doing," Yegar told him. "Yes, I know it,"
the doctor replied. "You can't break families and leave AIDS patients behind."[11] One Israeli who was involved in discussions about whether to reveal
this crisis told me, "We wanted to keep it under wraps. An entire population
would be social outcasts. Instead, we would identify them after they got [to
Israel]."[12] Besides, as Rick Hodes noted, "we were so busy keeping them
alive, we had no [time for] screening for AIDS." They did teach the use of
condoms, though. "We demonstrated on a Coke bottle," Hodes recalled.[13]

When Ethiopian officials continued to insist that they had stopped the
exits for "technical" reasons, meaning errors on the application forms, the
State Department stepped in. Herman Cohen dispatched Deputy Assistant
Secretary of State Irvin Hicks from Nairobi to express "serious U.S. concern
over any interruption in the emigration."[14] On the same day, Cohen also
sent a stern warning through Bob Houdek, who regarded the halt in exits as
pure extortion. Houdek pressed Kassa very hard. Cohen's message was that
the United States saw the shutdown of the emigration as a violation of the
accords reached at the tripartite meeting in November. This invalidated their
entire agreement, Cohen reportedly warned.[15] That was a clear threat: the
United States would play no role in peace negotiations unless Kassa renewed
the aliyah. Washington was in a better position to adopt a hard line than it
had been a few months earlier, since Ethiopia's term on the Security Council
had expired. The United States no longer needed its goodwill as it had in the
run-up to the Gulf War.

Kassa, for his part, accused the Jewish organizations and Israel of smear-
ing him. He was particularly furious about reports in the *Jerusalem Post* that
the Ethiopians had stopped the aliyah to extract arms and supplies from
Israel. Kassa told Houdek that the emigration would resume only if the Israeli government told the media that the interruption had happened for purely
technical reasons. In addition, the Israeli spokesman cited in the article would
have to apologize, and the exit forms would have to be filled out properly.[16]
On these conditions, Kassa informed Ambassador Asher Naim the next day,
March 13, the exits would begin again. At that meeting, Naim too got tough
with Kassa, then told him that he wanted to raise the emigration rate to

thirteen hundred a month. "We still have twenty-two thousand refugees after five months," he complained. "I am the ambassador to a refugee camp." Kassa acquiesced.[17]

The overtures to Baker and to Scowcroft had worked. Still, the American Jewish leaders agreed to speak of the blockage publicly as "technical" to satisfy Kassa, and Lubrani played along. On March 18, the Ethiopian embassy in Washington announced that five hundred Ethiopian Jews had been given exit visas.[18] But many Israelis distrusted the Ethiopians. "There is an agreement for a flight this week and next," said one Jewish Agency official. "After that, God only knows."[19]

On Friday, March 22, the first planeload of Ethiopian *olim* to arrive in Israel for over three weeks set down at Ben-Gurion Airport. On board were 202 people. In all, over 500 Ethiopian Jews reached Israel in March.[20] Babu Yacov, the spokesman for the United Ethiopian Organization in Tel Aviv, asked, however, "What will be the fate of the other 17,000 Jews left in Addis Ababa? We are afraid because no one knows what will happen there tomorrow."[21]

## "HE DIDN'T BELIEVE WE COULD PULL IT OFF"

Against this volatile background, Lubrani sought to persuade the American Jewish leaders to pursue a massive one-shot exodus. "What kind of crazy idea is this?" Schneider had asked himself when he first heard this scheme. "I thought it my duty to humor him." Schneider had imagined that they would have to move the Jews behind rebel lines somehow, away from government control, to rescue them. "I never thought it would take place with permission," he said.[22] But an airlift with Mengistu's assent was precisely what Lubrani now proposed.

A rescue operation went against the personal advice that Bob Frasure gave the Jewish leaders in mid-March. "If the Mengistu regime is terminated in the next few weeks, no rush situation by us will work," he said. "Instead, we should ride out the storm. We have political and relief relationships with the EPLF and the TPLF."[23]

And yet Frasure was distressed about the Jews' safety in Addis; he had serious misgivings about leaving them in harm's way, but doubted that there would be time for a single huge airlift. "He didn't believe we could pull it off," Lubrani said later.[24]

## "MENGISTU'S CHESTNUTS"

Lubrani, who came to the States in mid-March, was not sanguine about how the rebels might treat the Falashas in Addis Ababa. He refused American overtures to meet with them, he recalled. "They made the right noises," he said of the rebels, "but always with conditions. . . . I expected more extortion." A rescue operation sooner rather than later was the wise course, he believed. "We had to find a way, and fast," he said.[25]

Early in March, Naim had cabled Lubrani from Addis Ababa, urging him to ask the Israel Defense Forces to plan ahead for an evacuation. Lubrani did, and Lieutenant General Dan Shomron, the Israeli chief of the general staff, sent a team led by Meir Dagan to Ethiopia to explore the options. On March 20, Dagan's group proposed several possible courses of action, including one radical option: for the Israeli military to seize the airport at Addis, then conduct an airlift. "Madness!" Lubrani responded when he heard about Dagan's plan. "Dagan examined an option with force! I couldn't imagine this," Lubrani said. "I knew this was impossible. This made it hard for me to do diplomacy."[26]

The Ethiopian government had to consent to an air rescue, Lubrani knew, and for that to happen, American pressure would be the key.[27] While he was in the States, he and Schneider kicked around ideas about ways to get this to happen and decided to push for a special presidential envoy to Mengistu. Every effort they made failed.

First they met in Palm Beach, Florida, with the industrialist Max Fisher, known as "Mr. Jewish Republican," who had advised Nixon, Reagan, and Bush on Jewish affairs. Lubrani and Schneider asked him to request that the administration appoint a special representative to go to Addis. "Fisher wasn't excited," though, Lubrani recalled later. "He was an old man. I saw he couldn't do it." Fisher spoke with Deputy Secretary of State Lawrence Eagleburger, but nothing came of it.

Lubrani, Schneider, and Eliezri then asked Congressman Stephen Solarz to be the envoy. Solarz had projected a powerful image on CNN during the Gulf War, and Schneider felt that he was the best man for the job. But Solarz warned that, as a Democrat, he might not be acceptable, and in the end Scowcroft rejected him.

"I didn't give up on this," Lubrani said later. He was getting phone calls from Israel at four o'clock every morning, updating him on the situation in Lebanon, and he was tired. But he persisted. He met next with Herman Cohen at the State Department, who also turned him down.[28] Cohen wanted the aliyah to go forward, but not in haste, and not in isolation. It had to be addressed in the larger context of bringing peace to Ethiopia. That was one reason that Cohen had canceled the second tripartite meeting, which had been set for February in Addis. "We felt that the Falasha issue had to be on hold until the overall political situation sorted itself out. It had to come to a climax. The Falashas had to wait," he said later.[29] Unlike Lubrani, Cohen and his colleagues at State believed that the Beta Israel were in no imminent danger in Addis Ababa. Still, Cohen was concerned about the chaos that might result if a general battle for the city should occur. It would be best to negotiate peace in order to avoid such a battle, he thought. That way, they could get the Jews out more easily. Cohen was planning to return to Ethiopia soon and felt that he could do the negotiating himself, so he did not support appointing a presidential emissary to press for a quick exodus immediately.[30]

Cohen did instruct Houdek at the end of March, however, to make a strong démarche in Addis to reinforce America's insistence on the expedited emigration of the Jews. "Go in to the president and beat up on Mengistu," Houdek recalled being told. He carried out his instructions, but privately he wondered why the dictator would worry about fifteen thousand people at a time when his country was falling apart. In Houdek's estimation, sending a presidential emissary and simply having him say, "Let my people go" would not work. Instead, the United States needed a plan, and it needed carrots. To create an incentive, Houdek proposed that the State Department make a strong pitch for a conference in London to negotiate a solution to the war and allow Mengistu to exit safely. He suggested conditioning the proposed peace conference on "parallel momentum" in the emigration.[31] That would establish linkage without using the word.

Lubrani, by contrast, wanted a presidential envoy immediately, to push the Ethiopians to agree to an airlift before Mengistu's regime collapsed. "Time is of the essence," he told Schneider and others. "Someone in the name of the Chief has to go, to say that the president wants a one-shot deal."[32]

The opposition was formidable, though. At the National Security Council, Scowcroft had his own reasons for opposing such an appointment: it would make the rebels think that the United States was propping up Mengistu, and the dictator would boast that he had American support.[33] Frasure, who worked for Scowcroft on the NSC, put it colorfully, as usual: "Scowcroft hates these guys," Frasure told Lubrani. "He will want to insist that no goodies be promised by the U.S. government, political or otherwise. The White House said, 'Nobody pulls Mengistu's chestnuts out of the fire. He gets nothing.'"[34]

## THE ANTE

As March 1991 ended, Lubrani's hopes for a one-off air operation were still frustrated, but he already had begun negotiating the terms under which it would take place. Kassa had refused to discuss an airlift when Lubrani had brought it up in February. But in March, Kassa began to agree in vague terms in what became a series of conversations between them over a direct phone line.[35] These talks achieved a focus quickly: the price. It was clear that the terms of this emigration would be based on the "Ceausescu model," in which Israel paid a large sum for each Jew who was permitted to leave Romania, supposedly to cover expenses. Now the game would be to determine how high the cost would be. As early as March 13, Lubrani notified the American Jewish leaders that the ante was up to $20 million. Perhaps not by coincidence, this was the same day that Kassa agreed to restart the emigration. He must have seen Mengistu's demise coming, and he bet his family's future on Israel: on that same day he filed an application for an Israeli visa for his younger daughter, whose sister was already a student at Hebrew University. The next day, Naim received a visa application for Kassa's wife as well.[36] The collapsing military situation and the American pressure had had a profound effect. An airlift and the hard cash that it would bring in were beginning to appeal to the Ethiopians. Kassa was ready to talk about it.[37] On March 14, Marty Kraar, the executive vice president of the Council of Jewish Federations (CJF), told the JDC that $20 million was an amount that the American Jewish community could raise.[38] It was early in the game, though, and the stakes could go higher.

Lubrani and the American Jews knew that the price would be steep. "The Ethiopians wanted to spread it out. This was the goose that lay golden eggs," Lubrani recalled, using a phrase that was becoming popular among the Israelis who dealt with Ethiopia.[39] But he was determined to get a one-shot mission, and he was thinking in terms of poker, not golden eggs in fairy tales. Lubrani now brought the IDF into the picture. Up to this point, groups of Beta Israel were being flown out of Addis on Ethiopian Airlines planes, usually bound for Rome or Athens, and from there were taken to Israel. Lubrani had in mind something very different: a mass exodus carried out by the IDF. Reuven Merhav had selected him in part because of his clout in the Ministry of Defense. Lubrani now demonstrated it, walking into the office of Dan Shomron, the chief of the General Staff. "I told him there will be a *mivtsah* [operation]," Lubrani recalled matter-of-factly. Shomron, who had led the raid on Entebbe in 1976, ordered his staff to begin planning for this rescue.[40]

## NUMBERS

Even though the planning of the operation had begun, the Israelis did not know how many Falashas they were trying to rescue. Despite the JDC's computerized "bible" of names, the Jewish Agency's scrutiny in distributing stipends only to Jews, and the JDC health care workers' visits to the Jewish families in Addis, no one could agree on how many Jews actually were there.

Merhav had been told in 1989 that there were 7,000 to 9,000 Falashas left in Ethiopia. The mass migration into Addis in 1990 had changed that estimate quickly.[41] In early January 1991, JDC documents reported that there were some 23,000 Jews in the capital, of whom the health-care visitors were seeing 22,000. Yet Micha Feldman counted only 17,000.[42] Eli Eliezri, in an intelligence report to the Joint, noted on January 16 that between 21,500 and 23,000 Jews must be in the capital city, but Feldman continued to count 17,000, attributing the larger numbers to duplication.[43] Discrepancies persisted until the day of the operation. In the end, Feldman's conservative numbers would prove to be closest to the truth.[44]

Still, Lubrani needed something to cite as the basis for negotiating payment, and he was not going to be daunted by conflicts in the tallies. "I used the figure eighteen thousand," he recalled.[45] It seemed as good a number as any.

# EIGHT

# Taking the Chips Away—
# The Cordon Sanitaire—
# Rudy Boschwitz

**APRIL 1–18, 1991**

April 1991 opened in expectation and impasse, with military indecision in Ethiopia and diplomatic deadlock. The rebels slowed their advance toward Addis; in the United States, efforts to have Bush appoint an envoy to Mengistu stalled. What was needed was an integrated plan to ease Mengistu out of office, evacuate the Jews from Addis Ababa, and bring peace to Ethiopia.

## THE MAYOR OF ADDIS ABABA

Rather than closing on Addis Ababa quickly, the EPRDF chose in April to tighten the noose around the capital. That gave them time to identify their partners in a transitional government. More importantly, the insurgents hoped to avoid a battle for the city in which civilians might be caught in the crossfire. Mengistu had vowed to fight, and some observers feared that he might employ a scorched-earth policy, damaging the capital as he had done to Massawa after it fell. Even if the dictator fled, the Amharic residents of Addis Ababa might defend the capital themselves against the ethnic Tigrean rebels. Many of these civilians were armed, having bought Russian-made AK-47 Kalashnikov assault rifles from soldiers fleeing the army. The EPRDF strategy therefore was to strangle the city, moving in on it gradually, in the hope that the government would collapse in the interim.[1]

Bob Frasure continued to estimate that it was only a matter of weeks, at most months, until Mengistu fell.[2] And yet the dictator hung on. "He's like a cancer patient," one diplomat said at the time. "He'll get a little worse, then a little better, but no one expects him to ever get well."[3] The Ethiopian president's forces had lost so much land that a joke now went around the capital that his title had been changed to mayor of Addis Ababa. Still, the regime harbored hopes of putting up resistance, and resorted to the desperate measure of drafting the children of the elite: during the first weeks of April, the government closed the university in Addis and conscripted seven busloads of students into the army, then closed the high schools and drafted children as young as fourteen.[4]

On the diplomatic front, matters were stalled as well. The American effort to remove Mengistu was not progressing. President Robert Mugabe of Zimbabwe had offered the dictator asylum, an escape route for which Mengistu had paved the way. The Ethiopian president had appointed his uncle as Ethiopia's ambassador to Zimbabwe, and had acquired a farm in a town outside of Harare. His wife went to live in Zimbabwe in late March, according to members of Zimbabwe's Ethiopian community, and was trying to enroll their two sons in an exclusive school there.[5] But Zimbabwe's parliament criticized Mugabe for making this gesture without consulting them, and the plan did not go ahead.[6]

## FRASURE BROKE THE IMPASSE

Within the administration, only Bob Frasure was openly saying that the Jewish community could be in immediate danger if they remained in Addis. Frasure covertly had played a crucial role in major events that had led up to this point, and now it was he who secretly broke the impasse.

Frasure had realized back in February that the military situation had shifted irrevocably. "I saw that . . . Mengistu's nine lives had run out," he said in an interview. The giveaway was that the Tigrean rebels previously had been fighting and winning in their own regions, but by February they were moving easily through Amharic territory.[7] This told him that Mengistu had no support anymore. Till then, the NSC "had been standoffish on Ethiopia," Frasure recalled, and "we wanted State out of it too." By March, however, the situation in Ethiopia had deteriorated to the point that Frasure felt that the United States would have to get involved, to prevent chaos during a rebel takeover of the capital. But how could he persuade Scowcroft? Frasure was aware that his boss was not inclined to ask a favor of someone like Mengistu. He also knew that Scowcroft never wanted to make a move without knowing what his next step would be. Frasure concluded that he would have to propose an integrated game plan. And so in the first week of April he wrote a situation paper for Scowcroft recommending that the United States coordinate all of its goals in Ethiopia. Frasure's plan was that in return for Mengistu's stepping down and allowing the Jews to leave en masse, the Americans would guarantee him a personal soft landing.[8] As far as Frasure was concerned, that could include a financial incentive. "A couple of million dollars is a lot of money to these guys," he told the American Jewish leaders.[9] The United States then would sponsor talks leading to a transitional government. "I saw Scowcroft," Frasure said in the interview. "He was skeptical, as usual. We spent a couple of hours, and he was taken by the idea."[10]

A key factor motivating Scowcroft, Frasure recalled, was the recent Iraqi slaughter of Kurds who, with American encouragement, had risen against

Saddam Hussein after the Gulf War. The United States had not helped them, and they had been crushed. "We were awash in TV pictures of the Kurdish," Frasure said. "We were held responsible." The United States did not want to be similarly powerless to act if there were chaos in Addis, he noted.[11] Another event influencing the Americans was the disaster that had occurred in January in Mogadishu, the capital of Somalia, Ethiopia's neighbor to the east. There had been a civil war there too, and, in the end, Mogadishu had descended into violence. The Americans had stood by and watched it happen. Something like that could not be allowed to occur in Addis Ababa. Ethiopia was much more important and more fragile, and thousands of potential Jewish victims were sitting in the capital. Scowcroft had other political concerns too, Frasure recalled: "He wanted to deal with domestic Jewish pressure, and to help Israel."[12] Scowcroft himself later confirmed that it was the humanitarian aspect of Frasure's scheme that persuaded him to accept it.[13]

"Scowcroft asked me to talk to State," Frasure said. The State Department was wary of this kind of "adventurous engagement. State said, 'You're trying to overturn a government!'" They accused the NSC of saying to the Ethiopians, "You can jump off a bridge, or we'll push you."[14] Herman Cohen still opposed sending a presidential envoy to Mengistu. He intended to go himself on April 24 and planned to try to persuade Mengistu then to accept a democratic solution. At the same time, he would deal with the issue of the Ethiopian Jews.[15] But the White House rejected Cohen's proposal. With that, Frasure's plan became the centerpiece of the American initiative, and the exodus of the Jews was a crucial element in it. "The White House said the mission will be Falasha-centered, a high-level appeal based on the Falashas, with peace thrown in," a State Department official later recalled unhappily.

Whether or not that was Frasure's view of the mission, it was not far from what Lubrani and the American Jewish leaders hoped for. For them, a crucial aspect of Frasure's plan was that it conditioned a peace conference on the release of the Jews, just as Houdek had suggested in his proposal for "parallel momentum." Schneider later suggested, in fact, that the idea of this "linkage" between the two goals had originated with them. "We shared the linkage idea with Will [Recant], who took it to Frasure," he recalled.[16] Nate Shapiro conceded that many people, particularly in the State Department, felt that it was inappropriate to tie peace talks to the Jewish emigration. There was "tremendous soul-searching within the administration" about this, he said. If the Ethiopians did not let the Jews go, and if consequently there was no chance to negotiate peace, "thousands could be slaughtered," Shapiro acknowledged. But he and Schneider argued at the time that a peace conference had to be linked to the aliyah. The Jews were Mengistu's bargaining chips for holding on to power. "He would never agree to a transition if the Jews were still there, hostage to chaos. . . . We had to take the chips away,"

Shapiro said later.[17] Frasure endorsed the idea of linkage, and Cohen ultimately did as well.[18] Scowcroft said later, however, that there was never any operational connection between the emigration and peace talks; in the end, the NSC would use the linkage only as a bluff to get Mengistu to let the Ethiopian Jews go.[19] At this moment, though, the American Jewish leaders believed that the policy was firm and were counting on it.

Frasure now also supported Bush's appointing a presidential as envoy to Mengistu—exactly what Lubrani had been working toward. Frasure reasoned that an emissary would be able to coordinate the multipronged strategy he had proposed. He went further and let Lubrani in on the potential policy change that he had set in motion with Scowcroft. Would Jewish pressure on the White House help? Lubrani asked him in one of their daily telephone conversations. Yes, Frasure answered in his disarmingly straightforward way. So Lubrani told the American Jewish leaders, "I have reason to believe that pressure will bring results. This is not a Mission Impossible."[20] On Monday, April 8, a "summit conference" of American Jewish leaders therefore delegated Hoenlein to ask former Senator Rudy Boschwitz to press the case for appointing a presidential envoy. In addition, Hoenlein would meet with Scowcroft personally and raise the issue with him. "Scowcroft is the key obstacle," noted a memo of a meeting of the "kitchen cabinet" of key Jewish American leaders. "Malcolm's meeting with him is a key meeting."[21] "This is decision-making time," Schneider wrote in a private memo that Wednesday. "The time to move is NOW." The Jewish leaders would have to keep hammering the Doomsday Scenario, he wrote. "By [the] end of the week some decisions will be reached."[22]

## "OK. AND YOU OUGHT TO GO"

It was the Doomsday Scenario that persuaded Boschwitz of the need for an envoy. "I got a call from Malcolm Hoenlein," he recorded later in a handwritten memoir. Hoenlein told him that "the Falasha community was in danger of destruction because the rebels were approaching the gates of Addis." He stressed to Boschwitz two points that Lubrani emphasized in the Doomsday vision: that changes in African governments are often violent, and that the Jews in Addis Ababa were vulnerable. The Israelis were prepared to do an airlift, and the State Department and Frasure were favorable, Hoenlein said. But, evidently not knowing of Scowcroft's recent change of position, he told Boschwitz that the national security adviser was resisting. "Malcolm said that we need to get to the president and ask him to send a special envoy to Ethiopia to spring them," Boschwitz wrote in his memoir, "and that others were unable to reach the president. So I did, made the case to him." Boschwitz repeated the Doomsday Scenario to Bush, who called him back a few hours later and said, "OK. And you ought to go."[23]

Frasure planned to accompany Boschwitz on the mission and to meet with the Ethiopian rebels in Khartoum during the return flight. He had granted Lubrani's wish. Lubrani would brief Boschwitz on the best way to close the deal for a mass exodus, but after that he could do little more than watch from the sidelines. As things turned out, though, Boschwitz did not like Lubrani and did not trust his judgment.

## THE PRICE: $35 MILLION

Even before Bush had decided to appoint Boschwitz, Lubrani and Cohen began to shape the outline of a deal. In a meeting on April 10, they discussed an ingenious plan that Bob Houdek had conceived for tying an air rescue to a payment to the Ethiopians. First, the United States would pay for chartered planes to airlift the Ethiopian Jews to Israel. "My superiors would approve such a scheme," Cohen told Lubrani. Then, in a separate transaction, the Israelis would give the Ethiopian authorities a large sum of money, representing the profit that Ethiopian Airlines would have made if it had continued to fly the Beta Israel to Europe.[24] These flights were a major source of hard currency for Ethiopia, and there was some logic in offering to compensate the government for the lost airfares. Proposing a generous dollar amount for airfare per head, Houdek had calculated that this would result in a total payment of about $35 million. Shortly after Lubrani's conversation with Cohen, Congress approved a classified amendment, introduced by Senator Daniel Inouye of Hawaii, to sequester $15 million for the Defense Department to pay for the airlift itself.[25] The $35 million "compensation" to the Ethiopian government would have to come from private American Jewish sources.[26] On April 11, Marty Kraar confirmed that the American Jewish community "will have to procure whatever it takes." "I promised Uri Lubrani, 'When the time comes, you won't be left holding the bag,'" Kraar said later. "I wasn't sure I could keep the promise. I kept telling him, 'Don't worry about the money.'"[27]

Despite its ongoing opposition to Israel's sending weapons to Mengistu, Washington thus was willing to allow a substantial infusion of cash into his treasury, funds that conceivably could go toward arms purchases. In Cohen's estimation, though, the Mengistu regime essentially was crumbling. Even if they did turn the money to that purpose, it would have little effect by that point.[28]

## "KASSA WILL NOT BE
## ABLE TO TURN THE KEY"

Cohen told Lubrani that when he went to Ethiopia in two weeks, he would meet with Kassa to raise the question of this compensation. It never happened. First, the White House did not permit Cohen to make the trip, as noted above. In addition, and surprisingly, it was becoming unclear whether Kassa was still the man to talk to. For more than a year, he had been the only one with whom to negotiate on the Ethiopian Jewish question, everybody's contact. But now, as the end approached and a lot of money was about to change hands, several informed observers believed that Kassa had lost his influence. "Kassa will not be able to turn the key," Bob Frasure told the American Jewish leaders on April 8.[29] Bob Houdek at the U.S. embassy in Addis observed that Kassa was listless and discouraged. "The game is flowing away from Kassa," he said. "He is less relevant than he was six months or even six weeks ago."[30] Naim also reported that Kassa was out, and the Italian ambassador in Addis told the JDC's Manlio Dell'Ariccia that Kassa was seen as being too connected to Israel and the American Jewish lobby.[31] These observations may have been astute. Kassa feared for his life and was planning to leave Ethiopia at this time.[32]

Despite these doubts about his efficacy, there was no harm in "feather-bedding Kassa's landing," Frasure said at the time. The American view was that Kassa had not been involved in bloodletting, so it would be okay to secure his future.[33] The AAEJ, which had a special relationship with Kassa, took the lead. Three years earlier, Gil Kulick had brought him to Nate Shapiro's attention. Then, after Kassa's visit to the States in spring 1990, they had promised to assist him when the time came. In return, they expected Kassa to be helpful in the emigration of the Jews.

Kulik now wrote a personal letter to Kassa, offering him the help that the AAEJ had promised. Shapiro also wrote to Kassa, then spoke with him by phone.[34] He told Schneider, Lubrani, and Eli Eliezri that, in this conversation, Kassa "reminded me of my promise" to help him. Shapiro's goal, as always, was the early exit of the Jews, and Kassa was "definitely thinking on our lines," he said.[35]

Surprisingly, the AAEJ leaders were not the only ones looking out for Kassa's welfare. Lubrani revealed later that he too had agreed to protect Kassa, but only "if he behaved." "Kassa knew that his situation might become dicey," Lubrani told me. "I made him a promise that I would take him with me. He knew, if he behaved, I would take care of him physically. I did this early on." If Kassa's life might depend on the Israelis, surely he knew that he would have to accept the Israeli terms in the end. Did this mean that the entire negotiation had been a charade? "Not necessarily," Lubrani said. "He had to reflect the wishes of his boss. He knew Mengistu could wake up one morning and get him beheaded."[36]

So Kassa was treading a delicate line, and by early April he had security on his mind. He requested a visa to Israel for six generals. At about the same time Mersha, the Ethiopian official who approved or rejected the exit forms, asked for visas for his wife and two children.[37] "He said that his wife's grand-mother kept Jewish customs, and was Jewish," Naim recalled. "This was a very broad hint. . . . We had agreed to take his wife and kids. It was obvious where this leads": with his family in Israel, the principle of family reunification ensured that Mersha would be entitled to live there as well.[38]

Despite the uncertainty of the situation, Lubrani and the American Jewish leaders decided to treat Kassa as if he were still influential. In fact, Lubrani declared that he was now trying to "turn" Kassa, to bring him wholly over to their side. Shapiro, whose letter to Kassa was being hand-delivered by a colleague named Peter Jackson, now said that he would help Kassa even if he did not cooperate; he was not willing to sacrifice him.[39]

## A PASSOVER WITHOUT MATZO

Innocent of these negotiations in their behalf that April, the Beta Israel in Addis observed Passover, the first that most of them had spent away from their villages. In order to display the symbols and rites of the Passover ceremony familiar to Western Jews, NACOEJ's Joe Feit organized a huge seder on the grounds of the Israeli embassy. He met with the *qessotch* beforehand to explain the nature of the service and was surprised when they readily agreed to conduct the ceremony in the Western manner. "Why are you agreeing with everything I say?" Feit asked them.

"You told us that this is how they do it in Israel," a *qes* replied. "From Zion comes the Torah and the word of God from Jerusalem," the *qes* said simply, quoting Isaiah 2:3.[40] At the same time, though, the *qessotch* wanted to instruct the Beta Israel in how to observe their own Passover traditions in a setting far from their homes.

And so a very curious service began with Hebrew and Aramaic readings and songs, and ended with a half hour during which the *qessotch* sang in Ge'ez, the holy language of Ethiopian Jews (as well as Christians). There was no matzo—or any other food—because, given the danger in the city at night, the ceremony was held on the afternoon before Passover arrived. As the *qessotch* explained, that is a limbo period in which neither food contaminated by leavened bread nor matzo can be eaten. That was just as well, since twenty-two thousand pounds of matzo that had been ordered had not yet been delivered.

In the Gondar region, according to the *qessotch*, the Jews ate only in their own houses and so could maintain the ritual cleanliness of the holiday. In the slums of Addis, the religious leaders wanted to ensure that at least minimal standards were met. First, out of respect for the Beta Israel emphasis on extreme purity, food was not to be prepared by any woman who was menstruating. In addition, one *qes* warned, in putting together the family seder meals, they should be sure that the sheep did not have the "tail of a dog." That was a new concept to the Western Jews, and, as it turned out, one of the eleven sheep that NACOEJ delivered did have a long furry tail like a dog's. It was sold to a non-Jew.[41]

## PETER JACKSON

On the weekend of April 13, as plans for the Boschwitz appointment were taking shape in Washington, Peter Jackson flew into Addis Ababa to deliver Nate Shapiro's letter offering to help Kassa. Then sixty-one years old and a member of the AAEJ board, Jackson also was charged with negotiating a cash inducement to the Ethiopian government, which the American Jewish leaders called the "cordon sanitaire."[42]

In their first meeting, over lunch the day after Jackson arrived, Kassa told him that he felt betrayed by Israel. Kassa complained that he had been the champion of friendship with the Jewish state and had been hurt because of it.[43] Ethiopia's military and economic hopes and expectations had been dashed, Kassa said. Israel was embarrassing him, and so he would concentrate on developing relations with the United States, rather than Israel. (Despite its impoverished economy, Ethiopia had been paying a Washington lobbyist $25,000 a month since August to nurture those relations.)[44] But no matter how the connection with America might develop, Kassa noted, Mengistu would not flee. "All other leaders are useless," Kassa told Jackson; he saw no alternative to Mengistu. Besides, Mengistu would not feel safe in Zimbabwe or any other place outside of Ethiopia. He therefore had no incentive to move on.[45]

In this first meeting, Jackson offered a $17 million cash payment and presented Kassa with a rationale for it. "I said that we have the financial resources to support our people over the next eighteen months, but it would be better all around if you allow the Jews to go more quickly. The money we save could go to the Ethiopian government."[46] However sensible this may have seemed on its face, it undermined the plan that Lubrani had developed with Cohen. Their approach would reimburse the Ethiopian government the money lost in airfares on Ethiopian Airlines. Jackson, by contrast, offered a payment amounting to the cost of maintaining the entire Jewish community in Addis for at least eighteen months. There could be creative ways of calculating a fare per ticket, and it would be on those numbers that the negotiations could turn. The results from Jackson's proposed scheme could be very different, however. Besides, there was no reason now for Kassa not to demand both.

Shapiro had given Jackson a list of code names he was supposed to use to report on his negotiations. Kassa was "the Broker," Mengistu was "Coca-

Cola," and so on, Jackson recalled in an interview. "It was a waste of time," he said. Not only was Kassa listening in on Jackson's conversations, he actually complained to him that the code names were not clever enough. Certainly the Americans could do better than "Casablanca" as a code for the Arabs, Kassa said. "They must think I'm stupid if I don't understand this," he told Jackson.[47]

## BRIEFING BOSCHWITZ

The appointment of Boschwitz was a personal diplomatic victory for the Jewish American leaders. Now they considered it essential that he share their determination to arrange an early mass exodus of the Ethiopian Jews. So on Thursday, April 18, Schneider briefed him in a telephone conference call that included Hoenlein and Taylor.

Schneider first of all established Lubrani's credentials, and Boschwitz agreed to speak with the Israeli personally. Schneider then reviewed the Ethiopians' long-standing request for weapons and matériel, and Israel's refusal to comply. He referred Boschwitz to Shapiro, who would explain the cash payment that the American Jews were preparing to offer. Schneider knew that the Jewish question was not the only item on Frasure's agenda; he was going to discuss a peaceful transition to a new government as well. But Schneider hoped that Boschwitz "could help develop the talks so that Falasha exits become the sine qua non."[48]

"Boschwitz had been the first senator to take an interest in the Falashas," Schneider observed later. "He was a Holocaust refugee. It was not hard to convince him."[49] The former senator accepted the idea of linkage between the aliyah and a peace conference, according to Shapiro.[50] As for the crucial demand for a one-shot airlift, the American Jews and Lubrani "stressed this point very, very hard," Schneider recalled.[51] But the Ethiopians would prove to be elusive on that issue.

# NINE

# The Boschwitz Mission—Setting the Price

## APRIL 24–29, 1991

As American Jewish leaders conceived of it, the presidential envoy's role was solely to persuade Mengistu to release the Beta Israel. The Boschwitz mission, however, also offered the possibility of a negotiated end to the Ethiopian civil war. It remained to be seen whether Mengistu would accept a linkage between these goals, and whether he would bargain in good faith.

### "AN EXTREME NEED FELT BY THE ETHIOPIANS FOR INTERVENTION"

Boschwitz was scheduled to arrive in Addis on Friday, April 26, 1991. "The timing of the mission is excellent," Lubrani told Schneider by phone on Wednesday, the twenty-fourth. "There is an extreme need felt by the Ethiopians for intervention."

"In the town, everyone speaks of the delegation," a JDC-Rome official reported on the same day. "Everyone hopes there will be peace talks . . . to convince Mengistu to do the same as with Marcos," the dictator who had stepped down from power in the Philippines without bloodshed.[1]

There was a special urgency in Addis because the Tigrean rebels took the town of Ambo, some sixty-five miles west of the capital, on the twenty-fourth. This was a crucial victory. The circumstances of Ambo's fall disturbed Mengistu's supporters: the town reportedly fell through collusion among the army generals and politicians, and five hundred army special forces defected to the rebels.[2] So in the days before Boschwitz arrived, Addis Ababa awaited disaster. Naim noted at the time that between eleven and fifteen Libyan tanks had been sighted among rebel forces in Bahr-Dar. Farther north, in the port of Assab, merchants had been told to get all goods out of the city in anticipation of an EPLF assault. Meanwhile, in the capital, Mengistu's relationship with formerly close associates became tense, and the dictator was drinking heavily.[3]

Not everyone in Addis Ababa welcomed Boschwitz's visit; Kassa was less than euphoric about it. He put off his own plans to leave Ethiopia because of the mission, but he did not have high expectations for it.[4] Boschwitz had met with Kassa briefly in Washington the previous May and had helped arrange for him to meet Deputy Secretary of State Eagleburger. Now, however, Kassa would have preferred to have Frasure come alone. He had learned, somehow, of Boschwitz's meeting with Lubrani and had concluded that the Jews were the former senator's principal issue. The Falasha emigration was in fact at the top of the American agenda, but the Boschwitz mission's wider goal was to integrate it into a plan for peace and democracy.[5] Kassa said at the time, however, that Boschwitz's focus on the Falashas devalued his standing even before he arrived. The Ethiopian now bitterly declared that he expected nothing from Israel.[6]

## FLYING TO ADDIS

As he prepared to leave for Addis, Boschwitz wondered how much he could expect from Mengistu, and whether his efforts would be wasted. "Frasure told me that Mengistu and the Ethiopians were always a day late and a dollar short," he said later. That was ominous. If Frasure was right, Boschwitz could not know if the Ethiopian president would act in time to save the Jews or himself. Boschwitz's concern for the Falashas was deep and long-standing. He had been involved with them even before he was elected senator in 1978. His own experience as a Holocaust refugee whose father took him out of Berlin in 1938 had inspired his sympathy toward them. "One of the things that always motivated me was that nobody helped the Jews while they were being led to the slaughter" in Europe, he said. As he flew out of Dulles Airport outside Washington on Thursday night, April 25, he believed that his mission was to help save the Beta Israel from their own holocaust—the Doomsday massacre that Hoenlein had foretold. "The intelligence was that the army was arming the *kebeles*," he recalled. "There was fear of all hell breaking loose."[7]

Boschwitz was traveling with Frasure, whom he had just met and whom he admired at once. With them was Irvin Hicks, the State Department expert on northern Africa who had traveled to Addis the month before to protest the slowdown in the aliyah. John Hall, the Ethiopia desk officer at State, also was in the party. The former senator was impressed by Hicks and Hall too.

But Boschwitz met one person earlier that day whom he did not admire: Uri Lubrani. The Israeli had briefed him before his flight and had urged him to get tough with the Ethiopians, as, Lubrani said, he himself had done. Boschwitz did not take this well. He was no fan of Israeli foreign policy in Ethiopia. "The Israelis . . . overplayed their cards here, as they have done elsewhere in Africa," he recorded in his memoir later. "They have promised fast and loose up and down the continent" to provide arms, but in Ethiopia, "we wouldn't let them." And Israel had been "sloppy and high-handed" in filling out the emigration forms, he wrote. Boschwitz was unimpressed by Lubrani in particular. He judged the Israeli to be a paper tiger, "the last of the one-upmen," a very shrewd man who nonetheless had misjudged his adversaries. Lubrani "suggested I be very aggressive and confrontational," Boschwitz wrote. "He said he stormed out on Kas[s]a, had 27 hours with Mengistu and was tough with him, etc.[8] It wouldn't have worked. . . . If I had followed his advice, we would have blown the whole thing."[9] Boschwitz "disparaged Uri's judgment," Michael Schneider observed later. "The chemistry was not good."[10]

## "IS THIS THE TIME HE INVITES ME TO THE WINE CELLAR?"

On Saturday, April 27, in Addis, the Boschwitz delegation had its first meeting, with Tesfaye Dinka, a moderate acceptable to the West who had been promoted from foreign minister to prime minister in a cabinet reshuffle the day before. The Ethiopians had let the Americans know in advance that they would not be restricted to the Jewish issue. "They wanted a broader agenda," Boschwitz wrote in his memoir. "Mengistu wanted a peace parley convened to save his skin and allegedly to keep Ethiopia unified, and maybe end his regime on a more positive note." Since Boschwitz was focused on the Falashas, he spoke only briefly at this first meeting, noting that free emigration is fundamental in the American psyche. Frasure, by contrast, made quite a few points about the Jews. He then listed the American preconditions for a peace conference: a standstill cease-fire, permission for relief supplies to continue to enter through Massawa, enfranchisement of all political groups, and free elections with international monitoring within one year. Tesfaye was cooperative, though he noted that the very idea of emigration was hard for Ethiopians. He agreed that the government would enhance the flow of Falashas to Israel, however, as long as the United States did not insist on specific numbers that others could use later to accuse them of not living up to their word.[11] At this meeting, the Americans raised a potentially explosive topic: an orderly transfer of power. "They agreed to this!" Boschwitz recalled in an interview. "We were surprised. This implied a change of government."[12]

The next meeting was with the internal affairs minister, Tesfaye Wolde Selassie. A straightforward man who was in charge of the state security apparatus, he was said to keep intelligence files on his colleagues and opponents. It was he, along with East German advisers, who had suppressed the coup attempt against Mengistu in May 1989. His deputy, Mersha, joined him for this discussion, which dealt chiefly with the aliyah. "I and the others— at my lead—took a really tough, demanding line that we get the Falashas out and don't make all these excuses about paperwork, etc.," Boschwitz wrote in his memoir. "We really drummed them. . . . They said that 9,000 (we thought 6,000) [exit] applications were cleared, and we hammered them. The U.S.

government would do nothing unless they allowed all Falashas to emigrate. We set the tone and bore in, and this meeting was all Falashas.

"Then on to Mengistu," Boschwitz wrote. "Up to this point," he observed, Mengistu "is known principally as a butcher—many thousands have died; hundreds of thousands have died in the civil war in recent years.... Mengistu slaughtered all who opposed him. He participated in many executions and performed some of them in the cellar." Prior to the meeting, the Americans had joked about not accepting his invitation to go to the wine cellar with him. Then, "when I particularly bore in on the Falashas during our meeting and drove the points home directly and frequently, I passed a note to Bob Frasure, who sat next to me, asking, 'Is this the time he invites me to the wine cellar?'"[13]

The meetings with Mengistu "were interminable," Boschwitz said, "as if he had all the time in the world. It was bizarre." Boschwitz handed Mengistu a letter from President Bush, who, Boschwitz told the Ethiopian leader, "has been my friend for twenty years." Bush's letter thanked Mengistu for his help on the UN Security Council during the Gulf crisis, offered American assistance in restoring peace, and expressed strong support for Ethiopia's unity and territorial integrity. It also contained a "humanitarian appeal" for the "expedited departure" of the Jews "as soon as possible." What "expedited" meant was left open, though. A little over a thousand Ethiopian Jews left for Israel in April. At that rate, Boschwitz noted, the emigration could take another year and a half. "Expedited," by contrast, could mean a few days, he said later.[14]

"I cannot overemphasize the importance of this issue, to our President, to Congress, to the American people," Boschwitz told Mengistu. "When it comes to emigration, America is an extraordinary place. Every one of us is an immigrant. I myself am Jewish. Most of my family perished. There is an enormous American interest in emigration. We are consumed by it."

"Get it over with!" Boschwitz urged. "Why wait another one and a half years? Do it. Get it over with. Get the credit.... No other single act of your government would have a better effect." Boschwitz appealed to Mengistu's patriotism, to his sense of his place in Ethiopian history. He acknowledged that the Arabs could respond negatively to an airlift, but argued that it would probably be worse if Ethiopia dragged it out. Despite the formal denials of a political quid pro quo, the former senator backed up his appeal with a very clear message: "It simply will not be possible for the Ethiopian government to have a normal political relationship with the United States while the issue of Ethiopian Jewish emigration remains unresolved."[15]

"Mengistu responded for 1½ hours in a rather warm room at 8200' elevation to several pretty jet-lagged envoys," the American wrote in his memoir.[16] Mengistu questioned whether the Falashas were ethnically different from other Ethiopians, and pointed out that the Ethiopian government was under no obligation to promote their emigration to Israel. He asserted that he nevertheless was "enthusiastic" about it, though, because having them there would create an ethnic link between the two countries, to go with the historical and political links. The Ethiopian government had no problem with the number who left, Mengistu declared, as long as it was done cautiously, within the framework of family reunification.[17] Then "Frasure presented his points about the Roundtable conference"—the term that the Ethiopians used to refer to the potential peace talks. Frasure "strongly emphasized the need for 'parallel action' on the Falashas."[18] "The basic pitch to Mengistu," Frasure recalled in an interview, "was that we would help with an orderly transition if they would let the Falashas go. We would convene a [peace] conference in London."[19]

Whether Frasure realized it or not, merely by presenting the peace plan he was offending Mengistu. Boschwitz had expressed American and Jewish sensibilities eloquently, but, Kassa said later, the Americans were unaware of Ethiopian sensitivities. Frasure was the junior person in Mengistu's eyes, Kassa recalled. Boschwitz was the senior one, and, as presidential emissary, he had the greater authority. Yet "the junior people came about peace, the senior person about the Falashas. . . . Mengistu was mad about this," Kassa said. "This is the Ethiopian mentality."[20]

Frasure had a far ruder shock in store for the Ethiopian ruler, however: he brought up the topic of his resignation! Frasure was fed up with Mengistu's deviousness. "He wanted to buy time, to sucker the Americans," Frasure said in the interview. If a peace conference could drag on for six weeks, the rainy season would begin, and Mengistu could feel safe from rebel attack until the rains had ended. Frasure wanted a much more immediate result and, characteristically, he expressed himself directly: he asked under what circumstances Mengistu was prepared to step down. "Great leaders sometimes make great sacrifices for their countries," he observed. Upon hearing this, "Mengistu was shocked," he said later. "I used the analogy of Lyndon Johnson in '68. I wanted the other Ethiopians to hear that his job is on the table."

In showing Mengistu the door so bluntly, Frasure was working within clear parameters agreed to by Scowcroft. The national security adviser "knew that we had to make it up as we went along," Frasure recalled, but had eliminated any future role for Mengistu.[21] Frasure and Houdek advised the Ethiopian president that stepping down was the only way that he could hope to save his life.[22] If the dictator had agreed to leave immediately, the Americans would have taken him out the next day with the Boschwitz mission on a U.S. government plane.[23] Mengistu was so stunned that he managed to answer only indirectly. "He replied, waltzed around, was evasive," Frasure recalled.

To resign would mean running away from his obligations to his people, Mengistu told him.[24]

Boschwitz spoke, using the word *linkage* "freely and with great emphasis." Then Houdek closed, "again strongly about the Falashas—he's excellent!! He left nothing in doubt," Boschwitz wrote in his memoir.[25] "I said, 'Do it once and for all, put it behind us,'" Houdek recalled later.[26]

"And the first day ended," Boschwitz wrote. "We hammered them, but as yet there was no response." He was optimistic, though, that linking an exodus to the American carrot, the peace conference, would work. "It was apparent," he wrote, "(though not so much on the first day) that they badly wanted this, so badly that we could get them to cash their Falasha chips—whether all or most we'll have to see, but surely there could be a much-enhanced rate of departure."[27]

## "D-DAY IS HERE"

Lubrani and the American Jewish leaders were aiming for much more than an enhanced rate of departure, however. What they had in mind was an evacuation. They were monitoring events literally day and night, and their back-channel information, passed on by Peter Jackson, was that Bob Houdek had told the Ethiopians that merely doubling the rate of exit, to two thousand a month, would be acceptable. In fact, Jackson was wrong. Houdek had said no such thing, but in New York the kitchen cabinet became alarmed when they heard about it. "It has to be driven home aggressively by Boschwitz that D-Day is here and there must be no more nonsense," said Lubrani. Boschwitz's scheduled meeting with Kassa the next morning could be vital, he added. "There must be a final statement that 'This is it!'" Kassa would have to know that this was the final offer. He expected "Byzantine haggling" about the payment but insisted, "Now is the time to put pressure on them!" They decided to press Boschwitz again to demand a single mass rescue. Shapiro would call both Boschwitz and Jackson, and Jackson then would drive home the message to Boschwitz in person. They would have to reach closure on that.[28]

"Following this call," the JDC memo went on, "we received new information, which confirms that Kassa will try to obstruct any agreement reached in principle with the delegation." This was based on a telephone call Kassa had made to Naim on Saturday night, Ethiopia time, in which he had tried yet again to raise the question of errors on the exit forms. Naim cut Kassa short and angrily told him "to stop using pretexts and excuses for disqualification in order to apply a quota system. There should be no bureaucratic excuses to stop emigration. Forms could be corrected; they should not be a bargaining chip." Naim "chided Kassa about the '16,500' Jews languishing in

Addis and said this would harm their absorption process in Israel." Kassa responded, "Who's talking about 16,500? There are only 9,000. What do you want? For them to leave immediately—in one week?" No, in three days, Naim responded. Kassa parried that this had nothing to do with the Boschwitz mission. "With them we only discuss principles. With you we discuss modalities," he told the Israeli. "The practicalities are a bilateral affair between Israel and Ethiopia. If you do not like the modalities, we can change them."[29]

This was exactly what the American Jewish leaders had feared: that the Ethiopians would agree to the airlift in principle but then, after Boschwitz had gone, would sabotage it with "modalities"—a word that the Ethiopians loved, Boschwitz noted later.[30]

Hearing about this conversation late that Saturday afternoon New York time, Shapiro said that it would be good to repeat it to Boschwitz. "It will get him angry," he said.[31] So Naim got a transcript to him, and Lubrani followed up with a letter that reached Boschwitz on Sunday morning. "The meeting with Kassa today is the most critical of the entire trip," Lubrani wrote. "What Kassa relays to [Mengistu] will determine the issue. This is why Kassa must be convinced himself, and therefore convince [Mengistu], that there is no way they can hope for any assistance from the United States without them giving an absolute and irrevocable decision to let the Falashas go in one integrated operation. This can only be done by brinksmanship, which has worked in the past with Kassa. If this can be put clearly and, if necessary, brutally, to the other side, and not let go, there is chance of success."[32]

## "THE OPTIMUM POSSIBLE MATERIAL RETURN"

That Sunday morning in Addis Ababa, Micha Feldman and Asher Naim took Boschwitz to see some of the worst housing areas in which the Jews were living. The small Falasha compound they visited "wasn't really a compound, but hovels" that the people shared with animals, Boschwitz wrote later. "In the first room were three cows in filth, flies all around; in the eyes, on the lips of the people (they didn't even brush them away). . . . They really live like animals."[33] "I hope that the next time we meet will be in Jerusalem," he told one of the children. "I will do my best to get them out of this pigsty," he promised.[34] "Boschwitz got very emotional about it," Lubrani (who was following events from abroad) reported to Schneider, Shapiro, and Taylor in New York.[35]

"From there to Kassa Kebede," Boschwitz wrote in his memoir. This, Lubrani had told him, would be the make-or-break meeting for the mission. It was not. Boschwitz ignored Lubrani's exhortation to be tough, even brutal. And Kassa, far from engaging in Byzantine haggling, did not bargain at all. Rather, he "gave us a lecture," Boschwitz wrote: "two hours [about] the history of Christianity in Ethiopia . . . the history of Ethiopia in Jerusalem, the 150 year lawsuit [over the Deir al-Sultan monastery in Jerusalem], the Israelis and how they misbehaved (mostly because they wouldn't trade guns for Falashas)."[36] As far as Boschwitz was concerned, this meeting proved that Kassa was no longer the man to deal with. Tesfaye Dinka and Tesfaye Wolde Selassie had taken charge of the Jewish question, he concluded. Any deal would have to be cut with them.

Kassa later conceded in an interview that he had had the job of getting "the optimum possible material return" in these negotiations. But, he said, that this was against his wishes. And, as always, he argued that it was never a question of Falashas for arms, or Falashas for anything. There were Israeli promises, there were Ethiopian promises, he said, but there was no linkage between them. Rather, as Kassa recalled it, if the Ethiopians accommodated the Israelis on religious grounds, they should reciprocate in kind: they should guarantee Ethiopian authority over the monastery of Deir al-Sultan, which comprises a group of huts on top of the Church of the Holy Sepulcher in Jerusalem. The Ethiopians and the Egyptian Coptic Church had argued over the control of this monastery since 1838, and Kassa wanted Israel to resolve the dispute in Ethiopia's favor once and for all. It was not his idea to ask for money in exchange for the expedited aliyah, Kassa stated in the interview. "I told my colleagues we wouldn't make money out of the Falasha issue," he recalled. But, he said, Tesfaye Wolde Selassie, the internal affairs minister, asked, "If Sudan can make a lot from Operation Moses, why can't Ethiopia?" "This was easy to say," Kassa commented. "The idea of a religious return was overtaken by a material return," Kassa said.[37]

## "DON'T WORRY. WE HAVE FIXED THE PRESIDENT"

The final meeting of the trip was with Mengistu again, and during that discussion, Boschwitz thought that his mission may have succeeded. "All were excited, except for Mengistu—always cool," he wrote in his memoir. "But the two Tesfayes must have gotten to Mengistu."[38]

In fact, Tesfaye Dinka, the new prime minister, claimed that he had, according to Frasure. Tesfaye took Frasure aside, and the two spoke in a parking lot, where Frasure told him, "We are deadly serious. You are in deep shit."

"Don't worry," Tesfaye replied, "we have fixed the president."[39]

At the meeting, Mengistu agreed to "accelerate" the emigration, contingent on three conditions: the operation would have to be totally secret, it would be carried out with Ethiopian and Israeli (not American) planes, and there would be "generous financial assistance" for Ethiopia.[40]

The Americans were not excessively optimistic but were willing to see what came of this. As they went to lunch with Mengistu after the meeting, Boschwitz wrote later, "Bob Frasure whispered in my ear, 'Bingo! Now we'll see if they perform.'"[41] Later, however, Frasure had a more jaundiced take on this conversation with the Ethiopian leader. "Mengistu had to play the game," he said. "Mengistu was all sweetness and light. . . . Some understood that Mengistu promised that the Falashas could leave before [the peace conference in] London, but Mengistu is a pathological liar." Why had Frasure accepted a promise merely for accelerated emigration instead of a one-shot airlift? "It was clear that they wouldn't go for 'one shot,'" he said. "We had to come up with a euphemism: 'accelerated.' That left a lot of room for interpretation. We knew we were playing a game."[42]

After lunch, Boschwitz wrote, the Americans went "back to the [U.S.] Embassy and we debriefed ourselves . . . and were somewhat self-congratulatory—though the proof is in the next steps. The Israelis insist I'm Moses," Boschwitz wrote.[43]

Privately, though, the Israelis were frustrated that the mission had not yielded an instant exodus. "The Ethiopians will now try to play games," Lubrani predicted. The problem, Schneider concluded in New York, was that Mengistu still thought that he could survive politically. The offer of a peaceful transition after the Jews were let go would be effective only if Mengistu thought he was finished, Schneider said.[44]

Boschwitz's intervention, however, had marked a turning point in the aliyah. It had presented a plan that unified the goals of ending the civil war, accelerating the emigration, and offering a financial incentive to the Ethiopians. It had placed the prestige of the American president behind the process. And it had won Mengistu's formal commitment to speed the departures. One immediate consequence was that the negotiations about the price now would proceed more urgently and openly. An extremely important side benefit was the fact that the Americans had put Mengistu on notice that they wanted him out of office. Within days, Frasure would act to get him out. In addition, a week later Boschwitz would brief Bush on his trip, arguing that it was imperative that Israel take the Jews out of Addis Ababa quickly. From this point on, the former senator would be a close and influential ally of the American Jewish leaders and Israelis who were driving events forward toward an airlift. And, as a result of the Boschwitz mission, the Ethiopians significantly hastened the aliyah, increasing the pace of the departures by about 50 percent: from an average of 235 each week in April, it would rise to some 350 a week in May, until the start of Operation Solomon.[45]

In New York, the kitchen cabinet pushed ahead. They began to put together the plans to raise the "financial aid," noting that Lubrani, Simcha Dinitz, and American Jewish leaders would deal with the specifics. And they concluded that, in view of Kassa's apparent loss of influence, the "Jackson piece"—the cash incentives for helpful Ethiopian officials—"may have to be directed toward other individuals."[46]

## MELES PROMISED TO COOPERATE

That Sunday, April 28, the Boschwitz party stopped over in Khartoum, the capital of Sudan, where they met with the leaders of the principal Ethiopian rebel movements. Frasure stayed on there, spending ten hours with the EPRDF's Meles Zenawi, who was eager to develop good relations with the United States. Frasure told him that he wanted the Falashas out of Ethiopia and Meles agreed to cooperate. In fact, the Tigrean insurgents, who spoke with pride of having protected Falashas in the past, now feared that the Jews were in danger in Addis Ababa.[47] The Jews were seen as a prominent and privileged group who were not suffering as the rest of the Ethiopian people were. As a result, popular resentment and enmity were rising against them. So the EPRDF wanted the Falashas to be taken out of Addis immediately, in case there was a gap between the fall of the government and the rebels' taking over.[48] But if the Jews remained in the city, Meles said, he would give instructions to his people to safeguard them. The rebel leader also promised to work with the Americans toward a dignified transition to democracy. He did not want disorder. "His nightmare was to have to shoot his way into Addis Ababa," Frasure recalled later. "He was nervous about '36"—a reference to the violence that had occurred when Haile Selassie fled Mussolini's advancing troops in 1936. Knowing how close Mengistu was to collapse, Meles was unenthusiastic about a peace conference in London. He told the American that he would come, though, if the United States needed him to for political reasons.

While he was in Khartoum, Frasure told the Eritrean leader, Isaias Afewerki, that Eritrea would get its chance for independence, but not right away. Frasure proposed a "deferred guaranteed referendum," to be held in two to three years. Unlike Meles, Isaias did not commit to attending the London talks.[49]

That same day, Meles confirmed his cooperation with the United States, while Mengistu quickly displayed the opposite. The rebel leader had promised military restraint if the government behaved reciprocally. "We passed this on to Mengistu," Frasure recalled. On that Sunday, April 28, the EPRDF forces withdrew from Ambo. Far from exercising restraint, Mengistu airlifted three army divisions to the town and launched an offensive. The government claimed on state radio on Sunday night that the army had driven the EPRDF from Ambo "after a great struggle."[50] Meles told Frasure that he would teach Mengistu a lesson: he would break the back of the offensive and tighten the ring around the capital. But he promised Frasure not to go into Addis Ababa without consulting him. Frasure was very impressed with Meles and had had enough of Mengistu. When he got back to Washington, he told Scowcroft that they could not deal with the Ethiopian president. They should get him out immediately.[51]

Meanwhile, Boschwitz and Hall flew on toward home. During a stopover in Frankfurt, they debriefed Lubrani, who did not like what he heard. Lubrani distrusted the Ethiopians, especially their demand for secrecy. "The secrecy thing is bullshit," he told the kitchen cabinet by phone. "It's a way to blame Israel." Kassa could leak the story to a newspaper himself, then accuse Israel of breaching its commitment.[52]

### "WE HAVE THE CARDS"

The day after Boschwitz and his entourage left Addis, negotiations began in earnest to set the price for the release of the Jews. Lubrani believed, optimistically, that he had the advantage. "We have the cards," he declared that Monday, April 29. The hour was late, and Lubrani confidently was playing what he hoped would be the last hand with Kassa. The point of the game now was to win the release of the Jews at the least possible expense. As the Israeli assessed things, Kassa was beginning to panic.[53] The EPRDF had advanced to within sixty-five miles of Addis Ababa, and civilians were walking the streets of the capital with weapons.[54] To arrange the cash payment before Mengistu's time ran out, Kassa would have to come to the Israelis, and quickly.

Kassa called Naim early on Monday, asking him to calculate the cost of getting the Jews from Gondar to Addis, maintaining them there for a year, then flying them to Israel.[55] That amount would be the basis of the Ethiopian demand for compensation. Lubrani had anticipated this and had instructed Naim not to respond, so the ambassador told Kassa that he would have to refer the question to Tel Aviv. Lubrani's next move was to wait for Kassa to come back to Naim. But instead, Kassa contacted Peter Jackson, asking for a more extensive schedule of costs. "Kassa is wily, cunning," Lubrani told Schneider and Taylor by phone. "He's playing Peter [against] Naim. We must play it very cool."[56] The Israeli's gut instinct told him that they had the time to go slowly and wait Kassa out. Besides, Lubrani still did not know whether Kassa could deliver what he promised. "There is a great likelihood that Kassa is playing the lone wolf," he said at the time. "He probably has Mengistu in tow, but not the other two," referring to the prime minister and the internal affairs minister. Lubrani suspected that Kassa was trying to intrude himself into the loop solely for personal gain. Boschwitz and Hall had concluded that the aid would end up in private pockets, and Lubrani agreed.

"It could be that the big money is personal," he said at the time.[57] It was a realistic expectation: at some point the Ethiopian leaders would realize that their time was running short and would think about securing their personal futures financially. That would present the Israelis with a window of opportunity to fix the price for the release of the Jews. According to one report, this brilliant bit of foresight had shaped Lubrani's strategy for months.[58] The question now was whether the right moment had arrived.

At their meeting, Kassa told Jackson that he was forty-six years old and had done a lot for his country but was expecting to be executed when the rebels took the city. He was ready to allow the seventeen thousand Jews to leave, he said, but first he needed to set the amount of the payment. Then he raised the stakes from his earlier conversation with Naim. The government should be compensated not only for the cost of the flights, he told Jackson, but also for the expense of maintaining the Jews in Addis for eighteen to twenty-four months, as Jackson had proposed in their first conversation. For good measure, Kassa wanted calculations as well for the cost of the Jews' health and education.

Kassa then told Jackson that his "personal situation" was solved.[59] It was indeed! Numerous sources confirm that, without checking with the Israelis, Jackson had offered Kassa a $3.4 million cash side deal on behalf of Nate Shapiro and the AAEJ. Using the rough figure of seventeen thousand Jews, this amounted to a $200-a-head personal payment to Kassa upon completion of the airlift, in addition to the larger sum being negotiated. Naim was flabbergasted when he heard about it, and Lubrani expressed his disbelief succinctly: "Bullshit!" he said to Schneider. "The handling of the whole affair is out of our hands," Lubrani complained.[60]

Schneider also was unhappy with the payment to Kassa, but he secretly agreed to it, he revealed in 2001, ten years after the event. Once Jackson made the offer, Schneider feared that Shapiro would approve it, Lubrani would oppose it, and the entire rescue would unravel. So he got authority from the JDC leadership, fudged the issue until the operation was over, and the JDC paid Kassa. This, Schneider reasoned, would ensure Kassa's commitment to the aliyah in case circumstances became unstable in Addis. "The whole deal could have fallen apart had we not taken [that] additional step," he said.[61]

Kassa went to the AAEJ compound for a second meeting with Jackson that day, then a third. He now asked for a detailed schedule of virtually every dollar ever expended on the Ethiopian Jews. He wanted to know the cost of supporting them in Addis, itemized for each individual, including the price of food, clothing, shelter, medical treatment, social workers, and teachers. He also wanted to know how much the JDC had spent maintaining the Jews back in their villages in Gondar province, as well as the transportation costs for those who had emigrated, including hotel charges in Rome for people in transit.[62] Kassa was preparing to ask for a cash payment equal to all of these expenses, which would dwarf the $15 to $20 million that Jackson had put on the table. But Lubrani had instructed Jackson to put him off. A schedule of costs was a matter for the government of Israel. Jackson would provide a list of the AAEJ's expenses, but Kassa should take up the other costs with Naim or with Lubrani himself. Besides, "the request for a breakdown is bullshit," Lubrani said. "Really we are talking lump sums."[63]

Lubrani was concerned that Kassa could sabotage the aliyah if he did not get the deal he wanted. Mengistu had conditioned the agreement on secrecy, but "Kassa is giving visas to journalists," Lubrani noted.[64] Meanwhile, there were leaks about the negotiations and the airlift. And Ethiopian activists in Israel now began to plan a demonstration in Jerusalem, a distraction that Lubrani definitely did not want at this delicate moment.

Meanwhile, although the rescue had not been approved, plans for its execution went forward. It had not yet been decided if it would be done under military or (as the Mossad urged) civilian auspices.[65] And the American Jewish leaders still had to raise the cash, however much that turned out to be. "Whatever it is, it will be paid," Schneider told the kitchen cabinet. "Marty and Corky will ensure that there is enough," he said, referring to Marty Kraar and Charles "Corky" Goodman, the executive vice president and president of the CJF, respectively. They were thinking of a ceiling of $20 million, or $1,111 per head. Nate Shapiro insisted that money should not be paid in advance, but only in stages, as the Jews were leaving. The Ethiopian government had a history of starting exits, then stopping them, he said. The Americans would need to monitor the actual departures and the transfer of these funds.[66]

# TEN

# Playing Poker with *Sechel*

## MAY 1–19, 1991

As May 1991 began, Lubrani and American Jewish leaders were betting that linkage—the U.S. policy that there would be no London peace conference unless Mengistu released the Jews—had given them the winning hand in the negotiations in Addis Ababa. What they did not know was that their closest ally in Washington had abandoned that strategy. Meanwhile, in Addis, Kassa and Lubrani bargained to set the price for a mass exodus, and the Ethiopian opened the bidding with an astonishing figure.

### "A THEATRICAL STAGE PROP"

Bob Frasure had helped the aliyah along at every crucial point. In the first days of May 1991, however, he dropped his own game plan that the exodus of the Falashas from Addis would be the price for the London peace talks. Immediately after his return from Africa, there was a shift in policy at the White House, reducing this linkage to "a theatrical stage prop," Frasure recalled later. The new approach, he said, was, "We threaten them with canceling London, but won't really."

The turning point had come at the end of April, when Mengistu broke the truce by sending forces to seize Ambo after the EPRDF had vacated the town. To Frasure and Brent Scowcroft, that double-cross was the final sign that Mengistu had to go. They determined to get rid of him quickly, and the London Roundtable conference, which would lead to a new government, would be the engine to do that. The principle of parallel momentum on the Falashas and the peace talks remained good policy, and the State Department was still behind it. But Scowcroft and Frasure would not allow it to preclude the Roundtable.[1] If they did and Mengistu held on to the Jews, there would be no talks. He could then remain in power a while longer, the Falashas would be stuck where they were, and there would be needless bloodshed as the insurgents advanced—all very unhappy prospects. And for the EPRDF to enter Addis Ababa shooting would have been the most dangerous and destabilizing outcome for everyone, including the Jews. Scowcroft, who had never felt committed to the linkage policy, wanted to prevent those things from happening. "We can't pull the rug out from under the rebels," he told Frasure. "Use linkage as theater till it works." They would keep saying that the negotiations were linked to the airlift, to bluff Mengistu into letting the Jews go. In reality, though, the London talks would proceed at any cost, even if the Falashas were still in Addis. Frasure worried about the Jews' fate if the rebels attacked the capital, as he had for months, but he continued to believe that they could weather the storm.[2] Meles' recent promises to protect them could only strengthen that conviction.

The Americans wanted to remove Mengistu even before London, if possible. Frasure thought that the dictator would use the talks to stall for time anyway. So he started organizing for a "clean kill"—to remove the Ethiopian president from power. On Scowcroft's instructions, Frasure pressed President Robert Mugabe to offer Mengistu asylum in Zimbabwe, despite the opposition that had arisen there a month earlier.[3] This would take a few weeks to mature.

Meanwhile, the American Jewish leaders, unaware of the change in policy at the NSC, continued to pursue the concept of linkage. Schneider and Nate Shapiro flew to Minneapolis on Friday, May 3, to stress to Boschwitz one crucial point: that American participation in the London talks had to be predicated on the exodus of all of the Jews by May 15, the date the Roundtable was scheduled to begin.[4]

When Boschwitz met with Bush at the White House on Monday, May 6, he pointed out that the Ethiopians had broken their promise to expedite the Jews' departure. "As long as they have the Falashas they will feel they will have leverage over us and will not complete the Roundtable," he warned. Or, more likely, the rebels would see that Mengistu was dragging out the negotiations and would lose patience and attack Addis Ababa. The United States had to act immediately to get the Falasha exodus under way by the time of the peace conference, he advised the president.[5] There was no dissent by anyone in the room, and Bush was supportive. "The big man reacted favorably. He seemed well briefed on the issue," a JDC memo of May 6 said of him.[6]

## "HE CAN HINDER US"

During the weekend of May 4 and 5, 1991, while Schneider and Shapiro were still in Minnesota with Boschwitz, Lubrani planned to go to Addis Ababa. He had met with Israeli editors and had had military censorship put in place. This backfired. The uncharacteristic Israeli silence about the Ethiopian Jews tipped off the world press that something was about to happen, and reporters started making their way to Addis.

Lubrani also had gotten Prime Minister Shamir's approval to reach a final agreement for the airlift. Now he needed to close the deal at last. His plan was to reach the final terms with the internal affairs minister, Tesfaye Wolde Selassie, sidestepping Kassa, who, he still thought, was "playing on his own."

Lubrani wanted to keep Kassa sweet and polite, but at arm's length. "Kassa may not be able to help, but he can hinder us," he said.[7]

Kassa had a very different plan in mind, however. He was setting the pace, slowing things down, and had not yet called Naim in to discuss evacuation "modalities." Now Kassa asked Lubrani not to come to Addis until Wednesday, May 8, which would leave only seven days before start of the London Roundtable. "We are reaching an impossible timeframe," Lubrani warned.[8] He rarely displayed anger, but Lubrani was visibly angry now. He faxed a letter to Boschwitz, who then let Scowcroft and Bush know about the delay. "It seems pretty clear that they are stalling for time," Lubrani wrote. "They would like to concede as little as possible without risking cancellation or postponement of the London talks."[9]

Over Kassa's objections, Lubrani arrived in Addis Ababa on Monday, May 6, and brought with him Major-General Amnon Lipkin-Shahak, the Israel Defense Forces deputy chief of staff, who had been appointed overall commander of the airlift. "I saw that it was necessary for Shahak to come, to feel the cloth, to know what the fiber was like," Lubrani told me later.[10] Driving from the airport to Addis, Shahak "studied the intersections and rooftops" and concluded that "there was no way to evacuate fifteen thousand civilians with guns blazing."[11] The operation could happen only with the Ethiopian government's consent. The general "planned to the last detail," examining all contingencies and building solutions to cope with all possible pitfalls, Lubrani said. After four days in Addis, Shahak went home and assigned to the operation "the best possible people, from the Air Force and the Army," Lubrani added. Once the military plan was in place, the operation had to happen soon. "You can't have a military structure of planning in abeyance," Lubrani said. "You can for a week, or three weeks. But either you do this or you get off the pot."[12]

## "KASSA PLAYS POKER"

"Kassa plays poker, just like me," Lubrani observed later.[13] When they finally met, for seven hours on Wednesday, May 8, 1991, the Israeli found out just how high the Ethiopians had raised the stakes. Mengistu wanted $180 million! But the Ethiopian president had reached this number without offering any rationale, Naim observed. Kassa, by contrast, at least presented his case "with *sechel* [good sense]. . . . He put it in a package." He had quantified all of the previous expenses on the Jews, including "health care! Schooling!" Asher Naim told me later, laughing. Kassa had added to that a price for the "trouble, sacrifice and risks" that the government was taking. That resulted in a sum of $100 million, less than Mengistu had demanded initially but still drastically beyond anything that the Israelis were willing to consider.[14] Kassa confirmed this opening figure in an interview in 1992 but said, "It came from the two Tesfayes," Tesfaye Dinka and Tesfaye Wolde Selassie—a claim that Tesfaye Dinka denied forcefully when he heard it ten years later.[15] In any case, Lubrani had in mind $10 to $12 million, a figure to which Simcha Dinitz had committed the Jewish Agency.

The next day, May 9, Lubrani told Houdek that Mengistu wanted to get enough money from the Falasha departure to purchase weapons for yet another counteroffensive.[16] By delaying the negotiations, the dictator hoped to buy time for the army to prepare for this.

By Friday, May 10, Kassa had come down to $60 million, a package that would cover the cost of the airlift as well as the "financial assistance" to the government—and to himself. Still, the figure was too high. Lubrani now was aiming for $30 million.[17] To give himself some negotiating room, Lubrani called Schneider in New York and asked, "What about $40 million?"

"He asked me to sound out the establishment . . . to get a picture of what was acceptable," Schneider said. Schneider knew that, in the worst case, the JDC's endowment could cover the entire payment. But he wanted to get the Jewish federations and the United Jewish Appeal to commit to raising the money. So now, about seven o'clock in the evening, he called Marty Kraar and Corky Goodman of the CJF, and Marvin Lender, the national chairman of the United Jewish Appeal (UJA).[18]

The support of these three officials was essential, given the source from which the money ultimately would come. American Jews gave charitable donations to 189 Jewish federations, each of which decided how much would be assigned to overseas rescue and aliyah missions. This money went to the UJA, which funded the JDC, and to the United Israel Appeal, which funded the Jewish Agency. The CJF represented the interest of the federations, and when an issue such as the Ethiopian rescue was involved, the CJF helped the federations to act collectively.[19] This made the support of Kraar, Goodman, and Lender important, and each of them gave Schneider the go-ahead. "I phoned Uri twenty minutes later," Schneider recalled, "and told him, 'Two bananas'"—their secret code for $40 million.

But Schneider added one thing that did not delight Lubrani. "I told Uri he would have to talk to Simcha Dinitz," Schneider recalled.[20] The Jewish Agency, with its large budget, would have the necessary cash or lines of credit, and they would be the ones to make the actual transfer of funds. Dinitz, as chairman of the Jewish Agency, would have to authorize the transaction. But Lubrani did not want to deal with him. Now that the figure had jumped to $30 million or more, he worried that Dinitz would second-guess him. Zvi Barak, the Jewish Agency treasurer, had fought with Lubrani about the $10 million package that he had offered Mengistu a few months earlier, "so on the big money I was afraid to talk to them," Lubrani said later. He was reluctant to tell Dinitz any actual figures at all while the negotiations were under way, and he certainly did not want to tell him about the $3.4 million side deal with Kassa. "Simcha thinks he can buy cheaper," Lubrani complained at the time.[21]

At this time in Israel, Reuven Merhav, Haim Divon, and key figures at the Defense Ministry made their final recommendation to Prime Minister Shamir to approve the operation, to which the Israeli Air Force had given the code name Gishmei Za'af, or "Torrential Rain."[22] Now it was up to Lubrani to make it happen.

## "HOW CAN YOU DEAL WITH THIS GANG OF THUGS?"

By Wednesday, May 15, one week into negotiations, Lubrani was getting nowhere. This was the day on which the Roundtable had been scheduled to begin and the intended deadline for conducting the airlift, but the Eritrean rebels had asked for a delay. They needed time "to tighten the noose on Asmara," Bob Frasure recalled.[23] The delay also served Mengistu, however, since they were now only a month away from the rainy season. If he could hold out till then, he would have a good chance of surviving into September, when the rains would end. The conference was put off till May 20, and then until May 27.

The American pressure on the Ethiopians was not working: Kassa would not budge on the price. Lubrani dressed him down, insisting that he would not engage in horse-trading for human lives. Kassa called Lubrani insensitive and made himself unavailable. To break the stalemate, each tried to unnerve the other. Knowing that Kassa had tapped his phone, Lubrani would call Israel to say that he was sick of the negotiations and was leaving. "That rattled Kassa," he recalled later. For his part, Kassa threatened to have the Jews conscripted into the army, Lubrani said. The Israeli responded by threatening to meet with the rebels, which, he told Kassa, he had avoided doing till then.[24]

At one point, Kassa confided his dilemma. Mengistu was surrounded by two groups, he said: moderates who wanted a peace conference and radicals who did not. The radicals had blood on their hands, and, if Mengistu went from power, they would too. So they opposed a compromise, and they had a strong influence on Mengistu. Kassa had to contend with both groups, which made his position untenable, he told Lubrani. His wife was nagging him, "How can you deal with this gang of thugs?" "My life is not a life," Kassa told the Israeli in Hebrew. "I will soon be regarded as a traitor."[25]

The problem as Kassa described it was insoluble. His government already had agreed to release the Jews, and he supposedly was merely negotiating the "modalities." In reality, the Beta Israel had become a shield for the hard-liners, who feared a peaceful end to the war, and for Mengistu, who felt safe only in power and in Addis Ababa. Kassa had only one tactic left: to protract the bargaining. But the rebel advance was sure to put an end to that. To complicate his situation even further, Kassa was dependent on his adversaries. He would have to rely on Israel for his immediate safety, and on American Jews for his future financial security. He had been playing a game that he could not win, and now he had shown his hand. He told Lubrani that he wanted to leave Ethiopia. Lubrani replied that Kassa could make a successful new life if he came out at the right time—after the release of the Falashas. He threatened Kassa that no previous arrangement would be honored unless he stayed until Israel got permission for the airlift.[26]

Still, the gap between the sides remained the same. Lubrani offered $30 million, Kassa asked for twice that amount. "This is all the dowry this bride has," Lubrani told him. "She has nothing more to offer."[27] And still the question lingered: for whom was Kassa speaking? "Everyone thinks Kassa is freelancing," said Frasure.[28]

Kassa now made himself accessible only by phone.[29] "We were supposed to reach a situation where Kassa cooperated or we got him out," Lubrani said in an interview. He had guaranteed Kassa's safety—if he behaved; by being uncooperative, Kassa jeopardized his chance for a financially comfortable new life, as Boschwitz noted later. But now Kassa "was making trouble," creating a stalemate, Lubrani recalled. "It became very tense at the end. We seriously considered removing him. We sought a way to the interior minister [Tesfaye Wolde Selassie], but there was no time. We didn't know what to do."[30] So, to shock Kassa, Lubrani announced in earnest that he was going to leave. By Friday evening, May 17, he would be in London. "That is the way the game is played," Bob Houdek said approvingly in Addis when he heard about that move.[31]

Kassa was faced with the prospect of having no one with whom to negotiate, but the distance between the dollar amounts remained undiminished. "We have to hold their feet to the fire," Houdek advised. Later that Thursday, he made it clear to Kassa that there would have to be movement by May 27, the new date for the Roundtable. But Lubrani wanted more. He wanted Boschwitz to return to Ethiopia, to "put American weight on the financial gap" between the two sides.[32]

To spur Kassa further, Schneider, Jackson, and Shapiro agreed that Jackson should tell Kassa that there was no U.S. money to help pay for the airlift. The Ethiopian replied that he knew about the funds that secretly had been set aside in the Defense Department budget. How could Kassa possibly have

known that? asked the kitchen cabinet back in New York when Jackson reported to them. (Kassa revealed later that the Americans had told him.)
Obviously that ploy had not worked.[33]

Ultimately it was the rebels who broke this impasse. On Friday, May 17,
they surrounded the town of Debre Birhan, which the Americans considered a red line, equal in strategic importance to Ambo. The insurgents also
cut the crucial road to Assab, the last port in government hands. The Ethiopian Third Army had been destroyed. The rebels now declared that they
would agree to the peace talks only if the government would capitulate in
London, rather than attempting to form a coalition. If there were no talks,
they said, they would take Addis Ababa before the rainy season began, in
mid-June. Under no circumstances would they allow Mengistu to drag the
negotiations out beyond that point.[34]

Lubrani met with Kassa again that Friday, before leaving Ethiopia. Kassa
conceded that the military situation was irreversible. Houdek, who attended
this meeting, told the Ethiopian that the Americans would "pull the plug"
on the Roundtable talks if there was no progress. Kassa proposed that American organizations should help bridge the financial gap in the negotiations
with Lubrani. The Israeli countered, however, that a payment of more than
$30 million would be called a ransom, a word that Kassa did not want to
hear. Kassa mentioned the figure $50 million. Lubrani replied that he might
be able to go an extra $1 or $2 million to show improvement and "might go
an extra five." But he would not budge on this, he told Kassa. Shamir might
oppose a larger amount, he warned.[35]

After Lubrani left, Houdek told Kassa that his intransigence had lost
Ethiopia $30 million, the goodwill of the Israelis and the Americans, and,
maybe, the peace conference in London.[36]

### "THEY ARE BECOMING DESPERATE"

"They are becoming desperate," Lubrani said of the Ethiopians the next
morning, when he and Eliezri joined Schneider and Taylor in London.
Lubrani met with Herman Cohen, who had come to London for discussions
prior to the Roundtable, and suggested that another statement by Bush could
help to soften up Mengistu. The president could reiterate the American commitment to the unity of Ethiopia and could put Mengistu in a humanitarian
light for letting the Jews go. Cohen was concerned that having Bush affirm
Ethiopian unity would undermine the Eritrean rebels' demand for independence, and so could jeopardize the peace conference. "We can get around it
by wording it suitably," Cohen told him, however.[37]

They now seemed close enough to success for Lubrani to talk to Schneider
about meeting the planes that would bring the Ethiopian Jews to Israel.

They also would have to arrange a PR campaign to help fund-raising in the United States. And they would need a name for the mission. An Israeli at the embassy in London supplied it: Operation Solomon.[38] It was a fitting name for the rescue of a people whose foundational narrative established their descent from King Solomon. And just as Solomon had gambled that a mother's love would not allow her child to be cut in two, this mission would unite the Beta Israel, half of whom were already in Israel.[39]

The next morning, Sunday, May 19, Kassa called Lubrani in London. "Where are you? When are you coming back?" Kassa asked, and told him that he required "only a little more."[40] This was what Lubrani had been waiting to hear. He agreed to return, and in fact had already made plans to leave for Addis late the next day.

# ELEVEN

# The Final Week:
# Mengistu's Flight—
# Closing the Deal

## MONDAY, MAY 20–WEDNESDAY, MAY 22, 1991

The plans for the newly named Operation Solomon were nearing fruition, and as the weekend of May 18–19 drew to a close, Lubrani and the American Jewish leaders could start to feel secure that the rescue would happen soon. But the next day brought a series of sudden changes and startling setbacks that put the entire mission in doubt.

### MONDAY, MAY 20: THE "CLEAN KILL"

Monday had barely begun, London time, when a momentous message reached Schneider and the other American Jewish leaders there: Mengistu was about to flee. It arrived in the form of a riddle. There is "a place down south where s.o. [someone] will go and make a trip to visit a home of his," the message said. He was "likely to go very soon" and it "may be a very short trip."[1] The "visitor" would be Mengistu, who would leave Ethiopia the next day, and the place down south was Zimbabwe.

There had been speculation in the press for weeks that Mengistu would step down, but the proximate cause of his decision to go at that moment was a process that Frasure had set in motion. At Frasure's instigation, Zimbabwe's president, Robert Mugabe, dispatched an envoy to Mengistu that Monday with a message: "I will help you in exile, but come now. This offer is not for long."[2] The "clean kill" toward which Frasure was working was about to take place.

Mengistu's flight would be welcome news from a humanitarian perspective, but it put the airlift in question. The release of the Beta Israel was predicated on his consent. With Mengistu gone, would all bets be off? And what if the dictator's departure led to political instability followed by chaos in Addis Ababa and the Doomsday Scenario for the Jews? With this turn of events, the future of Operation Solomon had become imponderable.

Then, early Monday morning London time, Lubrani and the American Jewish leaders were confronted with extremely bad news. First, they received a cable from the Israeli embassy in Washington saying that Boschwitz would not be allowed to return to Addis Ababa. Brent Scowcroft, the national security adviser, wanted to strengthen relations with the rebels, especially now that they were near to victory, so he did not want to send an envoy as a further gesture to Mengistu. For the same reason, President Bush would not send a second message to the Ethiopian government to ask them to permit the airlift.[3] Now Lubrani revealed another major blow: he had learned that the NSC had abandoned the strategy of linkage. This shift conflicted with the policy at the State Department, where Herman Cohen had received orders to give the Falasha departure the highest priority. Insisting that the United States stand by its commitment to condition peace talks on the release of the Jews, Cohen denied Frasure's recommendation to inform the Israelis of a delinkage.[4] The message reached Lubrani anyway, though. "We will have to manage," Lubrani told Schneider and the others in the kitchen cabinet. Everyone would have to keep a poker face.[5] These were serious tactical setbacks, but if Israel could maintain the bluff of linkage for a few more days, the operation still might happen.

There was more bad news that Monday morning in London. Eli Eliezri told Michael Schneider and Gideon Taylor that a conversation between Lubrani and Simcha Dinitz the day before had not gone as well as Lubrani had reported. Dinitz was still angry that Lubrani was trying to go around him and the Jewish Agency. That Sunday afternoon they finally had spoken, and Lubrani had been irritated by the conversation. "I cannot say that he is not a pompous ass," he had said of Dinitz. Still, he had told Schneider that the discussion had gone reasonably well. Dinitz was making difficulties, but he had not placed a ceiling on the payment, and he had agreed to meet with the fund-raisers in New York to ask for the $35 million.[6] This was better than if Dinitz had demanded to go to Addis to do the negotiating himself, as Lubrani had feared. Now, on Monday, however, Eliezri said that the conversation had been "worse than Uri painted it." Dinitz had been "iffy," saying that it was not his job to find the money. Lubrani was playing poker again, Eliezri said, gambling that the Jewish Agency would foot the bill when the time came.[7]

Still, the news was not all unwelcome. The American government continued to support the rescue in principle. Frasure said that they had the rebels in hand, and though he would not delay the conference again, he promised to act as if linkage were still on. And, if Lubrani reported progress in Addis, Frasure would arrange for a second letter from President Bush after all. Lubrani had until the end of the week.[8]

Before leaving London, Lubrani arranged to have Peter Jackson call Kassa. "He should tell Kassa that he should play the game," Lubrani said. "Peter should say it is his last chance." The Americans were losing patience, Lubrani noted.[9] The rebels were becoming impatient as well.

Lubrani and Eliezri traveled from London to Israel on Monday. Before dawn on Tuesday morning, they left for Ethiopia, stopping over in Nairobi, Kenya, then getting on a flight to Addis Ababa. Ironically, their plane may have crossed paths in the air with the craft that was carrying Mengistu to exile. Mengistu was fleeing in secrecy and deception. He had left Addis in a small DASH-6 plane with about a dozen senior military officers on the pretext that they were going to observe the training of new recruits in south-central Ethiopia. In midflight, however, Mengistu abruptly had the pilot change the itinerary and proceed to Nairobi instead. From there he boarded a commercial craft that took him to Zimbabwe, and all or most of the officers who had flown with him went directly back to Ethiopia.[10] Mengistu's wife, who had returned to Ethiopia from Zimbabwe a week earlier, left that same day for their farm outside of Harare on a commercial flight. Mengistu had vowed to fight "to the last bullet." His departure therefore surprised many of his colleagues, some of whom had appointments with him that afternoon.[11]

## TUESDAY, MAY 21:
### "ARE WE BACK TO SQUARE ONE?"

At 10:00 on Tuesday morning, May 21, in Addis Ababa, Kassa was called to an urgent meeting of the politburo in the president's office. There the vice president, General Tesfaye Gebre Kidan, announced that Mengistu had left. General Tesfaye was now the acting president.[12]

Why had Mengistu fled when he was only days away from a multimillion-dollar "incentive"? "The noose became too close for comfort," Lubrani told me. "He was wealthy enough by that time. He had a farm waiting for him in Zimbabwe. All dictators have these things. I had this all lined up."[13] According to one report, Mengistu was destitute when he left Ethiopia, and his uncle was seeking aid for him from embassies in Harare.[14] In actuality, however, he had looted everything of value that he could from the treasury room in the Jubilee Palace, including the crown jewels, gold boxes, ivory tusks, and state gifts.[15] Mengistu reportedly arrived in Zimbabwe with $3 million, and the *Sunday Times* noted that he had stashed away hundreds of millions of dollars in Swiss bank accounts. He later invested in real estate in Harare's affluent suburbs, buying opportunely at a time when white residents were fleeing the country. The former Ethiopian president paid $1.3 million in cash for one property alone.[16] The fact remains, though, that he had left Addis less than four days before a large sum changed hands.

Mengistu may have had had little choice but to leave when he did. Mugabe's envoy had told him on Monday that if he wanted to seek refuge in Zimbabwe, he would have to act fast. The Ethiopian Council of State reportedly had deliberated on Monday night, then had decided that the president should leave in the interest of preventing the disintegration of the country. After Mengistu was gone, the council spoke derisively of him. They then dismissed Mengistu's uncle from his post as ambassador to Zimbabwe on the grounds that he had greeted his nephew at the Harare airport "illegally" and had let him stay in the Ethiopian embassy.[17]

Perhaps Mengistu left without knowing that the multimillion-dollar payment was so near. The prime minister, Tesfaye Dinka, said at the time that he himself did not know—that Kassa was keeping it from him.[18] (Kassa, by contrast, said that the initial demand for $100 million was the idea of the prime minister and the internal affairs minister, as noted above.) In any case, Kassa said that he did tell Mengistu. That Monday night, Kassa remembered, he called his boss. "I told him Uri Lubrani is coming tomorrow to finalize the deal. Mengistu agreed to $35 million [and] gave orders to go ahead," Kassa said. That, however, conflicts with the account by Lubrani, who said that it was not until Tuesday, after Mengistu fled, that he raised the offer to $35 million.[19]

A third possibility is that Mengistu intended to get the money after all, from exile, as we shall see.

Soon after Mengistu's flight that Tuesday morning, General Tesfaye requested a meeting with Bob Houdek. The acting president informed the American chargé d'affaires that he was committed to the London talks and asked for help getting a cease-fire. As he had before, Houdek now intervened at a critical moment: he mentioned the Boschwitz mission and the need for parallel momentum on the Falashas. Tesfaye said that he had not been briefed about the issue of the Jews. Houdek filled him in and advised that Kassa should carry on the negotiating with Lubrani. Kassa does not make decisions, the general said contemptuously, so Houdek suggested that Kassa bring him the raw facts and that Tesfaye reserve the decision making for himself.[20] "We can resolve it in a matter of hours, and the [Jewish] community can depart in a matter of days," Houdek told him. "Like a military man," Tesfaye promptly said, "No problem. This can be done," Houdek recalled. "This is a drop in the ocean," the general told him. "We can discharge it just like that."[21] "This guy was scared," Herman Cohen said of the acting president later. "We told him it was absolutely necessary to let the Falashas out immediately. He was so desperate, he said, 'Okay.'"[22] General Tesfaye then met with Kassa and authorized him to make a deal allowing the Falashas to leave.[23]

Lubrani and Kassa met all day Tuesday, and that night Lubrani made his final offer. "I knew that I had to get this operation on, and I knew it had to cost some money," Lubrani remembered. "I said to Kassa, 'Go to Tesfaye and tell him, if he agrees now, there'll be another $5 million.'" This $35 million total would make Tesfaye look better than Mengistu, the Israeli recalled saying.[24]

That is not the complete story of how the payment went from $30 to $35 million, however. A well-informed Israeli source, speaking on condition of anonymity ten years after the event, gave a very different and somewhat scandalous account. Kassa's intelligence-gathering skills were always awesome, and at this point in the negotiations he applied them on a personal level to discover how much Lubrani was authorized to pay. Choosing his words carefully, this source said, "One of the people very close to Lubrani was in very close connection (and maybe more than that) to the chief negotiator for the Ethiopians [i.e., Kassa]. Maybe this contributed to the large payment." An Israeli diplomat confirmed this in an interview in November 2001.

And so the two sides agreed on the dollar amount at last. After the long course of bargaining, the histrionics, and the haggling, the $35 million final figure was precisely what Houdek had suggested, and Cohen and Lubrani had discussed, six weeks earlier. This amounted to $2,446 for each Ethiopian Jew who would be taken to Israel in Operation Solomon.[25] In addition, the United States would pay the $13 million cost of the airlift, and the JDC would cover the private payment to Kassa, which in the end was reduced to $2.8 million.[26]

At this dangerous moment for the Ethiopian leaders, political security also would be valuable currency, so Lubrani proposed getting a second letter from Bush. Kassa replied that he would have to consult with his colleagues. Lubrani specified that the Israelis would need formal approval of the operation. During Entebbe, Israel had been accused of acting without permission, so Shamir had required that the Ethiopians approve this mission in writing.[27]

### "PAY COD"

On Monday, May 20, as Mengistu was preparing to leave Ethiopia, Simcha Dinitz, the chairman of the Jewish Agency, flew from Israel to New York. The day before, at a state dinner in Jerusalem honoring Lech Walesa, the president of Poland, he had asked Prime Minister Shamir to fund half of the rescue. Shamir had agreed, Dinitz told me later. The Jewish Agency and the government each would pay $17.5 million. "Get out the Jews, then we'll settle accounts," Dinitz recalled the prime minister's telling him. Now, on Tuesday, at the Grand Hyatt Hotel in Manhattan, Dinitz called "an emergency meeting of the top brass in America," as he rather grandly referred to the American Jewish fund-raisers.[28] The group included Schneider, Max Fisher, Marvin Lender of the UJA, Corky Goodman and Marty Kraar of the CJF, Mendel Kaplan, the chairman of the Board of Governors of the Jewish Agency, and Sylvia Hassenfeld, the president of the JDC.

Dinitz announced at the meeting that the amount would be $35 million. (Schneider already had cleared this with them, but he let Dinitz take the credit.)[29] "We need the money, we need it now, and we need it secretly," he told his audience. "I told them, 'It's a matter of days,'" Dinitz recalled. "They okayed the $35 million."

"I called Zvi Barak," Dinitz told me. "Zvika wasn't happy." Barak, the Jewish Agency treasurer, had clashed with Lubrani over money before, as noted above. Now he thought that Lubrani had bargained badly, that $35 million was excessive. In fact, Barak thought that the operation should have been left in the hands of the Mossad in the first place, according to Dinitz.[30] That was one reason that Lubrani had wanted to keep Barak and Dinitz out of the loop in the negotiations with Kassa. In fact, Lubrani and Barak avoided speaking to each other at all. Distrust and misunderstanding between the leaders of the Jewish Agency, on the one hand, and Lubrani and Schneider, on the other, would lead to immediate conflict, and would threaten the operation itself a few days later.

That Tuesday evening, Lubrani called General Lipkin-Shahak from Addis to tell him that he was near an agreement with the Ethiopians. The operation could begin very soon. "Get ready for it," Lubrani said, and the IDF began to alert the pilots for the mission. Lubrani also reemphasized the need to continue to keep a lid on press leaks. But "I didn't say a word about the money," he noted later. He did not want the Jewish Agency to hear about the final plans for the timing of the payment. Lubrani believed that unless Israel paid as the Jews departed, the Ethiopians would halt the airlift. He was certain that Dinitz and Zvi Barak, by contrast, would insist that they pay nothing until the aliyah was completed. "I know them," Lubrani recalled. "Barak would say, 'I want to see all of the Jews in Israel, then pay COD.'"[31]

## WEDNESDAY, MAY 22:
### "LET'S SEAL IT WITH A LETTER FROM BUSH"

In Addis Ababa the next morning, Wednesday, May 22, Lubrani expected the worst.[32] Neither the Eritreans nor the Tigreans had accepted a cease-fire, and rebel forces, taking up the positions of the retreating Ethiopian army, were closing in on the capital. Frasure sent a message to the insurgents on several fronts, telling them to hold off.[33] Meles agreed, but added, "If I perceive anarchy, I reserve the right to go in and establish order." Even if the rebels stood down, there could be a military coup, leading to chaos. Or hungry, desperate armed soldiers running from the front could enter the capital and start shooting. Thirty thousand leaderless troops already were wandering the streets of Addis Ababa, Bob Houdek told me, mostly Oromo kids "who sold the boots off their feet and their guns. You could buy an AK-47 for . . . around $6, but it cost $50 to buy a clip of ammunition. We were scared we were going to have a Night of the Long Knives of revenge-taking against the Derg, who had victimized the population for so many years."[34] The soldiers were on foot and in trucks, some with bazookas slung over their shoulders.[35]

There were other hazards as well. Though the city seemed calm during the day, the Israelis heard more gunshots at night than usual. Many soldiers had sold their weapon to civilians, including Jews, who might get involved in firefights.[36] With these potential dangers encroaching, Lubrani decided to look for Kassa, to pester him for an answer, but Kassa had disappeared. "He was afraid to stay home," Lubrani recalled. Naim had a more charitable interpretation of Kassa's absence: "He was busy closing the deal," the ambassador said later.[37]

At three o'clock that Wednesday afternoon in Addis, Kassa finally met with Lubrani and reported that the new acting president had accepted the offer. There would be conditions, chiefly that the payment would be made under the guise of reimbursing Ethiopian Airlines for the cost of the Falashas' airfares. In that spirit, the Ethiopians did not want the planes involved to bear Israeli colors, so they could claim that the aircraft were their own.[38]

There were problems too. A big one arose when an Ethiopian official (presumably Kassa) insisted that the cash payment should begin immediately. He "almost threw a tantrum" when Lubrani said no, and he accused the Israeli of being inflexible. Lubrani declared that "difficulties in banking procedure" required that they pay COD instead. Giving this elegant excuse, Lubrani noted, was better "than appearing to doubt their credibility."[39]

Houdek decided that this was the time for President Bush to send a message to President Tesfaye. In a "wax and gold" environment, in which commitments can be multiply ambiguous, it would be useful to have the Ethiopians see something reduced to writing. So Houdek got on a classified phone and called Frasure in Washington, saying, "The man's ready. Let's seal it with a letter from Bush."[40] Frasure was still skeptical about airlifting the Jews when the war was so near its climax.[41] Nevertheless, he replied to Houdek, "It shall be done." The letter, written in Bush's name, pledged to support the peace effort and asked Tesfaye to make the "statesmanlike and profoundly humanitarian gesture" of allowing the Falasha emigration to be completed prior to the opening of the London conference. Frasure got the letter to Scowcroft and they dispatched it immediately. Given the urgency of events in Addis, the national security adviser decided to act quickly and get the president's approval retroactively. The cable went out at 6:15 p.m., Washington time. The Ethiopian president would receive it in the morning.[42]

In Israel that Wednesday evening, the IDF gave the tentative go-ahead to put the rescue in motion. In Tel Aviv, Haim Halachmi called fifty-four veteran Ethiopian-Israelis. Over the past year Halachmi had organized the mission minute by minute with the Israeli air force. Now he was selecting the Ethiopian-Israelis who would act as translators and guides in the rescue. He told each of them to report to the Jewish Agency office in Tel Aviv the next day.

In Jerusalem that night, Eli Alcalay, the head of the Jewish Agency's Manpower Department, and his eleven assistants faced the daunting problem of staffing forty-nine new absorption centers almost instantly to receive the Beta Israel. They would need to hire seven hundred new workers before the first planes landed, and they would have to keep the whole thing quiet so as not to jeopardize the airlift. The fifty existing absorption centers already were filled, mainly with immigrants from the former Soviet Union. So the Agency had contracted for new sites, secretly keeping many of them empty for months in anticipation of this day. Alcalay and his team devised a plan in which the existing centers would "adopt" the new ones. The Agency would transfer workers from the current sites to the new ones, leaving only skeleton crews behind. The eleven assistants then would do the hiring as quickly as possible.[43]

## "POLITICS AND EGO"

Ironically, though Israel and Ethiopia had reached an accord about the airlift, the Joint and the Jewish Agency had not. As morning arrived in New York that Wednesday, May 22, Schneider feared that Simcha Dinitz would be so dilatory in transferring the $35 million that the entire project would end in disaster. He had left the meeting with Dinitz the day before "with great discomfort, afraid that I was party to critical information that would cause the collapse of the operation," he told me later. The rebels were closing in on Addis Ababa, and the airlift would have to happen in the next few days. The Ethiopians would want the money in advance, but Schneider was afraid that Dinitz would only pay COD, as Lubrani had feared. Dinitz had said at the meeting that the cash would be paid when the operation was over, Schneider recalled, and Marty Kraar later confirmed that.[44] To make matters worse, Monday would be Memorial Day, a bank holiday, which meant that the Jewish Agency might not transfer the funds until Tuesday or even later. Taking the risk of offending Dinitz, Schneider sent him a memo, with copies to the American Jewish top leadership, that declared, "The Ethiopians will demand cash immediately in stages, based upon the numbers departing each day. . . . This means the cash must be available for immediate transfer as soon as the deal is concluded"—possibly as early as that night. If the money was not available, the mission could be delayed by days. That, in turn, could terminate the operation altogether, since the peace talks were set to start on Monday. If the Roundtable collapsed, Schneider warned, the rebels could march into Addis immediately, and the Jews could be trapped.[45]

The relations between the organizations, already raw, now became inflamed. When Zvi Barak heard about the memo in Israel, he told Schneider off.[46] Lubrani responded from Addis, "I will call Simcha and tell him that if Barak causes problems, he can bloody will come here and do it himself." He then threatened to tell people that the operation failed because of Barak.

"It is vital to clarify that it is payment by stages, not at the end," Schneider told Lubrani. "It is vital that you call the pompous ass (Simcha) in order to ensure there will be no five-day delay."

"You keep out of it," Lubrani responded. The Israelis would handle this among themselves. A few minutes later, Lubrani reached Dinitz, who was annoyed with Schneider for having implied that he did not know what to do. Dinitz agreed to transmit the money "as early as possible." The Ethiopian Central Bank had an account into which the payment would be deposited when the time came, Dinitz said. They would pay in increments, and the amounts would vary, depending on the number of passengers who were flown out, he said.

"I'm afraid that you can't help," Lubrani told Schneider, who still feared that there would be delays in the payment that could undermine the rescue. He suggested to Lubrani that Shamir should nominate someone to liaise with Dinitz, to make sure that the money was transferred in a timely way. "Impossible," Lubrani replied. Personal tensions between Dinitz and the Shamir would not permit that. "Simcha and the Prime Minister hate each other," Lubrani said. "It's a question of politics and ego." Schneider then promised to research "the formulae and the suitable means of transfer," to make sure that the funds would be paid at the right time to the right account. "We will pay in New York, where their central bank has an account," notes a JDC memorandum of this conversation. "The sum will be transmitted to an account number which Uri will get as early as possible."[47]

# TWELVE

# "The Wings of History"

## THURSDAY, MAY 23, 1991

On Thursday, May 23, the day before Operation Solomon was set to begin, the Ethiopian acting president officially approved the airlift. A number of dangers threatened to impede or sabotage the mission, however, not the least of which was the possibility that the $35 million payment would fall through.

### "WE WON'T PAY"

Early that Thursday morning in Jerusalem, Zvi Barak suffered a surprising setback as he tried to arrange the transfer of the $35 million. Simcha Dinitz had told him about Prime Minister Shamir's promise of four days earlier, that the Israeli government would pay half of the money. The night before, Barak had called the Israeli accountant general, Eli Yones, to collect. Yones checked with the finance minister, Yitzhak Modai, then called Barak back at 7:00 a.m. Thursday with bad news. "We don't know anything about it," Modai had told Yones. "We won't pay." The payment had never been authorized. That meant that Barak would have to find another $17.5 million in one day.

Barak suspected that officials in Jerusalem were not cooperating because they had questions about how the payment had jumped from the $10 million that Dinitz had approved to $35 million.[1] Reuven Merhav offered a different interpretation. "Shamir played with Dinitz his usual (but not very frequent) trick of 'WHO, ME?'" when it came to paying the $17.5 million, Merhav commented later. "Dinitz should have known better. After all, Shamir had said from the outset to whoever mentioned money, 'Do not come to me for money.'"[2]

Meanwhile, everything else went ahead on the Israeli side. The Jewish Agency began to activate the forty-nine absorption centers, including hotels, youth hostels, and mobile home sites. They were concentrated in Haifa and the Galilee in the north, but ranged as far south as Eilat on the Red Sea. Six were in Jerusalem, including the five-star Diplomat Hotel, the largest of the centers.[3] (In a sense it was lucky that many rooms were vacant because of a drastic fall in tourism during the Gulf War crisis.) Eli Alcalay's team hired hundreds of new employees, the majority of them veteran Ethiopian-Israelis. The Jewish Agency reserved over 250 buses from the Egged Corporation to transport the new immigrants from the airport, and planned to have an Amharic-speaker on each vehicle. They arranged for nurses and social workers. The Jewish Agency also recruited Ethiopian-Israeli volunteers, including hundreds of students from youth villages, to greet the *olim* at the airport and accompany them to the absorption centers.[4]

The Israel Defense Forces assigned an elite unit of soldiers to secure Bole Airport outside of Addis, assist the Foreign Ministry security guards at the embassy, and escort the buses. The IDF also drafted civilian El Al flight crews into reserve duty and called up reserve doctors and medics. Meanwhile, crews gutted planes, removing the seats and bathrooms to allow them to hold twice their normal number of passengers. They laid foam rubber, covered by thick black plastic, as flooring. And, in accordance with Lubrani's agreement with the Ethiopians, the Israeli crews painted over the El Al logos and Stars of David on a number of the aircraft.[5]

## "LET THEM ALL GO"

On Thursday morning in Addis Ababa, the cable from President Bush reached Bob Houdek at the American embassy. Houdek dictated a cover letter, then immediately sent Bush's message to Kassa, who brought it to the Ethiopian acting president, General Tesfaye. From the general's perspective, the letter established that he was acting in accordance with American wishes in a humanitarian venture, rather than conducting a questionable business transaction with Israel. Kassa called Houdek in an hour with a response. The general said, "Let them all go," Kassa told him.[6] "It was a very pleasant surprise," Frasure recalled later. "They caved in."[7]

Soon afterward, Naim received an urgent invitation to see the Ethiopian foreign minister, Tesfaye Tadesse, who gave him the go-ahead for the airlift. He told the Israelis to coordinate logistics with the internal affairs minister, and to see that all Falashas left before May 27.[8] "I almost fell off my chair," Naim said later. At about noon, Addis time, he cabled the green light to Israel.[9]

Four hours later the Ethiopians nearly canceled the mission. Colonel Mersha called Naim to his office in the Internal Affairs Ministry and informed him that the rebels had entered Addis. The government was losing control, and it was not safe to let the operation go forward, Mersha told him. Naim called Houdek, who said that he had heard the same, but that the information kept changing. Turning to Mersha, Naim dismissed the report as a mere rumor and informed the Ethiopian that the first planes would land the next morning at ten o'clock. Mersha, though dubious, announced that he was a religious man and said, "Let us hope."[10]

That Thursday afternoon at the Israeli embassy, the staff of Almaya waited nervously to be called into action. Almaya's Doron Tashteet, Ami Bergman, and Kobi Friedman, working with Micha Feldman and his deputy, Avi

Mizrachi, as well as Amir Maimon, the second in command at the Israeli embassy, had planned out the whole operation as far as their end was concerned. They had devised a system to gather the entire Jewish community in Addis, perform identity and security checks, and then bus them to the airport outside of town. Their plan began with a call-up procedure similar to the networking that the Zionist underground had used in mobilizing fighters during the period of the Palestine Mandate and that the IDF still uses when circumstances preclude public announcements.[11] Almaya would deploy a Silent Signals networking committee of Beta Israel, who would go to the homes of every Jewish family. The leader of this committee was in charge of 5 neighborhood heads, each of whom directed 120 unit heads. Each unit head was responsible for contacting between 30 and 35 families, thereby alerting the almost 4,000 households registered in the Israelis' computer to come to the embassy. There the Jews would pass through four stations, where staff would check their plastic-coated ID cards, each of which carried the family head's name and picture on the front and a list of his or her dependents on the back. Finally, the JDC and Almaya workers would put the groups on buses to the planes. To prevent infiltration by non-Jews, the workers at the embassy would pass out tickets with three copies. The first would update the computer records, the second was for the bus, and the third would serve as a "boarding pass" for the plane.[12]

The Almaya staff were not certain how many people they would be rescuing, but they were sure that the community would get hungry and thirsty during the operation. So Bergman and Friedman had set aside stores of water and wood for cooking fires, as well as thirty-four thousand eggs and seven thousand frozen rolls. In a country virtually without gasoline, they had bought twenty thousand liters of it on the black market, a supply sufficient for the buses and small vehicles that they would employ, and for the generators that the IDF would run at the airport. Since the previous weekend, Bergman and Tashteet had worked on the physical setup at the embassy, including the foundation for fences to create pathways, and the wiring for lighting. On Tuesday, Bergman and Friedman had rented twenty buses, on the pretext that they wanted them for an outing for four thousand children. Since they did not know the date of the "outing" yet, they arranged to rent the vehicles from 8:00 a.m. to 4:00 p.m. every day. In order to take the buses out on a trial run, Bergman concocted the excuse that they were bringing the children to the zoo (which consisted of five elderly lions). They also added thousands of fresh oranges and potatoes to their stock of food.[13]

Now, late on Thursday afternoon, Bergman, Feldman, and Friedman waited anxiously at the embassy. They had been told that the operation would begin early on Friday, but they did not know whether they would be asked to start summoning the community immediately or in the morning. Lubrani, Eliezri,

Former president Jimmy Carter and his wife, Rosalyn (center), visiting Ethiopian leader Mengistu Haile Mariam (far right) in Addis Ababa. Bob Houdek, the U.S. chargé d'affaires in Addis, is at the far left (August 17, 1988). *Courtesy of Bob Houdek*

Susan Pollack visiting an Ethiopian Jewish mother in her room in Addis to check that the woman has taken her medicine for typhoid (1990).
*Courtesy of Susan Pollack*

Israeli ambassador Asher Naim (in jacket) with his wife (center) and teachers from the Israeli embassy school at a huge Hanukkah party on the embassy grounds (December 12, 1990). *Courtesy of Asher Naim*

President George H.W. Bush and Senator Rudy Boschwitz in the White House Oval Office, looking at photos taken during Boschwitz's mission to Ethiopia (May 6, 1991). *Courtesy of Senator Boschwitz*

Micha Feldman helping an elderly man at the Israeli embassy during Operation Solomon. *Courtesy of the Jewish Agency*

Buses leaving the embassy compound, bringing Jews to the airport during the operation. *Courtesy of the Jewish Agency*

New Ethiopian immigrants on an Israeli Air Force jet en route from Addis Ababa to Israel. *Photograph by Alpert Nathan, courtesy of the Government Press Office of Israel*

Brigadier-General Azriel Nevo, Prime Minister Yitzhak Shamir, Lieutenant-General Ehud Barak, and Reuven Merhav, director-general of the Israeli Foreign Ministry (left to right), at Ben-Gurion Airport, awaiting the first flight from Ethiopia during Operation Solomon. *Courtesy of Reuven Merhav*

Ground crews helping the first Operation Solomon immigrants off of the plane from Addis Ababa. *Photograph by Israeli Tsvika, courtesy of the Government Press Office of Israel*

Ethiopian immigrants disembarking from a Boeing jet after arriving from Addis Ababa.
*Photograph by Israeli Tsvika, courtesy of the Government Press Office of Israel*

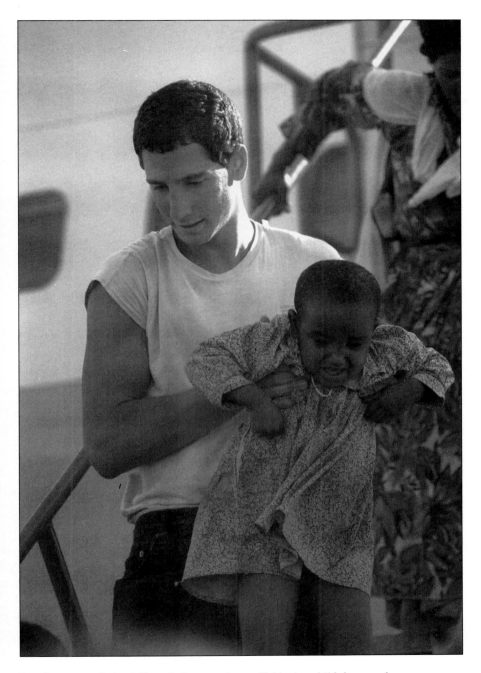

Israeli army medic in civilian clothes carrying an Ethiopian child down a plane ramp.
*Photograph by Israeli Tsvika, courtesy of the Government Press Office of Israel*

Line of Ethiopian immigrants streaming out of the belly of a Hercules C130 and walking toward buses that will take them to absorption centers. *Photograph by Israeli Tsvika, courtesy of the Government Press Office of Israel*

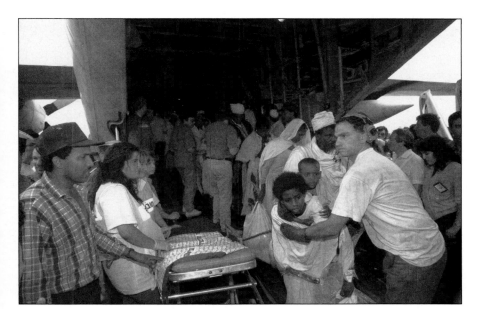

Part of air crew (R), in civilian clothes, helping immigrants out of the belly of a Hercules. *Photograph by Israeli Tsvika, courtesy of the Government Press Office of Israel*

Mother and two children arriving in Israel. *Photograph by Israeli Tsvika, courtesy of the Government Press Office of Israel*

New immigrants from Ethiopia just after arrival at Ben-Gurion Airport. *Photograph by Alpert Nathan, courtesy of the Government Press Office of Israel*

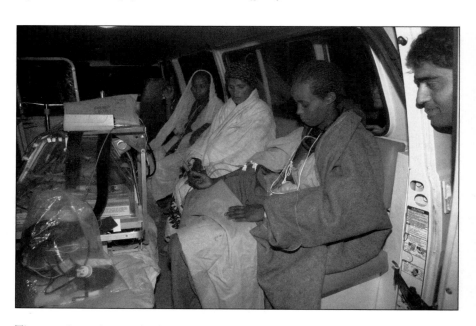

Three mothers who gave birth en route from Ethiopia, in a military ambulance taking them to the hospital. *Photograph by Israeli Tsvika, courtesy of the Government Press Office of Israel*

An Ethiopian-Israeli in Air Force uniform reunited with his mother at Ben-Gurion Airport.
*Photograph by Alpert Nathan, courtesy of the Government Press Office of Israel*

An Ethiopian-Israeli reunited with his sister, who tells him that their mother has died.
*Photograph by Richard Lobell, courtesy of Richard Lobell*

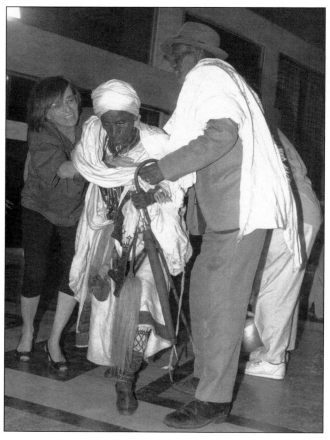

Smiling new immigrant at the Diplomat Hotel absorption center. *Photograph by Sa'ar Ya'acov, courtesy of the Government Press Office of Israel*

---

*Facing page, top*

An Ethiopian Jewish girl on her way to the Jewish Agency absorption center in Mikhmoret. *UJA Press Service Photo/Richard Lobell*

*Facing page, bottom*

Volunteer assisting an elderly Ethiopian immigrant at the Diplomat Hotel absorption center, Jerusalem. *Photograph by Sa'ar Ya'acov, courtesy of the Government Press Office of Israel*

Reuven Merhav and Uri Lubrani after the rescue.
*Courtesy of Reuven Merhav*

*To Bob Frasure.*
*Well Done! Best Wishes*
*Gg Bush*

President Bush presenting Bob Frasure with an award for exceptional service at a ceremony in the White House Rose Garden. Looking on are the other honorees: Boschwitz (second from left), U.S. Deputy Assistant Secretary of State Irvin Hicks, and Mary Houdek, who accepted an award for her husband, Bob (June 4, 1991). *Courtesy of Katharina Frasure*

Michael Schneider, Uri Lubrani, Eli Eliezri, and Gideon Taylor at a celebration honoring Operation Solomon. *Courtesy of Michael Schneider*

Dr. Rick Hodes praying with Jews who remained in Ethiopia after Operation Solomon (late 1991). *Photo by Robert Lyons, courtesy of the American Jewish Joint Distribution Committee*

and Naim had said that they would let them know by 5:30 p.m., but that deadline passed. The curfew, which was moved forward from midnight to 9:00 p.m. after Mengistu fled, was impending, so they decided to start at first light on Friday. Feldman recited a blessing in Amharic. Then Friedman told the networking committee that the airlift would begin the next day and instructed them to bring their families to the embassy at 6:00 a.m. He promised that their relatives would be the first to go to Israel, but the committee had to keep the operation secret through the night, and they had to commit to keep working until the mission was done.[14]

On Thursday evening at the embassy, Tashteet realized that no one had programmed the computer to keep track of how many people had passed through each stage of the operation. "If someone said, 'Stop,' we would need to know how many had left," he recalled. "It was a basic thing. No one had thought of it." He tried to adapt the program all Thursday night, he said. In the end, it did not work, an early omen of the massive disorder that would descend on them despite their plans.[15]

Tashteet went to sleep that night thinking about disaster. Still in his twenties, he had arrived in Addis in August and quickly had learned to cut through red tape to provide services for the Jews. He was, an observer on the scene said later, beloved by the entire Ethiopian Jewish community for his sensitivity to their needs and his respect and concern for them.[16] Now, on the night before the airlift, Tashteet was worried, and was certain that there would be no rescue at all on Friday. It would be too hazardous. What if someone threw a grenade into a crowd of Jews as they waited to get into the embassy, or fired on a bus carrying them to the airport? "Who could be sure that some rebel soldier, bored, or annoyed at the noise of the planes, wouldn't shoot one down for sport or spite?" he asked later. "Was it worth the risk? The security people knew about the risks. They had no way to prevent them. . . . It was playing with people's lives. . . . Why risk so many children in a military operation?"[17]

That Thursday at the AAEJ compound in Addis, LaDena Schnapper knew that something was up. Schnapper, a veteran AAEJ official, had taken over for Susan Pollack in Addis in October. A true representative of the AAEJ, she considered most of the Israelis at the embassy to be insensitive, chauvinistic brutes. Having learned Amharic during service in the Peace Corps in Ethiopia years before, she saw herself as a sympathetic listener whom the Jews could approach as a friend. "I was soon being called *Anatachin* ('our mother')," she wrote later in a memoir. That day, she and Berhanu Yiradu, the Ethiopian Christian who had run the transport program for Pollack, sensed the tension in the city and left the compound early. Schnapper decided to take a swim at the Hilton but was intercepted by an urgent invitation to meet Naim at the embassy at 5:30 p.m. "When I arrived, I was a bit overwhelmed to see a group of the most handsome, virile, and toughest-looking Israeli men I had ever seen," she wrote later. "They turned out to be a Mossad team brought in to support the operation. They exuded confidence."[18] Micha Feldman and Avi Mizrachi had realized that they would not have enough Jewish Agency workers to deal with the huge crowds that would come the next day. So, after a year of complaining that the AAEJ and NACOEJ were an unnecessary nuisance, Feldman now had to ask Schnapper and others from the American advocacy groups to help. Schnapper's job would be to check IDs and make sure that the Jews left their birr and luggage behind. The currency, she was told, would be useless in Israel, but could support further rescues of Jews left behind in Ethiopia. And the luggage would take up space on the planes that would be needed for people, and would be a security risk.

Schnapper left the embassy so excited that she stopped to tell some Ethiopian Jewish friends about the operation (thereby breaking the secrecy). She started on her way home shortly before the curfew and was stopped by two heavily armed policemen who wanted to take her in for questioning. With some flirtation and off-color jokes, and a 50-birr bribe, she convinced them to let her go. That night, she did not sleep.[19]

## "LET'S HAVE A GOOD DAY AND PRAY"

That Thursday evening in Jerusalem, Shamir gave Operation Solomon the OK at five o'clock, then again at eight o'clock. He would not give the final go-ahead until early Friday morning.[20]

In Tel Aviv, Hiam Halachmi summoned the veteran Ethiopian-Israelis to the Jewish Agency office. Every one of them reported within three hours, he recalled.[21] One who was not chosen was Rachamim Elezar, the director of the Amharic program on Kol Yisrael radio, who was determined to go anyway. Rachamim went by chance to the Jewish Agency office, he said later, where Halachmi told him that the operation was on for the next day and told him to stay behind and do radio reports. "Put me on the list" to go on the mission, Rachamim insisted. Halachmi pretended to, he said. Rachamim was an activist and believed that Halachmi resented him for criticizing Israeli policy on the aliyah and organizing demonstrations during operations in Sudan. The fact he that had worked on the AAEJ transport program in Addis also no doubt counted against him. But Rachamim was indefatigable. As a youngster in Ethiopia years before, he had made serial threats of suicide in order to force his family and officials to let him leave for Israel. Characteristically, he was not easily put off now, when he intended to return to help his relatives get out. A friend phoned that night to say that they had been called to the airport, so Rachamim went too.[22] He was not going to be stopped.

Yafet Alamu also was overlooked, and he was angry at the oversight. A veteran Ethiopian-Israeli and an activist, Yafet later would become the first Ethiopian rabbi in the history of Conservative Judaism. At this time in his life, however, he was a nurse. He therefore was assigned to work at one of the hotels in Jerusalem that had been converted into an absorption center, where his skills would be most useful. But Yafet, like Rachamim, believed that the real reason he had been passed over was his politics. He had agitated aggressively to have the Falash Mura, including his wife's family, brought over with all of the others. If he had been sent on the operation and the Falash Mura had been left behind, he would have started a fight on the tarmac at Addis Ababa, he told me.[23]

The first flight was scheduled to arrive in Addis at 10:00 a.m. the next day. The operation would continue through Friday night and into Saturday. That would desecrate the Shabbat (Sabbath), a profound offense to observant Jews, including the Beta Israel. But according to the principle of *pikuach nefesh* (preserving life), one may violate the Sabbath in order to save lives. Since the people who programmed the computers for Operation Solomon were Orthodox, an acceptable rabbi issued a *hechsher*, giving them permission to work during the Sabbath [24]

In New York that Thursday at noon, Michael Schneider held a conference call with a dozen American Jewish leaders who had been working toward this day. "Agreement has been reached," Schneider announced, "arrangements are being made. Rebel forces are coming from the northeast, and it's difficult to tell what complications will arise. This will contract into a very short time span."

The participants in the call feared that leaks might cause Operation Solomon to be aborted, as had happened with Operation Moses six years before. "Journalists are staking out the airport at Addis," Malcolm Hoenlein warned.

Marty Kraar added, "There is a great risk that the leak could come at the first plane that leaves, not the last plane."

Hoenlein recommended that they not spread the story beyond themselves. "Let's have a good day and pray," said Kraar.[25]

In London, representatives of the Ethiopian government and the rebels had gathered for informal talks prior to the Roundtable discussions. Boschwitz was there as well, at Frasure's request, and he met with the rebels to discuss the operation. The former senator was willing to return to Addis, but there would be no need for a second Boschwitz mission.[26]

Meanwhile, the Ethiopian rebels stood down outside of Addis. Frasure had sent them strong messages, telling them that the operation was about to start, that it was purely humanitarian, and that the West very much wanted it to succeed. He now asked them to hold off from attacking the capital for forty-eight to seventy-two hours, until the airlift was done. He also gave them the flight path that the planes would follow, warning them not to interfere.[27] "This was the touchiest part of Solomon," Frasure said later. The rebels' artillery was six miles away from the Addis Ababa airport, and they had patrols within two miles of the city. They could have stopped the operation, Frasure noted, but Meles cooperated.

"I'm not happy on this, but we discussed it in Khartoum," the EPRDF leader told Frasure. "I will order my forces to stand down."

"Do you trust this guy?" Scowcroft asked Frasure.

"Yes," Frasure replied.

"We had faith in his control—but we had no choice," Frasure said later. "We told Israel to go for it. They were waiting for this word."[28] If not for this American intervention, Operation Solomon might not have happened.

On Thursday night in Addis, Kassa feared for his life. Peter Jackson spoke to him on the phone and thought that Kassa sounded very concerned. Kassa even double-checked to make sure that it really was Jackson. "I need a flight. I cannot get a flight," the Ethiopian told him, adding, "The problem is not financial."[29] Kassa was drinking heavily, and by late that night was totally drunk.[30] He asked Lubrani to repeat his promise to protect him, which the Israeli did. Kassa "poured his heart out to Uri during those days," Eli Eliezri recalled later. The Ethiopian wanted to be out of the country by noon on Friday, but Eliezri insisted that he was still critical to the operation. He and Lubrani would look after Kassa until they got him out on Saturday, Eliezri told Schneider and Taylor. "We will take care of all of his apprehensions," Lubrani added.[31] They intended to keep Kassa with them, to reassure him, but also to make sure that he did not disappear. Then they would bring him to Israel before sending him to the United States.

Lubrani also arranged to look after Mersha, the man who once had discovered so many mistakes on the exit applications. Since his family had been taken to Israel, he had found far fewer errors. The government still required the forms, and Jewish Agency workers were urgently filling them out until 5:00 p.m. on Thursday. They certainly were making mistakes, but accuracy had ceased to be an issue.

Back in Jerusalem on Thursday night, Zvi Barak suspected that something was wrong. He had received a fax that day giving the number of the Ethiopian bank account into which to deposit the $35 million, Barak said in a series of interviews. But the route by which the fax had reached him aroused his suspicion. It had not come "via an official state of Israel channel," he recalled, "not from the Mossad, not the Foreign Ministry, not the Jewish Agency, not the Finance Ministry." Instead, "it came via a private company in Haifa." Surprised by this irregularity, Barak placed a call to Yair Seroussi, the chief fiscal officer of the Israeli Ministry of Finance, who was in New

York. He asked Seroussi to conduct an urgent check that the account number was in fact for the Ethiopian government account.[32] The question of the bank account number would threaten to end the operation almost before it began, as we shall see.

Also in Jerusalem that night, Reuven Merhav kept an open phone line with the embassy in Addis and pored over last-minute details, worrying about the unexpected. He had realized that the Egyptians and the Saudis would be seeing scores of aircraft on their radar screens the next day and would have to know their purpose. So Merhav had the U.S. convey the Israelis' intent to those Arab states. Then he took steps to make sure that the runway at the Addis airport would be clear for the Israeli planes. He instructed Naim's deputy, Amir Maimon, a former IDF lieutenant colonel whom he trusted, to check out the runway in the morning. Once Maimon gave him the go-ahead, Merhav would convey it to the IDF command post in Tel Aviv. At the same time Merhav would send a message thanking his colleagues in Addis and congratulating them on having the privilege to participate in this outstanding mission. "It is," he would say, "a realization of biblical prophecies and Zionist ideals on the ingathering of brethren from afar, on the wings of history."[33]

The Israelis were on the phone between Jerusalem and their headquarters in Addis Ababa (i.e., Naim's room at the Hilton) all that night. At 10:00 p.m. Lubrani told Shahak that a meeting with the Ethiopians to discuss the details of the operation had been postponed until the morning. This meant that the planes would have to leave Israel without official clearance to land.[34] Other problems, such as the fact that the 9:00 p.m. curfew could halt the rescue on Friday night, had not been solved yet either. But the Israelis were accustomed to improvising. They had been doing it all along, Merhav recalled, "on a daily-weekly-monthly basis," far more than even the Americans realized "then, and now."[35]

# THIRTEEN

# Operation Solomon

## 4:00 A.M.–3:00 P.M., FRIDAY, MAY 24, 1991

Through Thursday evening and into the early morning darkness of Friday, May 24, as Israelis and Americans waited sleeplessly in Addis Ababa, people across Israel set Operation Solomon in motion. In New York, Washington, and London, U.S. officials and American Jewish leaders monitored events keenly, attending to final details. Only a few people in the world knew that the single element on which everything else depended—the transfer of the $35 million—was not falling into place. Still, the mission went ahead.

### "THE PLANES ARE ON THE WAY"

At 4:00 a.m. on Friday, at an Israeli air force base adjacent to Ben-Gurion Airport, not far from Tel Aviv, the first planes were being readied to take off. Their flight plan called for them to traverse 1,560 miles, traveling southeast over the Red Sea, then cutting due south across Eritrea, and on to Addis Ababa. The air force estimated that they could complete the airlift in thirty-six hours if everything went according to plan.

Haim Halachmi's team of Ethiopian-Israelis had just been bused from Tel Aviv to the airbase. This was an intensely emotional day for most of them, since they had a double mission: to work on the rescue, but also to find relatives they had left behind years before, as children. Two hundred young Israeli elite soldiers stood around in civilian clothes, many in jeans and sneakers.[1] The Ethiopian officials did not want Israeli troops on the mission, so the soldiers were dressed as college students. As students often do, they wore backpacks—the contents of which were kept secret. "In their sacks were arms, in pieces, just in case," Halachmi recalled in an interview. Lieutenant General Ehud Barak, who had been promoted to chief of staff the month before, addressed them. "You are going to a military operation without any shooting," he told the soldiers. "Fire only if we are in danger."[2] If trouble did develop in Addis, a large ground force stood by in Israel, ready to enact Meir Dagan's most radical proposal: taking control of the capital.[3] Barak intended to monitor the mission very closely from Israel. Meanwhile, Amnon Lipkin-Shahak, the deputy chief of staff, also in jeans, would fly to Addis and take command on the scene.

The first plane lifted off at 4:41 a.m. A turboprop-driven Hercules C-130 Rhino, it was expected to take five to six hours to reach Addis.[4] The Boeing jets that followed would make the trip in three and a half hours or less.

At 4:00 a.m. in Addis Ababa, the phones rang in the rooms of the Americans who would be involved in the rescue. The Israeli caller said, "We need you to give blood," the code words telling them that the operation was under way.[5] In an hour the curfew would lift and it would be safe for them to go to the Israeli embassy.

At 5:40 that morning, Almaya's Kobi Friedman drove through the empty streets of Addis and came to the embassy. The others, from the Jewish Agency, Almaya and the JDC, the AAEJ, and NACOEJ, already had arrived. None of them had had much sleep the night before. Micha Feldman told the American volunteers that the planes would be bringing in Jewish Agency workers to relieve them. Till then, the Americans would have to man the first checkpoint, doing the initial identification checks, making sure that entire families had arrived together, and having them leave their luggage and money behind.[6]

The design for processing the Beta Israel sounded wonderfully organized and efficient. People would come in through the north entrance to the embassy compound, where the workers would check their ID cards and have them surrender their suitcases and birr. Families missing members would wait in an assembly area while the family head went to fetch the absent relatives. Once approved, the Jews would move up the hill, to the top of the embassy grounds, passing through a gate to a second station. There they would go through a more thorough ID check and receive two copies of their family boarding cards. The staff also would stick colored circular decals on the upper folds of their clothing, though they would realize later that it was easier to put them on people's foreheads. These stickers were numbered to correspond to the airplane flights. The goal was to organize the Jews into clusters of 190, assigning one batch to each Hercules Rhino. Three clusters would be designated for each Boeing 707, and five or six for each jumbo jet. Next, the Jews would go back down the hill, behind the embassy building, to a waiting area near the embassy's main exit. There the groups of 190 would wait in two holding areas. The trial excursion to the zoo the day before had shown that the people in each holding area would fill three buses. Finally, the Jews would board the buses, which would have backed into the embassy driveway. They would then wend their way to the airport, protected the whole way by Israeli air force security personnel and Ethiopian-Israeli soldiers. A reserve of three thousand people would be kept at the airport at all times, so planes could land, load, and take off without delay.[7] The plan had a reassuringly mathematical precision. But with the massive crowds that were about to descend on the embassy, the reality would nearly be a debacle.

At 7:00 a.m., Uri Lubrani padded around his room in the Addis Ababa Hilton, then looked outside and admired the weather. It was going to be a very nice day. He spoke to Michael Schneider in New York, where it was still midnight Thursday, and gave him the good news: "It's a go," he said, "the planes are on the way!" But they worried that the Jewish Agency was not ready to transfer the $35 million to the Ethiopians, which meant that this lovely morning could end in disaster for the mission.[8]

So Schneider wrote Simcha Dinitz a message, using Lubrani's name, urging him to have the money ready within two hours.[9] As it turned out, though, there was no way to get this message to Dinitz. After leaving New York, he had traveled to San Diego, and he had decided to return directly to Israel from there. That came as a total surprise to Schneider and Kraar in New York, and the result was chaos.[10] Dinitz had insisted that he had to be the one who would authorize the money transfer, but now, at the crucial moment, he was not available to do it. In fact, he had given Zvi Barak the responsibility for depositing the funds.[11] Nobody had told this to Schneider and Kraar, though. At 12:40 in the morning, New York time (9:40 p.m. in San Diego), Schneider tried urgently to reach Dinitz to convey "Lubrani's" request to make the deposit, but found that he was en route and inaccessible. "Typical!" Schneider said at the time. "It is critical that he be in phone contact for banking, but he prefers to be in Israel for the airport. For eight hours he will be out of contact!"[12]

"The whole operation nearly failed because Simcha was unavailable," Kraar remarked to Schneider later.[13]

"It was a problem of the relationship between Lubrani and Barak," Dinitz said later. "I didn't know that they were looking for me. They could do it all through Barak."[14]

## "WE WERE AFRAID TO OPEN THE GATES AND BE CRUSHED"

At the Israeli embassy in Addis, the Silent Signals networking committee members' families had been arriving since 6:00 a.m., and they were the first to go through the registration process. The system worked. The first sixty families passed through the sequence of ID checks, then went to wait in the cool breeze for the buses to arrive. Meanwhile, the committee gathered next to the embassy building to hear their charge: they were to rouse their fellow Jews, telling each family to come to the embassy, bringing only their ID cards and their medical records. Lubrani and the other key Israeli officials, who had set up a local headquarters in Naim's room at the Hilton, gave the green light. The call-up of the Beta Israel could begin. So at 7:30 a.m., the networking committee wove through the neighborhoods of Addis Ababa to summon their community to Zion.[15] They passed through "streets that had no names, with houses that were unknown to everyone except their inhabitants," observed Bergman, who had helped design the network.[16]

Then came a near disaster. At 7:50 a.m., Bergman and Friedman went to the bus depot to have the twenty buses sent over. They had planned the bus rental well in advance, but this morning the manager did not show up, potentially sabotaging the entire operation. He finally strolled in at 8:45 and agreed to extend the rental till 7:00 that evening. The Israelis knew that they would need the buses clear through the night but did not mention it for fear of giving away their plans. The manager then insisted that they stay for a receipt, which they did not have time to do. The first planes were due to land in little more than an hour! But, in a culture that requires politeness, they did not want to risk undermining the mission by offending the manager and losing the buses now. So Friedman waited for the receipt while Bergman went back with the vehicles.[17]

By the time the buses got to the embassy, shortly after 9:00 a.m., thousands of people were milling about in the street and inside the compound. Families who had been called up by the committee had arrived, as had local Christians who wanted to escape with them, or just to watch. Fathers in tattered suits stood outside the embassy wall with sons on their shoulders. Some held barefoot children by the hand while somehow carrying luggage as well. Mothers in colorfully embroidered robes, with scarves on their heads, had small children strapped on their backs in traditional fashion. At the same time, they held on to bigger children and managed to carry a basket of food or a cooking pan. There was a lot of shoving as a growing rush of people tried to force their way into the compound. Doron Tashteet and the veteran Ethiopian-Israeli Zimna Berhane, guarding the gate at the entry, were nearly overwhelmed by the crowd. Inside, there was terrible pressure at the checkpoint where the NACOEJ people checked IDs. LaDena Schnapper stood alone, taking suitcases and arguing in Amharic with those who refused to give theirs up.[18] It was still early morning, and perhaps ten thousand excited people were standing inside the embassy courtyard, waiting anxiously to be registered.[19]

In Jerusalem that Friday morning, Zvi Barak met with his legal adviser and his deputy in his office at the Jewish Agency to decide whether to pay the $35 million to the Ethiopian government. A forceful, intensely dedicated man, a former Israeli air force jet pilot, Barak insisted that everything be aboveboard before he transferred the money. But, he told me later, he had serious suspicions that something was wrong. "I was not sure if the Thursday night account was a government account," he said, referring to the bank account number that had been faxed to him the night before. He told his colleagues that the fax had come not from an official source but through an irregular route. They decided that the information "was not enough for me to pay," Barak recalled.[20]

## "IT ALL STARTED TOO QUICKLY"

This financial hang-up in itself threatened to end the operation. On top of that, just as the crowd was starting to gather at the Israeli embassy, the air mission nearly failed. At 8:00 a.m., the first Hercules C-130 flew over Eritrea. The pilot called ahead to the control tower at Addis Ababa, requesting permission to land. An air traffic controller, caught by surprise, demanded that the pilot disclose the purpose of the flight. The Americans had passed the Israelis' flight path on to the rebels, the Saudis, and the Egyptians, but the Ethiopian leaders, who had approved the operation less than twenty-four hours earlier, had not yet informed their own civil air authorities. "It all started too quickly," Naim said later.[21] Now the Israeli pilot was in a fix. If he revealed his mission, he would destroy the operation's secrecy. If he said nothing, he might be shot down. Brigadier General Amir Nachumi, the chief of IAF operations, sitting beside him in the cockpit, suggested saying that they were on a cargo mission.[22] The Ethiopian controller did not relent, so the pilot called the air force in Israel, who passed the problem on to Eli Eliezri in Addis. At the time, Eliezri was with Lubrani in Kassa's office, and he asked Kassa, "What should we do?" The normally stately Ethiopian, who had been drinking heavily the night before and was watching his world fall apart, suggested an off-color remark for the pilot to make. Eliezri had a more politic idea. He told Kassa to call Ethiopian Airlines and have them instruct the control tower to ask no questions. The Hercules was permitted to fly on.[23]

That morning in Addis, at a coordination meeting in Colonel Mersha's office in the Internal Affairs ministry, the Israelis announced that four Israeli aircraft were approaching: two Hercules C-130 Rhinos with equipment for setting up a command post and two Boeing 707s carrying three hundred people who would manage the departures. Mersha expressed amazement and asked whether all of the people onboard had visas. Micha Feldman replied that they did not even have passports with them, but assured him that no one would remain illegally after the airlift. Mersha then insisted on a passenger list before each takeoff, an impossible demand. Feldman agreed to provide the lists, knowing that they might have to be fictional, and at 9:45 a.m. the Ethiopians gave formal permission for the planes to land.[24] Lubrani said later that Mersha's bureaucratic pettiness in this meeting was in part an attempt to stall the operation until the $35 million had been deposited.[25]

At 10:00 a.m., two IAF Hercules transports set down at Bole Airport, on the runway at the northeast corner, which had been set aside for the mission. Hundreds of Ethiopian army soldiers surrounded one of them, watching curiously.[26] Ten minutes later, two 707s landed. On board the four craft were Generals Shahak and Nachumi and the Israeli soldiers, along with Haim Halachmi, Haim Divon, and other Foreign Ministry officials. With them were dozens of Jewish Agency staff, as well as Dr. David Raveh, who would be the doctor on duty at the embassy.[27] Amir Maimon, the chief of operations at the embassy, found Shahak and told him that between eight hundred and a thousand Jews already had been processed, more than enough to fill the first two planes. Shahak gave his OK to bring them to the airport. The plan called for the first plane to start loading at 11:00 a.m.[28]

## "WHERE IS THE MONEY?"

But the buses did not move, and four Israeli aircraft circling overhead were not permitted to set down. Instead, Operation Solomon was nearly aborted yet again that morning, causing alarm at headquarters in Israel.[29] Only a few minutes had passed since Mersha had given permission for the first planes to land, but now, in the antechamber to the acting president's office, a very nervous Kassa informed Lubrani that the entire mission had to stop. The Ethiopians were demanding the money in advance and, Lubrani said later, he had no intention of giving it to them. "I know my clients," he commented.[30]

There were three principal actors in the scene that transpired next: Lubrani, Kassa, and the newly appointed Ethiopian minister of finance. Each gave a different version of this episode, and these discrepancies obscure the question of who authorized the halt in the operation and under what circumstances it was allowed to resume. The incident that follows was perhaps little more than a comedy of errors played out in a setting of intense stress. But it takes on added significance because key Israelis soon concluded that someone was attempting to steal the $35 million. This episode may therefore have been part of an individual's attempt to get the money in the last hours or days before the regime fell.

According to Lubrani, Kassa came to him and announced that the operation would have to halt, saying that Tesfaye Dinka, the prime minister, had asked, "Where is the money?"

Lubrani offered the quick riposte, "Did you tell me who to give it to?"

Kassa said, "Oh, I forgot!" and slapped his forehead. "We didn't think about that!" Kassa then went off to find the Ethiopian government's bank account number in New York, into which the Jewish Agency could transfer the $35 million.

Returning with a sullen face, Kassa told Lubrani that the person or persons able to produce the account number had fled with Mengistu, and that the governor of the Ethiopian central bank also was out of the country, at a conference in Zaire. As a result, there was nobody to tell Kassa the bank account number.

Determined to have official permission for the rescue, as Shamir had required, Lubrani then urged Kassa to ask the finance minister to come over and help. While they waited, Lubrani reminded Kassa ominously, "If there is no operation, we have no arrangement."

In Lubrani's account of this episode, he knew the finance minister from more than twenty years earlier, during his time as ambassador, and when he arrived, they embraced. The minister had been in office for only two days, however, and he did not know the government bank account number either. Lubrani recalled saying to him, "Can you conceive that I represent a people and a government that will deceive you on a miserable $35 million?"

The minister replied, "I believe you."

Lubrani then asked him to lie about the deposit. "I told him to call the prime minister and tell him that the money was [already transferred]. We will give our word of honor that we will put it in [the bank account later]," said Lubrani.[31]

"What?" asked the minister, blanching at the thought of misleading his prime minister.

"This you are going to do, and you're going to be redeemed, because you know that our God and your God are the same," Lubrani exhorted.[32] "He did it," Lubrani said, "he called Dinka." They had lost an hour, but the mission was allowed to proceed.

"Then Kassa gave the account number later," Lubrani added.[33] The problem was that the number turned out to be wrong! In Lubrani's recollection of events, the finance minister then reappeared at a late stage in the operation, beseeching the Israelis for help in getting the right bank account number.[34]

This delightful scene contains several elements that are out of character, even antic. Kassa was a canny professional who had negotiated tenaciously since March to get the money. It would be ironic, to say the least, if he simply forgot to think about how it would be transferred. In fact, Kassa had said the night before that he would provide the number, according to a reliable Israeli source who asked not to be named. Granted, providing the government's bank account number could have been the responsibility of the previous finance minister, who had just been replaced in a cabinet shuffle. But getting the number was not difficult, as will soon become evident. Another surprising aspect of Lubrani's story is the finance minister's willingness to lie to his prime minister, based solely on his faith in Israel and Lubrani.

Kassa gave a different account of this episode, saying that it was not he but the new finance minister who supplied the bank account number. He declared, moreover, that the minister deliberately provided the false number in order to halt the operation and the financial transfer, fearing that the money would end up in the hands of the rebels if they came to power.[35]

Kassa's story contradicts Lubrani's, in which the finance minister, far from trying to stop the emigration, allowed it to proceed even before the Israelis had transferred the money. It is also totally incongruous with Lubrani's report that the minister later returned to ask for help in getting the right account number. Significantly, in Kassa's version of events, the error in the bank account number was no mere clerical mistake. Rather, the minister deliberately gave a wrong number for personal reasons. But Eli Eliezri, who was present during Lubrani's conversation with Kassa, recalled emphatically that "Kassa, not the finance minister, gave us a wrong account number." He thus corroborated Lubrani's story, as does Asher Naim.[36] Whether the error in the bank account number was an honest clerical blunder or a deliberate attempt to have the Israelis deposit the money in the wrong account is a question that we shall consider in Chapter 14.

Kassa's claim to be unable to get the bank account number also merits scrutiny. Kassa's predicament, as Lubrani reported it, was that the officials who could have provided the number were gone: they had absconded with Mengistu or were otherwise out of the country. But none of the people in authority at the Ethiopian central bank had fled, according to a source who was a very high-ranking Ethiopian official at that time; this source added that they certainly had not gone into exile with Mengistu, who had taken no one from the government along. Paul Henze confirms that Mengistu abandoned his officials and that only his family went into exile with him. Bob Houdek, too, corroborated this in a series of interviews: when Mengistu set out for Zimbabwe, he brought only military officers with him, and he left them behind in Nairobi.[37] Kassa's story, then, at least as Lubrani recounted it, appears to be problematic.

The finance minister, Bekele Tamrat, later denied some of Lubrani's and Kassa's most important claims. In Bekele's account, he did not misinform his prime minister, and he did not give the Israelis any bank account number, no less a false one.[38] Lubrani assured him that the money would certainly come, but said that they could not get the right account number. Bekele, who had been the governor of the Ethiopian central bank until two days earlier, responded that the central bank would readily provide it. As Bekele recalled the event, he then phoned the acting bank governor. Far from being away at a conference, the governor was at his post. He told Bekele that he already had given the number to Kassa and was willing to give it again.

Bekele said that Mersha had told him that the mission would not proceed until he verified that the deposit had been made. Shortly after his meeting with Kassa and Lubrani that morning, Bekele told me, the acting bank governor gave him the word that the money had in fact been placed in the government's account in New York. Bekele duly notified Mersha and the rescue mission resumed.[39] There is a serious problem in this chronology of events, though: as these conversations took place, it was still the middle of the night in New York and the banks were closed; the funds were not transferred until ten hours later. The mission, by contrast, was allowed to recommence within one hour. This means that either Bekele's version of the episode is wrong or some-one was deceived that morning about the deposit having been made in New York.[40] In any case, his story bears out Lubrani's: the finance minister did give his authorization, and the mission resumed before the payment went through.

Asher Naim added a very curious detail to this episode. That Friday after-noon at 3:00 in Addis, Naim wrote later, Lubrani "completed the deal: a bank check was handed over to Kabede, who scurried to check the account number before the New York banks closed for the weekend."[41] This story is peculiar. Lubrani did not have a $35 million bank check in his pocket, and if he had, he would not have put it in Kassa's hands.

Although they overlap in some respects, these narratives are so elaborately contradictory as to suggest that at least one of them was designed to cover what actually happened that morning. In view of Zvi Barak's report that the account number already had been faxed to him the night before, the entire interaction was mysterious. The mystery would soon deepen, as we shall see. The general outline of events is well documented, however. Several witnesses attest that Kassa asked for immediate payment, that the finance minister was brought in, and that the mission went ahead before Israel paid the $35 million.

That was lucky for Lubrani, who could not have transferred the money at that point even if he had wanted to. Barak was in charge of that, and he had not verified the account number yet, or found a source for the other $17.5 million. In any case, it was 4:00 a.m. in New York and the banks were closed.

One thing that Lubrani had not left to luck was the loyalty of Kassa and Mersha, both of whom were deeply invested in having the airlift succeed. Lubrani had guaranteed their lives, and they expected to be safely in Israel the next day. Both already had family members there, and, as key officials attest, Kassa had a big financial incentive as well. Kassa and Mersha were not about to let the mission fail. So the immediate crisis was resolved, and Operation Solomon went ahead, with no transfer of funds.

## "IN TWENTY-FOUR DAYS WE WILL NOT FINISH"

By the time the operation was allowed to resume, the situation at the em-bassy had almost gotten out of hand. The huge crowd had become a mob. There was disorder and crying, and people shouted, "Take us with you!"[42] Zimna said later that it reminded him of Saigon in the days before that city fell to the Communists.[43] Families arriving late were being pulled apart, with some of them unable to pass through the human flood outside. The Jewish Agency support team had not arrived. "Where is everybody?" Tashteet yelled. "There's no one here." "We were afraid to open the gates and be crushed," he recalled later.[44]

Eight buses were full and ready to go, the children peering through the windows, the numbers 1, 2, and 3 stuck on their foreheads. But there were strict orders that they should not leave the compound until Israeli security escorts arrived. Even if they had tried, they would have had a hard time passing through the congested streets. Some of the Israelis at the embassy now began to fear that the mission would fail.[45]

At the Addis Ababa airport, General Shahak's team had set up a command post with tents, equipment, and communications. On that day, the Israel Defense Forces essentially took control of the airport, except for the tower, which the Ethiopian air traffic controllers refused to surrender. So the IDF directed the air traffic from a tent. In a notoriously bureaucratic country, Israelis now arrived and departed at will.[46]

About 11:30 a.m., the Israelis bused reinforcements from the airport to the embassy, including the newly arrived Jewish Agency workers. A second bus brought Foreign Ministry staff, as well as security people and soldiers, many of whom were Ethiopian-Israelis. The Amharic-speakers talked to people while the others saw to their safety. They soon began to restore order inside the compound, and the processing started to flow more smoothly.[47]

Feldman told the support workers that, by agreement with the rebels, they had twenty-four hours in which to complete the rescue. Addisu Massele, a veteran Ethiopian-Israeli activist who had been on one of the planes that were made to circle above Addis, had just arrived. He looked at the thousands of people inside the embassy. "I said to myself, 'In twenty-four days we will not finish,'" he recalled. From that point on, he said, "we never drink, sleep, eat. Everyone has a role to do."[48]

Meanwhile, Rick Hodes, who had been rounding up Beta Israel patients from area hospitals, wandered through the compound, checking for people suffering from fever or dehydration. Rumors reached him that someone had died outside the north entrance. "I shoved my way out the gate into the overwhelming mass of humanity," he wrote later. "People were getting crushed by the crowd, passing out from dehydration, and old people and infants were weakening in the sun. . . . Pushing my way into the crowd, it took me fifteen minutes to go thirty yards, shouting '*Beshitegna yet new?*' [Where is the patient?] the entire time." The patient turned out to be an eighty-year-old woman who had fainted from dehydration. Hodes led her down the road, sat her down, and gave her some water. He knew many people in the throng, and tried to explain that there was no need to push. Everyone would get to Israel, he assured them. His words had no effect.[49]

At around noon, also outside the embassy gate, a Beta Israel woman gave birth. Ami Bergman heard about it and brought the mother and child inside. "The kid wasn't registered!" Bergman joked later.[50]

Then, at 12:50 p.m., there was another bureaucratic snag. Mersha demanded the lists with the names of everyone who got on a plane, which Feldman had promised to supply. That was absurd, Maimon told Mersha. The computer program had failed and could not provide this information. In fact, as the day wore on, Israelis manning the computer in the embassy basement could not even tell how many of the Jews had left at any given point. They would have to estimate, based on the number of buses that had gone to the airport. After negotiation, the Israelis offered to give Mersha the "boarding pass" copy from each three-part card. He agreed, and the mission resumed. But they had lost time because of "Mersha's nonsense," Maimon said later.[51]

Mersha then gave permission for the first Jews to leave for the airport. Armed security men boarded the eight loaded yellow and red buses, which very slowly pulled away from the embassy grounds. Israeli security guards battled the crowd outside, to open the roads so the buses could inch past. They pushed people back from the streets, including pregnant women and the elderly, in an effort that would continue well into the night.[52] The Jews inside the buses watched through the windows, their faces marked by tranquility and wonder. Some of them waved and called out to people they knew as their buses slowly passed through the multitude that lined the roads.

## "THEY MADE A TRILLING SOUND"

The buses passed through the back streets of Addis Ababa, then reached the airport at last. As the Jews got off, despite the magnitude of the event, they were silent, betraying no emotion. "They weren't panicked," Feldman recalled. "Ethiopians do not show emotion anyhow. They are not allowed to do so by their culture. But seeing the planes at the airport, they sat calmly and waited for their turn."[53] That was one of the main reasons that the operation succeeded, one of the Israelis recalled later: the Falashas were so quiet and cooperative. Even the children did not cry.[54]

One of those waiting on the tarmac to help them was Rachamim Elezar, the Ethiopian-Israeli director of the Amharic radio program in Israel. Halachmi had told him early that morning in Israel to stay behind to be in charge of assigning one or two other Ethiopian-Israelis to each plane. Rachamim did, briefly. Then he got impatient and boarded the third plane that went out.

On reaching the Addis airport, Rachamim was overtaken by the significance of what he was about to take part in. "You are there to save people, rescue human beings," he told me later. The airport "was full of Israelis, young boys. So full of planes. Everything was upside down. Like an astronaut, I was as if floating." They began to load a plane. "There are trees at the end of the airport," Rachamim said. "The Jews were told to lie down there. Suddenly they stood up." Four young Israeli soldiers had them move through a roped-off pathway toward the plane. As they walked, Rachamim watched his people pass before him, and saw how they had suffered. "They were weak, using walking sticks," he recalled. "Mothers were holding babies on their backs and with both hands."[55]

At 1:30 p.m., the first plane, an unmarked Israeli air force Boeing 707, painted in camouflage colors, took off for Israel with nearly four hundred people on board.[56]

Rachamim took responsibility for loading one aircraft, then got on himself. "There were no seats," he recalled. The Jews sat in rows along the walls from the back to the front. "People were pushed in," he said. "They were quiet, calm, happy, anxious," though they did not express it. When the plane took off, "I told the kids, there is no bathroom. In three and one-half hours of flight, nobody opened their mouths. . . . The pilot says, tell them they're flying to the Holy City, Jerusalem." Rachamim translated this into Amharic for them. "They made a trilling sound," expressing their joy, he said.[57]

## "YOU HAD TO FIGHT TO SURVIVE"

Back at the embassy, a deep anxiety was overtaking the workers. By afternoon, there were over twenty thousand people at the embassy gate, most of them local Christians. The Israelis had expected three or four thousand Falash Mura to try to get in, but nothing like this.[58] Waves of people kept pressing to enter the compound, as children and elders suffered in the heat. Hundreds of non-Jews tried to scale the embassy fences but were pushed back. "We were very, very close to disaster," one of the Israelis told me later. "I thought, a lot of people will be crushed and die . . . children will die."[59] A few dozen more Israelis were shifted from the airport to the embassy to help, but the pressure at the entrance continued. The street flooded with people, and the buses had difficulty moving. Security men set up fences along the access roads to prevent accidents as the buses passed, but that did not help. Nothing did.[60]

Lubrani went to the embassy several times that day to meet reporters. "I saw the mob at the embassy and prayed," he said later.[61]

Almaya's Doron Tashteet stood at the embassy gate, saw what looked to him like fifty thousand people pushing and shoving, and concluded that the operation had failed. Zimna, who was with him, had registered the Jews when they had arrived in Addis, and he knew most of them. At times he would see children torn from their families by the rush of humanity, and would pull them into the embassy. Tashteet was strong and stocky like an American football player, but he had not had anything to drink all day, and by 2:00 p.m. he nearly fainted. He took a fifteen-minute break to get a drink, leaving Zimna to guard the entrance alone. When he returned, he found Zimna using his body to prevent the crowds from entering. He also saw a mass of Christians blocking the Jews from reaching the gate. He called for help from several Ethiopian Jews, and they beat the non-Jews with sticks. "God should forgive me," Tashteet said later. He had been a manager at Angel's Bakery in Jerusalem before this, and his job during the mission was supposed to be preparing food and locating stragglers. Instead, this man, whom the Ethiopian Jews esteemed for his sensitivity, found himself using force to stop a tidal wave of people.

The chaos was slowing the whole operation. Maimon yelled that planes were sitting empty at the airport and demanded to know why. Tashteet grabbed a bullhorn and warned the Christians, "If you come in, we will take you to the police!" For another two hours, Tashteet continued to push people back from the entrance. Meanwhile, in the confusion, Christians stole ID cards from Jews, police took their money, and locals in the crowd picked their pockets. Others offered to sell the Jews colas in the heat of the day for 50 birr (nearly $25).[62]

Addisu Massele came to help check IDs at the embassy entrance. "Everyone was pushing and shoving, even climbing on top of the others," he said. Then he saw a ninety-year-old uncle whom he had not seen in fifteen years. The old man didn't recognize him, so Addisu kissed him and told him in his ear that he was the son of his sister. "He hugged me and called out, 'Praise God!'" Addisu recalled.[63]

Inside the embassy, another nephew had a much more disquieting experience. Avi Beita, another Ethiopian-Israeli activist, was assigned to check ID cards against the "bible" of approved names. Suddenly, to his surprise, his aunt Sagedu Dinku appeared before him. Sagedu was not on the list. The Jewish Agency considered her a Falash Mura, perhaps because she had married a man who had studied at a Christian missionary school, Avi said later. Nine of Sagedu's thirteen children had made aliyah since 1984, but she and the four others had been left behind. "She begged me, and we both cried," Avi recalled, "but there was nothing I could do. It was the first time I had seen her in thirteen years; she recognized me, grabbed me, and pleaded with me to let her on the plane. I told her I couldn't, and we both cried. I told her to have patience, and then ran from her."[64]

Meanwhile, the pressure at the checkpoint gates was becoming dangerous. "I physically held people back," said LaDena Schnapper. "I called for help. Avi Mizrachi and Micha Feldman would come and scream and push."[65] Throughout the day, Feldman darted through the crowd, making decisions on questionable cases, his face and clothes dirty and his shirttails outside his pants.[66] Though the buses gradually were filling and moving out, thousands of people continued to pack the embassy grounds.

# FOURTEEN

# Operation Solomon, Continued

## 3:00 P.M., FRIDAY, MAY 24–3:00 P.M., SATURDAY, MAY 25, 1991

### "THE NUMBER *WAS* RIGHT"

At 3:00 on the afternoon of Friday, May 24, it became apparent to some of the Israelis that something shady had almost happened with the $35 million payment. Zvi Barak called Naim in Addis Ababa with bad news for him to pass on to Lubrani: Barak's source in New York had discovered that the account number that had been faxed to him was wrong.[1] That account was configured to receive bonds or securities, not cash, a fact that Lubrani later cited as the reason that the $35 million could not be placed into it.[2] Tad Szulc also says that the Israelis could not authorize the transfer because they were "erroneously given the number of the bonds account instead of the cash account."[3] But that was not the obstacle, Barak remarked in an interview. If it had been, the Jewish Agency could simply have deposited $35 million in bonds or securities. The real problem was that the number was not for an official government account at all.[4] Rather, it was for a private individual account, as half a dozen highly placed Israeli and American sources later confirmed. It is improbable that the Ethiopian central bank made a clerical mistake in providing the number.[5] Rather, some key Israeli informants believe that somebody was trying to steal the $35 million.

The account number revealed the bearer's name, Barak told me. In view of the legal implications, however, he refused to disclose the name—though he did say that it was Ethiopian. "It can be published in ten years," he said.[6]

Since Kassa had supplied the bank account number earlier that day, suspicion fell on him. A senior Israeli official who played a principal role in Operation Solomon told me with certainty that Kassa was the one trying to take the $35 million. Why didn't Kassa have the right account number? I asked him. "The number *was* right," he replied, but "it wasn't the government account number! I'm sure that Kassa wanted the money for himself. . . . Kassa tried to get it in his pocket. He couldn't. We were smarter." A former top officer in the Mengistu government, one of Kassa's colleagues at the time, said of the financial dealings, "Kassa was playing many games."

Other informed sources differ, however, about whether Kassa was aware of a deception, and about the intended recipient of the diverted funds. Simcha Dinitz, the chairman of the Jewish Agency at the time of the airlift, told an interviewer in 1995 that the $35 million was obviously intended for the former

Ethiopian president; two years later he told me specifically that the account "was apparently the personal account of Mengistu."[7] If Kassa was involved, this would be consistent with a report in the *Times* of London that he supervised Mengistu's bank accounts.[8] Paul Henze also raises the possibility that the money was to go to Mengistu, or to Kassa.[9] Barak said that neither Mengistu's nor Kassa's name was on the account, but noted that it may have borne a name that was merely a front.[10]

If someone was aiming to dupe the Jewish Agency into transferring the $35 million into his personal bank account, though, why would he supply a number for an account that would not accept cash? The mystery is compounded by Barak's report that he had received the number the night before. The true story of who was behind the erroneous bank account number therefore remains to be told. Rudy Boschwitz had predicted that the "generous financial gesture" would end up in private pockets, and Barak believed that he had acted in time to prevent that. Not everyone was so sure, though, as we shall see.

When Lubrani told Kassa that the number was not right, Kassa exclaimed, jokingly, "It's not? Israeli intelligence knows everything!"[11] According to Lubrani, the hapless finance minister then reappeared very late in the operation, asking, "What do we do? We have no bank account number." The minister's face soon brightened, Lubrani recalled, and he importuned the Israeli, "You have such good intelligence. Can't you ask your intelligence [agents] in New York . . . to find out our bank account number?"[12] Lubrani later recalled that he suggested that Israeli officials (perhaps through Zvi Barak) contact the World Bank in Washington, D.C., to get the Ethiopian account number. The correct account number came back quickly from New York, Lubrani said.[13] He conveyed it to the finance minister, who asked him if he was certain about it. "He was thinking maybe it was my own number!" Lubrani joked later.[14]

That does not appear to be the way that the Israelis in Addis got the account number that they passed on to the Jewish Agency, however.[15] All of the other principals agree that it was actually the American chargé d'affaires, Bob Houdek, who found it. Out of desperation, the Israelis asked Houdek for help at about 3:00 p.m. on Friday. They told him that Kassa was unable to produce a valid number—an idea that struck Houdek as hilarious, given Kassa's single-minded attempts to negotiate the amount for so long. So Houdek called Wolie Chekol, the former Ethiopian deputy prime minister (whose responsibilities had included the central bank), and got the correct number. He then gave it to Naim, who phoned Barak in Israel early that evening to pass it on.[16]

Almost incredibly, when Naim called Barak's home with the account number, Barak was at the airport welcoming planes from Ethiopia, so his young daughter took the message. Following her father's instructions, she called the Jewish Agency in New York and repeated the number. The future of thousands of Ethiopian Jews and the fate of this epic operation depended at that moment on the note-taking skills of a thirteen-year-old girl.[17]

## "SINGING, AND CLAPPING, AND PURE JOY"

Operation Solomon went ahead despite these curious financial dealings. At 4:45 p.m., the first plane to leave Addis landed at Ben-Gurion, to the delight of the officials and the crowd who awaited it. Prime Minister Shamir was there to greet the new arrivals, as were Moshe Arens, David Levy, Ariel Sharon, and Ehud Barak. Arens, now the defense minister, had helped launch the aliyah, as noted above. Levy, who had succeeded him as foreign minister, had shown little interest in the Ethiopian Jews until recently. Barak and Sharon were about to intercede in an unexpected way.

The Ethiopian Jews, many in Western garb, others wearing traditional white *shammas* (togalike garments), emerged from the plane and descended the ramp shakily. Several, especially the children, still had the numbered round decals stuck on their foreheads. They seemed stunned as they looked into the forest of microphones and cameras, and the smiling, nearly hysterical crowd.[18] "They were very, very tired and bewildered, and facing the totally unknown," said the Jewish Agency's David Harman, who participated in the operation.[19]

In contrast to the new arrivals' quiet, the Israelis jostled and chattered noisily on cell phones and walkie-talkies. Hundreds of excited Jewish Agency workers, IDF personnel, dignitaries, and airport employees welcomed them with spontaneous, joyous applause. Shamir declared, "They are the remnants of a Jewish community that lasted for thousands of years, who are now coming back to their country. . . . They have come back to their homeland." Ehud Barak greeted the Ethiopians warmly, then briefed Shamir. "In half an hour, another plane will land," he whispered. For symbolic purposes, the Ethiopian government had insisted that this second flight be an Ethiopian Airlines plane. "Then 2,000 [Ethiopian Jews] are coming, then another 5,000," Barak told the prime minister. The curfew could suspend the mission, the general warned. But if it did not, planes would arrive every half hour all through the night. "Is it possible to finish by morning?" Shamir asked. "It's possible, but mistakes can happen," Barak replied.[20]

The Israeli air force chief, General Avihu Bin-Nun, told a reporter at the airbase that it was important to keep total press silence on the rescue. Censorship remained in effect in Israel until the operation was completed. But the BBC World Service broke the story prematurely, and broadcast it every hour.

That infuriated Tesfaye Dinka, and once again, the Ethiopians almost halted the mission.[21]

Through the day, as the new arrivals descended the ramps from the planes, each child was given an orange. Then Jewish Agency workers and Youth Aliyah volunteers virtually pushed the Ethiopians into overpacked buses, each of which had an Amharic-speaking guide onboard. The new *olim* were taken to one of three refreshment stands that the IDF had specially created, where they were shown to toilet facilities and were presented with sweets, biscuits, and coffee. Finally, they were brought to the absorption centers, which would be their homes for some time to come.

As the planes continued to land at Ben-Gurion Airport and at the adjacent military airbase, elation and wonder swept through the waiting Israelis. "It's like watching a scene from the Bible," said an IDF spokesman. Former Knesset Speaker Shlomo Hillel said, "Today is one of the biggest days for the Jews of the world and for Israel. It is what Israel is all about. We won't abandon Jews." The controversial member of Knesset Geula Cohen said that the aliyah was miraculous, a sign that the age of redemption is upon us.[22] (Soon after Operation Solomon, an ad in the *Jerusalem Post* claimed that three things presaged the immediate arrival of the Messiah: the fall of the Iron Curtain, the defeat of Iraq, and the airlift of the Ethiopian Jews. This ad was reproduced in the Israeli and American press.)[23] Natan Sharansky, the former Soviet dissident and "Prisoner of Zion," had a more modest impression. He went along on one of the flights and gave water to the Ethiopians on board. When asked later if they had recognized him, Sharansky replied, "They recognized me as one of the people who handed out bottles of water— one of the crew." One reporter, occasionally crying, said that he had never seen such warmth and fraternity among the Sabras ("native-born Israelis") as he had in the hundreds of them who helped in the rescue. "The singing, and clapping, and pure joy was the kind of thing that makes you forget about all the trials of living in this country," he said. Several people commented that they were seeing the wheels of history turning very quickly.[24]

## "JERUSALEM OF GOLD"

Back in Addis Ababa that afternoon, though, Operation Solomon still was moving quite slowly. Amir Maimon had promised the Israeli air force that they would send a thousand people an hour to the airport, and he worried because they were busing far fewer.[25] Micha Feldman considered the twenty thousand people outside, many of them Falash Mura and residents of Addis, and wondered if the mission would fail.[26] But Maimon looked forward to the curfew. The non-Jews would be gone by then, he hoped.[27]

The Ethiopian authorities were creating difficulties about landing the planes, and the delays in getting the Jews to the airport made matters worse. So many Israeli aircraft were waiting on the ground for the buses to arrive that there was no more parking available and planes had to circle in the air.[28] General Shahak decided to suspend further takeoffs from Ben-Gurion for two to three hours, and ordered five aircraft that already were in the air to set down at a military base in southern Israel.[29] By 5:30 only three planes, carrying a thousand passengers, had taken off, including the one that had just touched down in Israel. Another two were being loaded at the Addis airport, and one had just landed.[30]

An El Al 747 jumbo jet, marked only by a blue and green stripe and the word CARGO in red, landed, arousing great excitement. Only forty minutes later it took off, carrying more people than had left for Israel in an entire month in the past. There were 1,078 passengers packed onboard, El Al's Aryeh Oz recalled in an interview. This set a record for civil aviation, as the *Guinness Book of World Records* noted later. "We counted after they were in," Oz said, then "we found another forty kids covered by shawls on the backs of their mothers when they left the plane." The Israelis had converted it from a cargo plane to a passenger plane in a little more than a day, installing 760 seats. "Four kids sat on one seat," Oz said, and people sat on the floor between seats.[31] Among the three hundred children on board was a baby who was born prematurely, immediately before takeoff.[32] Typically the passengers on El Al flights to Israel are "wandering Jews," moving around and talking constantly, the chief pilot of the jumbo jet said later. But the Ethiopians on this trip were almost completely still, until they flew over Jerusalem.[33] Then the kids sang "Jerusalem of Gold," the hauntingly beautiful Israeli song that they had learned in the JDC school in Addis.[34]

This huge craft set down at Ben-Gurion that evening. Hundreds of reporters and cameramen and dozens of buses were waiting as the jumbo taxied to a halt. An eight- or nine-year-old boy in a running suit top and jeans was the first Ethiopian to walk out of the aircraft door, cautiously. Then he smiled broadly for the TV cameras, and as he descended the long ramp, he raised his hands to the sky and started playing to the crowd. He was followed by several old people, walking slowly. One was a man with a gold and pink parasol, which he closed only as he entered one of the buses. The father of the newborn premature baby emerged cradling the infant, then walked to an ambulance. Mystified, he let a nurse place the tiny child in an incubator.[35]

The first person to disembark from the jumbo, however, was not an Ethiopian. It was Simcha Dinitz, carrying a small Ethiopian boy! After his plane from California had set down in Budapest, Dinitz had caught a connecting flight on a plane carrying Russian olim. When it landed at Ben-Gurion, he had his pilot stop his plane so he could board the 747 while it was still on the landing strip. The jumbo then taxied a hundred yards to unload, and out came Dinitz, holding the child, to greet the camera crews. The Jewish Agency needs publicity, but a number of Israelis involved in the rescue saw this as excessively self-promoting. Dinitz then approached some of the new arrivals as they disembarked. He told a barefoot young man in Hebrew that the buses were full and they were waiting for another bus. "*Shalom*," the man replied, evidently the only Hebrew that he knew.[36]

Two more jumbos approached Addis, but the Ethiopian government threatened to halt the operation if the Israelis used planes of this type. They were so large that they could damage the small airfield, the Ethiopians complained. Lubrani acceded to their demand.[37]

### "THERE ARE NO OBSTACLES!"

The Israelis now had to overcome yet another obstacle that could have halted the mission: the curfew. The police in Addis made a practice of shooting anyone who was out past 9:00 p.m., so the bus drivers made it clear that they had no intention of working past 8:00 p.m. Shahak considered the fallback possibility of having the Jews walk to the airport.[38] But Eli Eliezri stepped in, calling a meeting with Mersha and the manager of the bus depot. In an interview, he recalled telling them, "No one can stop this operation!"[39]

The hapless depot manager pleaded, "I can't. They'll kill me."

But, according to Eliezri, he insisted, "I am telling you that either you will give the order to your drivers to continue or I will bring in my own drivers. I don't want to discuss anything!" Eliezri put $2,000 in American dollars in the pocket of the depot manager as "motivation money." He also gave $50 in birr to every driver. He could not take a chance on having police shoot at the buses, so, passing out more birr to the police, he said, "From now on, you are a motorcycle escort. You will escort each bus to the airport and back. From now on I am your commander! I'm telling you, there will be no curfew!"[40]

Next Eliezri went to the airport and instructed the Israeli army officers there to give bribes, if necessary. He handed them money, he said, to distribute in case problems arose later. "The army wasn't used to it," he said later.[41] The advice came in handy that night when an impasse occurred, General Nachumi, the IAF mission commander, recalled in an interview. An Israeli plane carrying drinking water landed, but there was no Ethiopian driver willing to convey the water to the embassy at night. Taking Eliezri's advice, Nachumi tore a 100-birr note in two and gave half to a driver. He promised to give him the other half when he delivered the water.[42]

When I interviewed him in October 1996, Eliezri expressed the philosophy behind his actions: "There are no obstacles! There is nothing you cannot do!" Michael Schneider told me later that Eliezri was the most creative operative he had ever met.[43]

## "A VERY DISORGANIZED MIRACLE"

As sunset approached that Friday, Micha Feldman got a loaf of bread and a bottle of wine, took a salami out of a knapsack, and movingly sang the prayers to usher in the Sabbath.[44] It would be the last one in Ethiopia for most of them.

The pressure outside the embassy began to ease after 9:00 p.m. Many Christians and Falash Mura in the street went home when the curfew fell, and at about midnight, the Jewish Agency's Avi Mizrachi opened all of the gates to the embassy and let the remaining five thousand Jews into the compound.[45] This created an even greater crush inside, however. "It's impossible!" one of the workers shouted.[46] To restore order, three Israelis pushed the crowd back and put up a barrier of fencing. In the process, families were split, with some children were briefly separated from their parents.

To accommodate the mass of people, the Israelis moved the first checkpoint back up the hill, then again, farther back. The fence at the top of the compound collapsed under the swell of the crowd, and a stream of people poured over it, toward the registry station.[47] At that point, the scene became violent. "Micha broke down," Schnapper said later of Micha Feldman. "He screamed and hit people. Kobi Friedman too."[48]

"Most of the Jewish community pushed toward a [narrow] gate," Feldman recalled later. "We feared that the children on the mother's backs would die. So we had to fight against them, even to beat them. . . . You had to fight to survive."[49] The experience shook Feldman. "It was very difficult, you know," he said months later, "hitting people you had previously taken care of."[50]

Tashteet and his assistants distributed the thousands of oranges, potatoes, and rolls they had stored, and the Israelis delivered huge canisters of water that Shahak's team had brought with them on the planes. The Americans, who had expected to be relieved that morning by Jewish Agency workers, continued to labor, without eating, drinking, or sleeping for very long stretches, if at all. Everyone was exhausted, but the processing went more smoothly now. "Everyone knows a miracle is taking place," observed Micha Odenheimer, a rabbi who came to cover the story as a journalist but joined in the rescue effort when Shabbat began.[51]

"It was a very disorganized miracle," Schnapper commented later.[52]

## "WHAT IF THE RESCUE FAILED?"

While the Israelis and Americans worked in the crisp air outside the embassy, and as the planes hurtled the Jews through the dark skies to Zion, the Israeli diplomats and Foreign Ministry officials passed the evening happily in Ambassador Naim's room at the Hilton. They drank and joked as Kassa sat with them and finished a full bottle of Chivas Regal by himself.[53] Kassa told them of his special emotional connection with Israel. "I may have sounded rough and tough here and there," he said to Naim, "but I had Mengistu to deal with."[54] Moshe Yegar said in an interview that he, Naim, and the Israeli journalist Tamar Golan watched with fascination as Lubrani talked to Kassa the whole time.[55] Kassa "was worried and sad," Naim observed later.[56] The money had not been transferred yet and they still were discussing the payment.[57] Kassa had tried to pull a fast one with the bank account, one of the key Israelis told me. Now "some people said that we should have sent him to hell," he noted. But what if the rescue failed as a result? "It was too much of a gamble," this source said.

Kassa still was "deathly afraid that we'd leave him," Lubrani recalled.[58] "If I remain here, the rebels will kill me," the Ethiopian told Naim. Lubrani approached Naim about bringing Kassa to Israel, telling him they had to take Kassa because otherwise he would definitely die. "We both agreed in this decision," Naim told me. But he did not know at the time that Lubrani already had made that commitment to Kassa months before. "If I knew Uri had guaranteed Kassa's life, it would have affected the $35 million," he commented years later.[59]

In the chaos of the moment, the Israelis were in a position to decide if they should refuse to pay the $35 million. Lubrani argued later that they were absolutely right not to hold back on the money. If they had, he said, somewhat grandly, "it would have gone down in history that the Jewish people reneged."[60] A more pragmatic reason for them to pay was to preclude any possibility of last-minute Ethiopian interference that might have sabotaged the operation. In any case, the financial transfer was already in motion. At about 2:00 that afternoon in New York, 9:00 p.m. in Addis, the money finally was deposited.

A few days earlier, Mendel Kaplan, the chairman of the Jewish Agency Board of Governors, had recommended that Israel delay the payment until the end of business in New York, by which time perhaps half of the Ethiopian Jews would be on their way to Israel.[61] Through a combination of indirection, happenstance, and intent, that was almost exactly what happened.

Barak had located a source for the $35 million in the Jewish Agency budget, but it was Marty Kraar in New York, acting in behalf of the American Jewish Federations, who actually had found the money that had been allocated to fund that budget. The federations already had put money in the pipeline, intended for the Jewish Agency's use. Secretly, Kraar and Schneider had met on Thursday night and sequestered $27 million that was designated to go to the Jewish Agency and $8 million that was headed to the Joint. Then Kraar got permission from the federations to divert the funds to pay for the operation instead.[62]

## THE FALASH MURA:
## "IT'S LIKE AN ONION—THE MORE PEEL
## YOU TAKE AWAY, THE MORE YOU CRY"

At last, well into the evening, the operation began to run smoothly. From 10:00 p.m. on, they bused people to the planes "at a terrific pace, more people than we needed," Maimon recalled.[63] At that point, six hundred Jews were sitting and waiting at the airport, and the planes were filling as soon as they landed, then taking off again without turning off their engines.[64] As midnight approached, the embassy had sent over seven thousand Jews on their way to Israel, roughly as many as had been brought over during the entire six weeks of Operation Moses.[65] The operation originally was expected to run into Saturday night, but there were fewer people to transport than expected, and Shahak now anticipated that it would be over by 9:00 the next morning. The Ethiopian government had demanded, in fact, that the last Israeli plane be off their soil by 11:30 a.m.[66]

Then, shortly before midnight, there came yet another hitch: the bus drivers complained that the work was too hard for them. The police, whom Eliezri had recruited to escort the buses, spoke with the bus drivers and suddenly were smitten with fatigue themselves. Friedman got them some food and promised that the Israelis would reward them the next morning.[67] They did, with cash taken from the huge piles of birr that people had surrendered at the embassy.[68]

At 11:45 p.m., Lubrani updated Schneider, adding, "I presume you feel relieved."

"So far, so good," Schneider replied. "I hope you get some rest tonight."[69]

As midnight approached, Operation Solomon took another surprising turn, this time concerning the convert families, the Falash Mura. Israeli officials feared that if they brought this group, they could be obliged to accept tens of thousands of other Ethiopians, all of whom might claim to be the descendants of converts returning to Judaism, or relatives of Falash Mura who had reached Israel. "When you solve one problem, you create another twenty," one of the Israelis who worked at the embassy at the time told me. "It's like an onion," he said—the more peel you take away, the more you cry.[70] The Israelis had decided months before not to bring the Falash Mura along on this mission. At the least, this question would require further study and debate.

But now, at midnight, Lubrani informed Schneider of a crisis with the Falash Mura. Powerful political and religious forces in Israel were insisting that the converts be brought along that night after all. The Sephardi chief rabbi, Mordechai Eliyahu, had sent a fax saying that the Falash Mura were in fact Jews. Aryeh Deri, the Israeli interior minister, had said the same in a phone call to Micha Feldman.[71] General Ehud Barak, who had been calling the Israeli embassy every hour to monitor events, also asked that Friday about bringing the converts along. Why not use this opportunity to take the Falash Mura too? Barak asked Amir Maimon. "There are only 3,000 people," the general said. "Why not? We can't say how many there are, and we have to check if there are lists identifying them," Maimon replied. Barak then called Shahak at the airport, and he too called the Israeli embassy to ask about bringing the Falash Mura. "Let's finish what we have, then go into the others," Maimon responded at the time. Later he said, "I asked others at the embassy and found out that we can't do it technically. There was no list," no way to check their identification.[72]

Evidently in order to surmount Maimon's objection, the prime minister's office had called Micha Feldman that afternoon to ask if he could identify the converts. Feldman had rejected the Falash Mura precisely because they were not named in the computerized "bible" of Ethiopian Jews. So he walked over to Andy Goldman and Solomon Ezra, whose organization, NACOEJ, had been taking care of the convert families in Addis. "Micha asked if we can organize them," Goldman recalled. Yes, he replied, they had yellow ID cards. Feldman reported that the answer was yes.[73]

It almost happened. At about 2:30 p.m., Shahak received a cable instructing him to bring the three thousand Falash Mura back with him. Shahak brought the cable to Lubrani at the embassy, and Lubrani called Jerusalem to check it out. It is unclear who sent the order, but it was canceled two hours later.[74] If the sender was trying to make an end run around Shamir, he had failed.

But the question still had not been put to rest. Around 11:30 that night, the pressure to bring the Falash Mura had increased. Simcha Dinitz called Lubrani and Naim to say that Sharon and others were pressing to get them on the planes. They referred Dinitz to the prime minister for an answer.[75] "I called Shamir and asked, 'Mr. Prime Minister, what do we do?'" Dinitz told me in an interview. "Shamir said, 'Let's get the undisputed Jews first.' I called [Addis Ababa] and said, 'Take the Jews first and the rest afterwards.'"[76] The matter was resolved shortly after midnight.

General Barak's interest in the converts was unexpected. "I don't have any idea how Ehud got to the matter of the Falash Mura," Maimon said later. "He never discussed this before."[77] In fact, the last-minute move to bring the Falash Mura was driven by the religious nationalist Gush Emunim, several highly placed Israeli sources revealed. This group believed that maintaining Israeli sovereignty over the West Bank was crucial to the messianic redemption, which was already underway. Gush Emunim leaders saw the Ethiopian Jews as a reservoir for populating the settlements in those territories. So they put pressure on Sharon, who in turn pressed Barak. Sharon reportedly made a direct appeal to Shamir as well.[78]

Sharon evidently was enthusiastic about this. He was then housing minister and aliyah cabinet head, and was a principal architect of the plan to expand the Jewish settlements in the occupied territories. In fact, Sharon now went so far as to make the false claim that Prime Minister Shamir already had approved bringing the Falash Mura, said a high Israeli official who asked not to be named.

It may seem surprising in retrospect that Israel had made contingency plans to bring the Falash Mura during Operation Solomon. "The Jewish Agency had located three thousand temporary rooms [for them] as part of the preparations for the operation," Avi Mizrachi said in an interview.[79] But the question had been decided for now. The converts would stay behind. That decision would trigger a debate that still persists in Israel.

## THE AERIAL RAILROAD

### Saturday, May 25, 1991

The Israelis, the Americans, and the Ethiopian-Israelis worked through that chilly night. By 3:00 a.m., eight thousand Jews had already left for Israel on the *rakevet avirit*, or "aerial railroad," and three thousand more were waiting to go at the Addis airport.[80] Things were moving at a fast clip. The Israelis got the timing down to only forty minutes from touchdown to takeoff—an extraordinary pace, considering the number of passengers that they were boarding onto the planes.[81] At one point, eight huge aircraft landed almost nose to tail on the small, curved runway, then took off, overloaded, through the thin air. Israeli planes sat so close together on the ground that the parking apron looked like the deck of an aircraft carrier. Planes passed each other in the dark with their wings practically touching.[82] A group of Soviet officers whose planes were at the airport watched the rescue in disbelief.[83]

Israelis wearing purple and orange parkas and carrying blue neon torches maintained order in the darkness along the airstrip. General Nachumi recalled later that the Hercules C-130 Rhinos, with their red lights, looked like dragons blowing hot air into the crisp night. "What is this?" the Ethiopian Jews asked. They had to go into the belly of a monster! "It made a hell of a noise," Nachumi observed. "We had to take them up by their hands to the plane."[84] The soldiers treated the Jews tenderly, he noted. "To watch soldiers taught and trained in a unit to be aggressive and, in fact, to kill—to watch how these fighters hugged the Jews in their care was extraordinarily moving."[85]

The JDC's Amos Avgar, who had worked all day at the embassy, went to help out at the airport late that night and saw what he called "the other side of the miracle" taking place. There, a teenage mother carried a child on her back and another in her arms while a third held her hand. She was unable to carry her fourth child, so Israeli security and Jewish Agency personnel shepherded the family from the bus to the plane. Then the Israelis received a panicked call from one of the planes: a mother already onboard had realized that they had left one of her children behind. The message was passed on to the embassy, where workers found the child and made sure that he got on a plane.[86]

The airlift moved very quickly and efficiently now. As many as twenty-eight planes shuttled through the nighttime sky simultaneously, sometimes passing each other nearly wingtip to wingtip.[87]

## ESKEDER

As dawn approached on Saturday, the last Jews at the embassy were being registered, and buses were waiting longer to fill. The network committee moved through town one last time to round up stragglers.[88]

Some of the most moving final moments of the mission involved Falash Mura families who had managed to get inside the embassy.[89] At 5:30 a.m., an exhausted LaDena Schnapper walked down the hill to the embassy building to see if there was anything more she could do. There she saw Eskeder and her four daughters, ages three to eight. Eskeder was a Jew who had married a Christian and moved to a non-Jewish area in Gondar, said Schnapper. Her husband had been shot by the rebels, and Eskeder had come to Addis Ababa with her parents and seven siblings. The Jewish Agency had accepted all of them as Jews except Eskeder and her children, who had to live on handouts. Schnapper had appealed the case. So had Peter Jackson, who, during his stay in Addis, had been touched by the sight of the four exquisitely beautiful, barefoot little girls dressed in rags. According to Jackson, Kobi Friedman shouted at him that they were Christians and instructed Zimna not to give them papers. Still, he said, Zimna reassured him that it would be okay.[90]

Now, almost at the last moment on the last day, Eskeder's brother ran up to tell Schnapper that she and the girls had been turned away at the final checkpoint. Schnapper found her, and "she threw herself at my feet and the children, all sobbing, grabbed my dress." Schnapper went to find Zimna, but instead found Feldman, whom Schnapper considered to be one of the con-descending, paternalistic Israelis. In this instance, though, exhausted and hoarse, Feldman accommodated her: he approved Eskeder and her daughters. When the Israelis stuck the numbered yellow decals on Eskeder's and the children's heads, "they all started crying and kissed my feet," the Ethiopian way of giving thanks, Schnapper recalled.[91]

## SILENCE IN THE EMBASSY

Between 7:00 and 8:00 that morning, the American volunteers and the Israeli staff started leaving. The last busload of Beta Israel went to the airport at 9:00. By 10:00 a.m., twenty-four hours after the first plane had landed in Addis Ababa, there was silence in the embassy compound. But isolated families trickled in, and the Israelis knew that a number of them must have missed their chance.[92] They also were aware that hundreds, perhaps thousands, of Jews remained in the north, particularly in an isolated region called Quara, near Sudan. Someone needed to remain to take them in. Someone also would have to look after the Falash Mura, and pay for the rented buses and the other expenses of the operation. Tashteet agreed to stay behind. The AAEJ's Berhanu and the JDC's Dr. Girma, who were Ethiopian Christians, would be there too, at least for a time.[93]

Remarkably, Naim and Maimon also volunteered to stay in Addis. The Tigrean rebels were virtually at the outskirts of the city. They "had advance units eyeballing us at the airport," Bob Houdek recalled.[94] The capital certainly would fall within days. When that happened, the Israelis wanted to have an official presence there, to establish ties with the new government and advocate for the Jews who had been left behind. Agreeing to stay was an act of courage by the two diplomats. They might face the very dangers that they had warned could befall the Jews, including a firefight for the city, or even the Doomsday Scenario. To make matters worse, they could not be sure how the new government would treat them. The insurgents had, after all, accused Israel of supplying cluster bombs to the detested Mengistu. And the Mossad had reported that troops from the vehemently anti-Zionist Arab state of Libya were with the rebels.

Maimon wanted Naim to leave, but for an entirely different reason. Lubrani and the others would be back in Israel on Saturday afternoon, and the world press would be eager to get their stories. Maimon wished that Naim could be there too, to make sure that others did not take all of the credit for the success of Operation Solomon.[95]

## "I HAVEN'T GOT THE HEART
## TO LEAVE THEM"

When it came time to go, Lubrani, Eliezri, Divon, Yegar, Harel, and the others from the Hilton went to the airport, accompanied by Naim and Maimon. Feldman, Friedman, and Bergman, all exhausted, left the embassy and joined them. Houdek went as well, to see them off.

Rick Hodes flew back on a Hercules C-130 with a couple of patients. "Despite hordes of people, dehydration, malaria, women in labor, hospitalized patients, and appendicitis, nobody had died" during the mission, Hodes observed. That was miraculous, he said.[96]

The Israelis smuggled Kassa and Mersha out of Addis disguised as patients, sedated and covered in blankets taken from the Hilton to hide their identities. An Israeli intelligence agent drove them to the airport, passing through Ethiopian security checkpoints on the way, then slipped the two officials onto the next-to-last plane to leave. "Kassa went to Israel on a stretcher!" Lubrani told me, perhaps with satisfaction.[97] On the tarmac, an Israeli crew was in the process of repairing one of the four engines of the plane, a Hercules C-130 that carried spare tires and aircraft parts. But it was necessary to get Kassa out of the country quickly because the Ethiopian president had summoned him to an urgent meeting and his colleagues would be looking for him.[98] So the plane took off immediately, flying sluggishly on only three propellers. The takeoff was precarious as the Hercules climbed over the surrounding mountains, and Kassa and Mersha had a long, slow trip to Israel. They arrived late in the day.

There was one final, wrenching scene at the airport. The last of the Israelis had gotten on a 757 jet, with Shahak and Feldman still standing outside the plane when, amazingly, two taxis pulled up to the tarmac and eight Ethiopian women climbed out. They represented four generations from a single family: a great-grandmother, her daughter, and the daughter's three daughters: one with twin girls on her back, one with a baby, and one unmarried. All were listed on their plastic-coated ID card and so were placed on the Hercules with the damaged engine, except the grandmother and her unmarried daughter, who had not been certified as Jews. The grandmother suddenly threw herself on Feldman's leg and screamed that she would not move unless they took her and her daughter to Israel.[99] "The engines were on. It was an ugly picture," Shahak recalled.[100] Addisu, who was seated on the 757, saw the women tearing at their faces and clothes and he started shouting that they should be brought on board.[101] On the tarmac, Feldman told Shahak that they did not have the proper plastic ID cards. "Plastic, shmastic—put them onto our plane!" the general told him.[102] "I haven't got the heart to leave them," Shahak told Lubrani as he sat down next to him in the front row.[103]

As they took off, Lubrani looked back to see who else was on the plane. "There were some Ethiopians there," he said. "But most were Israelis who did the operation. I saw their elation. Then I understood. They had come the day before. They said, 'You don't know what is going on in Israel. Everyone is at the airport, the prime minister, everyone!'"[104] The euphoria that Lubrani saw on their faces would be shared by very many Israelis when Operation Solomon was made public after the mission ended.

Back at the airport outside Addis, Houdek and Naim stood on an empty and eerily silent parking apron watching the last jet disappear into the clouds.

Spontaneously the two veteran diplomats hugged each other and jumped for joy, almost like kids. "We did it! We did it!" they exclaimed.[105]

The last plane lifted off at 11:35 a.m., slightly more than twenty-five hours after the first Israeli planes had landed in Addis. It reached Israel at 2:45 p.m. Waiting at Ben-Gurion Airport to greet Lubrani and the others were Shamir, Arens, Ehud Barak, Merhav, and Nachum Admoni, the former head of the Mossad, who had been in charge of Operation Moses. Admoni had been one of the officials who met with Kassa at the renewal of diplomatic ties more than eighteen months earlier. When Lubrani debarked, Merhav, Shamir, Arens, and Barak each embraced him warmly. Admoni stood by and congratulated them all. "You have finished what we began," he told them.[106]

And so Operation Solomon concluded, thirty-four hours and four minutes after the first plane had left Ben-Gurion Airport. Forty-one military and El Al aircraft were employed in the mission: eighteen Hercules C-130s, twelve Boeing 707s, three 747s, five 767s, and three 757s.[107] One Ethiopian Airlines plane had made a single round trip, and two of the Israeli Boeing 747 jumbos had not been permitted to land in Addis. The operation brought 14,310 Ethiopians to Israel, including eight babies who were born during the mission.[108] Most of the *olim* were children: over 60 percent of the Beta Israel who reached Israel in 1991 were nineteen years old or younger, more than twice the average figure for this age group among all new immigrants to Israel. The median age of these Ethiopian *olim* was 14.7 years, with only 7.2 percent of them over sixty years old.[109]

In Washington, D.C., watching the airlift on TV, Susan Pollack wept. The Israelis had done just what Israel was founded to do, she thought—pluck Jews out of danger.[110]

# Chomanesh Crosses the Red Sea

Chomanesh did not have to wait for the silent networking committee to tell her that the time had come to go to Jerusalem as Operation Solomon began. Word of mouth already had spread the news very early that Friday morning, and everyone in her family was up and packing. Tagenich was afraid, though. Her son, Or, was in the Yekatit 12 Hospital with meningitis. Now Tagenich would have to go to the hospital and get him. But what if he was too ill to leave? Chomanesh told her to go ahead, assuring her that she would meet her at the hospital and they would talk to the doctor together.

Meanwhile, Chomanesh's parents packed. They had arrived in Addis five months before and had saved some birr from their stipends. Now they were making a futile effort to hide it in their bags, to smuggle it with them to Jerusalem. Finally, the family left for the embassy, slowed down by Chomanesh, who walked tentatively and needed to rest her feet at one point. As they came near the embassy compound, she was dismayed to see thousands of people in the street, carrying children and luggage, and pushing forward. The crowd grew behind her, then surged, and someone accidentally knocked her down. A man carrying his elderly father on his back fell as well, and the old man landed hard on Chomanesh's leg and foot. The pain was too great for her to stand up, and she knew at once that she would be unable to walk to the hospital to meet Tagenich.

Chomanesh did not know that Rick Hodes was making his rounds of the city hospitals that morning to fetch the Jewish patients, including Or. Hodes examined the boy quickly, then took Tagenich aside and told her quietly that he was going to bring them to the embassy. This was the day for them to fly to Israel, he said. Amazingly, Tagenich refused, nervously speaking such rapid Amharic that Hodes could not follow. He found a Christian who could translate, and took the risk of letting out the news of the airlift, in case Tagenich had not understood his Amharic. Still she refused.

"You can get out of the country!" the newfound translator told her. "Go! Are you crazy?"

"My sister said that she would meet me here," Tagenich insisted.

"They teach you in medical school that you're not supposed to strangle your patients," Hodes told me later, but he wanted to strangle Tagenich. Instead, he tried a new approach, telling her that her sister was waiting for her at the embassy. It was a lie, as far as he knew, and even so, it did not work. He considered disconnecting Or's IV without her permission, but thought better of it.

Hot, thirsty, and frustrated, Hodes returned to the embassy. He made his way toward the embassy gate, wading through the confluence of thousands of people. As Hodes walked, Chomanesh saw him and hobbled over through the crowd, somehow managing to intercept him. "My sister and her son are in the emergency room at Yekatit 12 Hospital," she told him. "What should I do?"

Hodes smiled and said, "You're the one I need. Let's go."
He drove her to the hospital, where Tagenich readily agreed to let him disconnect the IV.

Did Hodes think it was a miracle that she had found him in that sea of people? I asked him later. "Of course it was," he answered, looking at me a bit strangely for having to ask. "God does everything."

Hodes drove the women and the boy to the clinic and put Or on one of the "Ethiopian futons" there, a mattress of wheat sacks stuffed with straw. He injected the boy with a powerful antibiotic and let him rest. A nurse offered Chomanesh and Tagenich an improbable snack: matzo and Slim-Fast. The twenty-two thousand pounds of matzo that had not arrived in time for Passover finally had come and were being stored in the clinic. For whatever reason, in a country of skinny people, NACOEJ had donated the Slim-Fast.

While this was happening, Dan'el got to work at the Addis Ababa airport. He had left Israel at six-thirty that morning on the same flight as Addisu Massele. Their plane circled in the air for thirty-five minutes while Lubrani worked out the terms of payment with Kassa, then set down at about the time that Chomanesh found Hodes. On landing, everybody did his assigned task. "My job was to arrange the stairs, to help the airplanes," Dan'el told me. "Then I was to come with the *olim* in the plane and explain to them."

When the first plane left Addis for Israel that afternoon, Dan'el was on board. "There were no chairs, only mattresses," he said. "Everyone stood till the plane was full. 'Now you can sit down,'" he told them. "Everyone was so quiet," he recalled. "They just wanted to go and not make a problem. Even the children didn't cry."

Dan'el told the new immigrants, "In three and a half hours we will be in Israel." That struck them as unlikely. It had taken their relatives months or years to reach Jerusalem. "Who are you to say that in three and a half hours we will be in Israel?" they asked him.

"All flights went over the Red Sea," Dan'el told me. "The second exodus. Moses crossed the Red Sea on foot. Now we crossed it on air." Finally Dan'el announced, "Now we are in Israel airspace. On the left side is Jerusalem." All of the passengers stood at once and looked out the windows on the left of the plane. "I was afraid we maybe lost balance, you know?" he remembered, smiling.

When they landed, "I told them, 'Welcome to the Holy Land. You are in Israel.' You can see the shining of the faces," Dan'el recalled. Then, as Prime Minister Shamir made his welcoming speech at the airport, Dan'el looked for the next flight back to Addis.

That Friday night in Addis, Hodes left the Israeli embassy with Ami Bergman and returned to the clinic to bring his patients to the airport. In small movements, the American and the Israeli helped them into two vans, then drove slowly through the same back roads that the buses loaded with *olim* were taking. They passed several of the buses, each with Israeli soldiers at the front and back, and Hodes noticed Israeli guards along the streets as well. As they approached the airport, buses pulled up every few minutes. Jews got off quietly and sat along the tarmac, many with their numbered stickers on their foreheads.

The vans with the patients drove directly up to a Boeing 707. Its seats and bathrooms had been removed, and two Israeli physicians waited on board. As Hodes and Bergman carried the patients up the ramp, Dan'el came over to assist them, and his face brightened when he saw Chomanesh helping her sister and nephew out of the van. Flying back with them, he sat close to Chomanesh, his betrothed from childhood, as they crossed the Red Sea.[1]

# EPILOGUE

Operation Solomon ignited a joyous mood among Israelis, who celebrated the key participants generously but unevenly. Lubrani in particular was lionized, though privately he was the target of attack over the payment to Ethiopia and the side deal with Kassa. It remained in doubt, in fact, to whom the $35 million actually had been paid. In the subsequent months and years, the Israeli effort to gather in the Jews who had been left behind in Ethiopia proved difficult, especially in the controversial case of the Falash Mura.

## "THE FESTIVAL OF CREDIT"

"In Israel, the festival of credit began immediately," Moshe Yegar recalled.[1] Most of the honor for Operation Solomon was focused on the IDF, the Jewish Agency, and Lubrani personally. The *Jerusalem Post*, for example, devoted much of its first section on Sunday, May 26, to the operation under the banner headline "Ethiopian Jewry Rescued." The paper included a large picture of Lubrani, whom a companion article characterized as the "conductor of a symphony." Soon after that, the *Jerusalem Report* put Lubrani on its cover, with a story titled "The Fixer—Uri Lubrani: The Mystery Man Who Saved the Jews."[2] Within the next few months, Lubrani was chosen the *Jerusalem Post*'s Personality of the Year, awarded the Ben-Gurion Prize for advancing the principles of David Ben-Gurion, and given a one-third share of the $100,000 Defender of Jerusalem Award. In January, he was the subject of a two-part *This Is Your Life* program on Israeli television.

"Uri got all of the credit," said one Foreign Ministry official who was involved in the mission. "I got a pen." Other participants in the operation felt that Lubrani had not properly credited Haim Divon, who had played a pivotal role for a year, or the Mossad, which had had people in every meeting, giving intelligence and estimates. And the staff of JDC-Israel were disturbed not to have received enough recognition. Michael Schneider felt obliged to remind them that they had acted out of humanitarian considerations, not for self-aggrandizement.[3]

The AAEJ was nearly ignored. Some press releases mentioned that the group had assisted with the Jews in Addis, but did not name Susan Pollack.

In Washington, by contrast, President Bush held a ceremony in the White House Rose Garden on June 4, 1991, and presented the Presidential Citizens

Medal to Boschwitz and special awards for exceptional service to Frasure, Hicks, and Houdek.[4]

In Jerusalem, Reuven Merhav was not that lucky. His boss, Foreign Minister David Levy, had missed out on the glory and was furious, Merhav told me. Except for a short appearance at Ben Gurion Airport on Saturday afternoon, May 25, Levy had spent most of the day at home. As a result, the news accounts barely mentioned him. "Levy blew his top," Merhav noted, and "made it practically impossible for me to work for him." Merhav resigned from the Foreign Ministry a few weeks later.[5]

Perhaps to set these matters right after ten years, Merhav, in his gentle but persistent way, urged me to express his gratitude to all of the Israelis and Americans who made the mission a success. He praised Shamir and Arens, "who acted as statesmen, not as politicians," Ambassador Naim, and his friends from the Foreign Ministry: Divon, Maimon, Yegar, and Michael Shilo. Lubrani was certainly the right man for the job, Merhav said, and the Jewish Agency's Feldman, Mantber, Mizrachi, and Uri Gordon also excelled. He spoke of Haim Halachmi's contributions to the Ethiopian aliyah and cited the Mossad's important role. He mentioned too his deep appreciation for the Jewish organizations, and for Susan Pollack in particular. He singled out the JDC/Almaya officials, who were quietly effective and politically astute "without becoming politicians." "Addis Ababa was not known for nurturing angels," he said. "But, given all the difficulties, the orchestra played well." Merhav also spoke of the extra measure of devotion of the American officials: Boschwitz, Cohen, Frasure, and Houdek.[6] Operating "under the instruction and with the full blessing of . . . the president, the secretary of state, NSC, etc," they were true colleagues and partners, he said.

Merhav offered a final thought about Kassa. The Ethiopian was a living bridge between the proud aristocracy to which he belonged and the Mengistu regime, which he tried to save, he said. Merhav thinks that Kassa acted as a "true but emotionally mixed admirer of Israel," who nevertheless could not forget to act like an Ethiopian during the negotiations, and to look after his own interests. Kassa's behavior may have been Byzantine, but he played the role history had assigned him. "Good luck to him—he well deserves it," Merhav concluded.[7]

Responses to Operation Solomon from Arab states were predictably hostile. Arab governments, media, and radical groups bitterly denounced the political agendas that, in their view, underlay the mission. Several newspaper editorials linked the airlift to Israeli policies of expansionism and population growth, predicting that Israel would settle the new immigrants in the occupied territories. Arab spokesmen deplored in particular the American support for the rescue, and President Bush's part in it. Washington's role, they argued, contradicted Secretary of State Baker's stated opposition to the extension of the West Bank settlements and proved that the United States did not truly seek to bring peace to the region. In an interesting contrast, Arab Israelis volunteered during Operation Solomon to assist the new arrivals, emphasizing the humanitarian rather than the Zionist aspect of the mission.[8]

Demographic growth would in fact be an overt consideration in the continued ingathering of Ethiopians in subsequent years, as we shall see. But there was no truth to the charge that the United States had been inconsistent in its position against settling the new arrivals in the occupied territories. Both before and after Operation Solomon, the American ambassador to Israel, William Brown, "emphasized the importance of ensuring that no Falashas were placed by the [government of Israel] beyond the Green Line," which demarcated Israel's pre-1967 borders.[9] Israeli authorities promised to honor this restriction. At the time, some two hundred Ethiopian Jews, *olim* from Operation Moses, were living in West Bank settlements. The *New York Times* reported that they wanted to leave, not out of political conviction, but to be closer to other Ethiopians, and to jobs. In 2004, small numbers of Ethiopian Jews reportedly were living in West Bank settlements.[10]

## THE RESENTMENT WENT DEEP

In the months and years that followed Operation Solomon, Lubrani absorbed some severe criticism over the personal payment to Kassa—and the fact that it was made in secret. Zvi Barak was particularly incensed that Lubrani had circumvented the proper Israeli authorities. If he had known about the side payment to Kassa, Barak said, he never would have paid the $35 million.[11] Barak saw himself as a trustee of the American Jewish community's charitable contributions, which he felt Lubrani had misused.

The resentment over these payments went deep. Though Lubrani had become a public hero, charges were leveled against him privately. Confidential documents to which I was given access reveal that officials of the Jewish Agency, the Foreign Ministry, and the Mossad jointly accused Lubrani of having panicked and paid the $35 million unnecessarily.

One of these documents notes that Dinitz and people in the Mossad were furious with Lubrani for lying about the payment to Kassa. Lubrani allegedly told Dinitz and the prime minister, in writing, that he did not know anything about this side deal. Lubrani's penchant for secrecy and loyalty evidently had only made matters worse for him.

Ironically, Lubrani had opposed the deal with Kassa initially, as noted above. And Kassa himself denied that he ever took any money. "I didn't take a cent," he said in an interview for this book. "It's all lies, nonsense from the land of nonsense," he told the Israeli newspaper *Yedi'ot Ahronot* in 2001.[12]

According to the same confidential document, Dinitz was so exercised about the money that he also turned on the JDC. He tried to convince Shamir that the Joint should be excluded from all future rescue operations, since it was they who ultimately had paid Kassa. Only the Jewish Agency could be trusted, he contended. Dinitz's argument failed, but it took time for the Jewish Agency and the Joint to find ways to work together again.

A number of Israeli officials and Ethiopians still feel that the $35 million need not have been paid. Some argue that Lubrani paid twice, both with Kassa's safety and with money. "None of us knew Lubrani had promised to save Kassa's life," an Israeli Foreign Ministry officer told me in 2001. When Mengistu fled, this source reasoned, Kassa had lost his power base and would be lucky to get away with his life. "I'm asking myself how a guy in [Kassa's] position, knowing that he'll be the first guy executed, continues to negotiate the deal as if nothing happened." But, he noted, Lubrani's guarantee of protection gave Kassa the security to negotiate. "Israel played this poker game very badly," he concluded. An Israeli who was centrally involved in Operation Solomon felt similarly. If he had known in advance that they were going to smuggle Kassa out, he told me, "I'm sure that we wouldn't pay. What is the logic? I asked him, 'Uri, why are you paying the money?'"

A respected Ethiopian scholar who monitored the mission closely assured me in 2001, "Kassa duped the UJA and Israel. He was a big zero in that government, believe me." Kassa could not have stopped the operation, despite his threats, this source continued. "The airport was under the control of the rebels. Ethiopians are very smart and easily duped Lubrani and the Israelis." He enthusiastically endorsed the Ethiopian proverb "The *farenj* [white man], like a child, believes anything that you tell him."

As Operation Solomon was under way, however, the circumstances were uncertain and the stakes were high. From the outset, unforeseen obstacles and mishaps had threatened to abort the mission. In the urgency of the moment, making the payment may well have seemed the best insurance against any further surprises in the rescue.

## THE $35 MILLION AND THE REBEL GOVERNMENT

While the Israelis celebrated, the Roundtable peace talks between the Ethiopian government and the Tigrean, Eritrean, and Oromo rebel groups convened on Monday, May 27, 1991. The military situation on the ground in Ethiopia dictated the terms of the discussion. Over the weekend, the Eritrean rebels had taken the port city of Assab, the last major urban center under government control other than Addis. On Sunday, the EPRDF had taken the main airbase of Debre Zeit, east of Addis Ababa, seizing much of the Derg's air force there.[13] These defeats left the government with little to negotiate other than surrender.

Although there had been gunfire in Addis Ababa on Sunday, the main rebel forces were camped on the outskirts of the city, honoring Meles' pledge to the Americans not to enter the capital before the parties came to an agreement in London. Then the United States unexpectedly invited the EPRDF to take Addis. On that Monday, Bob Houdek had cabled the State Department's Herman Cohen, who was in London for the Roundtable, saying that the situation in Addis was falling apart and acting president Tesfaye Gebre Kidan had instructed the state radio to welcome the Woyane (Tigrean rebels) into the capital.[14] Cohen then made a command decision: he held a news conference recommending that EPRDF forces enter the city as soon as possible. The insurgents moved into Addis the next day. "The rebels kept their word all along," Cohen noted. "They were an impressive bunch. . . . Meles is a remarkable man. And we knew they needed our help to get started."[15]

Asher Naim hoped that they would want Israel's help as well. He began by offering them something to eat. As rebel troops passed by his window in the Addis Ababa Hilton on Tuesday, Naim saw that many of them were children. He opened the window and gave them food.[16]

Naim offered a more substantial gift to the new provisional government in early June. "I was the second ambassador to meet with the new foreign minister," he recalled later. "I said, 'Listen, we are not friends of Mengistu. We are friends of the Ethiopian people, and what we did, we did for Ethiopia. We want to see the last Falasha out.'" The minister, Seyoum Mesfin, replied that they were not opposed and that the Falasha had freedom of movement; there was no cause for concern. Seyoum said that he was willing to forget about any aid that Israel may have given Mengistu, but that the rebel government was extremely upset with the Israelis for having taken Kassa with them.[17] One Israeli ambassador told me, "They hated Kassa even more than Mengistu. They thought that Mengistu was evil, but Kassa was the brains behind him, the one advising Mengistu to do evil." The press in Israel had made Naim's job harder by revealing within three days of Operation Solomon that the Israelis had brought Kassa back with them. Now the Ethiopian foreign minister said to Naim, "You did it! Get him back here! You took a criminal who must be put on trial," Naim recalled. "They really wanted him because he knew everything, to locate all of the enemies of the people." The Ethiopians kept pressuring Naim about this until Kassa left Israel. "We had an understanding with America that they would give him asylum," Naim noted.[18] Kassa could not enter the United States for seven months, however, according to Eli Eliezri. "The U.S. wouldn't give him a green card," he told me. "Finally we sent him to Geneva. He stayed there with his wife for a long time, till he got permission" to enter the United States.[19] After Kassa reached the States, the Meles government tried unsuccessfully to have him extradited.[20]

Was Naim in danger because Israel had taken Kassa out? "I was in personal danger several times," he said. "But I knew that Meles Zenawi needed America more than anything else, and needed money." He also knew that he had the $35 million to offer.[21]

The $35 million had been transferred to the Ethiopian government account on Friday, May 24, the first day of Operation Solomon. The following Monday was Memorial Day, a bank holiday in New York, and the rebels took Addis on Tuesday. The timing was "pure luck," Naim recalled.[22] The new government did not know about the account at first, and the money sat in New York.

Herman Cohen confirmed the general outline of this story, though with a startling twist. The $35 million became a gift to the new government—but Meles said that he would not take it! The Tigrean leader was ashamed of the deal in which it had been obtained. "He was an idealist," Cohen observed.[23]

Bob Houdek actually was the first to tell Meles about the $35 million, at the beginning of June. Meles promptly denounced the prior government for having "sold its citizens for money."[24] Naim suggested that if the Ethiopians would not take cash, they should accept the $35 million in the form of a development fund for agriculture and health. He told them that they were not taking it for the Falashas. But in the end the fund was not created.[25]

Who ended up with the $35 million? According to Herman Cohen, Meles told him in July that he had it but did not want it; it was "blood money."[26] It is unlikely that Meles actually returned it, though. He may have been offended by the deal that brought it to the government, but he knew that Ethiopia desperately needed hard currency. The Ethiopian treasury had only 96 million birr and only $3.6 million in foreign exchange. There was not enough money to pay for fuel, and a European Community consortium had to supply a $38 million credit to cover that expense.[27] So, though Meles let the "blood money" sit in the bank for a time, he was no position to give it back. Reuven Merhav confirmed this: "As far as I know, there was some talk about returning the money, but then their senses won the day. Just imagine, the notion of getting a $35 million green carpet as a welcome present! A rebel's dream. . . . I do not believe for one minute that it went back to Israel."[28] This is consistent with a confidential Israeli Foreign Ministry report of June 4, 1991, to which I was given access, which indicates that Seyoum, in his meeting with Naim, was determined to find the $35 million.

A surprising number of Israeli, American, and Ethiopian sources say that they are not sure who got the money. *Yedi'ot Ahronot* reported in June 1991 that the $35 million had "disappeared."[29] Howard M. Sachar, in his magisterial *History of Israel*, says that the Israelis deposited the payment in "the Swiss bank accounts of key Ethiopian ministers."[30] Several witnesses I spoke to also suspect that it wound up in private pockets after all. "God knows who has the $35 million today," a former Ethiopian government official told me in Addis. Did a government figure take it for himself? "For sure," he said.[31] Simcha Dinitz told me that, no, one cannot be confident that the money actually reached the new regime. "I will leave it in suspense," he said. "You cannot get [this information] from Ethiopian sources."[32] In fact, the Ethiopian ambassador in Washington did not respond to my calls or e-mail about this question. Nor did Prime Minister Meles' office answer my fax and letter to him in Addis Ababa.[33]

Rumors flew, and still do. "People in town [Addis Ababa] were sure the money might not have gone to the government. They said that Kassa might have taken it," a former senior Ethiopian official told me. One story that was still being passed around ten years later holds that, immediately after reaching Israel, Kassa flew to New York to try to get the $35 million from the account in Citibank. Haim Divon said, however, that Kassa was taken to a safe house in Israel, where he stayed for weeks. "Kassa definitely didn't go to New York," said Divon. "I was with him."[34] Kassa himself said in 2001 that all of the money was transferred into the bank account of the government of Ethiopia.[35]

Divon said the same. "I'm certain that the new government got the money," he told me. Divon, who became the Israeli ambassador to Addis in October 1991, was one of those who believed that Israel should not have paid anything at all during Operation Solomon; saving Kassa's life had been payment enough. So, late that fall, when Meles government officials expressed ethical objections to the way they had received the money, he told them that they could return it anytime; Israel could use it to help the Ethiopian Jews. They definitely had the money by then, he observed.[36]

Houdek confirmed this. "It's still there!" he recalled telling Meles when the Israelis informed him that the $35 million was sitting in the account. "Go ahead and use it!" Houdek urged the Ethiopian leader. "This was the only issue I've ever worked on in my life in which resources weren't a problem," Houdek told me, and yet he had to encourage Meles to accept the money. "They didn't touch it until well after I left" (on June 29, 1991), he said. "Months afterward, they drew on it."[37]

Paul Henze wrote at the time, "As of the end of 1991, the money has reportedly not been utilized."[38] Dinitz and Naim said that the $35 million remained locked in the account in New York after Operation Solomon and that only the State Department could release it. Indeed, Dinitz claimed that, months after the mission, Deputy Secretary of State Lawrence Eagleburger called to ask his advice about who was the legal heir to the money. As Dinitz recalled it, he told Eagleburger that the $35 million should go to the new government, but only after the last three thousand Jews had been evacuated from Ethiopia (i.e., by June 1992).[39] According to Eagleburger, however, the State Department neither froze the money in the account nor authorized its subsequent release.[40]

The fact is that the money was placed in the Ethiopian government bank account in New York on the first day of Operation Solomon and funds were moving out of the account soon after that. The Citibank official who made the deposit checked the records at my request. He confirmed that $35 million was transferred from Bank Leumi, where the Jewish Agency had its account, and deposited in the account of the Ethiopian National Bank in Citibank at about 2:00 p.m., New York time, on Friday, May 24, 1991.[41] This balance fell by July, continued to decline over the next month or two, and was down significantly by November. Deposits also were made into the account. All of this indicates that, despite his scruples, Meles did not return the $35 million. Rather, his government—or whoever had access to the account— drew on the funds over time. As noted above, Cohen reports that the new regime had the money by July, and officials of the Meles government acknowledged it to Divon by late fall. This was precisely the period in which the account balance fell, strongly suggesting that it was the government that made the withdrawals. Given the delay in forming a new government and Meles' attitude toward the money, it is possible that something irregular happened with the account. But the Ethiopian Central Bank had strict safeguards to prevent an unauthorized withdrawal.[42] And Meles gave oral confirmation to the JDC in 1993 that his government had received the $35 million.[43]

## THE JEWS WHO WERE LEFT BEHIND

Despite its concerns about the money, the provisional government established good relations with Jerusalem and in June reached an agreement permitting Israel to gather in the remaining Jews from Addis Ababa. In mid-September, the Jews began to leave on commercial Ethiopian Airlines flights via Rome to Israel. Naim himself flew home on September 21, and on October 15 he addressed the Third Committee of the United Nations, calling for the repeal of the 1975 General Assembly resolution that equated Zionism and racism. Operation Solomon proved to the world that Zionism is color-blind, Naim declared.[44] Two months later, the UN revoked the resolution. Though Naim seems to imply in his book, *Saving the Lost Tribe*, that his speech induced the UN to take this step, the vote to repeal was far more a demonstration of American influence after the Gulf War than it was a response to the Operation Solomon.[45] Still, Naim had made a cogent point.

Nearly a hundred people reached Israel each week that autumn. One of the first was Sagedu Dinku, the aunt whom Avi Beita had turned away in the Israeli embassy during the operation. After the mission, Avi had appealed in desperation to Qes Menashe Zimru, the senior spiritual leader of the Ethiopian community, who confirmed that Sagedu was Jewish. In late September, she was flown to Israel.[46] By early November, some 450 Ethiopian immigrants had been brought over. At that point, a Jewish Agency official announced that more than 40 percent of them were not Jewish. The non-Jews were mainly spouses in intermarriages, he said, and a number of the non-Jews who were arriving were Falash Mura.[47] That was a harbinger of things to come.

Ingathering the Jews of Quara proved to be another matter altogether. The Israeli Foreign Ministry said in August that the estimated two thousand Jews in that region and Gondar would reach Israel by the end of October.[48] Delays were caused, however, by the fact that the Jewish Agency had no idea who the Jews in Quara were. The region is geographically remote and had been cut off since the 1970s by a Maoist rebel group that opposed both Mengistu and the Tigreans, so the JDC's "bible" of names did not include the Quaran Jews. They were so isolated from the rest of Ethiopia, in fact, that they had not even heard about Operation Solomon.[49]

In the late summer of 1991, the rebels in Quara made peace with the new government and agreed to let the Jews go. The Quaran *qessotch* met with Micha Feldman in Gondar and listed the members of their community, naming some thirty-five hundred people.[50] In 1992, Israel, supported by the JDC, collected this community and brought most of them over. With that, the Ethiopian aliyah seemed nearly completed. Naim said in May 1992 that virtually the last of the Ethiopian Jews would reach Israel by June.[51] The *Jerusalem Post* ran a story late that July, when these Quaran Jews reached Ben-Gurion Airport, saying that "the exodus of Ethiopian Jewry officially came to an end yesterday morning."[52]

In fact, it would take at least seven more years for the balance of the Quaran community to arrive. During the interim, Israel's focus was not on the Jews of Quara, but on the Falash Mura.

## THE FALASH MURA

Some twenty-five hundred Falash Mura were left behind in Addis after the operation, according to the calculations of the JDC's Doron Tashteet.[53] The Joint and NACOEJ agreed to care for them. But thousands of Falash Mura descended on Addis, and in 1993 the JDC closed its list to new applicants for aid. The worrisome fact was that the number of Falash Mura still out in the countryside was incalculable. "We are on the tip of the iceberg. . . . Every number is good," Tashteet observed in 1996.[54]

The subject of the convert families was complex, the debate was bitter and politicized, and lives were at stake. Divisions grew between the Ethiopian-Israelis and the Falash Mura. The most urgent source of the tensions was the health danger that the Falash Mura faced in Addis, and that they in turn posed to the Ethiopian community already in Israel. The HIV infection rate among the Falash Mura was distressing. The Ministry of Health had determined that Ethiopian-Israelis were fifty times more likely than the general population to be HIV carriers, and the more recent arrivals from Addis were the most widely infected.[55] In October 1996, Shlomo Mula, secretary of the Unified Ethiopian Immigrants' Organization in Israel, said that the Falash Mura immigration should be stopped. The five hundred HIV-positive Ethiopians already in Israel were enough, he declared.[56]

Fear of HIV already had led to embarrassment for the Beta Israel, and to violence. In January 1996, Ethiopians in Israel had been infuriated when *Ma'ariv* broke the news that Magen David Adom, the state-run Israeli equivalent of the Red Cross, secretly was disposing of all blood donations by Ethiopians. The director of the blood bank, fearing HIV contamination, determined that the blood of Ethiopians had to be treated like that of homosexuals and drug addicts and discarded.[57] In fact, this was consistent with a larger pattern of keeping the Ethiopians' HIV rate from the public, apparently in order to protect the immigrants from stigmatization.[58] This attempt at sensitivity backfired, though, as outraged Ethiopian-Israelis held a demonstration in Jerusalem to protest what they considered racism. An estimated ten thousand of them shook their fists, shouted, threw stones, and tried to storm Prime Minister Shimon Peres' office. The police, surprised by such behavior in Ethiopians, responded with tear gas and water cannons. This outburst undoubtedly was driven in part by the frustration of many of the new Israelis who were challenged, disempowered, and socially dislocated by their experience in Israel. In response, the Labor Party chose Addisu Massele, who emerged as a forceful spokesman for the Ethiopian community, to sit in the Knesset. Addisu strongly advocated bringing the remaining Falash Mura in Addis to Israel quickly, specifically in order to arrest the spread of HIV among them.

Over the next year, virtually all of the Falash Mura who were then in Addis Ababa reached Israel. At the end of June 1998, in a gesture reminiscent of Shamir's seven years earlier, Prime Minister Netanyahu went to the airport to greet what was supposed to be the last plane of the aliyah, containing fifty-eight Falash Mura.[59] According to one sympathetic source, though, two hundred remained in the compound in Addis, awaiting clarification of their status. Then thousands of additional Falash Mura began to appear in the capital and Gondar town.

By the year 2000, activists claimed that there were twenty-six thousand Falash Mura still in Ethiopia. Hebrew University scholar Steven Kaplan predicted that "as soon as these are brought to Israel, more will be discovered. This has been the pattern in the past and there is no reason to believe that the people who are brought will not also have relatives who want to make aliyah."[60] The count of twenty-six thousand was based on a census taken the year before, which was overseen by David Efrati, a former director of population registry for the Israeli Interior Ministry. "The census was denigrated originally, but is now accepted as excellent and definitive," NACOEJ's Barbara Ribakove Gordon told me in 2001. "There will be no other thousands of people showing up," claiming to be Jews, she concluded. "That's a straw man we've had to put up with over and over again." Gordon argued that all twenty-six thousand should be brought to Israel. Many Falash Mura "never became genuine practicing Christians," she said. "I have no reason in the world to doubt the authenticity of their Jewish practice now. Come to Ethiopia. Take a look. They'd have to be fantastic actors. Their neighbors say the people there are so religious, they won't even have a cup of coffee on the Sabbath. . . . The rabbis in Israel have told us that they remain observant Jews."[61]

The JDC's Michael Schneider took a radically different position. "It's a travesty," he commented, also in 2001. "It's a matter of Third World people seeking First World comforts. A relatively self-sufficient agrarian population voluntarily left their villages and transformed themselves into a slum-dwelling urban population. They created a sorry sight, which attracted the sympathy of NACOEJ and the South Wing to Zion," an Ethiopian-Israeli activist group. The problem was fostered and allowed to continue, he said, by "an overzealous grass-roots organization [i.e., NACOEJ], a neglectful Israeli government without a consistent policy, a wavering chief rabbinate, and a slow-to-act Ministry of the Interior. We had our finger in the dike all these years. We were asked to provide cash and maintenance. We were willing to do so, so the government of Israel didn't have to hurry. They wanted to bring in enough to shut everybody up."[62]

The Falash Mura were reenacting the events of 1991 under different names. They had cast themselves in the role of the Beta Israel while NACOEJ had taken the place of the AAEJ. Ten years after Operation Solomon, several observers insisted that there was no conclusion in sight. "In hindsight, Mengistu was right," an anthropologist at Hebrew University told me. The dictator had argued in his interview with Micha Odenheimer in 1990 that everyone in northern Ethiopia could claim to be descended from Jews. "Thousands of

Ethiopians have now declared themselves 'Jewish,'" she observed. "And it's not the end."[63]

In 2001, Jewish Agency officials explicitly linked the Falash Mura question to the state's demographic needs. Given the high Israeli Arab birth rate, Israel depends on the immigration of Jews in order to remain predominantly Jewish. The Jewish Agency estimated that forty thousand immigrants would have to arrive annually in order to maintain an 80 percent Jewish majority in Israel.[64] In May 2001, however, Jewish Agency chairman Sallai Meridor noted that the intifada and signs of economic and social stabilization in the former Soviet Union had led to a troubling decline in immigration. In response, he promised that the Jewish Agency would transport up to five thousand Ethiopian immigrants annually, more than doubling the 2,228 who arrived in the year 2000. In the event, this forecast turned out to be optimistic.[65]

In the fall of 2002, Rabbi Ovadiah Yosef again played a defining role in the Ethiopian aliyah, declaring that the Falash Mura had converted out of fear and persecution and so should be regarded as Jews rather than Christians. He thus equated them with the fifteenth-century Spanish Marranos, despite arguments to the contrary by academic scholars. (In subsequent years, a number of press reports repeated his conclusion uncritically as historical fact.) As Sephardi chief rabbi in 1973, Yosef's validation of the Beta Israel's Jewishness had initiated the process that resulted in their aliyah and, ultimately, in Operation Solomon. Now, as spiritual mentor of the Shas Party, he inspired similar resolve toward the Falash Mura.[66] In February 2003, Interior Minister Eli Yishai, not coincidentally a member of Shas, led the Israeli government to resolve to expedite the immigration of the eighteen thousand to twenty thousand Falash Mura who remained in Ethiopia. There would be new guidelines for admitting them, following halakhic (religious legal) rather than civil principles. Decisions about whom to accept would no longer be based on the Law of Return or family reunification, but on Jewish maternal lineage. Officials in the Absorption Ministry, the Interior Ministry, and the Jewish Agency reportedly objected to this change of criteria.[67]

Matters took an abrupt turn when Yishai was replaced as interior minister by Avraham Poraz of the Shinui Party, who opposed bringing the Falash Mura en masse. The costs of absorbing Ethiopian immigrants were exceptionally high, $100,000 each, Poraz noted, and the government could not take on the expense of a large-scale immigration during the current economic downturn. Rather, it would bring the Falash Mura at a rate of 250–300 a month. The Ethiopian aliyah "is a never-ending story," Poraz complained, adding provocatively that the Falash Mura were not Jews in any case, rabbinic opinions notwithstanding.[68] Faced with this opposition, 380 Ethiopian-Israeli family heads and an American advocacy group petitioned the Israeli High Court at the end of June 2003 to compel the government to speed the immigration. Supporters argued that the situation was urgent: the Falash Mura who remained in Ethiopia faced starvation, and dozens had died in recent months. In November, hundreds of Ethiopian-Israelis demonstrated outside of Prime Minister Ariel Sharon's offices in Jerusalem, claiming that they were victims of racism, criticizing Poraz, and carrying photos of their relatives who were waiting to make aliyah. A few days later Poraz surprised his critics by announcing that he would propose to a ministerial committee that the twenty thousand people still on the Efrati list should be brought to Israel. Under this plan, those eligible under the Law of Return would arrive by the end of 2004; those who did not so qualify but who had a first-degree relative living in Israel would be brought within six months after that. The list would then be closed permanently. As an informed official in a major American Jewish philanthropic organization observed privately, however, this commitment meant little practically, since it came with no promise of budgetary resources to back it up, and no firm guidelines for implementation.[69]

In January 2004, Foreign Minister Silvan Shalom, while leading a trade delegation to Ethiopia, visited the Falash Mura holding sites in Ethiopia and affirmed the commitment to bring the people on the Efrati list to Israel. As in the time of Operation Solomon, however, it was uncertain how many qualified. In the previous three years, 8,656 of the 26,000 Ethiopians on the list had emigrated to Israel, but estimates of those still eligible ranged widely, from 18,000 to 24,000.[70] Even those numbers were in dispute. Several *qessotch* told Israel's absorption minister, Tzipi Livni, that the list included undeserving non-Jews.[71] Veteran Ethiopian-Israelis warned against taking in charlatans and "hitchhikers." And critics accused NACOEJ of seeking to enlarge Israel's Jewish population, and specifically the Orthodox community, by "manufacturing Jews": enticing Ethiopian Christian villagers to claim Jewish descent and convert. NACOEJ officials denied this, asserting the sincerity of the Falash Muras' return to Judaism. But some Jewish religious leaders observed that there were actually only three thousand to four thousand Jews left in Ethiopia. In another echo of Operation Solomon, the *Times* of London reported that "Ethiopia, sensitive to allegations that it was auctioning citizens, is believed to have exacted a high price for its accord."[72]

"The problem will be closed once and for all," said Foreign Minister Shalom. Livni argued, though, that the budget simply did not have the funds to undertake a rapid, large-scale immigration, a claim that provoked familiar charges of racism.[73]

Since Operation Solomon, seven successive Israeli governments have failed to bring the issue of the Falash Mura to a conclusion. If Israel follows Poraz's schedule, it will complete the Ethiopian aliyah in 2005, thirty years after first authorizing it. The matter remains unresolved as of this writing.

## "RESCUE"

... the discovery of fact bursts
In a paroxysm of emotion
Now as always. Crusoe
We say was
"Rescued."
So we have chosen.[74]

"Rescue from what?" Steven Kaplan, the Hebrew University historian, asked me, citing my references in a manuscript of the present book to the rescue of the Ethiopian Jews.[75] He raised a serious question: whether removing a people from their social, religious, and economic base, then exposing them to health risks and refugee life in circumstances that ultimately resulted in an emergency airlift, can properly be called a rescue.

The Beta Israel themselves presented their situation as requiring rescue. Indeed, Ethiopian Jews made timely interventions that helped spur the AAEJ, and later the Israelis, to urgent action. The elders' petition in December 1989 that the AAEJ transport the community from Gondar evoked a desperate vision of an imminent tragedy, as Susan Pollack reported. The same was true of Zimna Berhane's request in February 1991 that Lubrani extract the Jews from Addis before their family heads were slaughtered. In fact, months before these conversations took place, both Pollack and Lubrani already had spoken of taking dramatic steps to remove the Jews from harm's way. They then cited the Ethiopians' arguments in order to persuade others to endorse these actions.

The AAEJ transport program moved thousands of Beta Israel away from present hardships and possible future danger. In the process, it exposed them to the degradation and perils of existence in Addis Ababa. Whether this constituted a rescue remains a matter of dispute. The American organization did fulfill the Jews' wishes, however, putting them on a course that culminated in their safe arrival in Israel far more quickly and efficiently than would have been possible had they remained in Gondar.

Operation Solomon unquestionably did rescue the Ethiopian Jews from the hazards of life in Addis, and delivered them from the impending rebel assault on the city. As events unfolded, the EPRDF takeover was remarkably smooth, the Doomsday Scenario was never realized, and the new Meles government allowed the Beta Israel who remained in Addis to leave gradually and safely. At the time of the airlift, however, Mengistu's flight and the insurgent advance on the capital had made the future of the Jews there imponderable. The Israelis took a bold chance in order to save the Ethiopian Jews from potential catastrophe. When they did, Operation Solomon succeeded brilliantly, becoming a highlight in the history of Israel.

## THE GENETIC EVIDENCE

As noted in the Introduction, the Ethiopian aliyah was predicated on Rabbi Yosef's ruling in 1973 that the Beta Israel are descendants of the lost tribe of Dan. In 1991 and subsequently, researchers conducted genetic tests of the Ethiopian Jews who had reached Israel, to subject this question to scientific scrutiny. Their findings do not support the rabbi's judgment. Indeed, the most recent studies refute it, noting that the Ethiopian Jews do not show a number of genetic markers that are characteristic of Jews whose ancestors lived in the Middle East.[76]

The Ethiopian Jews' biological connection to the people of King Solomon may be in question, but their spiritual commitment to the God of Abraham, Isaac, and Jacob is not. They endured generations of hardship to sustain their Jewish identity. That continues today in the land for which they yearned for so long.

# APPENDIX 1

| ANNUAL EMIGRATION FROM ADDIS ABABA TO ISRAEL[1] | | MONTHLY EMIGRATION FROM ADDIS ABABA TO ISRAEL, 1990–91[2] | |
|---|---|---|---|
| 1977 | 124 | January 1990 | 180[3] |
| 1978 | 3 | February | 129 |
| 1979 | 32 | March | 115 |
| 1980 | 677 | April | 554 |
| 1981 | 681 | May | 457 |
| 1982 | 800 | June | 438 |
| 1983 | 2,227 | July | 80 |
| 1984 | 8,413 | August | 128 |
| 1985 | 1,787 | September | 177 |
| 1986 | 216 | October | 58 |
| 1987 | 262 | November | 428 |
| 1988 | 604 | December | 532 |
| 1989 | 1,382 | | |
| 1990 | 4,153 | January 1991 | 1,038 |
| 1991 | 19,879 | February | 974 |
| 1992 | 3,527 | March | 508 |
| 1993 | 844 | April | 1,008 |
| 1994 | 1,190 | May 1–23 | 1,138 |
| 1995 | 1,259 | May 24–25 | 14,310 |
| 1996 | 1,348 | | |
| 1997 | 1,703 | | |
| 1998 | 3,105 | | |
| 1999 | 2,300 | | |
| 2000 | 2,228 | | |
| 2001 | 2,971 | | |
| 2002 | 2,656 | | |
| 2003 | 3,029 | | |

Using the figures above, one can determine the number of Jews who reached the capital during the mass migration that began in spring 1990:

Some 7,500 Jews made aliyah from Addis between April 1990 and Operation Solomon in May 1991; 4,310 were brought over during that mission; and 500 to 700 were left behind in the city. This yields a total of over 22,000 whom the Jewish Agency certified as Jews. Roughly 2,000–3,000 of these were already in the capital when the AAEJ transport program began in spring 1990, which means that 19,000 to 20,000 Jews came down from Gondar during the period in question. Perhaps 2500 Falash Mura joined them at that time.

# APPENDIX 2

## THE NUMBER OF PEOPLE BROUGHT TO ISRAEL IN OPERATION SOLOMON

The office of the director-general of immigration and absorption of the Jewish Agency cites 14,310 as the official number of people who were flown to Israel during Operation Solomon. This figure was determined by Micha Feldman, the Israeli consul in Addis in 1990–91, who oversaw the official list of emigrants from Addis.[1]

A report immediately after the operation by Arnon Mantber, then director-general of immigration and absorption of the Jewish Agency, indicated a somewhat lower figure based on the number of Ethiopians who were taken to absorption centers or hospitals during the operation. According to this report, 14,203 *olim* were brought to forty-nine absorption sites:

3,112 *olim* were brought to six sites in Jerusalem, including Ashkelon
3,130 *olim* were taken to six sites in the Negev, including three caravan sites
6,938 *olim* went to thirty-one sites in Haifa and the Galilee
  983 *olim* went to six sites in the nation's center
   40 *olim* went directly to hospitals

Total: 14,203[2]

# APPENDIX 3

## A CONVERSATION WITH KASSA KEBEDE

Kassa's heart is red, Riki Mullah told me, meaning that his heart is good. Riki, who appears in the Introduction to this book, met Kassa in 1988, after she had spent eight months bribing Ethiopian officials to allow her parents to go to Israel. Then Kassa agreed to see her and arranged for her parents to go. "Did you bribe him?" I asked. "No, his heart is red," she answered.[1]

"No one else but Kassa stayed to help" in those last days before Operation Solomon, the AAEJ's Nate Shapiro said. "Why? We asked him to. He says he could've left. He says it was good for Ethiopia and good for the Jews" for him to stay. "I really believe him."[2]

Kassa loved Israel and Judaism, said Asher Naim, the Israeli ambassador to Addis Ababa at the time of the airlift. He was the only one to stick his neck out for the Jews at a time when rivals in Mengistu's murderous regime were always looking to get him. "You can't take that away from him," Naim said.[3]

"Kebede was a shit," one Israeli who was intimately familiar with the negotiations observed succinctly. "He was tougher to Israel than Mengistu was. Mengistu didn't know Israel. Kassa knew what he could get."

"Kassa was a thief and a liar, but a pleasant one," said a key Israeli Foreign Ministry official.

As I drove to Bethesda, Maryland, on May 5, 1997, to meet Kassa, I was pretty sure that I was in for a memorable interview. For months I'd been hearing about his intelligence and complexity, his brilliant and frustrating public justifications and denials, and his almost Shakespearean theatricality. I wondered if he'd give a performance: Iago calmly insisting that he's Hamlet. Or would he offer the sincere perspective of a talented man who tried to save his country's disintegrating regime?

We spoke over coffee in a hotel lounge. Kassa was dressed casually, in a short-sleeved sport shirt. His manner was aristocratic, relaxed and secure, though seasoned by a hint of distrust. He lived outside of Washington now, and said that he worked at a think tank devoted to world peace.[4] Obviously he'd landed on his feet. As we spoke, Kassa seemed patiently forbearing of the fact that a stranger was going to help define his role in history. He clearly intended to guide me in that, and I could understand his motivation. We had scheduled two hours, which for him was just a warm-up. Then I would have to leave for my next interview, with Susan Pollack.

What I really wanted to hear was Kassa's side of the story about the exchange of money and weapons for Jews. I asked first about his negotiations with Lubrani for the "generous financial assistance." "Transport costs," Kassa corrected me tolerantly. That came late in the story, he said; "Uri Lubrani was a latecomer in the whole picture." Kassa now spent an hour giving me the background that he felt I needed. Over our first cup of coffee, he told me his account of Operation Moses. When I tried to return the conversation to Operation Solomon, he gently rebuked me: "This is a very unstructured interview," he said in his dignified way. Then he returned to his narrative. Speaking in formal, nearly perfect English, Kassa explained that during Operation Moses, the Ethiopian government did not make a deal to let the Jews pass into Sudan in return for Israeli arms, as people claimed. "That wasn't true," he said. "The Ethiopian government didn't want to obstruct this insofar as it didn't affect Ethiopia." Rather, "we wanted them to go to Israel."

Kassa stressed his deep personal sympathy for Jews. His most important schooling in Israel, he told me, was not at Hebrew University, but at Ulpan Akiva in Netanya, where he took an intensive course in Hebrew. There, he recalled, he met Jews of sixty-two nationalities and learned from them the history of Jewish suffering. The Americans told him about the civil rights movement, and taught him to sing "We Shall Overcome," he said. Kassa asked them, "Why do you Jews sing this?" "Because we were oppressed too," they answered.[5] As we sipped our coffee, Kassa reminisced that as a student in Jerusalem, he took written prayers from his Jewish friends and placed them in cracks in the Wailing Wall. That was a way for Jews to petition God, but at the time, Jordan, which controlled the Old City of Jerusalem until 1967, did not permit them to go to the wall themselves. So Kassa did it for them. This spiritual background, he implied, had inspired his benevolent treatment of the Falashas.

A chief motivation for him in Ethiopia had been to help the Jews to leave, Kassa told me. He had suffered a great deal of emotional pain because the Israeli press had not given him credit for this, he said. "The issue for us was, there are divided families," he told me. By stressing the concept of family reunification, he noted, "I can have the courage to go to the military bosses and my genuinely committed Communist colleagues" and make a humanitarian argument to let the Jews join their relatives in Israel.[6]

But Kassa also allowed that there were political reasons for him to permit the Jews to leave. American Jews supported the emigration. "Did we want the very strong Jewish lobbies in the U.S. against us? My problem was an image problem, improving relations with the U.S. and Western media. I wanted sympathetic authors in Jewish circles," he said, with an implication that was hard for me to miss. "I also believed Israel would give access to these lobbies."

Over our second cup of coffee I returned to the question of Jews for weapons. In addition to your humanitarian concern for the Jews, I said, it was also true that the military situation was becoming desperate. Didn't it make sense to ask Israel for arms in appreciation for Mengistu's giving them what they wanted? Kassa smiled at the formulation but offered an animated denial. "What would you do with Israeli arms?" he responded. "Brezhnev supplied everything, $11 billion in arms. If arms would have done it, it would have then. In 1991 it wasn't a lack of equipment. Ethiopia in 1991 had the largest army in Africa, air force, missiles, helicopter gunships." But, I interjected, I'd seen Mengistu's shopping list of lethal weapons. "It's true," Kassa conceded, smiling again, "Mengistu would ask. Mengistu went to Israel to ask for many things, and arms were stressed. He was spoiled by the Soviet Union." And Kassa asserted that yes, "Israel sent some arms."

I asked about the money. "Uri and I tried to work this out in a logical way," he said. Ethiopian Airlines told him that the cost of a ticket from Addis to Rome to Tel Aviv was $1,917. "I asked the Israelis, 'How many people?' and took their figure: around 18,000." This worked out to almost $35 million. "It was simply a question of arithmetic," he said.[7]

"Uri told me that the initial demand was for $180 million," I said.

Kassa smiled and replied, "Other figures were discussed, but Uri knew it wasn't serious. I told him, 'Let's not appear to be selling people.'"

As we approached the end of our talk, ironically, Kassa spoke warmly of the Israeli whose succinctly obscene opinion of him appears near the top of this profile. He spoke well of Lubrani too. "Uri was very friendly, helpful. There were no misunderstandings at all. We were very open." That didn't quite square with Lubrani's account of the staged confrontations and threats that went on between them, but it confirmed something that Michael Schneider had told me: that there was antagonism between Kassa and Lubrani on a professional level but love on a personal basis. Schneider had added that Kassa felt genuine affection for the Israelis.[8] This seemed to be true.

The meeting with Kassa then became a little surreal when I called Susan Pollack to let her know that I'd be there soon and Kassa got on the phone to complain that he hadn't seen her in a long time.

At Pollack's apartment, I told her that I'd spent two hours interviewing Kassa over two cups of coffee, and only toward the end had he started to tell me about the things I'd wanted to hear. It takes three cups of coffee with Ethiopians, she replied. Over the first they tell you generalities. Over the second, the conversation starts to get interesting. And over the third they tell you what you need to know. I'd had only two cups.[9]

Several weeks later, back in Jerusalem, Asher Naim told me that, whatever else one might say about him, Kassa was brilliant.[10] In retrospect, Naim

was right. Kassa was a favorite of Haile Selassie's who was dexterous enough—
or sufficiently well connected—to survive the brutal coup in 1974. Many of
the leading figures from the old regime were executed or imprisoned, but
Kassa made the transition successfully. Years later, when the civil war in his
country was all but lost, it was Kassa who realized the crucial role in which a
tiny religious minority, the Jews, could be cast. Then, even with a losing
hand, Kassa played poker with an old pro like Uri Lubrani until the last
moment, when he ran out of time. And, when it was all over, he managed the
softest of landings, into a safe, comfortable life outside of Washington, D.C.

# NOTES

The sources referenced below are listed by type in the Bibliography.

## Preface

1. Interview with Riki, August 11, 1996.
2. Interview with Weil, December 18, 1996.
3. Cf. Weil, "It Is Futile to Trust in Man," p. 2.
4. See Kay Kaufman Shelemay, *Music, Ritual, and Falasha History*, pp. 28–29.
5. Interview with Qes Adane, December 9, 1996. The *qes's* account describes events in 1984–85.
6. Interview with Qes Adane, December 9, 1996.
7. The phrase "the Operation Solomon in their memories" is inspired by Hagar Salamon's elegant assertion that her quest when she interviewed Ethiopian Jews was for "the Ethiopia within" (*The Hyena People*, p. 4).
8. White, *Tropics of Discourse*, p. 90.

## Introduction

1. See Appendix 2.
2. For a brief account of Pollack's story, see Rabinovich, "Down from the Hills." Berger, *Rescue the Ethiopian Jews!*, pp. 185–91, and Kaye, "On the Wings of Eagles: A History and Analysis of the Movement to Rescue Ethiopian Jewry," pp. 333 ff., draw largely on Rabinovich. Also see Rabinovich, "Exodus: The Sequel."
3. Abbink, in "The Enigma of the Beta Esra'el's Ethnogenesis: An Anthro-Historical Study," contrasts Beta Israel accounts of the Menelik story with that in the *Kebra Negast*, the Ethiopian national epic.
4. Ullendorff, "The Queen of Sheba in Ethiopian Tradition," p. 104.
5. See Rev. 5:5. Cf. Ullendorff, *The Ethiopians: An Introduction to Country and People*, pp. 2, 139, 187; Leslau, *Falasha Anthology*, p. xliii.
6. Gobat, *Journal of a Three-Years' Residence in Abyssinia*, p. 467; d'Abbadie, "Réponses des Falashas dit Juif d'Abyssinie aux questions faites à M. Luzzato," p. 183.
7. Kaplan, *The Beta Israel (Falasha) in Ethiopia: From Earliest Times to the Twentieth Century*, pp. 24–26, 165.
8. See Quirin, *The Evolution of Ethiopian Jews: A History of the Beta Israel (Falasha) to 1920*, p. 8; Leslau, p. xliii; Ullendorff, *The Ethiopians*, pp. 37–38.
9. See Ullendorff, *Ethiopia and the Bible*, pp. 16–17; Kaplan, pp. 26–30. Jeremiah 44:1 refers to Jews living in Egypt. See Bezalel Porten, *Archives from Elephantine*, p. ix, and, for a different perspective, Kessler, *The Falashas: The Forgotten Jews of Ethiopia*, pp. 41–49; also Quirin, *Evolution*, p. 9. See also Conti Rossini, *Storia d'Etiopia*, pp. 91–131, 144, 167–201; Ullendorff, *The Ethiopians*, pp. 48ff.
10. Quirin, *Evolution*, p. 10. See Tadesse Tamrat, *Church and State in Ethiopia*, p. 66, and "The Abbots of Dabra Hayq, 1248–1535."

11. Cf. Conti Rossini, "Appunti di storia e letteratura Falascia"; Rathjens, *Die Juden in Abessinien*, p. 92; Leslau, p. xliii; Hess, "Toward a History of the Falasha," p. 111; Ullendorff, *Ethiopia and the Bible*, pp. 17–23, and *The Ethiopians*, p. 51; Kaplan, 30–32. See also Aešcoly, *Recueil de textes falachas*, p. 3.

12. *The Ethiopians*, p. 96. See Polotsky, "Aramaic, Syriac and Ge'ez," pp. 1–10; Nöldeke, *Neue Beiträge zur Semitischen Sprachwissenschaft*; Ullendorff, "Hebrew, Aramaic, and Greek: The Versions Underlying Ethiopic Translations of Bible and Intertestamental Literature," pp. 249–57; also "Hebrew Element in the Ethiopic Old Testament," pp. 42–50, cited in Kaplan, p. 170 n. 30.

13. Ullendorff, *The Ethiopians*, p. 99. See "Circumcision," in Eliade, ed., *The Encyclopedia of Religion*. The Muslim Pashtuns (or Pathans) in Afghanistan also reportedly follow this practice (Weil, "Our Brethren the Taliban?").

14. See Tadesse, *Church and State*, pp. 207–9, 213–19, 224–30, 291.

15. *The Ethiopians*, p. 96. See Getachew, "The Forty-nine Hour Sabbath of the Ethiopian Church," p. 246.

16. See Ullendorff, *Ethiopia and the Bible*, pp. 18, 21; Kaplan, *The Beta Israel*, pp. 18–20. For a contrary view, cf. Rodinson, "Sur la question des 'influences juives' en Ethiopie," pp. 11–19.

17. See Quirin, *Evolution*, pp. 19–20; Kaplan, pp. 50–51.

18. Kaplan, pp. 9, 55. See Shelemay, *Music, Ritual, and Falasha History*, pp. 20–21. Quirin concludes that references to the Ayhud, Falashas, Beta Israel, Kayla, and Israel all designate the same people, at least since the fourteenth century ("The Beta Israel [Falasha] in Ethiopian History," pp. 34–35 n. 12).

19. For earlier contributions to this "integrated group model" (as opposed to the "lost tribe model" cited in Salamon, *The Hyena People: Ethiopian Jews in Christian Ethiopia*, p. 126 n. 8), see Conti Rossini, *Storia d'Etiopia*; Krempel, "Die Soziale und wirtschaftliche Stellung der Falascha in der christlich-amharischen wirtschaftliche von Nordwest-Äthiopien"; Ullendorff, *The Ethiopians* and *Ethiopia and the Bible*; and to a degree Leslau. Cf. Rathjens, *Juden in Abessinien*; Rodinson, pp. 1–19; and Dillmann, *Über die Regierung, insbesondere die Kirchenordnung des Königs Zar'a-Jacob*.

20. Cf. Gaguine, "The Falasha Version of the Testaments of Abraham, Isaac, and Jacob," pp. 46–47.

21. See, however, Alvarez-Pereyre and Ben-Dor, "The Formal Organisation of the Beta Israel Liturgy—Substance and Performance: Literary Structure," p. 240.

22. Shelemay, *Music* and *A Song of Longing*, ch. 9. For a wholly different theory, see Ephraim, "An Obscure Component in Ethiopian Church History."

23. See Krempel, "Eine Berufskaste in Nordwest-Athiopien—die Kayla (Falascha)," p. 41.

24. Quirin, "Beta Israel," pp. 192, 208–9.

25. Abbink, "A Socio-Structural Analysis of the Beta-Esra'el as an 'Infamous Group' in Traditional Ethiopia," pp. 145–53.

26. See Reminick, "The Structures and Functions of Religious Belief Among the Amhara of Ethiopia," pp. 33–34; Abbink, pp. 146–50; Salamon, chapter 3.

27. See Abbink, p. 149; Salamon, pp. 85–86.

28. Salamon, pp. 85–86. See Abbink, p. 150; also Hess, p. 120.

29. See Ullendorff, *The Ethiopians*, p. 106; Quirin, p. 12; and Salamon, p. 128 n. 14 and pp. 21–23.

30. "Tarika-Nagast," cited by Tadesse, *Church and State*, p. 201. See Salamon, pp. 32, 128 n. 14, 129 n. 1.

31. Salamon, p. 128 n. 14.

32. See Kaplan, p. 9, and Shelemay, *A Song of Longing*, p. 146.

33. See Kaplan, "Black and White, Blue and White and Beyond the Pale"; Salamon, p. 75.

34. Leslau, pp. xiii, xix, xl. See Salamon, pp. 18–20, 47–51, 98–99.
35. See Shelemay, *A Song of Longing*, p. 71; Feldman, *The Ethiopian Exodus*, pp. 187–88. Cf. Abbink, "Seged Celebrations in Ethiopia and Israel: Continuity and Change of a Falasha Religious Holiday," 789–810; Shoshana Ben-Dor, "Ha'sigd shel Beta Israel: Hag hidush ha'brith"; and Salamon, "Contacts and Communication Among the Beta-Israel in Ethiopia: Regional Aspects," pp. 62–68.
36. Kethuboth, the Babylonian Talmud, 62a; Ginsburg, *Sod ha-Shabbat*, p. 106 n. 87, p. 119 n. 168, p. 120 n. 174.
37. Leslau, pp. xxxii–xxxiii. Ethiopian Christians conceive of the Sabbath similarly. See Luzzato, "Mémoire sur les juifs d'Abyssinie ou Falashas." Cf. Shelemay, "Music and Text of the Falasha Sabbath," 3–22.
38. Kaplan, p. 123.
39. Shelemay, *Music*, pp. 47–48. Also see her chapter 2; Leslau, pp. xxi–xxxvi; and Feldman, p. 188.
40. Shelemay, *A Song of Longing*, p. 72; Halevi, "The Last Jewish Monk"; Quirin, p. 6.
41. See Shelemay, *A Song of Longing*, p. 36.
42. Kessler, p. 93. Cf. Bruce, *Travels to Discover the Source of the Nile*, p. 486; Kaplan, p. 189 n. 3. See also Aeścoly, *Recueil de textes falachas*, p. 1, and Baron, *A Social and Religious History of the Jews* 18:379–82; also, Quirin, p. 3.
43. Kaplan, p. 147.
44. In January 1990, the Jewish Agency's Feldman estimated that there were 17,000 Jews in Ethiopia (Feldman, p. 139).
45. Shimon Peres, for example, then David Ben-Gurion's defense minister, after spending a week in Ethiopia with Yitzhak Rabin, wrote in a top-secret report in 1963 that "Ethiopia is a vital element in our effort to break the Arab hostility around us with power, connections, and resourcefulness. . . . It is our goal to reach an alliance with Ethiopia—cultural, economic and military. We must spare no effort and resources in working toward this aim" (Erlich, *The Cross and the River*, p. 161).
46. Erlich, *Ethiopia and the Middle East*, chapter 10, and *The Cross and the River*, pp. 147–63.
47. Erlich, *The Struggle over Eritrea*, p. 106; Black and Morris, *Israel's Secret Wars: A History of Israel's Intelligence Services*, p. 187.
48. Erlich, *Ethiopia and the Middle East*, p. 140; Dawit, *Red Tears*, p. 318.
49. Sachar, p. 576; Erlich, *Ethiopia and the Middle East*, pp. 165–69.
50. Rapoport, *Redemption Song: The Story of Operation Moses*, p. xv. Cf. Bard, *From Tragedy to Triumph*, p. 19.
51. Westheimer and Kaplan, *Surviving Salvation: The Ethiopian Jewish Family in Transition*, pp. 23–24; M. Waldman, *Beyond the Rivers of Ethiopia* (Israel: Ministry of Defense, 1989), pp. 274–75; Kaplan, p. 25; Kessler, p. 161. See also Bard, *From Tragedy to Triumph: The Politics Behind the Rescue of Ethiopian Jewry*, p. 49, for a discussion of the role of Shlomo Hillel, who, while filling in as interior minister, endorsed the rabbinic decision in 1976.
52. Erlich, *Ethiopia and the Middle East*, pp. 179–80.
53. Black and Morris, p. 448.
54. Erlich, *Ethiopia and the Middle East*, p. 185.
55. Rapoport, p. 56; Dawit, p. 331.
56. Artzi'eli, "The Falashas: A Dying Community. The Weakness of Israel," cited in Bard, p. 63.
57. See, however, Bard, p. 64.
58. Interview with Shamir, May 23, 1997.
59. U.S. intelligence estimates, cited in Brzezinski, *Power and Principle*, p. 184.
60. Interview with Halachmi, July 21, 1997. See Henze, *Layers of Time: A History of Ethiopia*, pp. 298–302.

61. Erlich, *Ethiopia and the Middle East*, p. 184.
62. Collins, "Mossad Unable to Specify Fatality Toll for Ethiopian Jews." Cf. Rapoport, p. xv; Westheimer and Kaplan, p. 27; Schindler and Ribner, *The Trauma of Transition: The Psycho-Social Cost of Ethiopian Immigration to Israel,* p. 3. Haim Halachmi said in an interview (July 21, 1997) that the number was at most 1,500. Dawit Wolde Giorgis points out that this was the single greatest loss of life for the Falashas in the twentieth century. Arguing that the Western media have ignored the Ethiopian perspective on the emigration, he says that it was wrong to single out one of the many oppressed peoples of Ethiopia for rescue on the basis of religion. He claims that the Falashas were poor, hungry, uneducated people lured away from their homes, and that a fraction of the money spent on airlifting them would have been sufficient to help them had they remained in Ethiopia (pp. 318–19).
63. Ayalen, "To Live in Deed."
64. Rapoport, pp. 83, 93, 99, 106–17. Westheimer and Kaplan say that 6,500 Ethiopian Jews came to Israel in Operation Moses (p. 25). A JDC-Brookdale study refers to 7,000, while the JDC and the Ministry of Absorption use the number 8,000. Micha Feldman, who directed the aliyah for the Jewish Agency, says there were 6,364 (p. 153).
65. Safire, "Interrupted Exodus."
66. Bard, pp. 164–66; Black and Morris, p. 449. Feldman, citing foreign press reports, says that Operation Sheba brought 494 Jews to Israel (p. 153).
67. HIAS count (see Appendix 1). JDC figures agree, except for the 1988 immigration, which the JDC sets at 824, as against HIAS' 604 (JDC report of April 9, 1991, JDC archive). Feldman says that there were 16,000 Ethiopians in Israel by March 1990: 12,000 from twenty-five operations, and the rest via Europe with the assistance of the Intergovernmental Committee for Emigration (p. 153).
68. Jewish Agency Information Center, www.jafi.org.il/mission/history; see page 85 in this volume. The Statistical Abstract of Israel 2004 (Central Bureau of Statistics, 55:2.23) indicates that some 1,166,400 immigrants from the former Soviet Union lived in Israel by the end of 2003.
69. The Statistical Abstract of Israel 2004 (Central Bureau of Statistics, 55:2.26) notes that approximately 94,700 Ethiopians were in Israel at the end of 2003. Thirty percent of these (28,900) were born in Israel, and the median age of the Ethiopian-Israeli population was 19.8 years. See Appendix 1.
70. See Henze, *Layers of Time*, p. 324.
71. Ibid., p. 325 n. 13; Cohen, *Intervening in Africa,* p. 21.
72. Feldman, p. 165.
73. "Airlift of Jews Is Anti-Arab Plot: Syrian Paper" and "Syria, Palestinians Denounce Falasha Evacuation."
74. The United States had complained to Israel in 1985 about reports that hundreds of Ethiopian Jews who had been brought over in Operation Moses had been sent to the Kiryat Arba settlement on the West Bank. The Israeli minister of immigration responded that Kiryat Arba was one of five immigrant processing centers and would not necessarily be the Ethiopian Jews' permanent home (Gwertzman, "Ethiopian Jews Said to Resettle on West Bank"). As of early 2004, a few hundred Ethiopians were reportedly living on the West Bank.

## Chapter One

1. Interview with Mengistu in Orizio, "The Lion Sleeps Tonight," pp. 29, 31.
2. See Copson, "Ethiopia: War and Famine," p. 10; Henze, "Ethiopia in 1991—Peace Through Struggle," p. 8.

3. Gorbachev thereby confirmed his written warning to Mengistu in January 1989 (Cohen, *Intervening in Africa: Superpower Peacemaking in a Troubled Continent*, pp. 20, 230 n. 9). See Henze, "The Defeat of the Derg," p. 24; *Layers of Time*, p. 312. Erlich notes that the Soviets had grown impatient with Mengistu as early as 1987 (*Ethiopia and the Middle East*, pp. 184–85).

4. Marcus, *A History of Ethiopia*, p. 212; Cohen, p. 20; telephone interview with Bob Houdek, November 29, 2001.

5. Perlez, "Ethiopia's President Looks Toward Better U.S. Relations."

6. Henze, "The Fall of the Derg," p. 3; *Layers of Time*, pp. 314, 318.

7. Interviews with Bob Frasure, senior Africa officer on the National Security Council (1992), and American and Israeli diplomats who were posted in Addis Ababa at the time.

8. Cohen, p. 230 n. 3.

9. Marcus, *Ethiopia, Great Britain, and the United States*, pp. 2–5, 90–114; Lemmu Baissa, "United States Military Assistance to Ethiopia, 1953–1974: A Reappraisal of a Difficult Patron-Client Relationship," 51–70.

10. Marcus, *Ethiopia, Great Britain, and the United States*, p. 7.

11. Cohen, p. 17; Henze, *Layers of Time*, pp. 297–98; interview with Brent Scowcroft, June 12, 2003.

12. Cohen, pp. 17–18, 20; Henze, *Layers of Time*, pp. 297–98; Brzezinski, *Power and Principle: Memoirs of the National Security Adviser, 1977–1981*, pp. 179–80, 189, 203–4, and passim.

13. Cohen, pp. 18–21.

14. Cohen, pp. 24–25; interview with Cohen, 1992. See Perlez, "Ethiopian-Israeli Accord Eases Jewish Emigration."

15. Record of a conversation with Cohen, by Scott Cohen, September 19, 1989 (JDC archive), confirmed by Herman Cohen, telephone interview, April 11, 2003.

16. From January to June 1989, 133 emigrated directly from Ethiopia; from June to December, the number rose to 401 (Feldman, *The Ethiopian Exodus*, pp. 129, 137). The Jewish Agency's annual figures for the aliyah, which factor in emigration from Sudan, cite 1,382 arrivals in 1989. See Appendix 1.

17. Interview with Merhav, July 23, 1997.

18. Henze, *Layers of Time*, pp. 309–11; Orizio, "The Lion Sleeps Tonight," p. 39. See Sivini, "Famine and the Resettlement Program in Ethiopia."

19. Position paper prepared for the Foreign Ministry in September 1988 by Hanan Aynor, former Israeli ambassador to Addis; interview with Merhav, July 23, 1997.

20. Perlez, "Ethiopian-Israeli Accord Eases Jewish Emigration"; interviews with Israeli diplomatic sources.

21. Perlez, "Ethiopian-Israeli Accord Eases Jewish Emigration"; *New York Times*, November 5, 1989; *Sunday Times*, December 1, 1989; McManus, "U.S. Confronts Israel on Ethiopia Cluster Bombs." See Henze, *Layers of Time*, p. 315. That Israel resumed arms sales to Ethiopia prior to November 1989 was confirmed by Herman Cohen (interview, April 11, 2003) and a high-ranking official in the Israeli Foreign Ministry (interview, 1992).

22. In a meeting at the U.S. embassy in Addis Ababa in late 1989, Carter privately criticized Israeli officials forcefully for arming Mengistu. "That's one of the dumbest things you can do," he told them (telephone interview with Bob Houdek, May 24, 2004).

23. E-mail interview, December 14, 2001; confirmed by Haim Divon in a 1992 interview.

24. Interview with Merhav, July 23, 1997; Haim Divon, in a 1992 interview, credited Yossi Hadas, then deputy director-general for Asia and Africa at the Foreign Ministry, with being a moving force behind the policy change.

25. Interviews with Divon (1992) and Rachamim Elazar (1992).

26. Interview with Merhav, July 23, 1997.

27. Ibid.; Cohen, p. 35.

28. Interview with Merhav, June 23, 1997.
29. Makovsky, "U.S. Opposes Israeli Links with Ethiopia's Mengistu"; Perlez, "Israelis Widening Role in Ethiopia."
30. The Morrison Report, submitted to the House Subcommittee on Africa on February 3, 1990. Details about Morrison's sources were supplied by Bob Houdek, the American chargé d'affaires in Addis (interview, 1992).
31. Interview with Morrison, 1992.
32. *Ha'aretz*, March 23, 1990; Makovsky, "Israel Backs Mengistu Despite U.S. Pressure."
33. Merhav, e-mail interview, January 5, 2002; interview with Lubrani, 1992.
34. Interview with Naim, 1992.
35. Henze, "The Defeat of the Derg," p. 25.
36. Interview with Frasure, 1992.
37. Feldman, p. 139.
38. Interviews with Merhav (July 23, 1997) and Yoffe (1992). On the Ethiopian plateau there are small rains from March until May and torrential rains from June to September, which I refer to as the rainy season. See Ullendorff, *The Ethiopians*, p. 26.
39. See Feldman, p. 17.
40. Feldman, p. 155; interview with Ami Bergman, October 13, 1996.
41. Jewish Agency, "Summary of February 18th Meeting on Ethiopian Aliyah," February 18, 1990; Jewish Agency cable from Feldman to Arnon Mantber, April 17, 1990; interviews with Haim Halachmi (July 21, 1997) and Arnon Mantber (July 30, 1997).
42. Interview with Pollack, 1992; Rabinovich, "Down from the Hills"; Berger, *Rescue the Ethiopian Jews!*, p. 184.
43. Berger, pp. 7ff.; telephone interview with Will Recant, March 12, 2003.
44. Rapoport, *Redemption Song*, pp. 88–93; Bard, *From Tragedy to Triumph*, pp. 40–43 and passim; also, interviews with Nate Shapiro (1992 and May 27, 2003), Hiam Halachmi (July 21, 1997), Will Recant (1992 and October 9, 1997), and Howard Lenhoff (telephone interviews, December 2, 2002, and May 21, 2004).
45. AAEJ report, "'The People Who Get Money from the Sky': A Report on Ethiopia and Kenya," February 1989; Rabinovich, "Down from the Hills."
46. "'The People Who Get Money from the Sky.'"
47. Ibid.
48. A memo of March 17, 1988, from Ami Bergman to the JDC's Michael Schneider noted that there were 2,000 Jews then in Addis (JDC archive). Merhav, citing figures supplied by Micha Feldman, said that 3,000 were in the capital by March 1990 (interview, August 17, 1997). Feldman said in an interview, however, that there were as few as 1,500 in January 1990 (July 14, 1997).
49. Bob Houdek, the American chargé d'affaires in Addis Ababa, reported that non-Jews had "burned homes, stolen property, and killed Falashas in Gonder" in 1990 ("Falasha Round-up: 1990," Department of State document 1991ADDIS00753, February 20, 1991). His overall assessment, however, was that the Jews were at no particular risk relative to anyone else in the region (interview, May 18, 2004).
50. Interview with Pollack, May 5, 1997; Rabinovich, "Exodus: The Sequel."
51. Interviews with Shapiro (1992 and May 27, 2003) and Will Recant (October 9, 1997); Rabinovich, "Exodus: The Sequel."

## Chapter Two

1. Marcus, *A History of Ethiopia*, p. 230; Ullendorff, *The Ethiopians*, p. 222; Henze, *Layers of Time*, p. 290 n. 13.

2. Interviews with numerous Israeli diplomatic sources; Feldman, *The Ethiopian Exodus*, p. 132; Naim, *Saving the Lost Tribe: The Rescue and Redemption of the Ethiopian Jews*, p. 17. See Bergman's fascinating profile, "I, Kassa Kebede."

3. Korn, *Ethiopia, the United States, and the Soviet Union*, p. 107; Henze, *Layers of Time*, p. 290 n. 13, 316 n. 6; Erlich, *Ethiopia and the Challenge of Independence*, p. 241; Dawit, *Red Tears*, pp. 347–48.

4. Korn, *Ethiopia, the United States and the Soviet Union*, pp. 107–8. Kassa told Bergman that his father's life was in danger when Mengistu came to power ("I, Kassa Kebede"). Clapham notes, however, that Kassa's father was Mengistu's patron (*Transformation and Continuity in Revolutionary Ethiopia*, p. 105).

5. Interview with Kassa, 1992.

6. Henze, *Layers of Time*, p. 290 n. 13; Erlich, *Ethiopia and the Challenge of Independence*, p. 241; Korn, *Ethiopia, the United States, and the Soviet Union*, p. 108. Bergman's "I, Kassa Kebede" discusses Kebede Tessema's activities in Jerusalem after the emperor's stay there. See Pankhurst, *The Ethiopians*, pp. 236–37, and Orizio, "The Lion Sleeps Tonight," p. 24.

7. See Bergman, "I, Kassa Kebede," and Naim, *Saving the Lost Tribe*, pp. 17, 66.

8. Kraybill and Hostetter, *Anabaptist World USA*, p. 149.

9. Interviews with Kulick, 1992 and May 27, 2003, and with Shapiro, 1992 and May 27, 2003; confirmed, to some extent, by interview with Kassa, May 5, 1997.

10. Kassa later denied asking the Israelis to safeguard his life or accepting any money for his part in Operation Solomon. See pages 106, 121, 146, and 168 in this volume.

11. Some of Kassa's colleagues in Mengistu's government spoke of him in similar terms. See former Ethiopian deputy foreign minister Dawit Wolde Giorgis's *Red Tears*, pp. 322, 331. Cf. also page 161 in this volume.

12. Interview with Houdek, 1992.

13. See the discussion of this incident in the Introduction. Also, see Rapoport, *Redemption Song*, p. 88; Dawit, *Red Tears*, p. 331.

14. Interview with Naim, May 30, 1997. See Appendix 3.

15. Interview with Lubrani, February 11, 1997.

16. Cohen, *Intervening in Africa*, p. 27.

17. Copson, "Ethiopia: War and Famine," pp. 9–10; "Mengistu Plays Democracy Card to Save His Skin," *The Times*, April 2, 1990.

18. Erlich, *The Struggle over Eritrea*, p. 1.

19. Marcus, *Ethiopia, Great Britain, and the United States*, pp. 15–16.

20. Henze, *Layers of Time*, pp. 287–89, 303.

21. Marcus, *A History of Ethiopia*, pp. 196–99.

22. Cohen, *Intervening in Africa*, pp. 21, 22, 30, 38–39; Henze, "A Political Success Story," p. 42. Cf. Erlich, *Ethiopia and the Challenge of Independence*, ch. 10.

23. Young, *Peasant Revolution in Ethiopia*, p. 178; Henze, *Layers of Time*, pp. 248–50, 292, and "A Political Success Story," p. 43; Gilkes, *The Dying Lion: Feudalism and Modernization in Ethiopia*, p. 187ff.; Hammond, *Fire from the Ashes: A Chronicle of the Revolution in Tigray, Ethiopia*, p. 416; telephone interview with Bob Houdek, May 24, 2004.

24. Pankhurst, *The Ethiopians*, p. 276; Cohen, *Intervening in Africa*, pp. 21–23. Of the other insurgent groups, the Oromo Liberation Front (OLF) was the principal force, representing the largest ethnic group in Ethiopia.

25. Fitzgerald, "Marxist Armies Clash in Ruined Ethiopia"; Cohen, *Intervening in Africa*, p. 28; telephone interview with Bob Houdek, May 24, 2004.

26. Henze, "Ethiopia in 1991—Peace Through Struggle," p. 3. The 1990 U.S. Department of State Human Rights Report of February 1, 1991, said that Mengistu commanded

well over 300,000 troops, while the International Institute for Strategic Studies put the number at 438,000 (Associated Press, February 27, 1991). Cohen (*Intervening in Africa*, p. 21) refers to 200,000 men.

27. Henze, *Layers of Time*, p. 321; Cohen, *Intervening in Africa*, pp. 22, 39.

28. Cf. Macconi, "Africa, Tempo d'Eritrea."

29. Perlez, "Israelis Widening Role in Ethiopia."

30. Brilliant, "Eritrean Success Could Prove Dangerous to Israel's Interest"; Erlich, "Massawa: Catalyst for a Red Sea War?"

31. Erlich, *Ethiopia and the Middle East*, pp. 156–57.

32. Joe Feit said later that Frasure never told him that Ethiopian Jews were in danger in Gondar. Knowing of Feit's desire to bring them to Addis, though, Frasure pointed out that Ethiopian government planes flying weapons and ammunition to the north were returning empty. Frasure proposed that Feit contact an Ethiopian air force officer he knew, saying that it was on his recommendation, and ask the officer to bring back Jews on the return flights. This plan did not work out, however (telephone interview with Feit, May 24, 2004).

33. "Ethiopia Chronology, 12/89–9/90," Pollack's report to the AAEJ covering her time as resident director in Addis; confirmed by interviews with AAEJ officers. "It was Bob Frasure who told Pollack to get people out of Gondar," the veteran Israeli diplomat Uri Lubrani said later (JDC record of April 29, 1991).

34. Interview with Frasure, 1992. Bob Houdek, who conferred closely with his deputy Frasure in Addis, suggested later that Pollack may have overstated Frasure's warning. Frasure probably had expressed serious concern about the safety of the Falashas in their villages, he said, but had not presented the danger as urgent. Houdek added that the claim that the rebels were only hours from Addis at that time was exaggerated (telephone interviews, May 18 and 24, 2004).

35. Interview with Pollack, 1992, confirmed by Friedman, *Operation Solomon*, p. 161, and interview with Micha Feldman, December 22, 1996.

36. Interviews with Pollack, 1992, and Micha Feldman, December 22, 1996; Pollack, "Ethiopia Chronology."

37. See Appendix 1, note 2.

38. Feldman, *The Ethiopian Exodus*, p. 153; interview with Pollack, 1992.

39. Kalita, "Missed Chances." This policy of the Sudanese ruler, General Omar al-Bashir, was confirmed by Herman Cohen in a telephone interview, January 3, 2002.

40. Interview with Yoffe, 1992.

41. Interview with Pollack, 1992; e-mail interview with Pollack, March 31, 2004.

42. Feldman, *The Ethiopian Exodus*, p. 156. The emigration from Addis Ababa in that week exceeded the totals for any of the previous three months. In January, Feldman notes, 189 Jews left directly from Ethiopia; an additional 425 exited from Sudan (p. 140). The Jewish Agency's figure of 600 for January reflects the approximate total from these two departure sites (report by Arnon Mantber, director-general, Department of Immigration and Absorption, May 27, 1991). The Israeli embassy counted 180 leaving directly from Addis Ababa in that month. In February, the embassy recorded 129 exits, Feldman reported 146 (p. 149), and the Jewish Agency counted 152. In March, the embassy noted that 115 Jews left from Addis, and Feldman says that 344 left in a final airlift from Sudan (p. 153). The Jewish Agency count of 441 again roughly reflected the sum of these two figures.

43. Interview with Recant, 1992.

44. Interview with Shapiro, 1992.

45. Interviews with Schneider, October 9, 1997, and Recant, October 9, 1997. See page 53 in this volume.

46. Pollack, "Ethiopia Chronology," broadly confirmed by memos from Eli Eliezri and Ami Bergman to Michael Schneider, June 3 and 11, 1990, JDC archive, and also by "JDC in Ethiopia," a background report, December 1990, JDC archive. For brief accounts of the AAEJ's role in emptying the Jewish villages of Gondar, see Rabinovich, "Down from the Hills," and Berger, *Rescue the Ethiopian Jews!*, pp. 188–91.

47. Naim, *Saving the Lost Tribe*, p. 10; Cohen, *Intervening in Africa*, p. 31; interview with Bob Houdek in Kaye, "On the Wings of Eagles," p. 347.

48. Interview with Addisu Massele, January 7, 1997.

49. Interview with Shamay Balay, May 23, 1997.

50. "JDC in Ethiopia," December 1990, JDC archive.

51. Interviews with Gold, December 30, 1996, and Pollack, May 5, 1997.

52. Map 6 in Marcus's *History of Ethiopia* confirms that the Gondar region was one of the least affected by famine.

53. Hall's account of his familiarization trip to Ethiopia in March 1990, in a memo from Scott Cohen, April 5, 1990; confirmed by "Coordination of Activities Re Ethiopian Jews," minutes of Ministry of Foreign Affairs meeting of May 13, 1990; also confirmed by interview with Feldman, December 22, 1996.

54. Interview with Getahun Tizazu, July 1, 1997.

55. Memo from Cohen, April 5, 1990; interview with Feldman, December 22, 1996.

56. Interview with Hodes, April 29, 1997.

57. Memo from Ami Bergman to Michael Schneider, March 17, 1988, JDC archive.

58. Rosen and Chemtov, *Be "Gobez" for the Sake of Your Health*; Westheimer and Kaplan, *Surviving Salvation*, pp. 125–26.

59. Interview with Shamay, May 23, 1997.

60. Interviews with Babu Yacov, June 16, 1997, and Tevege Tegenye, July 21, 1997.

61. Odenheimer, "Jews in Ethiopia Getting Together."

62. Keinon, "Doyen of Spiritual Leaders."

63. Internal memo by Michael Schneider, "JDC in Ethiopia," December 1990, JDC archive.

64. Interview with Pollack, May 5, 1997.

65. Interviews with Recant, October 9, 1997, and March 12, 2003.

## Chapter Three

1. "Ethiopia Chronology," Susan Pollack's report to the AAEJ covering her time as resident director in Addis. See also Feldman, *The Ethiopian Exodus*, p. 157.

2. The tents were left over from the search for the body of Congressman Mickey Leland, who died in a plane crash in 1989 while leading a mission to a refugee camp in Ethiopia (interviews with Will Recant, October 9, 1997, and Bob Houdek, May 24, 2004; Pollack, "Ethiopia Chronology"; Feldman, *The Ethiopian Exodus*, pp. 158–59).

3. Pollack, "Ethiopia Chronology"; interview with Berhanu Yiradu, 1992.

4. Memos from Eli Eliezri and Ami Bergman to JDC officials in New York and Rome, May 21 and June 3, 1990, JDC archive.

5. Feldman, *The Ethiopian Exodus*, pp. 161–62.

6. Medical report from Dr. Micha Eladan and Dr. Moshe Efrat to Ami Bergman, June 9, 1990, JDC archive.

7. Pollack, "Ethiopia Chronology"; undated cable from Friedman to Ami Bergman, JDC archive.

8. Interview with Pollack, May 5, 1997; Pollack, "Ethiopia Chronology"; Feldman, *The Ethiopian Exodus*, p. 159. Another tent was set up on the embassy grounds as a synagogue for the Ethiopian Jews (interview with Andy Goldman, May 18, 2004).

9. Pollack, "Ethiopia Chronology"; interview with Pollack, May 5, 1997.
10. Feldman, *The Ethiopian Exodus*, p. 159.
11. Memos from Eliezri and Bergman to JDC officers, May 21 and June 3, 1990, JDC archive; memo from Ami Bergman to Michael Schneider, January 6, 1991, JDC archive.
12. Interview with Berhanu, 1992; also interview with Recant, in Kaye, "On the Wings of Eagles," p. 339.
13. Interview with Berhanu, 1992.
14. Interview with Girma, April 6, 1998.
15. Interview with Recant, 1992.
16. Interview with Pollack, May 5, 1997.
17. Pollack, "Ethiopia Chronology"; interview with Feldman, December 22, 1996.
18. Interview with Recant, 1992; Pollack, "Ethiopia Chronology." A memo from the JDC's Eliezri and Bergman (see note 4), June 3, 1990, in the JDC archive, confirms these events.
19. Interview with Micha Feldman, August 8, 1995, cited in Arbel, *Riding the Wave*, p. 137.
20. Interview with Hodes, April 29, 1997.
21. Interview with Zimna, 1992.
22. Interview with Recant, 1992.
23. Interview with Odenheimer, December 19, 1996.
24. Interview with Hodes, April 29, 1997.
25. Telephone interview with Houdek, May 24, 2004.
26. Telephone interview with Kobi Friedman, August 3, 1997; confirmed by Feldman, *The Ethiopian Exodus*, p. 171.
27. Feldman, *The Ethiopian Exodus*, p. 172; see Salamon, *The Hyena People*, p. 47.
28. Odenheimer, "Ethiopia: More Exits by Death than Immigration"; Myers, "A Medical Care Program."
29. Mangasha Nagast, "A Report Card of Ethiopian Jews in Addis Ababa" (Hebrew), August 20, 1990, JDC archive. See Odenheimer, "Medical Aid Reaches Addis Jews."
30. Myers, "A Medical Care Program," pp. 336–37.
31. J. Grant, "The State of the World's Children," 1990 UNICEF report, cited in Myers, "A Medical Care Program," p. 337; interview with Hodes, April 29, 1997.
32. Interview with Pollack, 1992; e-mail interview with Pollack, March 31, 2004. The use of biscuit boxes as baby coffins is noted in the June 1990 entry of Pollack, "Ethiopia Chronology."
33. Fax from Eli Eliezri and Ami Bergman to Michael Schneider, June 4, 1990, JDC archive.
34. "1990 Human Rights Report," U.S. Department of State dispatch, February 1, 1991.
35. Interviews with Kassa Kebede, May 5, 1997, and Will Recant, October 9, 1997; Gedda, "Ethiopian Envoy Can't Meet Conditions."
36. Interview with Kassa, 1992. In a report to the State Department, Bob Houdek noted the Ethiopian government's genuine surprise and shock at the massive influx of Falashas into Addis Ababa from May to August 1990 ("Falasha Roundup," February 20, 1991, Department of State document 1991ADDIS00753).
37. Henze, "The Defeat of the Derg," p. 23; Steve Morrison, confidential report on Israeli-Ethiopian relations submitted to Rep. Howard Wolpe, February 13, 1990; Dagne, "Ethiopian Jews," p. 4. Dawit notes that that the news leak about the episode contributed to the coup (*Red Tears*, p. 318), but Bard says that Nimeiri's falling from power soon after the airlift was coincidental (*From Tragedy to Triumph*, p. 166).
38. Interviews with Kassa, 1992 and May 5, 1997.
39. Interview with Recant, October 9, 1997; Rabinovich, "Exodus: the Sequel."

40. Pollack, "Ethiopia Chronology."
41. Interview with Kassa, 1992.
42. Interview with Mantber, August 18, 1997.
43. Interview with Kassa, 1992.
44. Interview with Yoffe, 1992.
45. Interview with Mantber, July 30, 1997.
46. Interview with Feldman, December 22, 1996.
47. Memo from Sherry Hyman to Ami Bergman, April 5, 1990, JDC archive.
48. Interview with Feldman, December 22, 1996.
49. Interview with Moshe Yegar, June 17, 1997.
50. Ibid.
51. Interview with Kassa, 1992.
52. Interview with Moshe Yegar, June 17, 1997.
53. Interview with Yoffe, 1992.
54. Interview with Addisu Massele, January 7, 1997.
55. Interview with Feldman, December 22, 1996.
56. "Coordination of Activities Re Ethiopian Jews," minutes of a meeting held in the Ministry of Foreign Affairs on May 13, 1990.
57. "Summary of Meeting on Ethiopian Aliyah: Monday, June 25, 1990," JDC archive; interviews with Will Recant, October 9, 1977, and Bob Houdek, in Kaye, p. 353.
58. Interview with Pollack, 1992.
59. Interview with Recant, 1992.
60. See, however, Naim, *Saving the Lost Tribe*, pp. 146–51. The Israelis would later revisit the question of who were Ethiopian Jews, as we shall see.
61. Rabinovich, "Down from the Hills."
62. Interview with Schneider, October 9, 1997, confirmed in a separate interview with Recant, October 9, 1997.
63. Pollack, "Ethiopia Chronology," entry for February 19, 1990; interview with Pollack, May 5, 1997; confirmed in an interview with Barbara Ribakove Gordon, 1992.
64. Interview with Feldman, December 22, 1996.
65. Interview with Pollack, May 5, 1997.
66. Interviews with Merhav, August 13, 1997, and Haim Divon, January 12, 1997; Rabinovich, "Down from the Hills."
67. Interview with Gold, December 30, 1996.
68. North American Conference on Ethiopian Jews 1990 annual report; interview with Gordon, 1992.
69. Interviews with Gordon, 1992 and November 1996; "NACOEJ: Our Mission" (2002), available at www.nacoej.org.
70. Telephone interview with Feit, May 24, 2004.
71. Interviews with Gordon, 1992 and November 1996; "NACOEJ: Our Mission"; interview with Goldman, 1992.
72. Interview with Strum, in Kaye, p. 367.
73. Interview with Strum, 1992.

## Chomanesh and Dan'el

1. Westheimer and Kaplan (*Surviving Salvation*, p. 96) cite this term used by Michelle Schoenberger to designate the Beta Israel girls who, by the early 1970s, began to delay their marriages well past the age of puberty.

## Chapter Four

1. JDC annual report, 1988; interviews with Bergman (October 13, 1996), Eli Eliezri (October 13, 1996), Michael Schneider (October 9, 1997), and other JDC officials; memos from Ami Bergman and Eli Eliezri to JDC offices in New York and Rome, June 3 and July 12, 1990, JDC archive; Michael Schneider, "JDC in Ethiopia," December 1990, JDC archive; Szulc, *The Secret Alliance,* pp. 297–300.
2. Field report from Eli Eliezri to the JDC, January 16, 1991, JDC archive.
3. Orna Mizrachi, "The Largest School in the World," in Toran, ed., "Operation Solomon: The Beta Israel Return Home," p. 59.
4. Interview with Orna Mizrachi, 1992.
5. Ibid.; interview with David Harman, July 11, 1997; see Feldman, *The Ethiopian Exodus,* p. 190.
6. Memo from Kobi Friedman to Ami Bergman, September 11, 1990, JDC archive; report from Manlio Dell'Ariccia to Steven Schwager, February 27, 1991, JDC archive. See Mizrachi, "The Largest School in the World," in Toran, ed., "Operation Solomon: The Beta Israel Return Home," pp. 58–60.
7. Feldman, *The Ethiopian Exodus,* pp. 170, 175; interviews with David Harman, July 11, 1997, and Orna Mizrachi, 1992.
8. Arbel, *Riding the Wave,* p. 139; Avi Mizrachi, "We Tried to Rescue, They Wanted to Survive," in Toran, ed., "Operation Solomon: The Beta Israel Return Home," p. 58.
9. Interview with Orna Mizrachi, 1992.
10. Westheimer and Kaplan, *Surviving Salvation,* p. 112; Shalva Weil in Herb Keinon, "The Ecology of Domestic Violence," *Jerusalem Post,* January 24, 1992.
11. Interview with Mizrachi, 1992. See the general report by Almaya's Kobi Friedman, September 11, 1990, JDC archive.
12. Memo by Ami Bergman, January 6, 1991, JDC archive.
13. Myers, "A Medical Care Program," p. 334.
14. Report by Almaya's Kobi Friedman, September 11, 1990, JDC archive; Myers, "A Medical Care Program," pp. 335–36.
15. Interview with Hodes, April 29, 1997.
16. Interview with Myers, 1992.
17. Interview with Hodes, April 29, 1997; Moshe Efrat, "Health Care for Ethiopian Jews in Addis Ababa: An Evaluation of the AJDC Medical Program, with Recommendations," October 14, 1990, JDC archive.
18. Interview with Myers, 1992; Feldman, *The Ethiopian Exodus,* pp. 162–63, 174.
19. Interview with Hodes, April 29, 1997; Myers, "A Medical Care Program," pp. 335–37; see Schachter, "Sharp Drop in Death Rate Among Stranded Ethiopian Jews."
20. Interview with Hodes, April 29, 1997; Myers, "A Medical Care Program," pp. 335–36.
21. See Hodes, "Cross-Cultural Medicine and Diverse Health Beliefs," p. 32, and Grisaru, Lezer, and Belmaker, "Ritual Female Genital Surgery Among Ethiopian Jews." Cf. Naim, *Saving the Lost Tribe,* pp. 163–64.
22. See Naim, *Saving the Lost Tribe,* p. 97.
23. U.S. Arms Control and Disarmament Agency, *World Military Expenditures and Arms Transfers, 1991–92* (Washington, DC: U.S. Government Printing Office, 1994), cited in Henze, "The Fall of the Derg," p. 4 n. 4; Henze, *Layers of Time,* pp. 312, 314, 318; Cohen, *Intervening in Africa,* p. 37.
24. Interview with Moshe Yegar, June 17, 1997.
25. Interview with Naim, May 30, 1997 .
26. From a confidential Foreign Ministry document to which I was given access, and confirmed by a reliable Israeli Foreign Ministry source and by Kassa himself in a 1992 interview. Cf. Feldman, *The Ethiopian Exodus,* pp. 171–72.

27. I extended an invitation to comment in faxes of August 3 and 17, 1997, to David Bar-Ilan, communications director for then Prime Minister Netanyahu, followed by a telephone conversation with Bar-Ilan.
28. Interview with Shamir, August 5, 1997.
29. Emigration figures are from Feldman, *The Ethiopian Exodus,* pp. 150, 169, and 178, and from the records of the Israeli embassy in Addis Ababa (which, however, note 80 exits in July). Other sources cite minor differences in the data. The Jewish Agency count was 153 in July, 103 in August, and 210 in September. The HIAS monthly records for 1990 start in September with 184 immigrants. These numbers represented a dramatic decline from the roughly 100 departures each week in May and June.
30. Naim, *Saving the Lost Tribe,* p. 4.
31. Feldman, *The Ethiopian Exodus,* pp. 175, 183.
32. Keinon, "Ethiopian Anger at Pace of Rescue Turns Violent."
33. Rudge, "A Man for All Missions."
34. Merhav, interview, July 23, 1997, and e-mail interview, September 21, 2001.
35. Interview with Lubrani, February 23, 1997.
36. Interview with Shamir, August 5, 1997.
37. Silver, "The Mystery Man Who Saved the Jews."
38. *Jewish Week,* June 21–27, 1991.
39. Interview with Lubrani, February 11, 1997.
40. Interview with Moshe Yegar, June 17, 1997.
41. Beeston, "Israeli Reveals Falasha Airlift Strategy"; La Guardia, "Falashas Used by Mengistu 'as Pawns for Weapons.'"
42. See Naim, *Saving the Lost Tribe,* p. 42.
43. Interview with Lubrani, 1992.
44. Rapoport, *Redemption Song,* p. 176.
45. Interviews with Naim, August 10, 1997, and Merhav, July 23, 1997; Naim, *Saving the Lost Tribe,* pp. 8–11.
46. Henze, "The Fall of the Derg," p. 4.
47. Ibid. See Cohen, *Intervening in Africa,* p. 21.
48. Telephone interview with Henze, December 18, 2001.
49. Cohen, *Intervening in Africa,* p. 35.
50. Walker and Stambler, ". . . and the Dirty Little Weapons."
51. See Hammond, *Fire from the Ashes,* p. 216.
52. Sciolino, "U.S. Officials Suspect Israelis Sent Ethiopia Cluster Bombs."
53. Steve Morrison, confidential report submitted to Howard Wolpe, chair of the Congressional Subcommittee on Africa, on February 3, 1990 (Morrison Report).
54. Sciolino, "U.S. Officials Suspect Israelis Sent Ethiopia Cluster Bombs"; Morrison Report; Blitzer, "U.S. Accepts Rabin's Denial of Cluster Bombs to Ethiopia."
55. Pound, "Explosive Issue."
56. Interview with Frasure, 1992; cf. similar sentiments in Cohen, *Intervening in Africa,* p. 35.
57. Sciolino, "U.S. Officials Suspect Israel Sent Ethiopia Cluster Bombs." Ethiopian foreign minister Tesfaye Dinka issued a similar denial in July (Rozenman, "Ethiopian FM Affirms Aliya" *Jerusalem Post,* July 27, 1990). See Ball and Ball, *The Passionate Attachment,* p. 290.
58. Merhav, e-mail interview, January 5, 2002.
59. Interview with Frasure, 1992.
60. Cohen, *Intervening in Africa,* p. 35.

## Chapter Five

1. Interview with Merhav, August 13, 1997.
2. The EPLF did not agree to allow food shipments to be delivered through Massawa until December 1990.

3. Cohen, *Intervening in Africa,* pp. 31–33.

4. Ibid., pp. 25–26, 32.

5. Interviews with Cohen, 1992 and April 11, 2003.

6. Cohen, *Intervening in Africa,* pp. 20–21; Cohen, private correspondence, October 29, 2001; telephone interview with Cohen, April 11, 2003; Makovsky, "Israel and Mengistu." The geostrategic perspective from State differed from that on the ground in Addis. Bob Houdek told me that he and Bob Frasure set three goals in 1988 and never diverged from them: end the civil war, remove Mengistu from office, and get the Falashas to Israel. The Russians were already disengaging by July 1988, and the U.S. embassy did not place a high priority on helping them leave gracefully (telephone interview, May 24, 2004).

7. Interview with Lubrani, February 11, 1997. See Arbel, *Riding the Wave,* p. 142.

8. Weil, *One-Parent Families,* 1991.

9. Ibid., p. 9.

10. Mizrachi, "We Tried to Rescue, They Wanted to Survive," p. 58.

11. Friedman, *Operation Solomon: A Year in Thirty-one Hours,* pp. 77–81; fax from Ami Bergman to Steve Schwager, February 5, 1991, JDC archive.

12. Odenheimer, "Jewish Justice, Ethiopian Style."

13. Interview with Zimna, 1992.

14. Susan Pollack, "The People Who Get Money from the Sky: A Report on Ethiopia and Kenya," prepared for the AAEJ, February 1989. See Arbel, *Riding the Wave,* p. 144.

15. "General Report for Discussion," Kobi Friedman to Ami Bergman, September 11, 1990, JDC archive; memo from Ami Bergman to Michael Schneider, January 6, 1991, JDC archive; interview with Haim Divon, 1992.

16. Interview with Zimna, 1992.

17. Naim, *Saving the Lost Tribe,* p. 70; Cohen, *Intervening in Africa,* p. 35; Feldman, *The Ethiopian Exodus,* p. 187.

18. Naim, *Saving the Lost Tribe,* p. 72; Cohen, *Intervening in Africa,* p. 36.

19. Interview with Lubrani, 1992.

20. Cohen, *Intervening in Africa,* p. 36.

21. See Dawit, *Red Tears,* pp. 331. Dawit notes that even after other African states had renewed relations with Israel following the Egyptian-Israeli peace agreement, Ethiopia had not.

22. A few days earlier, in a startling interview with Micha Odenheimer, Mengistu had positioned his government as Israel's natural ally against the Arabs. Ethiopia was the enemy of Iraq and other Arab states that were supplying arms to his enemies, Mengistu said. He argued that Egypt and Sudan were dependent on Ethiopian water and were waging a proxy war based on hydropolitics. The Arabs wanted to turn the Red Sea into an Arab lake, but, he declared, Ethiopia stood as an obstacle to the Islamization and Arabization of Africa (Micha Odenheimer, "Ethiopian Angst: Warm on Israel, Stone-cold on Iraq" and "'Wake Up,' Mengistu Urges Israel," *Jerusalem Post,* November 9 and 11, 1990).

23. See Cohen, *Intervening in Africa,* p. 33.

24. See Naim, *Saving the Lost Tribe,* p. 73.

25. Figures are from the Israeli embassy count and Feldman, *The Ethiopian Exodus,* p. 188. The Jewish Agency report of May 27, 1991, recorded 59 Ethiopian immigrants in October, 432 in November, and 527 in December. HIAS reported 438 in November and 540 in December.

26. Keinon, "Ethiopia Will Allow 1,000 Jews to Leave." See Naim, *Saving the Lost Tribe,* pp. 42–44.

27. Interview with Kassa, May 5, 1997.
28. Rosenthal, "The New Exodus," p. 49.
29. Interview with Naim, May 30, 1997.
30. Telephone interview with Tesfaye, January 3, 2002.
31. Feldman, *The Ethiopian Exodus,* pp. 154, 184. The Ethiopians also agreed that a rude and uncooperative official in the emigration bureau named Kifle would work with two Israeli embassy staff, an arrangement that ameliorated tensions (ibid., pp. 184, 187).
32. Interview with Feldman, December 22, 1996. See Naim, *Saving the Lost Tribe*, p. 72.
33. Interview with Feldman, December 22, 1996; Feldman, *The Ethiopian Exodus*, pp. 185–86. See Mizrachi, "Operation Solomon: The Beta Israel Return Home," p. 57.
34. Interview with Feldman, December 22, 1996. See Feldman, *The Ethiopian Exocus*, p. 189.
35. Notes by Michael Schneider, April 26, 1991, JDC archive; interview with Avi Mizrachi, 1992; confirmed in Taron, ed., *Operation Solomon*, p. 60.
36. Interview with Lubrani, February 11, 1997.
37. Bergman, "I, Kassa Kebede."
38. Interviews with Lubrani, 1992; Gideon Taylor, August 7, 1996; Schneider, 1992; and Eli Eliezri, October 19, 2001.
39. The Jewish Agency actually paid $7 million of that, according to Barak (telephone interview, April 19, 2001).
40. Telephone interview with Barak, April 19, 2001.
41. Interviews with Lubrani, 1992; Dinitz, January 1, 1998; Arnon Mantber, August 18, 1997, and May 22, 2001; and Barak, April 19, 2001.
42. Interviews with Lubrani, 1992; Schneider, April 12, 2001; and Arnon Mantber, May 22, 2001. Cf. Brzezinski, *Power and Principle,* p. 98.
43. Field report from Eli Eliezri to Michael Schneider, January 16, 1991, JDC archive.
44. Ibid.; interviews with Ackerman, 1992, and Kassa, 1992. For Ackerman's dealings with Mengistu in April 1990, see Cohen, *Intervening in Africa,* p. 31.
45. Interview with Morrison, 1992.

## Chapter Six

1. Feldman, *The Ethiopian Exodus*, pp. 189–90; aide-mémoire of meeting of Lubrani, Schneider, Divon, and Taylor, February 19, 1991, JDC archive.
2. Feldman, *The Ethiopian Exodus*, p. 149; interview with Kobi Friedman, 1992.
3. Memorandum from the Committee of Social Workers on Family Reunification to Comrade Mersha Ketsela, December 31, 1990.
4. Interview with Avi Mizrachi, 1992.
5. See Feldman, *The Ethiopian Exodus*, pp. 40–42; Bodovsky, David, and Eran, *Customs and Culture.*
6. Kaplan, "Everyday Resistance and the Study of Ethiopian Jews," pp. 10–11. See Toran, ed., "Operation Solomon: The Beta Israel Return Home," p. 61.
7. Mizrachi, "We Tried to Rescue," p. 58.
8. Interview with Naim, August 10, 1997.
9. Interview with the AAEJ's Glenn Stein, in Kaye, "On the Wings of Eagles," p. 379.
10. Interview with Barbara Ribakove Gordon, in Kaye, "On the Wings of Eagles," p. 379.
11. Interview with Hodes, April 29, 1997.
12. Keinon, "Doyen of Spiritual Leaders"; "Despite Threats of Iraqi Attack, Ethiopian Jews Are Relieved to Finally Be in Israel," AAEJ press release, February 1991, cited in Kaye, "On the Wings of Eagles," p. 380.

13. Figure from Feldman, *The Ethiopian Exodus,* p. 194, confirmed by HIAS. The Jewish Agency recorded 832. The Israeli embassy count of 1,038 was significantly higher.

14. "Aliyah from the Former Soviet Union," Jewish Agency Immigration and Absorption Home Page, February 1999 and June 2003, www.jafi.org.il; Report to the Jewish Agency Board of Governors, February 2003. While the war was the principal reason for the decline in Soviet emigration in January 1991, Absorption Minister Yitzhak Peretz said at the time that a drastic cut in the basket of services for new *olim* was another factor (Keinon, "1,000 Came from Ethiopia Last Month"). See Associated Press, "Soviet Immigration Picks Up with Cease-fire in the Gulf," and Rosenthal, "The New Exodus."

15. Field report from Eli Eliezri to the JDC, January 16, 1991; interview with Dinitz, January 1, 1998; Naim, *Saving the Lost Tribe,* pp. 166–69.

16. Interview with Lubrani, 1992.

17. JDC record of Lubrani's conversation with Michael Schneider and Gideon Taylor, January 28, 1991.

18. Keinon, "1,000 Came from Ethiopia Last Month."

19. Interview with Zimna, 1992, confirmed by Lubrani in 1992 interview.

20. Interview with Lubrani, 1992.

21. Toron, ed., *Operation Solomon: The Beta Israel Return Home,* p. 57. Simcha Dinitz recalled later that he too pressed for a one-time operation (Arbel, *Riding the Wave,* pp. 141–42).

22. Toron, ed., *Operation Solomon: The Beta Israel Return Home,* p. 57.

23. JDC record of Lubrani's conversation with Schneider and Taylor, January 28, 1991.

24. Interview with Michael Schneider, April 4, 2003; e-mail interview, May 13, 2003.

25. Field report, January 16, 1991, JDC archive.

26. JDC record of Michael Schneider's report on his visit to Ethiopia, March 1, 1991.

27. Interview with Lubrani, 1992; see Naim, *Saving the Lost Tribe,* pp. 174–78.

28. See Cohen, *Intervening in Africa,* p. 58; Naim, *Saving the Lost Tribe,* p. 182.

29. Report to the JDC by Manlio Dell'Ariccia, citing a "reliable source," April 24, 1991, JDC archive. See Cohen, *Intervening in Africa,* p. 43.

30. The Israeli embassy's figure for February was 974, the Jewish Agency's count was 986, and HIAS recorded 996. Feldman similarly speaks of 200 *olim* twice each week in the first half of the month (*The Ethiopian Exodus,* p. 196).

31. Aide-mémoire, February 14, 1991, JDC archive; Feldman, *The Ethiopian Exodus,* p. 190.

32. See Feldman, *The Ethiopian Exodus,* p. 159; Friedmann, "The Case of the Falas Mura."

33. Interview with Feldman, December 22, 1996.

34. Feldman, *The Ethiopian Exodus,* pp. 162, 165–66.

35. Interview with Hodes, 1992.

36. Michael Schneider, "Report on Visit to Ethiopia," March 1, 1991, JDC archive.

37. Kaplan, "Falasha Christians: A Brief History," much of which was published as "'Falasha Christians: Which of them is Jewish," *Jerusalem Post,* May 31, 1991.

38. Salamon, *The Hyena People,* pp. 65–71.

39. Feldman, *The Ethiopian Exodus,* p. 126.

40. Fishkoff, "The Ones Left Behind—Part I."

41. Naim, *Saving the Lost Tribe,* p. 238; also based on interviews with Foreign Ministry sources.

42. Cohler, "U.S. Calls Sharon's Words 'Hopeful' Sign"; Sheriden, "Israeli Settlements 'Anger U.S.'"

43. Mary A. Fitzgerald, "How Ethiopian Rebels Turned Struggle Around," *San Francisco Chronicle,* July 4, 1990, cited in Teshome, "The International Political Ramifications of Falasha Emigration," p. 577.

44. Confidential aide-mémoire of discussion of officers of the Jewish Agency, Foreign Ministry, HIAS, and JDC, February 14, 1991, JDC archive.

45. Interview with Strum, in Kaye, "On the Wings of Eagles," p. 362. See Feldman, *The Ethiopian Exodus*, p. 190. Joe Feit, as president of NACOEJ, initially ordered that his people keep the Falash Mura out of the NACOEJ compound. At the request of the Israeli chief rabbinate, he said, he reversed this position and took them in (telephone interview, May 24, 2004). Feit reviews rabbinic decisions in favor of the Falash Mura in "Falas Mura," www.nacoej.org/falas.htm.

46. Interview with Gordon, in Kaye, "On the Wings of Eagles," p. 438.

47. Naim, *Saving the Lost Tribe*, p. 238.

48. Feldman, *The Ethiopian Exodus*, p. 166.

## Chapter Seven

1. JDC record of Frasure's briefing to JDC, March 12, 1991, JDC archive; "Ethiopia—Phone Discussion with Robert Frasure," Sherry Hymen to Gideon Taylor, March 13, 1991, JDC archive; "Ethiopia Update," Michael Schneider and Gideon Taylor to Ethiopia Subcommittee, March 14, 1991, JDC archive. See Feldman, *The Ethiopian Exodus*, p. 196.

2. JDC record of Eliezri's conversation with Dell'Ariccia, Schneider, and Taylor, March 13, 1991, JDC archive.

3. Telephone interview with Houdek, February 17, 2004; Department of State document 1991ADDIS01106.

4. Odenheimer, "The Guns of April."

5. Ibid.; Feldman, *The Ethiopian Exodus*, p. 197.

6. Keinon, "Ethiopia: Emigration to Resume Soon."

7. Feldman, *The Ethiopian Exodus*, p. 198. Herman Cohen reports that on March 7, Lubrani told the U.S. ambassador to Tel Aviv, William Brown, that the Ethiopian government was increasing the pressure on Israel to provide lethal weapons (*Intervening in Africa*, p. 44).

8. JDC record of conference call, March 8, 1991; aide-mémoire, "Ethiopia: Conference Call," March 8, 1991, JDC archive.

9. "Ethiopia—Phone Discussion with Robert Frasure"; EPRDF radio announcement on March 10 (BBC Summary of World Broadcasts, March 11, 1991).

10. JDC record of phone conversation, March 11, 1991, JDC archive; "AIDS in Ethiopia," confidential report from Ami Bergman to Steven Schweger, April 9, 1991, JDC archive. According to Hodes, 3.6 percent of blood donations in Addis Ababa were HIV-positive in 1991 (interview with Hodes, 1992).

11. Interview with Yegar, June 17, 1997.

12. Interview with David Harman, July 11, 1997.

13. Interview with Hodes, 1992.

14. Letter from assistant secretary of state for legislative affairs, Janet Mullins, to Stephen Solarz, co-chair of Congressional Caucus for Ethiopian Jewry, April 12, 1991 (cited in Kaye, "On the Wings of Eagles," p. 386).

15. Michael Schneider, notes, March 8, 1991, JDC archive; JDC record of telephone conversation, Dell'Ariccia, Eliezri, Schneider, and Taylor, March 13, 1991, JDC archive.

16. Aide-mémoire of conference call involving Malcolm Hoenlein, Michael Shilo, Abe Bayer, and Gideon Taylor, March 13, 1991, JDC archive. See Keinon, "Revolt Disrupts Ethiopian Aliyah," and Keinon, "Mengistu Orders Halt to Aliyah."

17. Interview with Naim, 1992.

18. News Agencies, "Ethiopia: Emigration to Resume Soon."
19. Keinon, "Ethiopian Emigration Set to Resume Tomorrow."
20. The sources cite significantly divergent figures for March. The Israeli embassy recorded 508, and Feldman puts the number at over 500 (*The Ethiopian Exodus*, p. 200). HIAS, however, counted 696, and the Jewish Agency figure was 703.
21. News Agencies, "Ethiopia: Emigration to Resume Soon."
22. Interview with Schneider, 1992; *Jewish Week*, June 21-27, 1991.
23. "Ethiopia—Phone Discussion with Robert Frasure," memo from Sherry Hyman to Gideon Taylor, March 13, 1991, JDC archive; JDC record of conversation between Barbara Ribakove Gordon and Taylor, March 19, 1991, JDC archive.
24. Interviews with Frasure, 1992, and Lubrani, 1992.
25. Interview with Lubrani, 1992.
26. Ibid.; interview with Naim, 1992. See Rabinovich, "Exodus: The Sequel."
27. JDC record of Lubrani's report to American Jewish leaders, April 8, 1991, JDC archive.
28. Interviews with Lubrani, 1992; Schneider, 1992; and Michael Shilo, 1992.
29. Interview with Cohen, 1992.
30. Ibid.; JDC record of conversation between Shilo and Taylor, March 27, 1991, JDC archive.
31. Frasure had proposed the felicitous phrase "parallel momentum" (interviews with Houdek, 1992 and May 18, 2004).
32. Aide-mémoire of conference call involving Lubrani, Bayer, Gordon, Hoenlein, Recant, Solendar, Schneider, Schweger, and Taylor, March 25, 1991; interview with Lubrani, 1992.
33. "Ethiopia," fax from Michael Schneider to American Jewish leaders, March 27, 1991, JDC archive; interview with Malcolm Hoenlein, 1992.
34. JDC record of conference call involving Schneider, Taylor, Lubrani, and John Coleman, March 23, 1991, JDC archive; interview with Frasure, 1992.
35. Interview with Lubrani, 1992.
36. Naim, *Saving the Lost Tribe*, p. 183. JDC records indicate that Kassa sought the visa for his daughter on April 11, 1991.
37. Interview with Lubrani, 1992.
38. "Ethiopia Update," from Schneider and Taylor to the Ethiopia subcommittee, March 14, 1991, JDC archive.
39. Interview with Lubrani, 1992.
40. Ibid.
41. Interview with Merhav, July 23, 1997.
42. "Jewish Population—Ethiopia," report by Ami Bergman to Gideon Taylor, February 12, 1991, JDC archive.
43. Eliezri, "Field Report: Ethiopia," January 16, 1991, JDC archive; "Jewish Population—Ethiopia," JDC archive.
44. Between the beginning of March and Operation Solomon, 2,654 Ethiopians made aliyah. Since 14,310 were taken in the airlift, this meant that there were approximately 17,000 in early March.
45. Interview with Lubrani, 1992.

## Chapter Eight

1. Interview with Herman Cohen, 1992; JDC record of report by Taylor to Lubrani and Shilo, April 1, 1991, JDC archive; Department of State document 1991STATE122531.
2. JDC record of Recant's briefing of Shapiro, Schweger, Schneider, and Taylor, April 1, 1991, JDC archive.

3. "Ethiopian Rebels Making Gains; Regime Fading."

4. Odenheimer, "The Guns of April" and "Countdown in Ethiopia."

5. Biles, "Mengistu Flees After 14 Years of Brutal Rule"; Brown, "Despite Mengistu Departure, Rebels Press Offensive." Bob Houdek noted at the time that Mengistu's daughter would graduate from the lycée in Addis that spring and that the Ethiopian president had asked his foreign minister, Tesfaye Dinka, to arrange a position for her at the University of Zimbabwe. This, he said later, was a sign that Mengistu would bolt with sufficient inducement (telephone interview, May 24, 2004)

6. Telephone interview with Bob Houdek, November 29, 2001; Associated Press, "Mengistu Flees Ethiopia Under Heavy Pressure From Rebels"; summary of Schneider's briefing of Rudy Boschwitz, April 18, 1991, JDC archive.

7. See Henze, *Layers of Time*, p. 313.

8. Interview with Frasure, 1992.

9. JDC record, April 1, 1991, JDC archive.

10. Interviews with Frasure, 1992, and Scowcroft, June 12, 2003.

11. Herman Cohen, assistant secretary of state for African affairs, did not share the NSC's concern about repeating the fiasco with the Kurds. "The Kurds in Iraq were not a consideration," he told me. "No one feared genocide" in Addis Ababa (telephone interview with Cohen, April 11, 2003).

12. Interview with Frasure, 1992.

13. Interview with Scowcroft, June 12, 2003.

14. Interview with Frasure, 1992.

15. Interview with Cohen, 1992; aide-mémoire of Cohen's conversation with Lubrani, April 11, 1991, JDC archive.

16. Interview with Schneider, 1992.

17. Interview with Shapiro, 1992.

18. Cohen, *Intervening in Africa*, p. 47.

19. Interviews with Scowcroft, June 12, 2003, and Frasure, 1992.

20. JDC record of American Jewish "summit meeting," April 8, 1991, JDC archive; interview with Lubrani, 1992.

21. Aide-mémoire of Jewish leadership "summit," April 8, 1991; JDC record of kitchen cabinet meeting, April 10, 1991, JDC archive; confirmed by Boschwitz in 1992 interview.

22. Memo by Schneider, April 1, 1991, JDC archive.

23. Memoir by Boschwitz, April 28, 1991, pp. 5–6, JDC archive.

24. JDC record of Lubrani's briefing of Schneider and Taylor, April 11, 1991, JDC archive; aide-mémoire of Lubrani's conversation with Cohen, April 11, 1991, JDC archive.

25. Classified amendment, Department of Defense Appropriations for fiscal year 1991, section 8021 (cited in Cohen, *Intervening in Africa*, p. 232 n. 40).

26. Interview with Cohen, 1992 and January 3, 2002; Cohen, *Intervening in Africa*, p. 45.

27. JDC record of Kraar's conversation with JDC leaders, April 11, 1991, JDC archive; interview with Kraar, 1992.

28. Telephone interview with Cohen, April 11, 2003.

29. JDC record of kitchen cabinet meeting, April 8, 1991, JDC archive.

30. JDC record of conversation involving Recant, Schneider, and Taylor, April 16, 1991, JDC archive.

31. JDC record of April 16, 1991, JDC archive.

32. Cable from Naim, reported in Jewish Agency staff meeting, April 22, 1991, cited in Toran, ed., "Operation Solomon: The Beta Israel Return Home," p. 53; interview with Kassa, 1992.

33. JDC records of kitchen cabinet conference call, April 8, 1991, and of Schneider's conversation with Taylor, April 12, 1991, JDC archive.

34. Letter from Kulik to Kassa, April 7, 1991, AAEJ archive; letter from Shapiro to Kassa, April 9, 1991, AAEJ archive.
35. JDC record of Shapiro's conversation with Schneider, Eliezri, and Lubrani, April 11, 1991, JDC archive.
36. Interview with Lubrani, February 11, 1997.
37. JDC record of kitchen cabinet conversation, April 11, 1991, JDC archive; Feldman, *The Ethiopian Exodus*, p. 203. See Naim, *Saving the Lost Tribe*, p. 183.
38. Interview with Naim, 1992.
39. JDC record of Lubrani's conversation with Shapiro, Schneider, and Eliezri, April 12, 1991, JDC archive.
40. Telephone interview with Joe Feit, May 24, 2004.
41. Odenheimer, "Why Is This Afternoon Different . . . ?"
42. Interview with Jackson, 1992; Berger, *Rescue the Ethiopian Jews!*, p. 201.
43. Dawit says that because of his close connections with Israel, Kassa was long suspected of being a Mossad agent. As a result, Dawit concludes, Kassa at times tried to prove his loyalty to Mengistu. Kassa therefore undermined officials who sought to moderate relations with Israel, even though it had been Kassa who had initiated the diplomatic step in the first place (*Red Tears*, p. 331).
44. Ellicott, "Lobbyists Ride Out the Recession in High Style."
45. JDC record of report to the JDC by Eli Eliezri (who ran into Jackson "by accident" and debriefed him), April 24, 1991, JDC archive.
46. Interview with Jackson, 1992.
47. Ibid.
48. JDC record of Schneider's briefing of Boschwitz, sent to Lubrani, April 18, 1991, JDC archive.
49. Interview with Schneider, 1992.
50. Interview with Shapiro, 1992.
51. Interview with Schneider, 1992.

## Chapter Nine

1. JDC records of Lubrani's conversation with Schneider and Taylor, April 24, 1991, and of a report by Manlio Dell'Ariccia to JDC-New York, April 24, 1991, JDC archive.
2. JDC record of Lubrani's conversation with Schneider and Taylor, April 24, 1991, JDC archive; report by Manlio Dell'Ariccia to the JDC, April 24, 1991, JDC archive.
3. Asher Naim, in JDC record of April 24, 1991, JDC archive.
4. Interview with Kassa, 1992.
5. Department of State document 1991ADDIS01786. Deputy Secretary of State Lawrence Eagleburger's "terms of reference" for the Boschwitz mission included assessing Mengistu's willingness to engage in negotiations as an alternative to war. If the United States then chose to involve itself in peace talks, it would consider the Falasha emigration a humanitarian issue rather than a political quid pro quo (Department of State document 1991STATE135266, April 25, 1991). Boschwitz observed later that Frasure had briefed him thoroughly about the plan to end the Ethiopian civil war (interview, May 18, 2004).
6. Report of Kassa's conversation with a Mossad agent, in JDC records of April 23 and 24, 1991, JDC archive.
7. Interview with Boschwitz, 1992.
8. This contradicts Lubrani's statements in his interview, cited on pages 69–70.
9. Boschwitz memoir, pp. 2, 7, 11, and 12, JDC archive.

10. Interview with Schneider, 1992.

11. Boschwitz memoir, pp. 6–7; Department of State documents 1991STATE144569 and 1991ADDIS02058.

12. Interview with Boschwitz, 1992. Present with Tesfaye Dinka were Deputy Prime Minister Ashagre, Attorney General Bililign, and Ambassador Alemayehu, director of the Foreign Ministry's Americas Department. Boschwitz was accompanied by Houdek, Frasure, and Hall (Department of State Document 1991STATE144569).

13. Boschwitz memoir, pp. 6–8; Department of State document 1991STATE144568.

14. Interview with Boschwitz, 1992; Department of State document 1991STATE144568; National Security Council, "Letter to Mengistu from President Re Allow Ethiopian Jews to Leave for Israel," April 17, 1991. The records of the Israeli embassy in Addis and HIAS show that the Ethiopians permitted 1,008 Jews to depart for Israel in April 1991.

15. Boschwitz's handwritten statement, prepared for his meeting with Mengistu, JDC archive; Department of State document 1991STATE144568.

16. Boschwitz memoir, p. 9.

17. Department of State document 1991STATE144568.

18. Boschwitz memoir, p. 9; Department of State document 1991STATE144568; interview with Houdek, May 18, 2004.

19. Interview with Frasure, 1992; Department of State document 1991STATE144568.

20. Interviews with Kassa, 1992 and May 5, 1997.

21. Interview with Frasure, 1992; interviews with Houdek and Boschwitz, May 18, 2004.

22. Henze, *Layers of Time*, p. 328 n. 18.

23. Scowcroft had approved in advance their removing Mengistu on the plane with the Boschwitz mission if the Ethiopian leader consented to go (interview with Houdek, May 18, 2004).

24. Interview with Frasure, 1992; Department of State document 1991STATE144568.

25. Boschwitz memoir, p. 9.

26. Interview with Houdek, 1992.

27. Boschwitz memoir, pp. 7, 9.

28. JDC memo, April 27, 1991, 4:40 p.m., JDC archive; JDC memo, "Phone call 17.15 PM NT time," April 28, 1991 (for conversation of April 27), JDC archive; Houdek, telephone interview, February 17, 2004.

29. Faxed message from Schneider to Lubrani, 12:39 p.m, April 28, 1991, JDC archive.

30. Interview with Boschwitz, 1992.

31. Record of kitchen cabinet discussion, JDC record of 4:40 p.m., April 27, 1991, JDC archive.

32. Letter from Lubrani to Naim, for delivery to Boschwitz, April 28, 1991, JDC archive.

33. Boschwitz memoir, p. 10. See Feldman, *The Ethiopian Exodus*, p. 205; Naim, *Saving the Lost Tribe*, p. 192.

34. Interview with Boschwitz, May 18, 2004; Naim, *Saving the Lost Tribe*, p. 192.

35. JDC record of Lubrani's discussion with Schneider, Shapiro, and Taylor, April 28, 1991, 3:20 a.m., JDC archive; Feldman, *The Ethiopian Exodus*, p. 205.

36. Boschwitz memoir, p. 11.

37. Interview with Kassa, 1992. See his similar comments in Bergman, "I, Kassa Kebede."

38. Boschwitz memoir, p. 11.

39. Interview with Frasure, 1992.

40. Boschwitz memoir, p. 12; JDC record, April 28, 1991, JDC archive. See Naim, *Saving the Lost Tribe*, p. 193.

41. Boschwitz memoir, p. 11.

42. Interview with Frasure, 1992.

43. Boschwitz memoir, pp. 11–12. In a similar idiom, John Hall said, "We were . . . helping the Jews cross the Red Sea to the Promised Land" (Kaye, "On the Wings of Eagles," p. 401).

44. JDC record of Eliezri's conversation with Schneider, Dell'Ariccia, and Taylor, April 28, 1991, JDC archive; JDC record of Lubrani's conversation with Taylor, April 29, 1991, JDC archive; JDC record of kitchen cabinet discussion, 6:05 p.m., May 15, 1991, JDC archive; interview with Maimon, 1992. See Feldman, *The Ethiopian Exodus*, p. 206; Naim, *Saving the Lost Tribe*, p. 193.

45. According to HIAS records, 1,138 Jews left Addis Ababa for Israel between May 1 and May 23, as compared to the 1,008 in all of April; the Jewish Agency count was 1,119 from May 1 to May 22.

46. Record of kitchen cabinet discussion, noon, April 28, 1991, JDC archive.

47. An EPRDF official, visiting Herman Cohen at the State Department in April, noted that the Tigrean rebels had been in control of many Falasha villages for nearly a decade without anyone's being harmed. During Operation Moses in the mid-1980s, he said, the rebels had tried to convince the Jews to stay, but, accepting the urgency of their desire to leave, they had escorted them safely to the Sudanese border. He added that the EPRDF had no quarrel with Israel (Department of State document 1991STATE122531).

48. Department of State document 1991KHART001026.

49. Interview with Frasure, 1992; Cohen, *Intervening in Africa*, p. 46.

50. Hutman, "Ethiopian Jews Now Fear for Their Lives."

51. Interview with Frasure, 1992; record of kitchen cabinet discussion, April 29, 1991, JDC archive.

52. JDC record of Lubrani's conversation with the kitchen cabinet, 8:10 a.m., April 29, 1991, JDC archive.

53. JDC record of Lubrani's conversation with Schneider and Taylor, 2:00 p.m., April 29, 1991, JDC archive.

54. JDC record of Ami Bergman's briefing of Taylor, 10:00 a.m., April 29, 1991, JDC archive; Perlez, "U.S. Team Seeking Exodus of Ethiopian Jews."

55. JDC record of April 29, 1991, 5:30 a.m.; Naim, *Saving the Lost Tribe*, p. 193.

56. JDC records of 5:30, 8:10, and 10:00 a.m., 1:45 p.m., April 29, 1991, JDC archive.

57. JDC records of kitchen cabinet discussions, 8:10 a.m., 7:15 p.m., April 29, 1991, JDC archive.

58. Telephone interview with Joe Feit, May 24, 2004. Asked to comment about this later, Lubrani neither confirmed nor denied it. "At the time, I was absolutely convinced that Mengistu's regime was doomed anyway—and no amount of money could save it," he said. "However, knowing a little about the nature of Mengistu's gang, I felt that money could produce permission to let our people go" (e-mail interview, May 27, 2004).

59. JDC aide-mémoire of Jackson's report on his meeting with Kassa, April 29, 1991, JDC archive.

60. JDC record of Lubrani's conversation with Schneider and Shapiro, 11:40 a.m., April 30, 1991, JDC archive; JDC record of 12:30 p.m. (London time), May 18, 1991; interview with Schneider, April 12, 2001; confirmed in interviews with several Israeli and American officials and by Eli Eliezri's e-mail of March 21, 2004. Naim also notes in *Saving the Lost Tribe* that Jackson told him of the deal to pay Kassa $200 for every Beta Israel (p. 195).

61. Interview with Schneider, April 12, 2001; e-mail interview, December 6, 2001.

62. AAEJ memo of Jackson's phone call of April 29, 1991; "For the Record," memo by Schneider, May 2, 1991, JDC archive. See Naim, *Saving the Lost Tribe*, p. 195.

63. JDC record of Lubrani's discussion with kitchen cabinet, April 29, 1991, JDC archive; JDC memos of April 29, 1991, and May 2, 1991, JDC archive.

64. JDC record of Lubrani's discussion with kitchen cabinet, April 29, 1991, JDC archive.
65. Zvi Barak, the treasurer of the Jewish Agency at the time, said later that he agreed with the Mossad on this point. Since Israel was not in a state of war with Ethiopia, he said, it was appropriate to use civilian rather than military aircraft (interview, April 8, 2004).
66. JDC record of kitchen cabinet meeting, 6:45 p.m., April 29, 1991, JDC archive.

## Chapter Ten

1. "We were never serious about linkage after Ambo," Frasure said, and added that the State Department and the Israelis didn't like this shift at the White House (interview with Frasure, 1992). He was right. The State Department's Herman Cohen said later that Frasure "decided unilaterally, sitting in the NSC, that the US should no longer insist on the release of the Falasha as a pre-condition for our moving forward on the final mediation. He said that the highest priority should be the collapse of the regime and its replacement by something else. . . . I had to overrule him because of President Bush's commitment on the Falasha issue" (private correspondence to Reuven Merhav, October 29, 2001, quoted with Cohen's permission). It appears that Frasure was not dissuaded, however. Bob Houdek observed in an interview that Frasure's formulation, "theatrical stage prop," was probably sharper than his intention. There were shifts in emphasis, depending on the circumstances, but parallel momentum remained the preferred goal, said Houdek (e-mail interview, May 28, 2004).
2. Interviews with Frasure, 1992, and Scowcroft, June 12, 2003.
3. Interview with Frasure, 1992. In an interview on June 12, 2003, Scowcroft confirmed that the United States removed Mengistu from office, but did not comment on the details. Frasure revealed his role in this event to Herman Cohen only after the fact, perhaps because he feared that Cohen might oppose the move (Cohen, e-mail interview, June 25, 2003). The State Department did not know about the "Mugabe gambit," Frasure noted in his 1992 interview.
4. Memo by Schneider, May 3, 1991, JDC archive; memo from Taylor, "Suggested Talking Points, meeting: Rudy, MS, NS," May 3, 1991, JDC archive; "Briefing Session for Boschwitz," May 4, 1991, JDC archive.
5. Boschwitz notes on his briefing of the president, May 7, 1991, JDC archive.
6. JDC record of conversation of Recant, Yossi Amrani, and Taylor, 3:30 p.m., May 6, 1991, JDC archive.
7. JDC record of Lubrani's conversation with Divon, Schneider, and Taylor, 10:15 a.m., May 1, 1991, JDC archive.
8. JDC record of Lubrani's conversation with the kitchen cabinet, 1:30 a.m., May 4, 1991, JDC archive.
9. Fax from Lubrani to Yossi Amrani, for delivery to Boschwitz, May 4, 1991, JDC archive.
10. Interview with Lubrani, February 23, 1997.
11. Rabinovich, "Exodus: The Sequel."
12. Interview with Lubrani, February 23, 1997.
13. Interview with Lubrani, 1992.
14. Interviews with Lubrani, 1992, and Naim, May 30, 1997. See Naim, "Operation Solomon Recalled: Countdown to a Miracle."
15. Interviews with Kassa, 1992, and Tesfaye Dinka, January 3, 2002. See Naim, *Saving the Lost Tribe*, pp. 193–95, 199.
16. Cohen, *Intervening in Africa*, p. 46.
17. JDC record of Lubrani's conversation with Eliezri, Schneider, and Taylor, 2:40 p.m., May 10, 1991, JDC archive.

18. Interviews with Schneider, October 9, 1997, and April 12, 2001.
19. Interview with Kraar, November 2, 2001. The CJF, UJA, and UIA have since merged into the United Jewish Communities.
20. Interviews with Schneider, 1992, October 9, 1997, and April 12, 2001; JDC records of conversation of Lubrani, Eliezri, and Taylor, 2:40 p.m., May 10, 1991, and of Schneider's phone message to Lubrani, May 10, 1991, JDC archive.
21. Interview with Lubrani, 1992; conversation of Lubrani, Eliezri, and Taylor in JDC record of 2:40 p.m., May 10, 1991, JDC archive.
22. Bergman, "I, Kassa Kebede."
23. Interview with Frasure, 1992.
24. Interview with Lubrani, February 23, 1991; JDC record, 12:30 p.m. (London time), May 18, 1991, JDC archive. See Naim, *Saving the Lost Tribe,* p. 199.
25. JDC record of Lubrani's report of this conversation to Schneider, Eliezri, and Taylor, 12:30 p.m. (London time), May 18, 1991, JDC archive.
26. Ibid.; interview with Lubrani, 1992.
27. Rabinovich, "Exodus: The Sequel."
28. JDC record of 12:40 a.m. (London time), May 19, 1991, JDC archive.
29. JDC record of Peter Jackson's conversation with Schneider, Taylor, Shapiro, and Recant, 6:05 p.m., May 15, 1991, JDC archive.
30. Interviews with Lubrani, 1992 and February 11, 1997, and Boschwitz, 1992; JDC record, 11:30 a.m. (London time), May 18, 1991, JDC archive.
31. Recant's report to Shapiro and Taylor, in JDC record of 11:00 a.m., May 16, 1991, JDC archive.
32. JDC records of 10:05 and 11:00 a.m., May 16, 1991, JDC archive.
33. Conversations of Recant, Shapiro, and Taylor in JDC record of 11:00 a.m. and of Recant, Shapiro, Taylor, and Jackson in JDC record of 3:15 p.m., May 16, 1991, JDC archive; interview with Kassa, 1992.
34. JDC record, 10:00 a.m., May 17, 1991; Frasure's briefing of Boschwitz, JDC records of 6:25 p.m. (London time), May 19, 1991, and 12:40 a.m. (London time), May 20, 1991, JDC archive.
35. JDC records of kitchen cabinet discussion, 9:15 and 11:30 a.m. (London time), May 18, 1991, JDC archive; Naim, *Saving the Lost Tribe,* p. 200.
36. Naim, *Saving the Lost Tribe,* p. 200.
37. Lubrani's conversations with Eliezri, Schneider, and Taylor, JDC records of 9:15 and 11:30 a.m. (London time), May 18, 1991, JDC archive.
38. JDC record, 12:30 p.m. (London time), May 18, 1991, JDC archive. The man who conceived of the appellation "Operation Solomon" was named Ilan Baruch (telephone interview with Schneider, October 19, 2001).
39. Cf. 1 Kings 3:16–28.
40. Interview with Lubrani, 1992; JDC record of Kassa's call to Lubrani, 6:45 a.m. (London time), May 19, 1991, JDC archive.

## Chapter Eleven

1. JDC record of 12:40 a.m. (London time), May 19, 1991, JDC archive. The words "to Zimbabwe" are interlineated after "make a trip." The riddle is bracketed, with an arrow pointing to the comment "N.B., short trip, sources impeccable." A notation on the document and its position among the surrounding pages indicate that this record actually was written shortly after midnight on Sunday night, May 20. The message was from Nate Shapiro, and the tip evidently came from Frasure.

2. Interview with Frasure, 1992; Associated Press, "Mengistu Flees Ethiopia Under Heavy Pressure from Rebels"; Raath, "Butcher of Addis Puts Out the Begging Bowl"; Raath, "Mugabe Role Is Revealed." The *Financial Times* reported that Moscow also had pressured Mengistu to quit; Ozanne, "Ethiopian President Is Forced to Flee Country." See Cohen, *Intervening in Africa*, p. 47, and Orizio, "The Lion Sleeps Tonight," p. 34.

3. Cable from Michael Shilo, JDC records, 6:00 a.m. and 2:15 p.m. (London time), May 20, 1991, JDC archive.

4. Cohen, *Intervening in Africa*, p. 47; Cohen, e-mail interview, June 25, 2003. See Chapter 10, note 1.

5. Lubrani's conversation with the kitchen cabinet, JDC record of 6:15 a.m. (London time), May 20, 1991, JDC archive; Shilo indicated the policy change in a cable (noted in JDC record of 6:00 a.m., London time, May 20, 1991, JDC archive). Lubrani first alluded to this shift on Sunday morning (JDC record of 8:30 a.m., London time, May 19, 1991, JDC archive).

6. JDC record 6:30 p.m. (London time), May 19, 1991, JDC archive.

7. Record of Eliezri's message to Taylor and Schneider, 11:50 a.m. (London time), May 20, 1991, JDC archive.

8. JDC records of kitchen cabinet discussions, 8:15 a.m. and 2:15 p.m. (London time), May 20, 1991, JDC archive; interview with Lubrani, 1992.

9. Lubrani's message to kitchen cabinet, 2:15 p.m., May 20, 1991, JDC archive.

10. Telephone interviews with Bob Houdek, November 29, 2001, and Herman Cohen, January 3, 2002; e-mail interview with Houdek, February 24, 2004; Krauss, "Ethiopia's Dictator Flees; Officials Seeking U.S. Help." See Henze, *Layers of Time*, p. 329; Cohen, *Intervening in Africa*, p. 47, and Zava, "Mengistu Under Attack," p. 29.

11. Telephone interviews with Tesfaye Dinka, January 8, 2002, and Bob Houdek, May 24, 2004; Meldrum, "Fleeing Mengistu Arrives in Zimbabwe"; Kiley, "Ethiopia Faces Anarchy as Troops Close In."

12. Interview with Kassa, 1992.

13. Interview with Lubrani, February 11, 1997.

14. Raath, "Butcher of Addis Puts Out the Begging Bowl."

15. Telephone interview with Bob Houdek, November 29, 2001.

16. Kiley, "Ethiopia Faces Anarchy as Troops Close In"; Zava, "Mengistu Under Attack"; Orizio, "The Lion Sleeps Tonight," pp. 24, 43. By 1996, the government of Zimbabwe reportedly had spent U.S. $900,000 to maintain Mengistu, including the cost of a luxury villa, security guards, and telephone bills (Agence France-Presse, "Exiled Ethiopian Dictator Drains Zimbabwe Treasury: Report," June 21, 1996, citing a story in the *Zimbabwe Independent*).

17. Krauss, "Ethiopia's Dictator Flees; Officials Seeking U.S. Help"; Biles, "Rebel Forces Close in on Addis Ababa." Bob Houdek later questioned whether the Council of State discussion really happened. If it did, said Houdek, then "Tesfaye Dinka sure put on a good act" of being taken by surprise by Mengistu's flight the next morning. And Mengistu's deceptive departure on the DASH-6 seems inconsistent with the idea of a council decision already having been made the night before (telephone interview, May 24, 2004). Tesfaye indicated to me the same sense of having been surprised by Mengistu's flight. Telephone interview, January 8, 2002.

18. Houdek's conversation with Tesfaye Dinka, reported by Lubrani, JDC record of May 18, 1991, JDC archive.

19. Interviews with Kassa, 1992, and Lubrani, February 11, 1997.

20. Telephone interview with Houdek, November 29, 2001; Naim, *Saving the Lost Tribe*, p. 204.

21. Telephone interviews with Houdek, November 29, 2001, and May 24, 2004.

22. Interview with Cohen, 1992.
23. Eliezri's report to Taylor, in JDC record of 9:40 a.m., May 22, 1991, JDC archive.
24. Interview with Lubrani, February 11, 1997.
25. This calculation is based on 14,310 people having been transported in Operation Solomon. If one uses the smaller figure of 14,203, people, the cost per person was $2,464. See Appendix 2.
26. Eli Eliezri, e-mail, March 21, 2004. I have been unable to determine if the United States paid for the cost of the flights in the end.
27. Interview with Lubrani, February 11, 1997; JDC record, 4:40 p.m., May 22, 1991, JDC archive.
28. Interview with Dinitz, January 1, 1998. See Arbel, *Riding the Wave,* p. 146.
29. Interview with Schneider, October 9, 1997.
30. Interview with Dinitz, January 1, 1998.
31. Interview with Lubrani, 1992.
32. Ibid.
33. JDC record of Recant's briefing of Taylor, 11:55 a.m., May 22, 1991, JDC archive.
34. Telephone interview with Houdek, November 29, 2001. See Hammond, *Fire from the Ashes,* chapter 22.
35. Friedman, *Operation Solomon,* p. 129.
36. Ibid., p. 130.
37. Interviews with Lubrani, 1992, and Naim, 1992.
38. Eliezri's briefing of Taylor, record of 9:40 a.m., May 22, 1991.
39. Lubrani's report to Schneider and Taylor, 6:35 p.m., May 22, 1991. Feldman notes that Kassa was sharp enough to demand all of the money in advance (p. 207).
40. Interview with Houdek, May 24, 2004.
41. Prior to the operation, Frasure told NACOEJ's Joe Feit that the odds against airlifting the entire community were ten thousand to one. Until Mengistu left power, those odds sounded right, Bob Houdek commented later (telephone interviews with Feit, May 24, 2004, and Houdek, May 27, 2004). A JDC record of April 24, 1991, notes that Feit reported Frasure's comment on that day.
42. "Ethiopian Jewish Emigration: From the President to Acting President Tesfaye," Department of State document 1991STATE169690; interviews with Houdek, 1992 and May 24, 2004, and Cohen, 1992; record of Lubrani's conversation with Schneider and Taylor, 6:35 p.m., May 22, 1991.
43. Hutman, "Mobilized for the Homecoming"; "Rescue in Ethiopia."
44. Interviews with Schneider, October 9, 1997, and Kraar, November 2, 2001.
45. Memo from Schneider to Dinitz, May 22, 1991, JDC archive.
46. JDC record, 5:30 p.m., May 22, 1991, JDC archive.
47. Lubrani's calls to Schneider and Taylor, in JDC records of 6:35 and 8:30 p.m., May 22, 1991, JDC archive.

## Chapter Twelve

1. Telephone interview with Barak, April 19, 2001.
2. Merhav, e-mail interview, October 2, 2001.
3. See Appendix 2.
4. Report by Arnon Mantber, director-general of the Jewish Agency Department of Immigration and Absorption, May 27, 1991, made available to the author; Rabinovich, "Africa Comes Through Door of Diplomat"; Hutman, "After the Euphoria, How to Integrate Them"; Hutman, "Mobilized for the Homecoming."

5. Burston, "IAF Reaches New Height in Ethiopian Airlift."
6. Interviews with Houdek, 1992 and November 29, 2001. The general told Houdek that he had ordered his people to "pull the plug" and let all of the Falasha out (phone interview with Houdek, May 27, 2004).
7. Interview with Frasure, 1992.
8. Naim, *Saving the Lost Tribe,* p. 210.
9. Interview with Naim, 1992.
10. Naim, *Saving the Lost Tribe,* pp. 210–12.
11. See ibid., p. 207.
12. Friedman, *Operation Solomon,* pp. 122–23; Feldman, *The Ethiopian Exodus,* p. 199; interviews with Avi Mizrachi, 1992, Doron Tashteet, 1992, and Ami Bergman, 1992.
13. Friedman, *Operation Solomon,* pp. 127–30; Feldman, *The Ethiopian Exodus,* pp. 210, 214; interview with Tashteet, 1992; report by Arnon Mantber, director-general of the Jewish Agency Department of Immigration and Absorption, May 27, 1991.
14. Friedman, *Operation Solomon,* pp. 123, 135–36; Feldman, *The Ethiopian Exodus,* p. 212; *Jewish Week,* July 26, 1991.
15. Interview with Tashteet, 1992; Friedman, *Operation Solomon,* p. 143.
16. Telephone interview with Andy Goldman, May 18, 2004.
17. Interview with Tashteet, 1992.
18. Berger, *Rescue the Ethiopian Jews!,* pp. 178, 199, 201–2.
19. Ibid., pp. 201–2; interviews with Schnapper, 1992, and Avi Mizrachi, 1992. Schnapper had been involved with the Ethiopian aliyah for ten years. She had expanded the AAEJ as Nate Shapiro's assistant, given lectures, and used her knowledge of Amharic to help organize the rescue of two hundred Ethiopian Jews a year between Operations Moses and Solomon. She had arranged phony marriages and college offers to help Jews leave Ethiopia legally and was central in getting together the committee of Ethiopians who carried out the AAEJ's transport program (Howard Lenhoff, telephone interview, May 21, 2004).
20. Interview with Brigadier General Amir Nachumi, 1992.
21. Interview with Halachmi, 1992; see Hutman, "Mobilized for the Homecoming."
22. Interview with Rachamim, 1992.
23. Interview with Yafet, December 9, 1996.
24. Avgar, "Operation Solomon."
25. JDC record of conference call, 12:00 p.m., May 23, 1991, JDC archive.
26. JDC record of Boschwitz's conversation with Shapiro and Schneider, 12:50 p.m., May 23, 1991, JDC archive.
27. Recant's report on his conversation with Frasure, JDC record, 9:25 a.m., May 23, 1991, JDC archive; interview with Amir Maimon, 1992. Simcha Dinitz recalled that he intervened from California with Scowcroft and Eagleburger that Thursday, asking them to halt the rebel advance (interview with Dinitz, January 1, 1998); see Arbel, *Riding the Wave,* p. 147. Shapiro recalled that he and Recant made a similar intervention with Frasure (telephone interview, May 27, 2003)
28. Interview with Frasure, 1992; confirmed by Bob Houdek, telephone interview, February 17, 2004.
29. Jackson's report to Shapiro, JDC record of 3:10 p.m., May 23, 1991, JDC archive; confirmed by interviews with Lubrani, 1992, and Shapiro, May 27, 2003.
30. Lubrani's report to Schneider and Taylor, JDC record of 6:35 p.m., May 23, 1991, JDC archive.
31. Ibid.; Jackson's report to Shapiro and Schneider, JDC record of 12:30 a.m., May 24, 1991, JDC archive; interview with Eliezri, 1992.

32. Interview with Barak, June 6, 2001, confirmed in interviews of April 19 and June 15, 2001; interview of April 8, 2004. Barak said that the fax bore Lubrani's signature. Asked about this, Lubrani denied sending a fax to Barak that Thursday night (telephone interview, February 12, 2004). After obtaining legal advice about making public a document obtained in a state operation, Barak declined to make the fax available to this author for examination. Without being able to verify its authorship and date, I choose to be circumspect in speculating about its provenance and its implications in interpreting the events that transpired on Friday morning, May 24, 1991 (see Chapter 13). Seroussi confirmed that Barak asked him on Thursday to conduct a check of the account, but recalled that Barak did not actually send him the account number until Friday morning (e-mail interview, May 17, 2004).
33. Interview with Merhav, July 23, 1997; Department of State document 1991RIYADH04783.
34. Interview with Shahak, October 31, 2001; see Rabinovich, "Exodus: The Sequel," *Jerusalem Post*, July 20, 2001.
35. Merhav, e-mail interview, November 4, 2001.

## Chapter Thirteen

1. Naim, *Saving the Lost Tribe*, p. 216.
2. Interview with Halachmi, July 21, 1997.
3. Bergman, "I, Kassa Kebede."
4. Details of the mission were supplied by the IDF spokesperson's office (private correspondence, January 13, 2002).
5. Odenheimer, "A Secret Gate Finally Swings Open."
6. Friedman, *Operation Solomon*, p. 138; Feldman, *The Ethiopian Exodus*, p. 213; interviews with LaDena Schnapper, 1992, and Barbara Ribakove Gordon, 1992.
7. Interviews with Avi Mizrachi, 1992, and Doron Tashteet, 1992; Friedman, *Operation Solomon*, p. 138; Feldman, *The Ethiopian Exodus*, pp. 210–11.
8. Lubrani's conversation with Schneider and Taylor, JDC record of midnight, May 24, 1991, JDC archive.
9. Ibid.; "Dictated by Uri Lubrani for immediate communication to Simcha Dinitz, 24th May, 1991," JDC archive; interview with Schneider, April 2, 2001.
10. JDC record of 5:00 p.m., May 12, 1991, JDC archive; also Lubrani's conversations with Schneider and Taylor, JDC records of 12:40 and 1:00 a.m., May 24, 1991, JDC archive.
11. JDC record of 5:00 p.m., May 12, 1991, JDC archive; interview with Dinitz, January 1, 1998, confirmed by Barak in an interview on April 19, 2001.
12. Schneider and Taylor, JDC record of 1:00 a.m., May 24, 1991, JDC archive; interview with Schneider, 1992.
13. Kraar's conversation with Schneider and Taylor, JDC record of 2:30 p.m., June 5, 1991, JDC archive.
14. Interview with Dinitz, January 1, 1998.
15. Friedman, *Operation Solomon*, p. 138.
16. Bergman, unpublished memoir, JDC archive.
17. Friedman, *Operation Solomon*, pp. 139–40. See Rabinovich, "We're Home."
18. Interviews with Tashteet, 1992, Schnapper, 1992, and Amir Maimon, 1992; Hodes, "Operation Solomon."
19. Friedman, *Operation Solomon*, pp. 140–41; JDC record of 7:00 a.m., May 24, 1991, JDC archive; Gideon Taylor, "Bulletin," 10:40 a.m., May 24, 1991, JDC archive. Naim (*Saving the Lost Tribe*, p. 216) says that there were 20,000 to 25,000 by 10:30 a.m. Cf. Feldman, *The Ethiopian Exodus*, p. 215.

20. Interview with Barak, April 19, 2001.
21. Interview with Naim, May 30, 1997.
22. Rabinovich, "We're Home."
23. Interview with an Israeli official who was on the scene, 1997.
24. Feldman, *The Ethiopian Exodus*, pp. 214–15. See Arbel, *Riding the Wave*, pp. 148, 150.
25. Interview with Lubrani, December 22, 1995, in Arbel, *Riding the Wave*, p. 150.
26. Shagrir, "The Tremendous Excitement of Being Part of an Historical Event," p. 48.
27. Naim, *Saving the Lost Tribe*, p. 216; Feldman, *The Ethiopian Exodus*, p. 215.
28. Interview with Maimon, 1992. Feldman says that nearly six hundred people were ready at that point, filling eight buses (*The Ethiopian Exodus*, p. 215).
29. Friedman, *Operation Solomon*, p. 141; Amos Avgar, "Operation Solomon: An Eyewitness Account of the Final Days of the Rescue of the Ethiopian Jews," JDC board briefing, JDC archive.
30. Interview with Lubrani, February 23, 1997.
31. Interview with Lubrani, 1992; substantially repeated in Lubrani's luncheon speech in New York City, June 5, 1996, celebrating the fifth anniversary of Operation Solomon; e-mail interview, February 16, 2004.
32. From tape recording of Lubrani's luncheon speech in New York City, June 5, 1996.
33. Interview with Lubrani, 1992; reiterated in an interview on February 23, 1997, and in an e-mail interview, February 16, 2004. Rabinovich, in "We're Home," repeats Lubrani's account but has the finance minister produce the account number. Tesfaye Dinka, the prime minister, later denied that he had ordered the mission to stop or had any involvement in the matter of the payment (telephone interview, January 3, 2002).
34. E-mail interview with Lubrani, February 16, 2004. Eli Eliezri, who witnessed the conversation with Kassa, later confirmed much of the substance of Lubrani's story. Eliezri stressed that he and Lubrani were playing with Kassa, trying to delay the payment so that perhaps they would not have to pay at all. Although he was not present for or did not remember some of the interactions, Eliezri corroborated Lubrani's exchange with the finance minister, adding that the conversation was polite and ended with a handshake (interview with Eliezri, October 19, 2001; e-mail interview, March 5, 2004).
35. Bergman, "I, Kassa Kebede."
36. Interview with Eliezri, October 19, 2001; Naim, *Saving the Lost Tribe*, p. 218. Naim also confirmed this at the time in a classified cable to the Israeli Foreign Ministry of June 3, 1991, to which I was given access.
37. E-mail interview with a former high-ranking Ethiopian official, February 2004; Bob Houdek, e-mail interviews, February 24 and 26, 2004; Henze, *Layers of Time*, p. 329; Kiley, "Ethiopia Faces Anarchy as Troops Close In."
38. Eliezri did not recall the finance minister's calling the prime minister. He did, however, confirm that it was Kassa, not the finance minister, who supplied the account number, as noted above (interview, October 19, 2001).
39. Telephone interview with Bekele, January 9, 2002. See the Epilogue in this volume. Lubrani confirmed that, after the transfer of the funds had been completed, a bank officer in New York phoned the Ethiopian finance minister to confirm the transaction (e-mail interview, February 16, 2004). The Citibank officer who made the transfer noted that there was an unusual amount of telephone activity concerning the transaction that day (interview, given on condition of anonymity, June 15, 2001).
40. Micha Feldman corroborates the finance minister's account on this point, saying that a phone call from New York early on Friday announced that the money had been deposited. The rest of his story does not agree with Bekele's, however. The Ethiopians tried to verify the deposit but could not, Feldman says, and that was why they stopped

the operation. The Israelis then gave the number a second time to the Ethiopians, who realized that they had called the wrong bank. They checked again and, satisfied, allowed the rescue to resume (Feldman, *The Ethiopian Exodus*, p. 216). This account, which Feldman evidently got from Naim, is extremely unlikely. That seasoned Ethiopian bank officials should, first, fail to call their own bank, then make a second error, mistakenly determining that a deposit had been made into their account, seems improbable.

41. Naim, "Operation Solomon Recalled: Countdown to a Miracle."
42. Interview with Victor Harel, August 18, 1997.
43. Rapoport, "14,400 Are Flown Here in a 24-Hour Airlift."
44. Interview with Tashteet, 1992.
45. Interview with Maimon, 1992; Friedman, *Operation Solomon*, p. 142; Feldman, *The Ethiopian Exodus*, p. 215.
46. Interviews with Maimon, 1992, and Eliezri, 1992; Friedman, *Operation Solomon*, pp. 143–44.
47. Friedman, *Operation Solomon*, p. 142; Hodes, "Operation Solomon."
48. Interview with Addisu, January 7, 1997.
49. Hodes, "Operation Solomon."
50. Interview with Bergman, 1992.
51. Interview with Maimon, 1992; Friedman, *Operation Solomon*, pp. 141–42; Feldman, *The Ethiopian Exodus*, p. 216.
52. Friedman, *Operation Solomon*, p. 142.
53. Interview with Feldman, December 22, 1997.
54. Telephone interview with Avi Mizrachi, October 15, 2001.
55. Interview with Rachamim, August 11, 1997.
56. JDC record, 7:00 a.m., May 24, 1991, JDC archive.
57. Interview with Rachamim, August 11, 1997.
58. Friedman, *Operation Solomon*, p. 144; Feldman, *The Ethiopian Exodus*, p. 217; confirmed by Naim in "Operation Solomon Recalled" and by interviews with Maimon, 1992, and Eliezri, 1992.
59. Telephone interview with Avi Mizrachi, October 15, 2001.
60. Friedman, *Operation Solomon*, pp. 145–46; Feldman, *The Ethiopian Exodus*, p. 217.
61. Interview with Lubrani, 1992.
62. Interview with Tashteet, 1992.
63. Hutman, "Mobilized for the Homecoming." Addisu later became the first Ethiopian member of the Israeli Knesset.
64. Keinon, "Man, Forced to Bar Aunt from Aliyah, Finally United with Her."
65. Interview with Schnapper, 1992.
66. Odenheimer, "A Secret Gate Finally Swings Open."

## Chapter Fourteen

1. Interviews with Barak, April 19 and June 6, 2001; April 8, 2004.
2. Lubrani's address at an event in New York celebrating the fifth anniversary of the rescue, June 5, 1996; Lubrani, interview, February 23, 1997, and e-mail interview, February 16, 2004. Lubrani also observed that the account was in the wrong bank.
3. Szulc, *The Secret Alliance*, p. 305.
4. Interview with Barak, June 6, 2001.
5. "It would be very, very unlikely for the central bank to give the wrong number," the former finance minister, Bekele Tamrat, told me. "We have only one or two or three

accounts" and the central bank does not keep accounts for individuals, he noted. In any case, he added, "the code characters would be different for an individual account" (telephone interview, January 9, 2002).

6. Interviews with Barak, June 6, 2001, and April 8, 2004.
7. Arbel, *Riding the Wave*, p. 153, citing an interview with Dinitz of August 15, 1995; interview with Dinitz, January 1, 1997.
8. Fitzgerald, "Tyrant for the Taking." The *Sunday Times* reported that Kassa had set up these accounts for Mengistu, who deposited hundreds of millions of dollars in them (Kiley, "Ethiopia Faces Anarchy as Troops Close In").
9. Henze, *Layers of Time*, p. 326.
10. Interviews with Barak, April 19 and June 6, 2001; April 8, 2004.
11. Interview with a reliable Israeli eyewitness who asked not to be identified, May 1997.
12. Interview with Lubrani, February 23, 1997, reiterated in e-mail interview, February 16, 2004.
13. Telephone and e-mail interviews with Lubrani, February 12 and 16, 2004.
14. From tape recording of Lubrani's luncheon speech in New York City, June 5, 1996.
15. The finance minister, in an interview, denied that the conversation between him and Lubrani ever took place. He added that it would have been unnecessary to ask Israeli intelligence for help, since the account number was readily available from the governor of the Ethiopian central bank (telephone interview, January 9, 2002). It seems improbable that their conversation would have occurred at a late stage in the operation, that is, on Saturday, as Lubrani recalled it, since the deposit had already gone through the night before.
16. Barak, Houdek, and Naim all confirmed this account. When told Lubrani's version of events, Barak said forcefully that Lubrani played no part in finding the correct account number (interviews with Barak, April 19 and June 6, 2001, and April 8, 2004; telephone interviews with Houdek, November 29, 2001 and February 17, 2004; e-mail interview with Naim, May 15, 2004); Department of State document 1991ADDIS02391.
17. Interviews with Barak, April 19 and June 6, 2001, confirmed by Naim (e-mail interview, May 15, 2004); see Arbel, *Riding the Wave*, p. 146.
18. Rapoport, "Ethiopian Jewry Rescued." Rapoport was an activist on behalf of the Ethiopian Jews and the author of *The Lost Jews: Last of the Ethiopian Falashas* and *Redemption Song: The Story of Operation Moses*.
19. Interview with Harman, July 11, 1997.
20. Rapoport, "Ethiopian Jewry Rescued."
21. Ibid.; Naim, "Operation Solomon Recalled"; Naim, *Saving the Lost Tribe*, p. 218.
22. Rapoport, "Ethiopian Jewry Rescued."
23. Beeston, "Rabbi Sees Messianic Pattern in Chaos."
24. Rapoport, "Ethiopian Jewry Rescued."
25. Interview with Maimon, 1992.
26. Feldman, *The Ethiopian Exodus*, p. 217. See Friedman, *Operation Solomon*, p. 145.
27. Interview with Maimon, 1992.
28. Telephone interview with General Shahak, October 31, 2001.
29. Rabinovich, "We're Home"; Feldman, *The Ethiopian Exodus*, p. 217.
30. JDC record of 10:30 a.m., May 24, 1991, JDC archive.
31. Interview with Oz, 1992; Micha Feldman (inteview, December 22, 1996), Naim, *Saving the Lost Tribe*, p. 220, and press reports said that 1,087 flew on the jumbo.
32. Horovitz and Hirschberg, "Homecoming"; also, Westheimer and Kaplan, *Surviving Salvation*, p. 1
33. Interview with Arie Fredilis, 1992.
34. Interview with Oz, 1992. See Rabinovich, "We're Home."

35. Horovitz and Hirschberg, "Homecoming."
36. Based on interviews with various participants and on Halevi, "Dinitz: Center Stage at Last."
37. Interviews with Amos Amir, 1992, Moshe Yegar, June 17, 1997, and Amir Maimon, 1992.
38. Interview with Maimon, 1992.
39. Interview with Eliezri, October 13, 1996.
40. Eliezri, "Anecdotal Memoirs," JDC archive; interview with Eliezri, October 13, 1996; "Eli greased all of the drivers of the buses, the policemen," JDC record of 9:20 p.m., May 24, 1991, JDC archive; broadly confirmed by Kassa in an interview, May 5, 1997. See Friedman, *Operation Solomon*, pp. 144, 147.
41. Interview with Eliezri, October 13, 1996.
42. Interview with Nachumi, 1992.
43. Interviews with Eliezri, October 13, 1996, and Schneider, August 9, 1997.
44. Interview with Barbara Ribakove Gordon, 1992.
45. Telephone interview with Avi Mizrachi, October 15, 2001; Feldman, *The Ethiopian Exodus*, p. 218.
46. Odenheimer, "A Secret Gate Finally Swings Open."
47. Ibid.; Friedman, *Operation Solomon*, p. 144; interviews with Odenheimer, December 19, 1996, and Barbara Ribakove Gordon, 1992.
48. Interview with Schnapper, 1992. See Arbel, *Riding the Wave*, p. 151.
49. Interview with Feldman, 1992; Feldman, *The Ethiopian Exodus*, p. 217.
50. Herb Keinon, "Ethiopian Olim Call Him Moses," *Jerusalem Post*, September 8, 1991.
51. Odenheimer, "A Secret Gate Finally Swings Open"; interviews with Odenheimer, December 19, 1996, and Barbara Ribakove Gordon, November 1996.
52. Interviews with Tashteet, 1992, Gordon, 1992, and Schnapper, 1992.
53. JDC record of 5:15 p.m., May 24, 1991, JDC archive; interviews with Harel, August 18, 1997, and Naim, May 30, 1997; also, Naim, "Operation Solomon Recalled," *Jerusalem Post*, May 22, 1992, and *Saving the Lost Tribe*, pp. 220–21.
54. Interview with Naim, May 30, 1997.
55. Interview with Yegar, June 17, 1997.
56. Naim, "Operation Solomon Recalled."
57. Interview with Yegar, June 17, 1997.
58. Interview with Lubrani, 1992.
59. Interview with Naim, May 30, 1997. See Naim, *Saving the Lost Tribe* p. 221. In an interview in *Yedi'ot Ahronot* (May 27, 2001), Kassa gave a completely different account of the conversation that resulted in his being brought to Israel.
60. Interview with Lubrani, February 23, 1997. Cf. Eli Eliezri's comment that he and Lubrani hoped that they would not have to pay the money at all (chapter 13, note 34).
61. Interview with Kaplan, April 23, 1995 (in Arbel, *Riding the Wave*, p. 150).
62. Interview with Kraar, November 2, 2001.
63. Interview with Maimon, 1992.
64. Eliezri and Manlio Dell'Ariccia's report to Taylor, JDC record of 2:50 p.m., May 24, 1991, JDC archive.
65. Conversation of Eliezri, Lubrani, Schneider, and Taylor, JDC record of 4:45 p.m., May 24, 1991, JDC archive.
66. Friedman, *Operation Solomon*, p. 148.
67. Ibid., p. 149.
68. Interviews with Victor Harel, August 18, 1997 and Tashteet, 1992.
69. Lubrani's conversation with Schneider, Eliezri, and Taylor, JDC record, 4:45 p.m., May 24, 1991, JDC archive.

70. Interview with Doron Tashteet, October 13, 1996.
71. Lubrani's call to Schneider and Taylor, JDC record of 5:00 p.m., May 24, 1991, JDC archive; Odenheimer, "Those Left Behind." Rabbi Ovadiah Yosef, who as Sephardi chief rabbi in 1973 had determined that the Beta Israel were Jews, now said the same of the Falash Mura and urged that they be brought to Israel during the rescue (Odenheimer, "The Next Dilemma"); see page 192 in this volume.
72. Interview with Maimon, 1992.
73. Interviews with Feldman, December 22, 1996, and Goldman, 1992; Fishkoff, "The Ones Left Behind—Part I"; Feldman, *The Ethiopian Exodus*, p. 217.
74. Interviews with Avi Mizrachi, October 15, 2001, and Shahak, October 31, 2001. See Feldman, *The Ethiopian Exodus*, p. 217.
75. Message from Lubrani to Schneider, record of 5:00 p.m. (midnight Addis Ababa time), May 24, 1991.
76. Interview with Dinitz, January 1, 1998.
77. Interview with Maimon, 1992.
78. Interviews with Victor Harel, August 18, 1997, and with a high official with the Jewish Agency; Hutman, "Dinitz: Jewish Converts Want a Way Out of Ethiopia."
79. Interview with Mizrachi, 1992.
80. Report from Amos Avgar and Ami Bergman, JDC record of 8:00 p.m., May 24, 1991, JDC archive.
81. Cable from Bob Houdek to Herman Cohen, May 25, 1991 (Department of State document 1991ADDIS02406).
82. Burston, "IAF Reaches New Height in Ethiopian Airlift"; Rabinovich, "We're Home."
83. Interview with Moshe Yegar, June 17, 1997.
84. Interview with Nachumi, 1992.
85. Burston, "IAF Reaches New Height in Ethiopian Airlift."
86. Avgar, "Operation Solomon: An Eyewitness Account of the Final Days."
87. Burston, "IAF Reaches New Height in Ethiopian Airlift"; Naim, *Saving the Lost Tribe*, p. 224.
88. Friedman, *Operation Solomon*, p. 149.
89. Ibid., p. 150.
90. Interview with Jackson, 1992.
91. Interview with Schnapper, 1992; Berger, *Rescue the Ethiopian Jews!*, pp. 203–4.
92. Interview with Maimon, 1992; Friedman, *Operation Solomon*, p. 150.
93. JDC records of 4:20 p.m., May 24, and 2:45 a.m., May 25, 1991, JDC archive; Friedman, *Operation Solomon*, p. 150.
94. Interview with Houdek, November 29, 2001.
95. Interview with Maimon, 1992.
96. Richard Hodes, "Operation Solomon," personal memoir made available to author.
97. Interview with Lubrani, February 23, 1997.
98. Interview with an eyewitness, 2002; Bergman, "I, Kassa Kebede"; Rabinovich, "We're Home"; Henze, *Layers of Time*, p. 326. Feldman gives an amusing analogue to this story in *The Ethiopian Exodus*, p. 221.
99. Feldman, *The Ethiopian Exodus*, pp. 222–23.
100. Telephone interview with Shahak, October 31, 2001.
101. Fishkoff, "The Ones Left Behind—Part I."
102. Feldman, *The Ethiopian Exodus*, p. 223.
103. Interview with Shahak, October 31, 2001; also, interviews with Harel, August 18, 1997, Maimon, 1992, and Lubrani, February 23, 1997. Cf. Odenheimer, "A Secret Gate Finally Swings Open," and Naim, *Saving the Lost Tribe*, p. 223.
104. Interview with Lubrani, 1992.

105. Telephone interview with Houdek, February 17, 2004.
106. Reuven Merhav, e-mail comments, September 21, 2001.
107. IDF Spokesperson's Unit, private correspondence, January 13, 2002; Feldman, *The Ethiopian Exodus*, pp. 209–10. Naim says that thirty-five planes made forty-one flights (*Saving the Lost Tribe*, p. 224).
108. See Appendix 2 and Feldman, *The Ethiopian Exodus*, p. 228, Krieger, "Operation Solomon Babies."
109. Rosen and Rubinstein, "The Demography of the Ethiopian Community in Israel." These figures are for Ethiopian immigrants in all of 1991, of whom those who arrived in Operation Solomon constituted nearly 72 percent. As a point of comparison, children under the age of seventeen made up 27 percent of all new immigrants to Israel (Efrat et al., *Young Children in Israel*).
110. Rabinovich, "We're Home."

## Chomanesh Crosses the Red Sea

1. This account is based on conversations with Rick Hodes (April 29, 1997) and with Ethiopian Jews.

## Epilogue

1. Interview with Yegar, June 17, 1997.
2. Kaplan, "Rescue Effort Result of Repeated Appeals to Both Ethiopian and U.S. Governments"; Silver, "The Fixer—Uri Lubrani: The Mystery Man Who Saved the Jews."
3. Interview with Schneider, October 8, 1997. Lubrani soon began to set things right in interviews and public appearances, praising the American Jewish community, Michael Schneider and Susan Pollack in particular, as well as Eli Eliezri and the Joint, the Foreign Ministry, and Shamir.
4. Houdek's wife, Mary, accepted the award in his behalf. Bush also credited Herman Cohen, whose service in the cause of the Ethiopian Jews went back to 1989. The president received appreciative letters from leaders of American Jewish organizations and communities around the country, praising his contribution to the rescue. "I share your feeling of joy," the president said in one response. "Thank God the Falashas are home now" (letter to David A. Harris, executive vice president of the American Jewish Committee, June 7, 1991, from the George H. W. Bush Presidential Library).
5. Interviews with Merhav, July 23, 1997 and September 9, 2001 (e-mail interview).
6. Bob Frasure died tragically in 1995 at the age of fifty-three when his car slid off a dangerous dirt road near Sarajevo. Thomas Oliphant wrote in "Real Icons Need No Tribute" that Frasure was running an effort to broker a peace settlement in the former Yugoslavia at the time, "trying to sneak through a window of opportunity against huge odds." Oliphant noted that Frasure had been at the center of "a decade's worth of unheralded crisis diplomacy" and that he "accomplished more in his time than most secretaries of state in American history."
7. Merhav, e-mail interview, September 21, 2001.
8. Department of State documents 1991DOHA01355, 1991BEIRUT01045, 1991CAIRO09793, 1991AMMAN04759, 1991DAMASC03610, 1991DAMASC-05983, 1991TELAVIV06649.
9. Department of State document 1991TELAV07162.
10. Brinkley, "200 Ethiopians Trapped in West Bank"; Agence France-Presse, "Israeli FM to Make Official Visit to Ethiopia."

11. Telephone interview with Barak, April 19, 2001.
12. Bergman, "I, Kassa Kebede." Lubrani told Bergman that Kassa may have received a small payment, enough to live on, when he reached Israel, but no more than that.
13. Henze, *Layers of Time*, pp. 329, 332; Hammond, *Fire from the Ashes*, p. 420.
14. Interviews with Cohen, 1992, and Houdek, May 27, 2004. For Houdek's key role at this crucial moment, see Henze, *Layers of Time*, p. 330. Meles said that it was his idea to enter Addis Ababa and take control, a decision he took when he learned that law and order were deteriorating. The U.S. government, he said, then consented (Associated Press, "Ethiopia's New Leader Says Rebels Took Capital Without U.S. Approval").
15. Interview with Cohen, 1992. Tesfaye Dinka and the rest of the Ethiopian delegation walked out of the Roundtable talks in London, accusing the United States of duplicity (Henze, *Layers of Time*, p. 330). Some Amhara called the episode "Cohen's coup." Bob Houdek later cited the Eritrean rebels' central role in the fall of Addis Ababa. Their tying down the best Ethiopian troops in the north greatly eased the EPRDF's advance toward the capital. And it was an Eritrean armored brigade, under the banner of the EPRDF, that actually entered and took Addis with very little resistance, Houdek observed (telephone interviews with Houdek, May 24 and 27, 2004).
16. Naim, *Saving the Lost Tribe*, pp. 231–32. For the role of women and children among the rebels, see Odenheimer, "Six Days That Shook Ethiopia"; Henze, "Ethiopia in 1991—Peace Through Struggle," p. 3; and Hammond, *Fire from the Ashes*, p. 426.
17. Interviews with Naim, 1992 and May 30, 1997; Naim, *Saving the Lost Tribe*, p. 236.
18. Ibid.
19. Interview with Eliezri, October 19, 2001; Naim, *Saving the Lost Tribe*, p. 236.
20. Telephone interview with Haim Divon, November 27, 2001.
21. Interview with Naim, May 30, 1997.
22. Ibid.
23. Interview with Cohen, 1992.
24. Agence France-Presse, "Falasha Evacuation 'Shameful,' Says Ethiopia's Acting President"; Department of State document 1991ADDIS03734.
25. Interview with Naim, May 30, 1997; Naim, *Saving the Lost Tribe*, p. 237.
26. Interview with Cohen, 1992, confirmed by Naim in a 1992 interview. See Cohen, *Intervening in Africa*, p. 233 n. 43.
27. Henze, *Layers of Time*, pp. 331–32.
28. Merhav, e-mail interview, November 4, 2001.
29. Yehezkeli, "Ethiopia is Investigating Where U.S. $35 Million Israel Paid Disappeared To."
30. Sachar, *A History of Israel*, p. 982; he puts the amount at $40 million.
31. Interview with Dr. Girma Tolossa, April 6, 1998.
32. Interview with Dinitz, January 1, 1998.
33. Letter and fax sent by author on December 18, 2001.
34. Telephone interview with Divon, November 27, 2001.
35. Bergman, "I, Kassa Kebede."
36. Telephone interview with Divon, November 27, 2001.
37. Telephone interview with Houdek, November 29, 2001.
38. Henze, "The Defeat of the Derg," p. 27.
39. Interview with Dinitz, January 1, 1998; "The $35m. Bribe Mengistu Never Got"; Arbel, *Riding the Wave*, p. 153; Naim, *Saving the Lost Tribe*, p. 219.
40. Lawrence Eagleburger, e-mail interview, November 19, 2001. In a 1992 interview, Herman Cohen did refer to having frozen the account, but in a telephone interview on October 23, 2001, he said specifically that he had not frozen it. The fact that the account balance was changing by July 1991 (as discussed below) confirms that by that point there certainly was no freeze in place.

41. Confirmed by the Jewish Agency's Susan Krupp, who transferred the funds, then checked that they had been received on Friday, May 24, 1991 (telephone interview of June 7, 2001); also corroborated by Kassa (Bergman, "I, Kassa Kebede").

42. Interview with Bekele Tamrat, January 9, 2002.

43. Interview with Amir Shaviv, May 22, 2001.

44. Naim, *Saving the Lost Tribe*, pp. 239–44; Associated Press, "Israel Asks Repeal of U.N. Zionism-Racism Resolution."

45. Naim, *Saving the Lost Tribe*, pp. 243–44. Yohannan Bein, Israel's acting permanent representative at the United Nations at the time, privately confirmed that although Operation Solomon was used as an argument, it did not really influence the vote (October 16, 2001). In a fascinating account, J. J. Goldberg explains the background to the Bush administration's prompting the UN to repeal the resolution: this was one of several gestures that Bush offered in order to make amends to American Jewish leaders for having appeared to denounce them in September 1991 (*Jewish Power*, pp. xv–xxiii).

46. Keinon, "Man, Forced to Bar Aunt from Aliyah, Finally Reunited with Her."

47. Keinon, "40% of New Ethiopian Olim Said to be Non-Jews."

48. Keinon, "Talks This Week on Immigration of Remaining 2,500 Ethiopia's Last Jews Expected Here Soon."

49. Odenheimer, "Victims of a Broken Promise."

50. Izenberg, "Left Behind."

51. Naim, "Operation Solomon Recalled."

52. Tsur, "Official End to Exodus from Ethiopia."

53. Interview with Tashteet, October 13, 1996. Other estimates range from 3,000 to 4,500.

54. Interview with Tashteet, October 13, 1996. See Fishkoff, "The Ones Left Behind—Part I."

55. Seeman, "One People, One Blood." See "Summary of Navon Commission Report on Blood Donations by Ethiopian Immigrants."

56. Tsur and Siegel, "Ethiopian Leaders Divided over Bringing Falash Mura Here."

57. Fischer, "The Lie of Ethiopian Blood"; Anidjar, "AIDS Scare Final Straw for Ethiopian Jews in Israel."

58. Seeman, "One People, One Blood."

59. Streit, "Last Planeload of Ethiopian Immigrants Arrives."

60. Turkienicz, "Speedy Solution Needed for Ethiopia's Falash Mura: Sharansky."

61. Telephone interview with Gordon, December 4, 2001.

62. Interview with Schneider, April 12, 2001.

63. Interview given on condition of anonymity, 2001.

64. Sheleg, "Jewish Agency Looks West for Immigrants."

65. Lazaroff, "Meridor: Immigration Rate Is in Crisis." In 2001, 2,971 Ethiopians immigrated to Israel; there were 2,656 in 2002 and 3,029 in 2003 (see Appendix 1).

66. During Operation Solomon, Rabbi Yosef had attempted to intercede in behalf of the Falash Mura, as noted above (see chapter 14, note 71).

67. Sheleg, "For the Falashmura, the Window of Opportunity May Be Closing."

68. Gilbert, "Interior Minister Poraz: No Budget to Absorb Falash Mura"; Gilbert, "US Jews Should Fund Ethiopian Aliya"; Lazaroff, "Ethiopians Complain About Poraz's Appointment to Immigration Committee."

69. Interview given on condition of anonymity, March 16, 2004.

70. See Appendix 1.

71. A senior official of the Ministry of Absorption who was present at the meeting later told colleagues that this discussion was a breakthrough because it disproved claims by Falash Mura advocates that all *qessotch* agreed on the accuracy of the list. (Based on confidential correspondence of January 27, 2004, to which I was given access.)

72. Agence France-Presse, "Ethiopian Jews to Rejoin Kin in Israel, but Their Numbers Still Unknown"; Krieger, "Local Ethiopian Jews Hail Visit"; Clayton, "Ethiopia's Last 20,000 Falashas Are Allowed to Fly to Israel"; Rabinowitz, "Israel Wavers on Entry of Ethiopian Immigrants Who Claim to Be Jewish"; Hammer, "The Promise of Exodus." I have been unable to confirm the claim that Israel paid the Meles government in return for permission to remove the Falash Mura. The idea seems questionable, though, given the current Ethiopian attitude toward emigration and Israel's budgetary problems.

73. Agence France-Presse, "Ethiopian Jews to Rejoin Kin in Israel, but Their Numbers Still Unknown"; Lynfield, "Definition of 'Jew' Confronts Israel."

74. Oppen, "Of Being Numerous," p. 166. I am grateful to Henry Abelove for suggesting this passage and to New Directions Press for giving me permission to reprint this portion of the poem.

75. Steven Kaplan, private correspondence, September 20, 1999.

76. See Mourant, Kope, and Domaniewska-Sobczak, *Genetics of the Jews*, p. 39; Zoossmann-Diskin et al., "Genetic Affinities of Ethiopian Jews," pp. 245–51; Ritte et al., "The Differences Among Jewish Communities—Maternal and Paternal Contributions," pp. 435–40; Lucotte and Smets, "Origins of Falasha Jews Studied by Haplotypes of the Y Chromosome," pp. 989–93; Hammer et al., "Jewish and Middle Eastern Non-Jewish Populations Share a Common Pool of Y-Chromosome Biallelic Haplotypes," pp. 6769–74. See Halkin, "Wandering Jews—and Their Genes," p. 54. I am grateful to my colleague Robert Sokal for bringing these references to my attention and to Bernie Dudock for vetting my summary of their findings. Cf. the inconclusive 1962 study by Tel Hashomer Government Hospital noted in "A Survey of Some Genetic Characters in Ethiopian Tribes."

## Appendix 1

1. Annual totals were supplied by the Jewish Agency, Department of Immigration and Absorption, Office of the Director-General, and confirmed for 1977–91 by HIAS. Updated figures for 1999–2003 are from the Jewish Agency Immigration and Absorption Department, Director-General's Reports, February 2000, February 2001, December 2002, and December 2003.

2. Monthly figures for 1990 and 1991 are from the records of the Israeli Embassy in Addis Ababa. Counts by HIAS and the JDC disagree with the embassy's in the following instances: in all of 1981 (598 emigrants); in 1989 (547); in 1990, September (184), November (438), and December (540); and in 1991, January (831), February (996), and March (696).

   A Jewish Agency report issued immediately after Operation Solomon differed from all of these other accounts for every month in 1990 and 1991, up to May 22 (report by Arnon Mantber, May 27, 1991). In addition, the Jewish Agency's annual immigration figures for 1990 and 1991 are larger than the total monthly figures cited by the other sources for those years. On both the monthly and annual levels, these differences for 1990 owe largely to the fact that the Jewish Agency count includes the *olim* who arrived via Sudan; they were not among the emigrants from Addis Ababa of whom the embassy kept track. See note 3 below. Presumably for the same reason, Bob Houdek cited 458 Jews brought to Israel in March 1990 ("Falasha Roundup," February 2, 1991, confidential Department of State document 1991ADDIS00753).

3. According to the AAEJ, an additional 430 Ethiopian Jews were flown from Sudan to Israel in January 1990, and 325 more the following March (confidential memo from

Will Recant to officials of JDC, NJCRAC, the Jewish Agency, and other Jewish organizations, November 8, 1990). Micha Feldman offers similar figures: he says that 189 Jews emigrated from Ethiopia and 425 from Sudan in January 1990 (*The Ethiopian Exodus*, p. 140). He adds that a final rescue from Sudan in March brought over another 344 Jews who remained after that country expelled 1,000 Jews in January 1990 (p. 153).

## Appendix 2

1. E-mail interview with Andrea Arbel, advisor to the director-general of the Jewish Agency's Immigration and Absorption Department, writing on behalf of Mike Rosenberg, the director-general, April 24, 2003; Feldman, *The Ethiopian Exodus*, p. 228; Arbel, *Riding the Wave*, p. 153.
2. Report to Mendel Kaplan, chairman of the Board of Governors of the Jewish Agency, on May 27, 1991. In a report the same day to Simcha Dinitz, the chairman of the Jewish Agency, Mantber cited a similar number of *olim*, saying that Israel had brought over 14,200 Ethiopian Jews in Operation Solomon. The Israeli Ministry of Immigrant Absorption gives a slightly lower number: 14,162 ("Aliyah Absorption 1989–2000," updated as of November 2001, www.moia.gov.il). Toran, ed., "Operation Solomon: The Beta Israel Return Home" (the Jewish Agency's undated report,) gives almost the same figure: 14,163 (p. 50).

## Appendix 3

1. Interview with Riki, August 11, 1996.
2. Interview with Shapiro, 1992.
3. Interview with Naim, August 10, 1997.
4. In fact, in 1996, the year prior to our conversation, Kassa was a financial supporter of the Gorbachev Foundation/USA in San Francisco. He had no deep connection with the organization, however, and discontinued his association after a few years (e-mail interview with James Garrison, president of the State of the World Forum, March 31, 2004). See "State of the World Forum: Honoring Our Past," www.worldforum.org.
5. Mark Winer, an American, shared a room with Kassa at Ulpan Akiva in 1962. He later confirmed the profound impact of the *ulpan* experience on Kassa's feeling for Jews and Judaism, specifically mentioning that Kassa remembered the jokes and songs that he had heard there. Beginning in January 1991, when Winer traveled to Ethiopia, he renewed his close friendship with Kassa. Winer then kept in regular touch with him, urging him to allow the Ethiopian Jews to leave (Goetz, "Visiting Rabbi Preaches Interfaith Understanding"; "Lessons from Ethiopian Jews, Visions for Our Future," Winer's High Holiday sermons at the West End Synagogue, where he is now senior rabbi, 1998).
6. Kassa reiterated this and other points cited here in a later interview with Ronan Bergman ("I, Kassa Kebede").
7. See, however, page 105 in this volume.
8. Interview with Schneider, October 9, 1997.
9. Interview with Pollack, May 5, 1997.
10. Interview with Naim, May 30, 1997.

# GLOSSARY OF NAMES AND TERMS

Titles and roles were those at the time of this story, until Operation Solomon. Ethiopians are listed alphabetically according to their first names.

**AAEJ:** American Association for Ethiopian Jews

**Ackerman, Gary:** Democratic United States congressman from New York

**Addis Ababa:** Established as Ethiopia's capital by Menelik II in 1889; often referred to as "Addis"

**Addisu Massele:** Ethiopian-Israeli activist, later a member of the Knesset

**aliyah:** (Hebrew) Emigration (literally "ascension") to Israel

**Almaya:** Quasi-official organization established by the JDC to carry on in Ethiopia if the JDC itself was forced to leave the country

**Amhara:** Inhabitants of the Ethiopian central highlands, one of the two largest ethnolinguistic groups in the country (along with the Oromo); politically dominant until May 1991

**Amharic:** An Afro-Asiatic language belonging to the Southwest Semitic group; the most widely diffused Ethiopian tongue and formerly the official language of the country

**Arens, Moshe:** Israeli foreign minister; as of June 1990, defense minister

**Avgar, Amos:** Official of JDC-Israel

**Baker, James:** U.S. secretary of state

**Barak, Ehud:** Lieutenant-general, IDF chief of general staff as of April 1991

**Barak, Zvi:** Director-general of the Jewish Agency Finance Department

**Bergman, Ami:** JDC-Israel official, deputy chairman of Almaya

243

**Berhanu Yiradu:** Ethiopian Christian AAEJ agent who organized the transport program

**Beta Israel:** The Ethiopian Jews' preferred name for themselves while they were in Ethiopia (as opposed to Falasha), meaning "House of Israel" in Amharic

**birr:** The Ethiopian currency

**Boschwitz, Rudy:** Former Republican U.S. senator from Minnesota, President Bush's special emissary to Mengistu in April 1991

*buda:* (Amharic) User of the evil eye, hyena-man

**CJF:** Council of Jewish Federations

**Cohen, Herman J.:** U.S. assistant secretary of state for African affairs

**Dell'Ariccia, Manlio:** Director of JDC-Rome

**Derg:** Secretive armed-forces coordinating committee formed in 1974; deposed Haile Selassie and took power in Ethiopia that year, transforming itself into the Workers' Party of Ethiopia in 1984 and established the People's Democratic Republic of Ethiopia in 1987

**Dinitz, Simcha:** Chairman of the Jewish Agency

**Divon, Haim:** Israeli Foreign Ministry desk officer for Ethiopia and special liaison to Uri Lubrani; formerly chargé d'affaires at Israeli embassy in Addis, then, in 1992, ambassador to Ethiopia

**Eagleburger, Lawrence:** U.S. deputy secretary of state

**Eliezri, Eli:** JDC operative, assigned to assist Uri Lubrani; chairman of Almaya; member of Reuven Merhav's Steering Committee

**EPLF:** Eritrean People's Liberation Front, founded and led by Isaias Afewerki

**EPRDF:** Ethiopian People's Revolutionary Democratic Front, rebel coalition led by the TPLF

**Falash Mura:** Beta Israel converts, or descendants of converts, to Christianity (alternatively, Feresmura, Felasmura, or other variants)

**Falasha:** Term for the Ethiopian Jews, meaning "stranger" or "landless one" in Amharic; *see* **Beta Israel**

**Feit, Joseph:** New York–based tax attorney and president of NACOEJ who worked with the Ethiopian Jews in Addis Ababa

**Feldman, Micha:** Jewish Agency official who specialized in Ethiopian-Jewish questions; in 1989, appointed Israeli consul in Addis Ababa, in charge of processing Ethiopian immigrants and determining their eligibility to emigrate to Israel

*ferenj*: (Amharic) Foreigner, white or non-Ethiopian person, literally meaning "Franks"

**Frasure, Robert:** Deputy chief of mission at the American embassy in Addis, then director of African affairs, National Security Council

**Friedman, Kobi:** Almaya official in Addis

**Ge'ez:** ancient Ethiopic, a southern Semitic language preserved in the Beta Israel and the Ethiopian Orthodox sacred writings and liturgy

**Girma Tolossa:** Ethiopian representing the JDC in Addis

**Goldman, Andy:** NACOEJ official in Addis

**Gondar:** Region north of Lake Tana where most Ethiopian Jewish villages were concentrated; also the name of the town there that is the provincial capital

**Goodman, Charles "Corky":** President of the Council of Jewish Federations

**Gordon, Barbara Ribakove:** Executive director of NACOEJ

**Gordon, Uri:** Head of the Jewish Agency's Immigration and Absorption Department

**halacha:** Talmudic literature dealing with law and the interpretation of laws in the Hebrew Scriptures

**Halachmi, Haim:** Official of HIAS, on loan to the Jewish Agency and the Israeli government to help oversee the Ethiopian aliyah

**Hall, John:** Ethiopian desk officer at the U.S. State Department

**Harel, Victor:** Official at Israeli Foreign Ministry, chief aide to Reuven Merhav

**Harman, David:** Jewish Agency official in charge of educational programs in the diaspora; developed the school curriculum at the JDC school in Addis

**HIAS:** Hebrew Immigrant Aid Society

**Hicks, Irvin:** U.S. deputy assistant secretary of state

**Hodes, Rick:** Director of JDC Medical Clinic in Addis

**Hoenlein, Malcolm:** Executive vice chairman of the Conference of Presidents of Major American Jewish Organizations

**Houdek, Robert G.:** Chargé d'affaires at the U.S. embassy in Addis

**IAF:** Israeli Air Force

**IDF:** Israel Defense Forces, comprising the Israeli army, air force, and navy

**injera:** Round, flat Ethiopian bread, usually made of *t'ef,* an indigenous grain

**Isaias Afewerki:** Secretary-general of the EPLF

**Jackson, Peter:** San Diego businessman who represented the AAEJ in Addis, April-May 1991

**JDC:** The American Jewish Joint Distribution Committee, or the "Joint"

**Jewish Agency for Israel (JAFI):** International body representing the World Zionist Organization and other prominent Jewish bodies, dedicated to assisting Jewish immigration to Israel and to helping develop and settle the country

**Joint, the:** *See* JDC

**Kaplan, Mendel:** Chairman of the Board of Governors of the Jewish Agency

**Kaplan, Steven:** Scholar of comparative religion and African studies at Hebrew University

**Kassa Kebede:** Secretary for foreign relations for the Central Committee of the Ethiopian Communist Party, head of the Cadre, Mengistu's chief adviser on Israel and the Ethiopian Jewish emigration

*kebeles*: Local Ethiopian Communist Party cadres

**Kimmit, Robert:** Undersecretary of state for political affairs

**Knesset:** The Israeli parliament

**Kraar, Marty:** Executive vice president of the Council of Jewish Federations

**Kulick, Gil:** AAEJ board member

**Lender, Marvin:** National chairman of the United Jewish Appeal (UJA)

**Levy, David:** Israeli foreign minister, succeeding Moshe Arens in June 1990

**Lipkin-Shahak, Amnon:** major general, IDF deputy chief of general staff

**Lubrani, Uri:** Coordinator of Ethiopian aliyah affairs, Prime Minister Shamir's special representative to Ethiopia

**Maimon, Amir:** Deputy chief of mission and chief of operations at the Israeli Embassy in Addis

**Mantber, Arnon:** Director-general of the Immigration and Absorption Department of the Jewish Agency; later, director of JDC-Israel

**Meles Zenawi:** EPRDF leader, later president and then prime minister of Ethiopia

**Mengistu Haile-Mariam:** lieutenant colonel, chairman of the Revolutionary Council of Ethiopia, then president

**Merhav, Reuven:** Director-general of the Israeli Foreign Ministry and chairman of the Steering Committee on the aliyah

**Mersha Ketsela:** Ethiopian deputy minister of internal affairs

**Mizrachi, Avi:** Senior Jewish Agency representative in Addis

**Mizrachi, Orna:** Wife of Avi Mizrachi; director of the JDC school in Addis

**Mossad:** The Israeli civil intelligence agency, answerable to the prime minister; charged with clandestine operations outside of Israel, including Operation Moses

**Myers, Ted:** JDC's director of East Africa medical programs

**Nachumi, Amir:** brigadier general, chief of Israeli Air Force operations, Shahak's deputy for Operation Solomon

**NACOEJ:** North American Conference on Ethiopian Jewry

**Naim, Asher:** Israeli ambassador to Ethiopia

**Odenheimer, Micha:** American-Israeli rabbi and journalist, later an activist for Ethiopian-Israeli causes

*oleh* (*pl. olim*): (Hebrew) Immigrant to Israel

**Oromo:** Also called the Galla, the largest of the Cushitic peoples in Ethiopia

**Pollack, Susan:** AAEJ representative in Addis Ababa

*qes* (*pl. qessotch*): (Ge'ez and Amharic; pl. in Hebrew is *kessim*) Jewish priest

**Rachamim Elezar:** Ethiopian-Israeli activist, director of Kol Israel radio program in Amharic

**Recant, Will:** AAEJ executive director

**Schnapper, Ladena:** AAEJ official, stationed in Addis

**Schneider, Michael:** Executive vice president of the JDC

**Scowcroft, Brent:** U.S. national security adviser

**Shabbat:** Sabbath (Hebrew)

**Shahak, Amnon:** *see* **Lipkin-Shahak, Amnon**

**Shamir, Yitzhak:** Prime minister of Israel

**Shapiro, Nate:** President of the AAEJ

**Sharansky, Natan:** Former Soviet dissident, involved in the Ethiopian aliyah as Israeli interior minister and in other capacities

**Sharon, Ariel:** Housing minister and aliyah cabinet head

**Shaviv, Amir:** JDC official in New York, dealing with the press and public relations

**Shilo, Michael:** Senior adviser to Foreign Minister Arens on diaspora affairs; as of 1991, deputy chief of mission at the Israeli Embassy in Washington

**Shomron, Dan:** Brigadier general, IDF chief of general staff until April 1991

**Solarz, Stephen:** Democratic U.S. congressman from New York

**Solomon Ezra:** Ethiopian-Israeli working for NACOEJ in Addis

**South Wing to Zion:** Ethiopian-Israeli activist group

**Tashteet, Doron:** Almaya official in Addis

**Taylor, Gideon:** JDC "desk officer" for Ethiopia; he later was involved in caring for the Quaran Jews

**Tesfaye Dinka:** Foreign minister, then prime minister, of Ethiopia

**Tesfaye Gebre Kidan:** General, then vice president, then acting president of Ethiopia

**Tesfaye Wolde Selassie:** Ethiopian minister for internal affairs

**TPLF:** Tigrean People's Liberation Front, led by Meles Zenawi

*tukul:* (Amharic) A circular hut with walls of tree trunks and branches covered by mud, clay, and straw, with a conical thatched roof

**Weil, Shalva:** Anthropologist at Hebrew University

**Yafet Alamu:** Ethiopian-Israeli activist

**Yegar, Moshe:** Deputy director-general for Asia and Africa at the Israeli Foreign Ministry

**Yoffe, Meir:** Israeli ambassador to Ethiopia from the renewal of relations until July 1990

**Yosef, Ovadiah:** Sephardi chief rabbi of Israel (1973–83) who recognized the Beta Israel's legitimacy as Jews in 1973

**Zimna Berhane:** Ethiopian-Israeli activist working with the Jewish Agency in Addis

# BIBLIOGRAPHY

## Books

Aešcoly, A. Z. *Recueil de textes falachas: Introduction. Textes éthiopiens.* Paris: Institut d'ethnologie, 1951.

Arbel, Andrea S. *Riding the Wave: The Jewish Agency's Role in the Mass Aliyah of Soviet and Ethiopian Jewry to Israel, 1987–95.* Jerusalem: Gefen, 2001.

Ball, George W., and Douglas B. Ball. *The Passionate Attachment: America's Involvement with Israel, 1947 to the Present.* New York: Norton, 1992.

Bard, Mitchell G. *From Tragedy to Triumph: The Politics Behind the Rescue of Ethiopian Jewry.* Westport, CT: Praeger, 2002.

Baron, Salo W. *A Social and Religious History of the Jews,* vol. 18. New York: Columbia University Press, 1983.

Berger, Graenum. *Rescue the Ethiopian Jews! A Memoir, 1955–1995.* New Rochelle, NY: J. W. Bleeker Hampton, 1996.

Black, Ian, and Benny Morris. *Israel's Secret Wars: A History of Israel's Intelligence Services.* New York: Grove Weidenfeld, 1991.

Bodovsky, D., Y. David, and Y. Eran. *Customs and Culture: Their Relevance to the Development of Professional Relations.* Jerusalem: Betachin No. 2, 1994 (Hebrew).

Bruce, James. *Travels to Discover the Source of the Nile.* 2nd ed. Edinburgh: A. Constable, 1805.

Brzezinski, Zbigniew. *Power and Principle: Memoirs of the National Security Adviser, 1977–1981.* New York: Farrar, Straus, and Giroux, 1983.

Clapham, Christopher. *Transformation and Continuity in Revolutionary Ethiopia.* Cambridge: Cambridge University Press, 1988.

Cohen, Herman J. *Intervening in Africa: Superpower Peacemaking in a Troubled Continent.* New York: St. Martin's Press, 2000.

Conti Rossini, Carlo. *Storia d'Etiopia.* Bergamo: Istituto Italiano d'Arti Grafiche, 1928.

Dawit Wolde Giorgis, *Red Tears: War, Famine and Revolution in Ethiopia.* Trenton: Red Sea Press, 1989.

Dillmann, August. *Über die Regierung, insbesondere die Kirchenordnung des Königs Zar'a-Jacob.* Berlin:Verlag der Koniglichen Akademie der Wissenschaften, 1884.

Efrat, Galia, Asher Ben-Arieh, John Gal, and Muhammad Haj-Yahia. *Young Children in Israel: A Country Study.* Jerusalem: National Council for the Child, 1998.

Erlich, Haggai. *The Struggle over Eritrea, 1962–1978: War and Revolution in the Horn of Africa.* Stanford, CA: Hoover International Studies, 1983.

———. *Ethiopia and the Challenge of Independence.* Boulder, CO: Lynne Rienner, 1986.

———. *Ethiopia and the Middle East.* Boulder, CO: Lynne Rienner, 1994.

———. *The Cross and the River: Ethiopia, Egypt, and the Nile.* Boulder, CO: Lynne Rienner, 2002.

Feldman, Micha. *The Ethiopian Exodus.* Jerusalem: Jewish Agency, 1998 (Hebrew).

Friedman, Ya'acov. *Operation Solomon: A Year in Thirty-one Hours.* Jerusalem, 1992 (Hebrew).

Gilkes, Patrick. *The Dying Lion: Feudalism and Modernization in Ethiopia.* London: Julian Friedmann, 1975.

Ginsburg, Elliot K. *Sod ha-Shabbat.* Albany: State University of New York Press, 1989.

Gobat, Samuel. *Journal of a Three-Years' Residence in Abyssinia.* 2nd ed. London, 1850.

Goldberg, J. J. *Jewish Power: Inside the American Jewish Establishment.* Reading, MA: Addison-Wesley, 1996.

Hammond, Jenny. *Fire from the Ashes: A Chronicle of the Revolution in Tigray, Ethiopia, 1975–91.* Lawrenceville, NJ: Red Sea Press, 1999.

Henze, Paul B. *Layers of Time: A History of Ethiopia.* New York: St. Martin's Press, 2000.

Kaplan, Steven. *The Beta Israel (Falasha) in Ethiopia: From Earliest Times to the Twentieth Century.* New York: New York University Press, 1992.

Kaplan, Steven, and Shoshana Ben-Dor. *Ethiopian Jewry: An Annotated Bibliography.* Jerusalem: Ben-Zvi Institute, 1988.

Kaplan, Steven, and Hagar Salamon. *Ethiopian Immigrants in Israel: Experience and Prospect.* London: Institute for Jewish Policy Research, 1998.

*Kebra Negast*, trans. and ed. Miguel F. Brooks. Lawrenceville, NJ: Red Sea Press, 1996.

Kessler, David. *The Falashas: The Forgotten Jews of Ethiopia.* New York: Africana Publishing, 1982.

———. *The Falashas: A Short History of the Ethiopian Jews.* 3rd ed. London: Frank Cass, 1996.

Korn, David A. *Ethiopia, the United States and the Soviet Union.* Carbondale: Southern Illinois University Press, 1986.

Kraybill, Donald B., and C. Nelson Hostetter. *Anabaptist World USA.* Scottdale, PA: Herald Press, 2001.

Leslau, Wolf. *Falasha Anthology: The Black Jews of Ethiopia.* New Haven: Yale University Press, 1951.

Levine, Donald N. *Wax and Gold.* Chicago: University of Chicago Press, 1965.

———. *Greater Ethiopia: The Evolution of a Multiethnic Society.* Chicago: University of Chicago Press, 1974.

Marcus, Harold G., ed. *Proceedings of the First United States Conference on Ethiopian Studies.* East Lansing: African Studies Center, Michigan State University, 1973.

———. *Ethiopia, Great Britain, and the United States, 1941–1974: The Politics of Empire.* Berkeley: University of California Press, 1983.

———. *A History of Ethiopia.* Berkeley: University of California Press, 1994.

Messing, Simon D. *The Story of the Falashas—Black Jews of Ethiopia.* Brooklyn: Balshon, 1982.

Mourant, A. E., Ada C. Kopec, and Kazimiera Domaniewska-Sobczak. *The Genetics of the Jews.* Oxford: Clarendon Press, 1978.

Naim, Asher. *Saving the Lost Tribe: The Rescue and Redemption of the Ethiopian Jews.* New York: Ballantine, 2003.

Nöldeke, Theodor. *Neue Beiträge zur Semitischen Sprachwissenschaft.* Strasbourg, 1910.

Pankhurst, Richard. *The Ethiopians.* Oxford: Blackwell, 1998.

Pankhurst, Sylvia. *Ethiopia: A Cultural History.* Essex: Lalibela House, 1955.

Parfitt, Tudor. *Operation Moses: The Untold Story of the Secret Exodus of the Falasha Jews from Ethiopia.* New York: Stein and Day, 1985.

Parfitt, Tudor, and Emanuela Trevisan Semi, eds. *The Beta Israel in Ethiopia and Israel: Studies on Ethiopian Jews.* Surrey: Curzon, 1999.

Porten, Bezalel. *Archives from Elephantine.* Berkeley: University of California Press, 1968.

Pritchard, James. B., ed. *Solomon and Sheba.* London: Phaidon, 1974.

Quirin, James. *The Evolution of Ethiopian Jews: A History of the Beta Israel (Falasha) to 1920.* Philadelphia: University of Pennsylvania Press, 1992.

Rapoport, Louis. *The Lost Jews: Last of the Ethiopian Falashas.* New York, Stein and Day, 1980.

———. *Redemption Song: The Story of Operation Moses.* New York: Harcourt Brace Jovanovich, 1986.

Rathjens, Carl. *Die Juden in Abessinien*. Hamburg: M. W. Kaufman, 1921.

Rosen, Haim, and Daniel Chemtov. *Be "Gobez" for the Sake of Your Health*. Jerusalem, 1992.

Sachar, Howard M. *A History of Israel from the Rise of Zionism to Our Time*. 2nd ed. New York: Knopf, 1996.

Salamon, Hagar. *The Hyena People: Ethiopian Jews in Christian Ethiopia*. Berkeley: University of California Press, 1999.

Salamon, Hagar, and Steven Kaplan. *Ethiopian Jewry: An Annotated Bibliography, 1988–1997*. Jerusalem: Ben-Zvi Institute, 1998.

Schindler, Ruben, and David Ribner. *The Trauma of Transition: The Psycho-Social Cost of Ethiopian Immigration to Israel*. Aldershot: Avebury, 1997.

Shelemay, Kay Kaufman. *Music, Ritual, and Falasha History*. East Lansing: Michigan State University Press, 1989.

———. *A Song of Longing: An Ethiopian Journey*. Urbana: University of Illinois Press, 1991.

Szulc, Tad. *The Secret Alliance: The Extraordinary Story of the Rescue of the Jews Since World War II*. New York: Farrar, Straus, and Giroux, 1991.

Tadesse Tamrat. *Church and State in Ethiopia, 1270–1527*. Oxford: Clarendon Press, 1972.

Ullendorff, Edward. *The Ethiopians: An Introduction to Country and People*, 3rd ed. Oxford: Oxford University Press, 1973.

———. *Ethiopia and the Bible*: The Schweich Lectures of the British Academy. Oxford: Oxford University Press, 1968.

Waldman, Menachem. *The Jews of Ethiopia: The Beta Israel Community*. Translated by Naftali Greenwood. Jerusalem: Ami-Shav, 1984.

Weil, Shalva. *The Religious Beliefs and Practices of Ethiopian Jews in Israel*. Jerusalem: Hebrew University, 1988 (Hebrew).

———. *One-Parent Families Among Ethiopian Immigrants in Israel*. Jerusalem: NCJW Research Institute for Innovation in Education, 1991 (Hebrew).

Westheimer, Ruth, and Steven Kaplan. *Surviving Salvation: The Ethiopian Jewish Family in Transition*. New York: New York University Press, 1992.

White, Hayden. *Tropics of Discourse: Essays in Cultural Criticism*. Baltimore: Johns Hopkins University Press, 1978.

Young, John. *Peasant Revolution in Ethiopia: The Tigray People's Liberation Front, 1975–1991*. Cambridge: Cambridge University Press, 1997.

## Scholarly Articles

Abbink, G. Jon. "*Seged* Celebration in Ethiopia and Israel: Continuity and Change of a Falasha Religious Holiday," *Anthropos* 78 (1983): 789–810.

———. "A Socio-Structural Analysis of the Beta-Esra'el as an 'Infamous Group' in Traditional Ethiopia," *Sociologus* 37 (1987): 140–54.

———. "The Enigma of Beta Esra'el Ethnogenesis: An Anthro-Historical Study." *Cahiers d'études africaines* 120 (1990): 397–449.

Alvarez-Pereyre, F., and S. Ben-Dor. "The Formal Organisation of the Beta Israel Liturgy—Substance and Performance: Literary Structure," pp. 235–51 in Tudor Parfitt and Emanuela Trevisan Semi, eds., *The Beta Israel in Ethiopia and Israel: Studies on Ethiopian Jews* (Surrey: Curzon, 1999).

Barnicot, N. A., et al. "A Survey of Some Genetic Characters in Ethiopian Tribes," *American Journal of Physical Anthropology* n.s. 20 (1962): 167–208B.

Bar-Yosef, Rivka W. "Children of Two Cultures: Immigrant Children from Ethiopia in Israel," *Journal of Comparative Family Studies* 32 (2001): 231–46.

"Circumcision." In Mircea Eliade, ed., *The Encyclopedia of Religion* (New York: Macmillan, 1987).

Conti Rossini, Carlo. "Appunti di storia e letteratura Falascià," *Rivista degli studi orientali* 8 (1919–20): 598–609.

Ephraim Isaac. "An Obscure Component in Ethiopian Church History," *Le Museon* 85 (1972): 238–45.

Friedmann, Daniel. "The Case of the Falas Mura," pp. 70–80 in Tudor Parfitt and Emanuela Trevisan Semi, eds., *The Beta Israel in Ethiopia and Israel: Studies on Ethiopian Jews* (Surrey: Curzon, 1999).

Getachew Haile. "The Forty-nine Hour Sabbath of the Ethiopian Church," *Journal of Semitic Studies* 32 (1988): 233–54.

Grisaru, Nimrod, Simcha Lezer, and R. H. Belmaker. "Ritual Female Genital Surgery Among Ethiopian Jews," *Archives of Sexual Behavior* 26 (April 1997): 211–16.

Hammer, M. F., et al. "Jewish and Middle Eastern Non-Jewish Populations Share a Common Pool of Y-chromosome Biallelic Haplotypes," *Proceedings of the National Academy of Sciences of the United States* 97 (2000): 6769–74.

Hess, Robert L. "Toward a History of the Falasha," pp. 106–32 in Daniel F. McCall et al., eds., *Eastern African History* (New York: Frederick A. Praeger, 1969).

Henze, Paul B. "Ethiopia in 1991—Peace Through Struggle." Rand Corp., 1991.

———. "The Defeat of the Derg and the Establishment of New Governments in Ethiopia and Eritrea." Rand Corp., 1992.

———. "The Fall of the Derg and the Beginning of Recovery Under the EPRDF (March 1990–March 1992)." Rand Corp., 1995.

———. "Political Success Story," *Journal of Democracy* 9 (1998): 40–54.

Hodes, Richard. "Cross-cultural Medicine and Diverse Health Beliefs: Ethiopians Abroad," *Western Journal of Medicine* 166 (January 1997): 29–36.

Hodes, Richard, and B. Teferedegne. "Traditional Beliefs and Disease Practices of Ethiopian Jews," *Israel Journal of Medical Sciences* 32 (1996): 561–67.

Kaplan, Steven. "The Beta Israel (Falasha) Encounter with Protestant Missionaries: 1860–1905," *Jewish Social Studies* 49 (1987): 27–42.

———. "Everyday Resistance and the Study of Ethiopian Jews," pp. 113–27 in Tudor Parfitt and Emanuela Trevisan Semi, eds., *The Beta Israel in Ethiopia and Israel: Studies on Ethiopian Jews* (Surrey: Curzon, 1999).

———. "Black and White, Blue and White and Beyond the Pale: Ethiopian Jews and the Discourse of Colour in Israel," *Jewish Culture and History* 5 (2002): 51–68.

Kaplan, Steven, and Haim Rosen. "Ethiopian Immigrants in Israel: Between Preservation of Culture and Invention of Tradition," *Jewish Journal of Sociology* 35 (1993): 35–48.

Krempel, Veronika. "Eine Berufskaste in Nordwest-Äthiopien—die Kayla (Falascha)," *Sociologus* 24 (1974): 37–55.

Lemmu Baissa. "United States Military Assistance to Ethiopia, 1953–1974: A Reappraisal of a Difficult Patron-Client Relationship," *Northeast African Studies* 11 (1989): 51–70.

Lucotte, Gérard, and Pierre Smets. "Origins of Falasha Jews Studied by Haplotypes of the Y Chromosome," *Human Biology* 71, 1999: 989–93.

Luzzato, Philoxene. "Mémoire sur les juifs d'Abyssinie ou Falashas," *Archives israélites* 13 (1852): 221, 655.

Macconi, Ennio. "Africa, Tempo d'Eritrea," *Ponte* 27 (1971): 37–42.

Myers, Theodore. "A Medical Care Program for Ethiopian Jewish Migrants in Addis Ababa," *Israel Journal of Medical Sciences* 29 (1993): 334–37.

Pateman, Roy. "Intelligence Agencies in Africa: A Preliminary Assessment," *Journal of Modern African Studies* 30 (1992): 569–85.

Polotsky, H. J. "Aramaic, Syriac and Ge'ez," *Journal of Semitic Studies* 9 (1964): 1–10.

Reminick, Ronald A. "The Structures and Functions of Religious Belief among the Amhara of Ethiopia," pp. 25–42 in Harold G. Marcus, ed., *Proceedings of the First United States*

*Conference on Ethiopian Studies* (East Lansing: African Studies Center, Michigan State University, 1973).

———. "The 'Evil Eye' Among the Amhara of Ethiopia," in Clarence Maloney, ed., *The Evil Eye* (New York: Columbia University Press, 1976).

Ritte, U., et al. "The Differences Among Jewish Communities—Maternal and Paternal Contributions," *Journal of Molecular Evolution* 37 (1993): 435–40.

Rodinson, Maxime. "Sur la question des 'influences juives' en Ethiopie," *Journal of Semitic Studies* 9 (1964): 11–19.

Rosen, Haim, and Ardon Rubinstein. "The Demography of the Ethiopian Community in Israel," *Israel Journal of Medical Sciences* 29 (1993): 333–34.

Rubenstein, Ardon, ed. "The Ethiopian Immigrations to Israel—Medical, Epidemiological and Health Aspects," special issue of *Israel Journal of Medical Sciences* 29 (1993).

Salamon, Hagar. "Metaphors as Corrective Exegesis: Three Proverbs of the Beta-Israel," *Proverbium* 12 (1995): 295–313.

———. "Blackness in Transition: Decoding Racial Constructs Through Stories of Ethiopian Jews," *Journal of Folklore Research* 40 (2003): 3–32.

Seeman, D. F. "One People, One Blood: Public Health, Political Violence, and HIV in an Ethiopian-Israeli Setting." *Culture, Medicine, and Psychiatry* 23 (1999): 159–95.

Shelemay, Kay Kaufman. "Music and Text of the Falasha Sabbath," *Orbis Musicae, Studies in the Arts* 8 (1982–83): 3–22.

Sivini, Giordano. "Famine and the Resettlement Program in Ethiopia," *Africa* 41 (1946): 211–42.

Tadesse Tamrat. "The Abbots of Dabra Hayq, 1248–1535," *Journal of Ethiopian Studies* 8 (1970): 37–117.

Teshome G. Wagaw. "The International Political Ramifications of Falasha Emigration," *Journal of Modern African Studies* 29 (1991): 557–81.

Ullendorff, Edward. "Hebrew, Aramaic, and Greek: The Versions Underlying Ethiopic Translations of Bible and Intertestamental Literature," pp. 249–57 in Gary Rendsburg et al., eds., *The Bible World: Essays in Honor of Cyrus R. Gordon* (New York: KTAV, 1980).

———. "Hebrew Element in the Ethiopic Old Testament," *Jerusalem Studies in Arabic and Islam* 9 (1987): 42–50.

———. "The Queen of Sheba in Ethiopian Tradition," pp. 104–14 in James. B. Pritchard, ed., *Solomon and Sheba* (London: Phaidon, 1974).

Weil, Shalva. "'It Is Futile to Trust in Man': Methodological Difficulties in Studying Non-Mainstream Populations with Reference to Ethiopian Jews in Israel," *Human Organization* 54 (1995): 1–9.

Zoossmann-Diskin, A., et al., "Genetic Affinities of Ethiopian Jews," *Israel Journal of Medical Sciences* 27 (1991): 245–51.

## Newspaper Articles, Articles in Popular Magazines, and Other Publications

Agence France-Presse. "Airlift of Jews Is Anti-Arab Plot: Syrian Paper," May 26, 1991.

———. "Syria, Palestinians Denounce Falasha Evacuation," May 26, 1991.

———. "Falasha Evacuation 'Shameful,' Says Ethiopia's Acting President," June 10, 1991.

———. "Israeli FM to Make Official Visit to Ethiopia," January 5, 2004.

———. "Ethiopian Jews to Rejoin Kin in Israel, but Their Numbers Still Unknown," January 8, 2004.

Anidjar, Patrick. "AIDS Scare Final Straw for Ethiopian Jews in Israel." Agence France-Presse, January 29, 1996.

Artzi'eli, Mordechai. "The Falashas: A Dying Community. The Weakness of Israel," *Ha'aretz*, December 17, 1982.

Associated Press. "Soviet Immigration Picks Up with Cease-fire in the Gulf," March 2, 1991.

———. "Mengistu Flees Ethiopia Under Heavy Pressure From Rebels," May 22, 1991.

———. "Ethiopia's New Leader Says Rebels Took Capital Without U.S. Approval," June 2, 1991.

———. "Israel Asks Repeal of U.N. Zionism-Racism Resolution," October 15, 1991.

Avgar, Amos. "Operation Solomon: An Eyewitness Account of the Final Days," *Jewish Telegraph Agency*, June 28, 1991.

Ayalen, Sophia. "To Live in Deed," *Jerusalem Post Magazine*, May 22, 1992.

Beeston, Richard. "Israeli Reveals Falasha Airlift Strategy," *The Times* (London), May 29, 1991.

———. "Rabbi Sees Messianic Pattern in Chaos," *The Times* (London), August 29, 1991.

Bergman, Ronan. "I, Kassa Kebede," *Yedi'ot Ahronot*, May 27, 2001.

Biles, Peter. "Mengistu Flees After 14 Years of Brutal Rule," *The Guardian*, May 22, 1991.

———. "Rebel Forces Close in on Addis Ababa," *The Guardian*, May 24, 1991.

Blitzer, Wolf. "U.S. Accepts Rabin's Denial of Cluster Bombs to Ethiopia," *Jerusalem Post*, January 24, 1990.

Brilliant, Joshua. "Eritrean Success Could Prove Dangerous to Israel's Interest," *Jerusalem Post*, February 12, 1990.

Brinkley, Joel. "200 Ethiopians Trapped in West Bank," *New York Times*, June 6, 1991.

Brown, Sarah. "Despite Mengistu Departure, Rebels Press Offensive," United Press International, May 22, 1991.

Burston, Bradley. "IAF Reaches New Height in Ethiopian Airlift," *Jerusalem Post*, May 26, 1991.

Clayton, Jonathan. "Ethiopia's Last 20,000 Falashas Are Allowed to Fly to Israel," *The Times* (London), January 9, 2004.

Cohler, Larry. "U.S. Calls Sharon's Words 'Hopeful' Sign," *Jerusalem Post*, June 26, 1990.

Collins, Liat. "Mossad Unable to Specify Fatality Toll for Ethiopian Jews," *Jerusalem Post*, July 22, 1998.

Ellicott, Susan. "Lobbyists Ride Out the Recession in High Style," *The Times* (London), June 3, 1991.

Erlich, Haggai. "Massawa: Catalyst for a Red Sea War?" *Jerusalem Post*, February 16, 1990.

"Ethiopian Rebels Making Gains; Regime Fading," *Los Angeles Times*, April 9, 1991.

Fischer, Ronal. "The Lie of Ethiopian Blood," *Ma'ariv*, January 24, 1996.

Fishkoff, Sue. "The Ones Left Behind—Part I," *Jerusalem Post*, May 31, 1996.

Fitzgerald, Mary Ann. "Marxist Armies Clash in Ruined Ethiopia," *Sunday Times* (London), March 4, 1990.

———. "Tyrant for the Taking," *The Times* (London), April 20, 1991.

Gedda, George. "Ethiopian Envoy Can't Meet Conditions," Associated Press, May 18, 1990.

Gilbert, Nina. "Interior Minister Poraz: No Budget to Absorb Falash Mura," *Jerusalem Post*, May 20, 2003.

———. "US Jews Should Fund Ethiopian Aliya," *Jerusalem Post*, November 20, 2003.

Goetz, Jill. "Visiting Rabbi Preaches Interfaith Understanding," *Cornell Chronicle*, May 16, 1996.

Gwertzman, Bernard. "Ethiopian Jews Said to Resttle on West Bank," *New York Times*, January 18, 1985.

Halevi, Yossi Klein. "The Last Jewish Monk," *Jerusalem Report*, January 28, 1993.

———. "Dinitz: Center Stage at Last," *Jerusalem Report*, June 27, 1991.

Halkin, Hillel. "Wandering Jews—and Their Genes," *Commentary* 110 (September 2000): 54–61.

Hammer, Joshua. "The Promise of Exodus," *Newsweek International*, February 2, 2004.

Hodes, Richard. "Broken Hearts," *Middlebury Magazine*, Fall 1996, 30–35.

Horovitz, David, and Peter Hirschberg. "Homecoming," *Jerusalem Report*, June 6, 1991.

Hutman, Bill. "Ethiopian Jews Now Fear for Their Lives," *Jerusalem Post*, April 30, 1991.

———. "After the Euphoria, How to Integrate Them," *Jerusalem Post*, May 26, 1991.

———. "Mobilized for the Homecoming," *Jerusalem Post*, May 31, 1991.

———. "Dinitz: Jewish Converts Want a Way out of Ethiopia," *Jerusalem Post*, June 9, 1991.

Izenberg, Dan. "Left Behind," *Jerusalem Post*, July 3, 1998.

Kalita, S. Mitra. "Missed Chances," *Newsday* (New York), December 2, 2001.

Kaplan, Allison. "Rescue Effort Result of Repeated Appeals to Both Ethiopian and U.S. Governments," *Jerusalem Post*, May 26, 1991.

Kaplan, Steven. "Falasha Christians: A Brief History," unpublished ms., much of which was published as "'Falasha Christians: Which of Them Is Jewish," *Jerusalem Post*, May 31, 1991.

Keinon, Herb. "Ethiopian Anger at Pace of Rescue Turns Violent," *Jerusalem Post*, October 22, 1990.

———. "Ethiopia Will Allow 1,000 Jews to Leave," *Jerusalem Post*, November 23, 1990.

———. "1,000 Came from Ethiopia Last Month," *Jerusalem Post*, February 3, 1991.

———. "Doyen of Spiritual Leaders Is Among Latest Group of Newcomers, 224 More Arrive from Ethiopia," *Jerusalem Post*, February 6, 1991.

———. "Revolt Disrupts Ethiopian Aliyah," *Jerusalem Post*, March 7, 1991.

———. "Mengistu Orders Halt to Aliyah," *Jerusalem Post*, March 11, 1991.

———. "Ethiopian Emigration Set to Resume Tomorrow," *Jerusalem Post*, March 21, 1991.

———. "Talks This Week on Immigration of Remaining 2,500 Ethiopia's Last Jews Expected Here Soon," *Jerusalem Post*, August 18, 1991.

———. "Man, Forced to Bar Aunt from Aliyah, Finally Reunited with Her," *Jerusalem Post*, October 3, 1991.

———. "40% of New Ethiopian Olim Said to Be Non-Jews," *Jerusalem Post*, November 6, 1991.

———. "The Eulogy of Domestic Violence," *Jerusalem Post*, January 24, 1992.

Kiley, Sam. "Ethiopia Faces Anarchy as Troops Close In," *Sunday Times* (London), May 26, 1991.

Krauss, Clifford. "Ethiopia's Dictator Flees; Officials Seeking U.S. Help," *New York Times*, May 22, 1991.

Krieger, Hilary Leila. "Local Ethiopian Jews Hail Visit," *Jerusalem Post*, January 8, 2004.

———. "Operation Solomon Babies Celebrate Bar Mitzva," *Jerusalem Post*, May 25, 2004.

La Guardia, Anton. "Falashas Used by Mengistu 'as Pawns for Weapons,'" *Daily Telegraph*, May 28, 1991.

Lazaroff, Tovah. "Meridor: Immigration Rate Is in Crisis," *Jerusalem Post*, May 7, 2001.

———. "Ethiopians Complain About Poraz's Appointment to Immigration Committee," *Jerusalem Post*, July 14, 2003.

Lynfield, Ben. "Definition of 'Jew' Confronts Israel," *Christian Science Monitor*, January 9, 2004.

"Mengistu Plays Democracy Card to Save His Skin," *The Times* (London), April 2, 1990.

Makovsky, David. "U.S. Opposes Israeli Links with Ethiopia's Mengistu," *Jerusalem Post*, January 17, 1990.

———. "Israel Backs Mengistu Despite U.S. Pressure," *Jerusalem Post*, March 23, 1990.

———. "Israel and Mengistu," *Jerusalem Post*, March 22, 1991.

McManus, Doyle. "U.S. Confronts Israel on Ethiopia Cluster Bombs," *Los Angeles Times*, January 22, 1990

Meldrum, Andrew. "Fleeing Mengistu Arrives in Zimbabwe," United Press International, May 22, 1991.

Mizrachi, Avi. "We Tried to Rescue, They Wanted to Survive," in Yaron Toran, ed., "Operation Solomon: The Beta Israel Return Home," Jewish Agency Department of Immigration and Absorption, n.d.

Naim, Asher. "Operation Solomon Recalled: Countdown to a Miracle," *Jerusalem Post*, May 22, 1992.

Odenheimer, Micha. "Medical Aid Reaches Addis Jews After 350 Said to Have Died," *Jerusalem Post*, August 30, 1990.

———. "Ethiopia: More Exits by Death than Immigration," *Jewish World*, August 20, 1990.

———. "Jews in Ethiopia Getting Together," *Jerusalem Post*, September 14, 1990.

———. "The Guns of April," *Jerusalem Report*, April 11, 1991.

———. "Why Is This Afternoon Different . . . ?" *Jerusalem Report*, April 11, 1991.

———. "Countdown in Ethiopia," *Jerusalem Report*, April 18, 1991.

———. "Jewish Justice, Ethiopian Style," *Jewish World*, April 18, 1991.

———. "A Secret Gate Finally Swings Open," *Jerusalem Report*, June 6, 1991.

———. "Those Left Behind," *Jerusalem Report*, June 6, 1991.

———. "Six Days That Shook Ethiopia," *Jerusalem Report*, June 13, 1991.

———. "Victims of a Broken Promise," *Jerusalem Report*, July 5, 1999.

———. "The Next Dilemma," *Jerusalem Report*, July 19, 1999.

Oliphant, Thomas. "Real Icons Need No Tribute," *Boston Globe*, August 27, 1995.

Oppen, George. "Of Being Numerous," in *George Oppen, New Collected Poems*, ed. Michael Davidson (New York: New Directions, 2002).

Orizio, Riccardo. "The Lion Sleeps Tonight," *Transition* 11 (2001): 20–43.

Ozanne, Julian. "Ethiopian President Is Forced to Flee Country," *Financial Times*, May 22, 1991.

Perlez, Jane. "Ethiopia's President Looks Toward Better U.S. Relations," *New York Times*, November 28, 1988.

———. "Ethiopian-Israeli Accord Eases Jewish Emigration," *New York Times*, November 5, 1989.

———. "Israelis Widening Role in Ethiopia," *New York Times*, February 7, 1990.

———. "U.S. Team Seeking Exodus of Ethiopian Jews," *New York Times*, May 2, 1991.

Pound, Edward T. "Explosive Issue: U.S. Sees New Signs Israel Resells Its Arms to China, South Africa," *Wall Street Journal*, March 13, 1992.

Raath, Jan. "Mugabe Role Is Revealed," *The Times* (London), May 30, 1991.

———. "Butcher of Addis Puts Out the Begging Bowl," *The Times* (London), October 5, 1991.

Rabinovich, Abraham. "Africa Comes Through Door of Diplomat," *Jerusalem Post*, May 26, 1991.

———. "Down from the Hills," *Jerusalem Post Magazine*, May 22, 1992.

———. "Exodus: The Sequel," *Jerusalem Post*, July 20, 2001.

———. "We're Home," *Jerusalem Post*, July 27, 2001.

Rabinowitz, Gavin. "Israel Wavers on Entry of Ethiopian Immigrants Who Claim to Be Jewish," Associated Press, January 10, 2004.

Rapoport, Louis. "Ethiopian Jewry Rescued," *Jerusalem Post*, May 26, 1991.

"Rescue in Ethiopia," *The HIAS Reporter*, summer 1991.

Rosenthal, Donna. "The New Exodus," *Atlantic*, May 1992.

Rozenman, Eric. "Ethiopian FM Affirms Aliya, Denies 'Cluster' Connection," *Jerusalem Post*, July 27, 1990.

Rudge, David. "A Man for All Missions," *Jerusalem Post*, September 8, 1991.

Safire, William. "Interrupted Exodus," *New York Times*, January 7, 1985.

Schachter, Jonathan. "Sharp Drop in Death Rate Among Stranded Ethiopian Jews," *Jerusalem Post*, September 30, 1990.

Sciolino, Elaine. "U.S. Officials Suspect Israelis Sent Ethiopia Cluster Bombs," *New York Times*, January 21, 1990.

Shagrir, Micha. "The Tremendous Excitement of Being Part of an Historical Event," in Yaron Toran, ed., "Operation Solomon: The Beta Israel Return Home," Jewish Agency Department of Immigration and Absorption, n.d.

Sheleg, Yair. "Jewish Agency Looks West for Immigrants," *Ha'aretz*, May 3, 2001.

———. "For the Falashmura, the Window of Opportunity May Be Closing," *Ha'aretz*, March 4, 2003.

Sheriden, Michael. "Israeli Settlements 'Anger U.S.,'" *The Independent*, April 8, 1991.

Silver, Eric. "The Fixer—Uri Lubrani: The Mystery Man Who Saved the Jews."*Jerusalem Report*, June 6, 1991, p. 10.

Streit, Noah. "Last Planeload of Ethiopian Immigrants Arrives," compiled from news agency reports, *Jerusalem Post*, June 26, 1998.

"Summary of Navon Commission Report on Blood Donations by Ethiopian Immigrants," July 29, 1996, available at www.mfa.gov.il.

"The $35m. Bribe Mengistu Never Got," *Jerusalem Report*, December 25, 1997.

Tsur, Batsheva. "Official End to Exodus from Ethiopia," *Jerusalem Post*, July 28, 1992.

Tsur, Batsheva, and Judy Siegel. "Ethiopian Leaders Divided over Bringing Falash Mura Here," *Jerusalem Post*, October 18, 1996.

Turkienicz, Anna. "Speedy Solution Needed for Ethiopia's Falash Mura: Sharansky," *Canadian Jewish News*, April 19, 2000.

Walker, Paul F., and Eric Stambler. ". . . and the Dirty Little Weapons," *Bulletin of the Atomic Scientists* 47 (1991).

Weil, Shalva. "Our Brethren the Taliban?" *Jerusalem Report*, October 22, 2001

Yehezkeli, Zadak. "Ethiopia Is Investigating Where U.S. $35 Million Israel Paid Disappeared To," *Yedi'ot Ahronot*, June 14, 1991.

Zava, Julius. "Mengistu Under Attack," *New African*, January 1996.

## Public Printed Documents

### U.S. Department of State

1990 Human Rights Report, February 1, 1991.

### Congressional Research Service

CRS Issue Brief. Copson, Raymond W. "Ethiopia: War and Famine," Library of Congress, April 10, 1990.

CRS Issue Brief. Dagne, Theodore S. "Ethiopian Jews," Library of Congress, September 13, 1990.

### U.S. Arms Control and Disarmament Agency

*World Military Expenditures and Arms Transfers, 1991–92* (Washington, D.C.: 1994).

### Jewish Agency for Israel

Toran, Yaron, ed. "Operation Solomon: The Beta Israel Return Home." Jewish Agency Department of Immigration and Absorption, n.d.

Director-General's Report, Jewish Agency Immigration and Absorption Department, December 2003.

### Israeli Central Bureau of Statistics

Statistical Abstract of Israel, 2004

**Hebrew Immigrant Aid Society (HIAS)**
"Rescue in Ethiopia," *The HIAS Reporter,* Summer 1991

**The North American Conference on Ethiopian Jewry (NACOEJ)**
North American Conference on Ethiopian Jewry 1990 Annual Report.
"NACOEJ: Our Mission" (2002), www.nacoej.org.


## Unpublished Documents

**United States Congress, Subcommittee on African Affairs**
Steve Morrison, confidential report re Israeli-Ethiopian relations, submitted to Rep. Howard
    Wolpe, February 13, 1990.

**United States Department of State**

Unclassified and Limited-Official-Use Documents
1991ADDIS02406
1991STATE087136
1991STATE130394
1991STATE142503
1991STATE172251
1991DOHA01355
1991STATE174567
1991STATE175812
1991BEIRUT01045
1991CAIRO09793
1991STATE178690
1991STATE182330
1991STATE185090
1991DOHA01494
1991STATE280016

Confidential and Secret Documents
1991ADDIS00753
1991ADDIS01106
1991LONDON05069
1991STATE122531
1991ADDIS01786
1991STATE133208
1991STATE135266
1991KHARTO01026
1991STATE144568
1991STATE144569
1991ADDIS02058
1991STATE172313
1991STATE172613
1991ADDIS02391
1991RIYADH04783
1991ADDIS02407
1991TELAV06649
1991TELAV07162

1991DAMASC03610
1991AMMAN04759
1991TELAV07007
1991TELAV10982
1991TELAV11077
1991ADDIS03734
1991STATE169690
1991STATE276969
1991DAMASC05983

### National Security Council

"Letter to Mengistu from President Re Allow Ethiopian Jews to Leave for Israel," April 17, 1991.

### George H. W. Bush Presidential Library

Ninety-eight-page file of correspondence between American Jewish leaders and President Bush in May and June 1991.

### Israeli Ministry of Foreign Affairs

H. S. Aynor, position paper, September 1988.
"Coordination of Activities Re Ethiopian Jews: Minutes of a Meeting Held in the Ministry of Foreign Affairs on May 13, 1990."

### Jewish Agency for Israel

Summary of February 18, 1990, Meeting on Ethiopian Aliyah.
Arnon Mantber, report to Simcha Dinitz, May 27, 1991.

### HIAS

"Yearly Arrivals of Ethiopian Jews to Israel," July 23, 1991 (courtesy of Haim Halachmi).
"The Number of Olim from Ethiopia, 1977 till Today, Correct to 1.12.2002" (courtesy of Haim Halachmi).

### Ethiopian Committee of Social Workers on Family Reunion

"Evaluation of Family Reunion Application," memo to Comrade Mersha Ketsela, December 31, 1990.

### Ethiopian Shengo (Parliament)

"Resolution of the Third Emergency Session of the National Shengo of the People's Democratic Republic of Ethiopia," April 22, 1991.

### The EPRDF (Ethiopian People's Revolutionary Democratic Front)

"EPRDF's Proposal for a Smooth and Peaceful Transition of Power in Ethiopia," March 1991.

### The American Jewish Joint Distribution Committee, New York

Two hundred and fifty-five pages of handwritten records that quote and paraphrase hundreds of meetings and telephone discussions involving JDC officers, other Jewish American leaders, and officials of Israel and the United States: January 28– June 5, 1991. Recorded chiefly by Gideon Taylor, with some in the hand of Michael Schneider. (I refer to these in the notes as "JDC records.")

JDC Reports, Memos, and Correspondence

JDC Annual Report, 1988.

"Summary of Meeting on Ethiopian Aliyah: Monday, June 25, 1990."

Dr. Moshe Efrat, "Health Care for Ethiopian Jews in Addis Ababa: An Evaluation of the AJDC Medical Program, with recommendations," October 14, 1990.

Michael Schneider, "JDC in Ethiopia," December 1990.

Aide-mémoire, meeting of Arnon Mantber, Moshe Gan, Micha Feldman, Haim Divon, Haim Halachmi, Michael Schneider, Ei Eliezri, Ami Bergman, Amos Avgar, Amir Shaviv, Gideon Taylor, February 14, 1991.

Aide-mémoire, meeting of Uri Lubrani, Michael Schneider, Haim Divon, Gideon Taylor, February 19, 1991.

"Field Trip Report: Addis Ababa—February 21–27, 1991," Manlio Dell'Ariccia.

Aide-mémoire, conference call, March 8, 1991.

"Ethiopia Update," Michael Schneider and Gideon Taylor, March 11, 1991.

"JDC Operations in Ethiopia," Michael Schneider and Gideon Taylor, March 11, 1991.

Aide-mémoire, conference call of Malcolm Hoenlein, Michael Shilo, Abe Bayer, and Gideon Taylor, March 13, 1991.

"Ethiopia Update," Michael Schneider and Gideon Taylor, March 14, 1991.

"Rebel Groups in Ethiopia—A Brief Summary," Gideon Taylor, March 14, 1991.

Aide-mémoire, conference call of Uri Lubrani, Abe Bayer, Barbara Gordon, Malcolm Hoenlein, Will Recant, Steve Solander, Michael Schneider, Steve Swhwager, and Gideon Taylor, March 25, 1991.

"Ethiopia," fax from Michael Schneider to Abe Bayer, Abe Foxman, Ken Jacobson, Barbara Gordon, David Harris, Malcolm Hoenlein, Marty Kraar, Will Recant, and Steve Solander, March 27, 1991.

Memo by Gideon Taylor, April 1, 1991.

Aide-mémoire, meeting of Abe Bayer, Amira Dotan, Eli Eliezri, Barbara Gordon, David Harris, Malcolm Hoenlein, Ken Jacobson, Marty Kraar, Uri Lubrani, Will Recant, Larry Rubin, Michael Schneider, Nate Shapiro, Michael Shilo, and Gideon Taylor, April 8, 1991.

Aide-mémoire, meeting of Abe Bayer, Barbara Gordon, David Harris, Malcolm Hoenlein, Ken Jacobson, Marty Kraar, Uri Lubrani, Will Recant, Larry Rubin, Michael Schneider, and Gideon Taylor, April 10, 1991.

Aide-mémoire, phone conversation of Herman Cohen and Uri Lubrani, recorded by Gideon Taylor, April 11, 1991.

Memo by Gideon Taylor, April 19, 1991.

"Briefing Points" [for Rudy Boschwitz], Gideon Taylor, April 24, 1991.

Record of Peter Jackson's conversation with Asher Naim, phone call of 5:15 p.m., April 28, 1991.

Record of Asher Naim's conversation with Kassa Kebede, April 28, 1991.

Message prepared with Uri Lubrani, sent to Rudy Boschwitz via Asher Naim, April 28, 1991

"Current Situation," Gideon Taylor, April 28, 1991.

"Current Issues: Ethiopia, Based on Conversations at 5:30 a.m., 2:30 p.m," Gideon Taylor, April 29, 1991.

Aide-mémoire, "Meeting with KK, Peter," April 29, 1991.

Aide-mémoire, "Discussion on Ethiopia—MDA, GT," April 30, 1991.

"Current Issues," Gideon Taylor, May 2, 1991.

"For the Record," Michael Schneider, May 2, 1991.

"Suggested Talking Points, Meeting: Rudy, M[ichael] S[chneider], N[ate] S[hapiro]," May 3, 1991.

Confidential memo on Michael Schneider and Nate Shapiro's briefing of Rudy Boschwitz, May 3, 1991.

"Briefing Session for Boschwitz," Michael Schneider, May 4, 1991.

"Notes," Gideon Taylor, May 6, 1991.

Aide-mémoire, meeting of Shoshana Cardin, Sylvia Hassenfeld, Neil Katz, Marty Kraar, Marvin Lender, Norman Lipoff, Herman Markowitz, Jay Yoskowitz, Michael Schneider, Steve Schwager, and Gideon Taylor, May 7, 1991.

"Ethiopia Update," Gideon Taylor, May 16, 1991.

"Bulletin," Gideon Taylor, May 24, 1991.

Amos Avgar, "Operation Solomon: An Eyewitness Account, The Final Days of the Rescue of the Ethiopian Jews," JDC board briefing (undated).

Anecdotal memoirs, distributed by JDC (undated):
> Ami Bergman
> Eli Eliezri
> Uri Lubrani
> Arnon Mantber

Memos sent by JDC officials in Addis Ababa, Jerusalem, Rome, and other locations to JDC headquarters in New York, written by:
> Sherry Hyman, April 5, 1990
> Ami Bergman and Eli Eliezri, May 21, 1990
> Eli Eliezri and Ami Bergman, June 3, 1990
> Eli Eliezri and Ami Bergman, June 4, 1990
> Ami Bergman and Eli Eliezri, June 11, 1990
> Ami Bergman and Eli Eliezri, June 12, 1990
> Kobi Friedman, September 11, 1990
> Amos Avgar, November 5, 1990
> Ami Bergman, January 6, 1991
> Eli Eliezri, January 16, 1991
> Ami Bergman, February 12, 1991
> Sherry Hyman, March 13, 1991
> Manlio Dell'Ariccia, March 15, 1991
> Ami Bergman, "Ethiopia—Report: Aids in Ethiopia," April 9, 1991
> Rick Hodes, April 26, 1991
> Manlio Dell'Ariccia, May 2, 1991.

Memos and correspondence sent from JDC headquarters in New York:
> Fax to Uri Lubrani, report on Michael Schneider's briefing of Rudy Boschwitz, April 17, 1991
> "Critical Factors Pertaining to U.S. Mission," "M," April 25, 1991
> Fax from Michael Schneider to Moshe Yegar, May 5, 1991
> Fax from Gideon Taylor to Uri Lubrani and Guest, May 17, 1991
> Michael Schneider to Simcha Dinitz, May 22, 1991
> "Re: Operation Solomon," by Michael Schneider, sent to Federation presidents and executives, May 29, 1991

Memos from Dr. Ted Myers:
> "Mortality Data," to JDC Medical Team in Addis Ababa, April 6, 1991
> "Mortality Data," to Michael Schneider, Steve Schwager, and Roxana Shalo, May 5, 1991
> "Childhood Mortality," to Gideon Taylor, May 13, 1991.

## The American Association for Ethiopian Jews (AAEJ)

Memos and Correspondence
Scott Cohen to Nate Shapiro, memorandum, September 19, 1989.

Scott Cohen to Nate Shapiro and Will Recant, "Meeting with John Hall, Ethiopian Desk Officer," April 5, 1990.
Will Recant, "Current Status and Suggested Action for Ethiopian Jewry," November 8, 1990.
Gil Kulick to Kassa Kebede, April 7, 1991.
Nate Shapiro to Kassa Kebede, April 9, 1991.
Will Recant, May 19, 1991.

Reports
Susan Pollack, "'The People Who Get Money from the Sky: A Report on Ethiopia and Kenya, Prepared for the AAEJ, February 1989."
Susan Pollack, "Ethiopia Chronology, 12/89–9/90" (undated).

## Miscellaneous Private Memoirs, Reports, Correspondence, and Notes

### Rudy Boschwitz
Handwritten prepared statement for meeting with President Mengistu, April 27, 1991.
Memoir of the Boschwitz Mission, handwritten, April 28, 1991.
Notes for meeting with President Bush, May 7, 1991.
"What a Difference 50 Years Makes: The Ethiopian Rescue, April 28, 1998."

### Uri Lubrani
Urgent fax to Rudy Boschwitz, via Yossi Amrani, May 4, 1991.
Memorandum, May 8, 1991.
Message, "Dictated by Uri Lubrani for immediate communication to Simcha Dinitz," May 24, 1991.

### Simcha Dinitz
Memo to Michael Schneider, May 26, 1991.

### Barbara Ribakove Gordon
"Operation Solomon—A First-hand Account," June 4, 1991.

### Dr. Richard Hodes
"From Gondar to Jerusalem: An Unfinished Journey," JDC luncheon commemorating the fifth anniversary of Operation Solomon, June 5, 1996.
"Operation Solomon."
"Broken Hearts."

### Rabbi Mark Winer
"Lessons from Ethiopian Jews, Visions for Our Future," High Holiday sermons at West London Synagogue, 1998.

## Unpublished M.A., Ph. D., and Rabbinic Theses

Abbink, G. J. "The Falashas in Ethiopia and Israel: The Problem of Ethnic Assimilation," Ph.D. dissertation, University of Nijmegen, 1984.
Ben-Dor, Shoshana. "The *Sigd* of the Beta Israel: Renewal of the Covenant," M.A. thesis, Hebrew University, 1985 (Hebrew).

Gaguine, Maurice. "The Falasha Version of the Testaments of Abraham, Isaac, and Jacob," Ph.D. dissertation, University of Manchester, 1965.

Kaye, Jeffrey A. "On the Wings of Eagles: A History and Analysis of the Movement to Rescue Ethiopian Jewry," rabbinic thesis, Hebrew Union College—Jewish Institute of Religion, 1993.

Krempel, Veronika. "Die soziale und wirtschaftliche Stellung der Falascha in der christlich-amharischen Gesellschaft von Nordwest-Äthiopien," Ph.D. dissertation, Freie Universität Berlin, 1972.

Quirin, James. "The Beta Israel (Falasha) in Ethiopian History: Caste Formation and Culture Change, 1270–1868," Ph.D. dissertation, University of Minnesota, 1977.

Salamon, Hagar. "Contacts and Communication Among the Beta-Israel in Ethiopia: Regional Aspects," M.A. thesis, Hebrew University, 1986 (Hebrew).

## Other Sources

Agence France-Presse
*Atlantic*
*The Boston Globe*
*The Canadian Jewish News*
*The Christian Science Monitor*
*The Financial Times*
*The Guardian*
*Ha'aretz*
*The Jerusalem Post*
*The Jerusalem Report*
*The Jewish Telegraph Agency*
*The Jewish Week*
*The Los Angeles Times*
*Ma'ariv*
*The New York Times*
*Newday*
*Newsweek International*
*The Times* (London)
UPI
*The Wall Street Journal*
*Yedi'ot Ahronot*

## Oral History Interviews

The late Charles Hoffman conducted the 1992 interviews listed below. Ethiopians are listed by first names first. Some informants spoke on condition of anonymity.

Ackerman, Congressman Gary: Washington, D.C., 1992

Addisu Massele: Jerusalem, January 7, 1997

Qes Adane: Beit Shemesh, Israel, December 9, 1996

Amir, Amos: Israel, 1992

Arbel, Andrea: Jerusalem, April 24, 2003 (e-mail interview)

Arge Mekonen: Netanya, Israel, July 21, 1997

Aviva Byne Saye: Jerusalem, February 1997

Babu Yacov: Ramle, Israel, June 16, 1997

Barak, Zvi: Jerusalem, April 19, 2001 (telephone interview); New York, June 6, 2001; Jerusalem, June 15 and 18, 2001 (telephone interviews); New York, April 8, 2004

Baitush Tegenya: Netanya, Israel, July 21, 1997

Bayer, Abe: New York, 1992 (two interviews)

Bekele Tamrat: Virginia, January 9, 2002 (telephone interview)

Ben-Dor, Shoshana: Jerusalem, December 12, 1996; October 30, 2000 (telephone interview)

Ben-Meir, Yoram ("Peachy"): Jerusalem, March 12, 1997

Bergman, Ami: 1992 (two interviews); Jerusalem, October 13, 1996

Bergman, Ronen: November 27, 2001 (telephone interview)

Berhanu Yiradu: Addis Ababa, 1992

Bin-Nun, General Avihu: Israel, May 24, 2004 (e-mail interview)

Boschwitz, Rudy: Minnesota, 1992; Washington, D.C., May 18, 2004; June 23, 2004 (e-mail interview)

Cohen, Herman J.: Washington, D.C., 1992; October 23 and 30, 2001, January 3, 2002, and April 11, 2003 (telephone interviews); June 25, 2003 (e-mail interview)

Cohen, Scott: Washington, D.C., 1992

Daniel Syoum: Netanya, Israel, January 9, 1997

Dell'Ariccia, Manlio: Rome, April 3, 1998

Dinitz, Simcha: Jerusalem, 1992; January 1, 1998

Divon, Chaim: Jerusalem, 1992 (two interviews); January 12, 1997; August 12, 1997; Ottowa, November 27, 2001 (telephone interview)

Eagleburger, Lawrence: November 19, 2001 (e-mail interview)

Eliezri, Eli: Jerusalem, 1992; October 13, 1996; New York, October 19, 2001; Belgrade, March 4, 2004 (e-mail interview)

Ephraim Isaac: Princeton, N.J., April 22, 2001

Esther Grma: Jerusalem, March 3, 1997

Ezra Dawit: Carmiel, Israel, April 16, 1997

Fantahun Mekonen: Israel, 1992

Feit, Joseph: New York, May 24, 2004

Feldman, Micha: Jerusalem, 1992; December 22, 1996; July 14, 1997

Frasure, Bob: Washington, D.C., 1992

Fredelis, Arie: Israel, 1992

Friedman, Kobi: Jerusalem, 1992; August 5, 1997 (telephone interview)

Garrison, James: San Francisco, March 31, 2004 (e-mail interview)

Gebeye Adamake: Jerusalem, December 26, 1996

Getahun Tizazu: Jerusalem, December 15, 1996; July 1, 1997

Gilkes, Patrick: England, November 26, 2001 and January 9, 2002 (telephone interviews)

Dr. Girma Tolossa: Addis Ababa, 1992; April 6, 1998

Gold, Henry: Jerusalem, December 30, 1996; May 22 and 23, 1997

Goldman, Andy: Addis Ababa, 1992; New York, May 18, 2004 (telephone interview)

Gordon, Barbara Ribakove: New York, 1992 (two interviews); Jerusalem, November 1996; New York, December 4, 2001 (telephone interview)

Gordon, Uri: Tel Aviv, 1992

Halachmi, Haim: Tel Aviv, 1992; July 21, 1997

Harel, Victor: Jerusalem, August 18, 1997

Harman, David: Jerusalem, July 11, 1997

Henze, Paul: Culpepper, VA, December 18, 2001 (telephone interview)

Hiwot Yemer: Jerusalem, December 19, 1996

Hodes, Dr. Richard: Addis Ababa, 1992; Jerusalem, April 29, 1997; Addis Ababa, April 6–8, 1998

Hoenlein, Malcolm: New York, 1992; April 11, 2003 (telephone interview)

Houdek, Robert: 1992; Washington, D.C., November 29, 2001, and February 17, 2004 (telephone interviews); February 24, 2004 (e-mail interview); May 18, 2004; May 24, 27, and 28, 2004 (e-mail interviews); July 28, 2004 (telephone interview)

Jackson, Peter: Washington, D.C., 1992

Kaplan, Steven: Jerusalem, April 26, 1997

Kassa Kabede: various locations, 1992 (two interviews); May 5, 1997

Sister Kolelich Alamu: Addis Ababa, 1992

Kraar, Marty: New York, 1992 (two interviews); November 2, 2001; November 14, 2001 (telephone interview)

Krupp, Susan: New York, June 7 and 14, 2001 (telephone interviews)

Kulick, Gil: Washington, D.C., 1992; May 27, 2003 (telephone interview)

Lenhoff, Howard: Oxford, Mississippi, December 2, 2001; May 21, 2004 (telephone interviews)

Lubrani, Uri: Various locations, 1992 (two interviews); February 11, 1997; February 23, 1997; February 12, 2004 (telephone interview); February 16, 2004 (e-mail interview)

Maimon, Amir: 1992

Mamit: Ramle, Israel, June 16, 1997

Mamuye Tezazu Zere: Jerusalem, October 13, 1996; July 24, 1997

Mantber, Arnon: Jerusalem, 1992; July 30, 1997; August 18, 1997; New York, May 22, 2001

Melese Sibabbat Avraham: Carmiel, Israel, April 16, 1997

Merhav, Reuven: Jerusalem, 1992; July 23, 1997; August 13, 1997; August 17, 1997; September 9 and 21, October 2, November 4, and December 14, 2001 (e-mail interviews); January 5, 2002 (e-mail interview)

Miller, Aida: Netanya, Israel, June 16, 1997

Mizrachi, Avi: Addis Ababa, 1992 (two interviews); Israel, October 15, 2001 (telephone interview)

Mizrachi, Orna: Addis Ababa, 1992 (two interviews)

Morrison, Steve: 1992

Myers, Dr. Theodore: New York, 1992

Nachumi, General Amir: Jerusalem, 1992

Naim, Asher: Jerusalem, 1992 (two interviews); May 30, 1997; August 10, 1997; April 9 and May 15, 2004 (e-mail interviews)

Nudelman, Anita: Tel Aviv, January 9, 1997

Odenheimer, Micha: Jerusalem, December 19, 1996

Or Mekonen: Netanya, Israel, July 21, 1997

Oz, Captain Aryeh: Israel, 1992

Pollack, Susan: various locations, 1992 (two interviews); May 5 and 23, 1997; March 31, 2004 (e-mail interview)

Rachamim Elazar: Jerusalem, 1992; August 11, 1997

Recant, Will: New York, 1992 (four interviews); October 9, 1997; April 12, 2001; March 12, 2003 (telephone interview)

Riki Mullah: New York, August 11, 1996.

Rosen, Chaim: Jerusalem, October 30, 2001, April 9, 2003 (telephone interviews)

Schnapper, LaDena: Highland Park, Illinois, 1992

Schneider, Michael: New York, 1992 (two interviews); October 9, 1997; April 12, 2001; October 19, 2001 (telephone interview); November 19, 2001; December 6, 2001 (e-mail interview); April 4, 2003; May 13, 2003 (e-mail interview)

Scowcroft, General Brent: Washington, June 12, 2003

Sendedkie Derebie: Carmiel, Israel, April 16, 1997

Seroussi, Yair: Israel, e-mail interview, May 17, 2004

Shahak, General Amnon Lipkin-: Israel, October 31, 2001 (telephone interview)

Shamay Balay: Jerusalem, May 23, 1997

Shamir, Yitzhak: Tel Aviv, August 5, 1997

Shapiro, Nate: Highland Park, Illinois, 1992; May 27, 2003 (telephone interview)

Shaviv, Amir: New York, October 19, 1997; December 19, 1997; April 12, 2001; May 22, 2001; November 14, 2001; December 21, 2001; April 4, 2003

Shilo, Michael: Washington, D.C., 1992; Jerusalem, November 27, 2001 (telephone interview)

Tagenich Mekonen: Netanya, Israel, July 21, 1997

Tashtit, Doron: Addis Ababa, 1992; Jerusalem, October 13, 1996

Taylor, Gideon: New York, August 7, 1996; September 18, 1997; October 19, 1997

Teruwork Mulat: Jerusalem, November 2, 2001(telephone interview)

Tesfaye Dinka: Washington, D.C., January 3 and 8, 2002 (telephone interviews); February 20, 2004 (e-mail interview)

Tevege Tegenye: Netanya, Israel, July 21, 1997

Truya Feleka: Netanya, Israel, July 21, 1997

Weil, Shalva: Jerusalem, December 18, 1996; October 23, 2001 (telephone interview)

Wubeyu Dawit: Carmiel, Israel, April 16, 1997

Yaacov Elias: Jerusalem, 1992

Yafet Alamu: Jerusalem, October 1996; Beit Shemesh, Israel, December 9, 1997

Yegar, Moshe: Jerusalem, June 17, 1997

Yoffe, Meir: Jerusalem, 1992

Zimna Berhane: Jerusalem, 1992 (two interviews)

Zwaditu Mekonen: Netanya, Israel, July 21, 1997

# INDEX

AAEJ. *See* American Association for Ethiopian Jews

Abbink, Jon, 5, 205n3

Ackerman, Gary, 81–82

Adane, Qes, xiii–xiv

Addisu Massele, 157, 160, 174, 178, 190

Admoni, Nachum, 175

Adwa, battle of, 35

Agaw, 3

Aksum, 3

Alcalay, Eli, 138, 140

aliyot: from Ethiopia, initiated, 10–12; from Iraq, 15; from Kurdistan, 15; from Soviet Union, 15, 85, 91, 192, 208n68, 220n14; from Yemen, 14–15. *See also* Operation Moses; Operation Sheba; Operation Solomon

Alliance, David, 88

Alliance Israelite Universelle, 8

Almaya, 63, 80, 141–42, 149, 182

Ambo, 110, 119, 123, 129, 227n1,

American Association for Ethiopian Jews (AAEJ): crisis in Addis and, 45–47, 51, 59; Falash Mura and, 89, 91, 191; history and makeup, 14, 17, 27–30, 44, 55; JDC and, 28, 30, 40–42, 48, 51–54; Kassa and, 33, 50–51, 106, 121–22; Operation Solomon and, 143–44, 149, 181; sidelined, 52; transport program, 31, 38–41, 43–47, 51, 55, 58, 66–67, 86, 89, 144, 194, 198, 212n33, 213n46, 231n19, 241n3; U.S. officials and, 74. *See also individual AAEJ officials*

American Jewish Joint Distribution Committee (JDC): AAEJ and, 28, 30, 40–42, 48, 51–54; Almaya, 63, 80, 141–42, 149, 182; Falash Mura and, 89, 92, 189–90; Jewish Agency and, 80–81, 184; list ("bible") of Ethiopian Jews, 27, 63, 99, 170, 189; Lubrani and, 73, 80; medical program, 65–66, 85, 99; Quaran Jews and, 189; school, 14, 63–65, 165; secret assistance to Mashav, 88; side-payment and, 121, 135; support of

Jews in Addis, 14, 43, 46–49, 52, 62–66, 76, 81, 85, 87–88; support of Jews in Gondar, 14, 121; thirty-five million dollars and, 99, 126, 188. *See also individual JDC officials*

Amin, Idi, 68

apocrypha, 6

Arab states: criticism of Operation Solomon, 17–18, 182–83; Dayan incident and, 11; Ethiopian rebels and, 24, 37, 110, 173, 218n22; Kassa on, 33; Mengistu and, 70, 218n22; notified of Operation Solomon, 147

Arad, Moshe, 25

Arafat, Yasser, 78

Arens, Moshe, 23, 25, 163, 175, 182

Argentina, 71

Ark of the Covenant, 2

Assab, 25, 93, 110, 129, 184

Avgar, Amos, 171–72

Avi Beita, 180, 189

*Ayhud,* 206n18

Bahr-Dar, 29, 37, 88, 93, 110

Baker, James, III: American Jewish leaders and, 94, 96; Arab criticism of, 182–83; meeting with Rabin, 71; meeting with Tesfaye Dinka, 73; West Bank settlements and, 91

Barak, Ehud, 148, 163, 170, 175

Barak, Zvi: Dinitz and, 136, 150; Lubrani and, 80–81, 127–28, 136, 139, 235n16; Mossad and, 136, 227n65; on secret payment to Ethiopia, 80–81; on side deal, 183; thirty-five million dollars and, 136, 139, 140, 146–47, 150–51, 156, 161–62, 183, 235n16

Bard, Mitchell, 214n37

Barre, Mohammed Siad, 35

Bashir, Omar al-, 212n39

Begin, Menachem, 11

Bein, Yohannan, 240n45

Beja, 4